Jane Williams was born in India, of missionary parents, and is one of five sisters. She took a degree in theology at Cambridge and has worked in theological publishing and Christian adult education. Currently, she is a lecturer at St Mellitus College, London, and a visiting lecturer at King's College London. Her other publications include *Angels, Approaching Christmas, Approaching Easter* and *Faces of Christ: Jesus in Art*, all published by Lion.

# Lectionary Reflections

## Year A, B and C

Jane Williams

*Lectionary Reflections: Year A* first published in 2004 and reprinted twice
*Lectionary Reflections: Year B* first published in 2005 and reprinted once
*Lectionary Reflections: Year C* first published in 2003 and reprinted twice

First published in Great Britain as *Lectionary Reflections:*
*Years A, B and C* in 2011

Society for Promoting Christian Knowledge
36 Causton Street
London SW1P 4ST
www.spckpublishing.co.uk

*British Library Cataloguing-in-Publication Data*
A catalogue record for this book is available from the British Library

ISBN 978–0–281–06579–0

First printed in Great Britain by MPG Books
Subsequently digitally printed in Great Britain

# Contents

— ∼ —

# Contents

# Contents

## YEAR C

*Lectionary Reflections*

# *Preface*

—— ∾ ——

These pieces originally appeared in the *Church Times* as a regular 'Sunday Readings' column. I am very grateful to Paul Handley, Rachel Boulding and the other staff at the paper for the opportunity and the support they offered. I am not a biblical scholar, and took on the task with some trepidation, but have been encouraged by many generous readers of the *Church Times* to think that these reflections may help preachers and congregations to engage with and enjoy the Sunday lectionary readings assigned for use with *Common Worship*.

# YEAR A

*Advent*

# The First Sunday of Advent

———— ❧ ————

*Isaiah 2.1–5*
*Romans 13.11–14*
*Matthew 24.36–44*

In *The Magician's Nephew*, one of his Narnia books, C. S. Lewis describes a wood, which the children reach by magic. It is a kind of no-place, which Polly and Diggory come to call 'the Wood between the Worlds'. From that place they enter Charn, a dying world, Narnia at the dawn of its creation, and return again, at last, to their own world. But in the wood, time is suspended, and they can hardly begin to imagine the trials and adventures that await them in the many different worlds they are to visit.[1]

Advent is a 'wood between the worlds'. It is a point in the Christian calendar where we stand between two worlds: the world that cannot imagine Christ, and the world in which he comes to be the only picture of reality we have. At this point, we stand in a world where God's great act of incarnation and redemption is just a shadow, a child growing in the womb, secretly, in the dark. We do not know yet what this child will be like, or what his impact on our lives will be.

So Advent is a time of preparing to choose again. Which world will we choose? Will we choose the world of the newly born child, where so many of our most dearly held ideas about God and ourselves will be challenged? Or will we choose the old world, where there is no life, no birth, but at least there is also no challenge?

The 'wood between the worlds' is a place of great drowsiness because it is not a real place, and both Romans and Matthew warn us that the danger of the waiting period is sleep, oblivion, unpreparedness.

Matthew reminds us that it is very easy to live as though our world is real and secure, and as though there is no need to be

---

[1] C. S. Lewis, *The Magician's Nephew*, The Bodley Head, 1955.

watchful or poised for action. Until the moment they were swept away by the flood, the people of Noah's day were carrying on their normal lives, oblivious to the frantic hammering and animal-herding that was going on in Noah's back yard. Only Noah was prepared for what happened. All the little vignettes Matthew paints, of people innocently getting on with their lives, or turning their backs at just the wrong moment – any one of those could be us, Matthew says.

Paul, too, warns of the dangers of dozing off during this vital period when we need to prepare to make life-and-death decisions. Being Paul, he does not like to admit ignorance, as Matthew does, of when the time will come. Instead, he urges us to get ready for the dawn – it's time to be polishing our armour so that it will gleam in the sun that is about to rise. Don't go back to sleep now: any minute the alarm will go off.

But if Matthew and Paul are proper Advent readings, with their emphasis on the importance of preparation, Isaiah reminds us what it is all for. Although the centre of these verses is the vision of the Lord's house, restored to its proper focal position, our eyes are drawn to the people streaming towards the holy mountain. What are they looking for? Why have they come? They are, apparently, people who are sick of war, and who know that they have lost any ability to judge whether or not the fight is just. They long for an arbiter, they long for peace and above all they long to learn a new way of living (v. 3). They are people who have learned the hard way the cost of wrong choices, and now they ache to be taught, to be prepared for a different world.

But Isaiah's own longing is betrayed in the last verse of this reading. 'O house of Jacob,' he pleads, 'come, let *us* walk in the light of the LORD.' Surely, surely, he begs, we can see what God is offering? If even the nations, who have not known God, can look to him and see him as their heart's desire, surely we, his people, can admit that this is the way of life. Indeed, perhaps the two are connected. Perhaps if we, God's people, prepare ourselves to walk in his light, we will make the path plain for others who are lost and longing. Or is it, shamingly, sometimes the other way round? Will perhaps the desperate, those utterly despairing of the world they know, lead us, who are supposed to be God's people, to his path?

Choosing between worlds is not easy. It needs to be prepared for and imagined, over and over again. When the child is born, will it be a shock of anguish or of joy?

# The Second Sunday of Advent

——— ❧ ———

Isaiah 11.1–10
Romans 15.4–13
Matthew 3.1–12

Paul's letter to the Romans is the most formal that he wrote. He is writing to a church that he does not know, and in whose setting up and history he has not played a part. But he is writing as one already known to them, by reputation, to announce that he hopes to pay them a visit. Since it is not written in the midst of white-hot pastoral crises or violent controversies, Paul is able to sit back a bit and write reflectively about the theological conclusions that his calling as apostle to the Gentiles have forced upon him over the years. The result is a great testimony to God's determination to save us, and it has inspired Christians throughout the centuries. Theologians of all generations have written commentaries on it. Arguably, it was the cause of Martin Luther's breakthrough, in the sixteenth century, into belief in God's forgiving love. He wrote that he longed to believe what he read in Romans, that faith is all God asks. In the first decades of the twentieth century, while writing a commentary on Romans, Karl Barth was reminded that we cannot domesticate God, who is sovereign, free and utterly beyond our petty religiosity.

So we come to the reading of Romans with this great cloud of witnesses, known and unknown, who have heard Paul's words as glorious good news. One of the great themes of Romans is that of God's faithfulness. Paul sets the redeeming work of God in Christ against the whole universal history of God's dealings with us, from creation onwards, to show that God faithfully, persistently, inexorably moves his saving work forward.

In a number of his letters, Paul worries away at the question of how God's old work and new work relate. In particular, how God's old covenant with his people relates to the new promises made to all in Jesus. This is clearly a personal question for him, since he was brought up as a devout and well-educated Jew, proud to be part of

4

God's covenant people (see Galatians 1. 13ff. for a bit of autobiography), and then became the leading evangelist to those outside the Jewish race. But today's reading is not concerned with his own tensions, but is a strong exhortation to unity, based upon God's own unifying vision, laid out in Scripture.

Paul is arguing that, if you see Jesus in the context of all that God has done in the past, you see the skilful weaving fingers of God, always building the diverse threads into a lovely pattern, and you see that all the pattern coalesces around that central figure of Christ. If you stand close, the colours around Christ blaze out, startlingly bright and new; if you stand back, however, you can see the reds and purples of his life gradually building, dimly traced, in the earlier pattern too.

In other places, Paul makes the same point by using the metaphor of the first and the last Adam (see Romans 5, 1 Corinthians 15). God does not drop threads, even if we, who are supposed to be helping him, keep pulling the pattern into the wrong shape. God still works our blunders into the pattern, and even uses them to point up the figure of Jesus in the middle.

But here in Romans 15, Paul is suggesting that we can learn to be more like God if we watch him at work. Just as he weaves everything together into one complex yet satisfying whole, so we, his people, can become apprentice weavers. But first, we have to learn to see the pattern, learn to see the strength and loveliness of weaving things together, rather than pulling them apart.

At the end of this section, Paul quotes from the Old Testament, from others who have realized that God's purpose is much bigger than you might think.

Isaiah, too, is exploring themes of faithfulness and novelty; he, too, has seen that God can do the stunningly unexpected things that turn out to make sense of all that has gone before. So it is from the same root as David that the new order is to spring. But if David's role was to be the King of Israel, his descendant's job is to bring all the peoples to God. Paul longs for the Christian community to see and mirror God's great unifying work, while Isaiah dreams of a time when the whole of creation will see that it is made to live in harmony. Creatures whose whole nature should set them at enmity will see God's righteousness and faithfulness (v. 5), and know peace.

So John the Baptist strides out of the desert, calling people to respond to God's great new action, which is his eternal action of love for what he has made.

# The Third Sunday of Advent

—— ❦ ——

*Isaiah 35.1–10*
*James 5.7–10*
*Matthew 11.2–11*

In last Sunday's Gospel reading (Matthew 3. 1–12), John the Baptist arrives to herald the beginning of Jesus's adult ministry. He is incredibly rude to the people who flock to hear him preach their judgement and downfall, and they just love it. But by this morning's Gospel reading, they have tired of him and the uncomfortable truths he tells, and he is in prison.

He sends some of his few remaining faithful followers to Jesus. Is he going to ask the new favourite to use his influence with the people to free John? Is he going to remind Jesus how much he owes to John, who was the first to recognize him and give him a helping hand up the ladder? Not at all. What John wants to know is whether it is safe for him to give up, to hand his mission on.

John has never been under any illusion about what he is. The centre of the stage is not for him. But equally, he does not under-value what he is called to do. He is the one who is to herald the coming of God's Messiah, and he cannot relax until he knows whether or not he has done his job. So he sends to ask, 'Are you the one who is to come, or are we to wait for another?' (v. 3).

So when John's disciples carry Jesus's answer back to him, did he hear it as a yes or a no? What Jesus says could not be more different from the message that John preached. John shouted for repentance in the face of the wrath of God: he spoke of the axe cutting down the dead trees, and the unquenchable fire waiting for the empty husks from the threshing-floor. Jesus, on the other hand, speaks of mercy, healing and rejoicing. Did John recognize the connection? Did he see that the mercy Jesus is offering is as much a judgement on the world as the terrible fire that John himself envisaged? Did he see it as God's forceful overturning of the complacent values of those John called a 'brood of vipers'? Perhaps he did. He comes across as a man of very little personal vanity and a huge, fierce

6

commitment to God's kingdom, so perhaps he could let go of his own interpretation and rejoice in God's new work in Christ.

Matthew specifically tells us that John's disciples have gone to carry their odd message back to their master by the time Jesus pays tribute to John. All the reassurance he is to get is that cryptic message, which he must interpret in terms of his own knowledge of God. Jesus's witness to John and his message is not for John, to boost his ego, but for the crowds who once followed him, then transferred their allegiance to Jesus, and who will soon be looking for the next, more palatable, sensation.

The tribute that Jesus pays to John is warm, perceptive and puzzling. He firmly identifies John with the fulfilment of prophecy, and says he is the greatest man ever born. And yet, he is still outside. He is the messenger, not the message. He has to stand behind and point forward. We, who lack John's courage, his love of God and his calling, are on the inside, partly because he was prepared to play just that role and no other, bigger one.

But Jesus's message to John is not just a take-it-or-leave-it summary of Jesus's own ministry, but is in a code that Jesus is sure John will be able to read. Jesus is quoting from Isaiah 35, as John would surely have known, and the message is all about John. The wilderness, John's home, is to break into flower, the fearful are to be comforted. John is in prison, awaiting certain death; how can he not be afraid? John preached the judgement and vengeance of God, and here in Isaiah, God's wrath is an instrument of salvation for the weak and the fearful.

So when, at last, we come to the words that Jesus uses in today's Gospel, John will know that Jesus is talking about the continuation and fulfilment of his own message. John can be certain that Jesus is indeed the one he came to herald.

But now, in Advent, we cannot run too fast to reach that great highway of the ransomed of the Lord, where even those of us who are fools will not be able to get lost. Now is the time for patience, as James reminds us. As the 'early and late rains' (v. 7) fall on us, we begin to grow into the coming kingdom.

# The Fourth Sunday of Advent

—— ∼ ——

*Isaiah 7.10–16*
*Romans 1.1–7*
*Matthew 1.18–25*

Why won't King Ahaz ask God for a sign? The reason he gives sounds like a good religious response, but the tone of the story makes it clear that it isn't. What he says is 'I will not put the Lord to the test' (v. 12). In the Gospels, we often see that Jesus is asked for a sign, and refuses to give one, so why is Ahaz not right to refuse to ask for a sign? The simple answer is that Ahaz is wrong because, in this case, God himself has told Ahaz to ask, so that Ahaz's refusal is a deliberate determination to turn his back on what God is offering.

This is the second time that God has spoken to Ahaz in the middle of the deep political crisis for his kingdom. Judah is the subject of a double-pronged attack, and Ahaz is very frightened. Two of the neighbouring kingdoms are trying to force Judah into an alliance against the king of Assyria. God has already told Ahaz that he has nothing to fear (cf. v. 4), but Ahaz does not believe God.

So when we come to today's readings, we see Ahaz's real reason for rejecting God – he no longer trusts. It is hard to tell which he fears most – that God will be proved wrong, or that God will make him change his mind. Because Ahaz has already decided what he will do – he will submit to the King of Assyria. He is going to put his trust in his own political intelligence rather than God, and he cannot risk letting God mess up his decision with signs. The result of Ahaz's failure of nerve is a sign that reverberates down the centuries, though Ahaz may never have understood it or seen its fulfilment.

Matthew picks up on this sign, and knows exactly how to interpret the young woman whose child is called 'God is with us'.

Joseph's encounter with the angel is told in very straightforward and pragmatic language. There are no bursts of blazing light, no drift of snow-white feathers, just Joseph asleep and dreaming. But

8

his response to God is so different from Ahaz's. He simply, immediately, follows his dream, marries Mary, and steps into the story of the world's salvation. Ahaz chooses, though he doesn't know it, to step out of the light, into the background, so that he becomes just a sign of what is to take place without him. But Joseph's trust puts him at the heart of what God is doing in Jesus Christ.

It is hard to value Joseph properly. We get so few insights into his character, and the story could so clearly have gone ahead without him. But Matthew is prepared to give him his due. Joseph trusts God, simply and immediately, although it involves him in heartache and shame; and so Ahaz's rejected sign of the woman and child becomes a family, a trinity, a sign that human beings are capable of responding to each other and to God. In Matthew's account of the birth of Jesus, Joseph's role, as the one who listens to God and protects his family, is vital. Joseph's function is to be there for others, to forget himself and his needs and desires, and to make room for God's action in the woman and the child. Even before we know what the child will be, we can see the presence of God in Joseph's self-abnegation.

So although Paul makes no mention of Joseph, in Romans or anywhere else, still the mission that he accepts is not unlike Joseph's. Paul is to protect the Word of God and make room for it in the world. Paul is called to bear witness to that sign that Ahaz rejected and Matthew accepted, which is 'God with us'.

Thanks, at least partly, to Joseph's willingness to be nothing more nor less than God asks him to be, Paul, the Romans and we can see the fulfilment of prophecy. God is infinitely patient in doing what he has promised, and he never forgets. The promise made to David, rejected by Ahaz, misunderstood and misinterpreted by many others, comes to completion in Jesus. And as the promise waits, it grows and grows, to include more and more of us in its scope.

In this last week of Advent, we can stand either with Ahaz or with Joseph. Either we can refuse God's sign, the sign of the coming child, and step out of the story, handing on our part to someone braver and more trusting, or we can accept the call to protect the child and to help the world see him as the sign that 'God is with us'.

*Christmas*

# Christmas Eve/Christmas Day

———— ∾ ————

*Isaiah 9.2–7*
*Titus 2.11–14*
*Luke 2.1–20*

Luke starts what is to be one of the world's most famous narratives on the world stage, as it is traditionally recounted. He starts with emperors and governors, who are, after all, the people who make history, aren't they? These gigantic figures decree and the little ant-like ordinary folk rush around madly in response to their orders. Augustus lifts a finger and the whole of the region is on the move. The roads are choked with slow-moving donkeys, impatient horses and carriages, trudging figures with bundles and wailing children, all off to be counted, because the Emperor and the Governor say so. That's power for you.

Luke then switches his focus to a different but equally vast stage. Now his scene is the sweep of Israel's history. Joseph goes, admittedly at the bidding of the rulers, but he goes as one who knows that he, too, represents history-makers, because he is a descendant of David. In the history of God's relationships with his people, David is pivotal, at least as important as any Roman emperor or governor.

So civil history and religious history are coming together to provide the gigantic backdrop, and we know that we are to witness something enormous. But then, hang on, whatever is going on? On to this massive stage comes a baby. The sense of anticlimax is huge. Everything is done to diminish this strange entrance of the principal character. His birth happens off stage, and he is shoved into a corner, because the stage is already full of other more important-looking people and events. We begin to get bewildered. History is being turned on its head.

Well, exactly. History *is* being turned on its head. The powerfully significant scenery of religious and political stature is quite proper – history is being changed here, but part of the change is in our understanding of how momentous events are to be judged. From the moment this baby is born and wrapped in bands of cloth and put in a corner somewhere, corners and dark insignificant places take on a whole new meaning. Rulers and governors can shout away centre-stage all they like, but we begin to see that they may not be taking part in anything at all important. Whatever they may think, their reigns are ephemeral. They are no longer the ones who are shaping the world.

This is what the angels tell the astonished shepherds, which is, in itself, part of this strange shift in history. Why send your heavenly hosts to a group of shepherds? If they were to go to an emperor or a governor, they might even be able to get the baby a proper start in life, or at least a decent room and a cradle. But no, the angels are sent to the shepherds, so the shepherds are the first to learn that the world has changed for ever. 'And don't go mistaking the sign,' the angels warn the stunned shepherds. 'We are not the sign, for all our winged brightness. The baby is the sign. He is the symbol of salvation.'

Nothing could be clearer than this set of contrasts that Luke sees attending the birth of the one who is the Saviour. The huge machinery put into operation to get him to the right place at the right time, of the right ancestors. And then, when he arrives, he is born into obscurity. The massed choir of angels is sent to announce the news, but to shepherds, who will have no power to broadcast what they have been told.

It is as though God is saying, 'Things can only be changed this way. Power and might, grandeur and status, only perpetuate themselves and draw people further and further into the world they have made themselves, a world that clearly does not work. Only this can draw them out of themselves and make them look at the world I created, the real world.'

God's way to draw us back to the real aim of our existence is a strange way. He comes to live with us, as one of us, in utter humility. He is born in fragility and danger, as a human baby, with no wealth or power of privilege to protect him. All the trappings of earth and heaven are held at arm's length, so that Jesus can be just what we are, but so often refuse to be – fully human, dependent only upon God the Father.

This humility is to be the source of our new life, if we are humble enough to accept it. Our nourishment lies in the animal trough. This is the bread of life. Are we too grand to feed with the animals, or can we join the shepherds in rejoicing and 'praising God for all we have seen and heard'?

# The First Sunday of Christmas

——— ❦ ———

*Isaiah 63.7–9*
*Hebrews 2.10–18*
*Matthew 2.13–23*

Isaiah and Hebrews show us God's way of being in the world, a way that should be blindingly obvious to us at Christmas.

Isaiah is reminding the people of all that God has done for them throughout the ages. But although he talks in general terms about God's 'praiseworthy acts' and 'great favour', the real cause of joy is not the deeds, but the presence of God himself with his people. Isaiah wants his people to remember, as though this is a formative memory from their childhood, the times when God has been with them, and shown them how much he loved and pitied them. They can almost feel again what it is like to be small enough and trusting enough to be carried on God's shoulders. It is as though God is a father and Israel a child, feeling the magical mixture of excitement and security that riding up so high on a father's shoulders can bring. This is what God offers his people, his own love and presence. And because he loves them, he makes himself vulnerable to them. They 'will not deal falsely', God thinks of his children, and he trusts himself and his message to them.

Through all the centuries that follow, when that trust proves false over and over again, God's purpose does not waver, and neither does his love. Still God gives himself to his people, and willingly risks what follows, until we reach the logical conclusion, here at Christmas time. God becomes a human being, sharing flesh and blood and suffering, to be with his people. God made us to share his life, but since we are too stupid or proud to see that, he comes instead and shares ours.

So Isaiah and Hebrews have an understanding of how God works. He desires closeness and intimacy. He works by sharing himself, trusting himself to us, long after we have, by all possible measures, proven ourselves untrustworthy. He is willing to be vulnerable, to see his plans apparently go awry, but still not to change direction, but patiently, persistently, unerringly to go on giving himself to us, finding new, creative, stunningly unexpected ways of offering us a share in his life.

Herod, on the other hand, chooses a different way of working. His way of bringing about what he longs for is to seize it by force, and without any concern for anyone else. Herod wants power, but he can never have enough of it. After all, he is already a king. Herod had options. He could, for example, have sought out the child and adopted it, thereby extending his own rule into the next generation. But such a thought never enters his head. Or he could have calculated his own age and that of the new-born child and reckoned on a good number of years still as king before the child could prove any threat to him. Or he could have looked at the three strange men who came looking for the new 'king' and simply laughed.

But because Herod's whole identity is bound up with his need for power, and because he trusts no one but himself to give him what he wants, he cannot see any of those options. And so he kills, madly and in vain, to try to get security for himself.

Rachel's weeping for her children is a sound that has echoed down the ages, and still fills our ears. This terrible grief is always the result of Herod's kind of way in the world. Trying to choose security and inviolability for ourselves seems to us to justify taking away the security and even the lives of others, one cycle of violence leading always to the next, until no one can even imagine any other way.

Although Matthew tells us that Herod's actions are the fulfilment of a prophecy in Jeremiah, that does not mean that Herod had no choice, or that God willed him to do what he did. But it does suggest that God knows and grieves over this response of ours. Deeply woven into the biblical picture of human nature is the knowledge that, endlessly, mindlessly, we choose security for ourselves at whatever cost to others. The story of Herod, like the stories we read day by day in the papers, suggests that this tactic simply never works.

But this is not God's way. God chooses to give himself and his security into our hands. He chooses to come close and still closer, giving and sharing, and never defending or retaliating. His way leads, admittedly, to the cross, but also to resurrection and life freely available for all. Perhaps his way would be worth a try.

# The Second Sunday of Christmas

——— ≈ ———

*Jeremiah 31.7–14*
*Ephesians 1.3–14*
*John 1.1–18*

It is very difficult, in the middle of the school run or the super-market shop, to remember that in us God is fulfilling the whole purpose of creation. It is even more difficult to look at the news or read the papers and believe that there even is a purpose to the world at all, let alone that it is in the process of being fulfilled. But both John and Ephesians assure us that it is.

God's purpose for his world is in-built from the moment of creation. We are created through our redeemer and redeemed by our creator. God in Christ is our source and our destiny. As the Father creates us in the image of the Son, through the agency of the Son and the Spirit, already the purpose is born that through them we will be recreated, so that we can share in the true life for which we were made, the life of God.

In Ephesians, the joy feels very close. Our inheritance is already ours (Ephesians 1.11), not something far off that we long for, but something that we already possess and can spend. Although we are still awed by God's generosity, and amazed that he should have chosen us, of all people, to share his joy, we can no longer doubt it, because we have it in our hands. Although we can hardly believe that God destined us – us! – to be a part of his family, even before he made the world, with the Holy Spirit beside us, we cannot doubt it for long. There is no temptation to preen and get too big for our boots, because we cannot fool ourselves that God chose us because of what we are. The very fact that we were chosen long before our birth, or even the birth of any of the most ancient of our relatives, makes it clear that it is none of our doing. It is God alone who gives this unearned, unimaginable joy.

It is vital to remember that, and to share what we are given by God, rather than hug it to ourselves with a sense of our own worth and superiority. Jeremiah has seen his people so take their own

16

worth for granted that they hardly bother to think of God at all. God never forgets them or abandons them, they never cease to be his people, but they get complacent, and hardly care what their role in God's great work of creation is to be. They just want the land and the glory. They will get it, Jeremiah assures them, because it is what God has promised, and God does not break his promise. But the people Jeremiah sees pouring into Israel are not a mighty and triumphant horde, but a broken, tearful, hobbling mass, who can hardly believe what is happening to them. The remnant of the once proud people have long given up believing that they deserve to inherit God's promise. They are overwhelmed with gratitude and joy when they realize that God has never given up on them. As they limp and hobble home, helping each other along, they weep with amazed gladness. As God leads them in safety and comfort into his promises, they remember that God has always been their Father, only they didn't think, before, that they needed one. Now they know that they do. They thought that they could manage the world by themselves, but now they know that they can't: only God is their protector and their life. Now the joy that they feel is not vain and self-congratulatory, but full of awe and gratitude.

Jeremiah's rescued people and the Ephesians could join hands across the centuries and describe the experience they have in common. They know themselves to be vital to God and loved beyond anything they ever expected. But they also know that this is nothing to do with them. They have not deserved it in any way. It is one of God's inexplicable peculiarities that he has chosen them to be witnesses to his purposes for the world. They are allowed to feel the joy, always, but at all costs they must avoid complacency. Now that they know what God is like and what he plans for the world, they – and we – have a job to do. It is a job very like John the Baptist's. We are not the light, but we know who is.

Of course, it is possible to reject our role in God's purposes, but that will simply be our own loss. It is God's world and it will be what he has designed it to be, whether we join in or opt out. But when you hear about the joy of the Ephesians and the people of Jeremiah, why miss out?

*Epiphany*

# The Epiphany

—— ❦ ——

*Isaiah 60.1–6*
*Ephesians 3.1–12*
*Matthew 2.1–12*

What strange people God chooses to be witnesses and messengers of his coming! They hardly seem the best way to announce to the world that its salvation is at hand. For example, this letter to the Ephesians – whether written by Paul or not – explicitly admits that the great missionary is in prison. How is he going to get on with his work there? Surely the Ephesians might be forgiven for taking him with a pinch of salt, when he writes about the great commission that has been given to him. He sits there in chains, and has the nerve to tell them that something is being revealed through him that has never been known before. The great prophets and men of God of all the preceding ages failed to notice this thing, and yet it is central to the whole plan of God. Do the Ephesians snigger behind their hands and say, 'If God tells him secrets, how come he didn't know enough to avoid being captured?'

Perhaps the Ephesians have more understanding than many. After all, the letter suggests that they have already accepted the gospel of Jesus Christ, and have at least heard of the Apostle Paul and his work, even if they have never met him. What's more, many of them have already been directly affected by this great secret that God has been revealing through the work of Paul. The secret is that God chooses all people to know him and share his mission, not just one race, as used to be claimed. Many of the Ephesians know that they would not be Christians if God had not revealed to Paul that Gentiles, too, were to be included.

But if the Ephesians are prepared to believe that step, what about the next? Next it is claimed that the Christian Church, now that it includes Gentiles as well as Jews, can be used to show the world the 'wisdom of God' (Ephesians 3.10). At that point, even if the Ephesians don't laugh out loud, some of us might be tempted to. We have got rather more used to thinking of the Church as a kind of

20

tolerated, slightly senile old relative. We wouldn't dream of getting rid of it, but we really can't expect much from it.

Ephesians, on the other hand, thinks of the Church as a major player in the cosmos. Before the coming of the Church, the 'rulers and authorities in the heavenly places' (Ephesians 3.10) managed to gain control and status for themselves, and persuade themselves and many others that they, not God, were in charge of the destiny of the world. But now the Church, with its intimate knowledge of the mind of God, can challenge these other powers. Ephesians sees the Church as God's secret weapon in the struggle to bring the world to freedom and to worship of the true God.

But if, looking round at the congregations that we know and love, that seems like a ludicrous assumption, it may be that we have, ourselves, been taken in by the other 'rulers and authorities'. It may be that they have persuaded us to accept their definition of power and success. But we, the Church, are created with an entirely different set of assumptions and priorities, and we must not let ourselves be tempted.

That's why it is quite right and proper that Paul witnesses in chains to this stupendous calling. That is why the passage emphasizes Paul's humility. This great secret was not revealed to him because he was clever, and because he alone was prepared to understand what God had been trying to say for ages. On the contrary, he knows that he is the 'very least of all the saints' (Ephesians 3.8), and that his story starts with wilful misunderstanding and even persecution of God's Church. What fits him to be a carrier of God's secret is his knowledge of his own inadequacy and dependence upon God.

Perhaps the wise men started off with other ideas. Perhaps they believed that it was their wisdom and observational accuracy that allowed them alone to chart the rising of the star and follow it. They certainly believed that the sign they were witnessing was the stuff for kings, which is why they called on Herod. Possibly they expected to be rewarded and to play a large part in this new reign they had come to announce. But at last, at last, they come to the stable and the child. Whatever their previous misconceptions, like Paul, they recognize Christ when they meet him. As they rise from the floor and make their joyful way out of the story, they have helped to witness, yet again, to the way in which God plans to free the universe and bring it into union with himself.

21

# The First Sunday of Epiphany

———— ∾ ————

*Isaiah 42.1–9*
*Acts 10.34–43*
*Matthew 3.13–17*

Matthew's is the only Gospel that shows any embarrassment about Jesus's baptism by John the Baptist. In all of the Gospels, John knows that his baptism is a temporary measure, but he also knows that it is a necessary one, and that his own message of repentance through baptism is part of the build-up to the coming of the Messiah. John's Gospel, which, typically, does not directly refer to Jesus being baptized, though it undoubtedly knows about it, shows John recognizing Jesus at once as the fulfilment of his work. It is what John has been destined to do since the beginning of time, as the magnificent opening verses of the Gospel make clear. Luke and Mark give the Baptist a less pivotal role. In both of these Gospels, it is possible to read God's affirmation of Jesus and his mission as something heard and seen by Jesus alone. But none of these three Gospels is worried about the fact that John exhorts people to come to baptism to be washed clean of their sins.

But in Matthew, we have some conversation between Jesus and John, which places John's witness at the heart of the event. John knows that Jesus does not need to repent and be made clean, and he tries to reverse their roles and get Jesus to baptize him, rather than vice versa. So when Jesus insists, John too, presumably, hears the words of the Father, as confirmation not only of Jesus's own calling, but also of the completion of John's. Jesus's acceptance of this unnecessary baptism marks the end of an era. He takes on baptism 'for now' (Matthew 3.15) because until the voice of the Father initiates the new age, we are still in the period of the forerunner. It is John's task to carry the baton to this point, and Jesus accepts it. From the moment he comes out of the water, however, everything changes. John's baptism becomes obsolete. A new baptism is to mark the new age – baptism into the Son, through the Holy Spirit. But even this will not start while Jesus is physically

22

present. Jesus and his followers do not baptize during Jesus's earthly ministry, because they need no other symbol of unity with God. They are walking and talking with the source of all symbols.

This slight display of uneasiness about the baptism on Matthew's part is intriguing, though it is equally interesting that the other Gospels don't feel it at all. But all of them are clear that this marks a turning-point. From now on, the hidden years of Jesus's childhood and youth are over, and he steps out on to the public stage. His birth into the human condition is his first public act of obedience to the Father, although it is witnessed and understood only by a few. Presumably the human mind of the tiny child could only be implicitly involved in that act of obedience. But here at baptism Jesus submits himself to his calling. He may not know exactly what it will involve, but he knows it is the will of the Father, and he knows that it is symbolized by this act of solidarity with the state of all humanity. If, in the world that we have made for ourselves to live in, we need to repent and be cleansed from our sins, then that is the world that Jesus, in obedience to the Father, chooses too. He chooses to be like us, and his choice brings forth the Father's words of love and approval.

So now he knows, if he ever doubted it, that this is the path he is to walk. It is one of identification, not of superiority. It will involve the painful truths of being human, not to be avoided but to be embraced. And through his embrace of the symbol of baptism, Jesus wrenches all the polite fictions away from it and reveals it for what it is. This is not a superficial matter of washing away a little dirt. This is about sin, which leads to our death. As Jesus steps into the water, he accepts the cross, too, because they go together.

After Jesus's death and resurrection, we accept that too. Christian baptism is an acceptance of death, the death of all the things that create a world that is separate from God. Jesus receives our baptism and death so that we can receive his resurrection and life. He shares our reality so that we can share his. It may be hard and painful to let go of the approximation of reality that we thought was the world, but as we step down into the waters, we hear the voice of Truth, calling us beloved and pleasing.

# The Second Sunday of Epiphany

———— ❦ ————

*Isaiah 49.1–7*
*1 Corinthians 1.1–9*
*John 1.29–42*

To be called by God is a thing of joy and terror, in about equal measures. The Corinthians are largely experiencing the excitement, at present, but their walk of discipleship will certainly lead them to sympathize, at times, with the prophet who speaks in Isaiah 49.

The prophet speaks of his calling as something about which he had no choice. Like Jeremiah (see Jeremiah 1.5), this prophet cannot remember a time when he was unaware that he had been called by God, and that that calling was the foundation of his whole being. Not that that was necessarily obvious to others. Indeed, he specifically says that God hides him away, at least for a while. He doesn't say why – perhaps he didn't know. Another recurrent theme in the lives of those called by God is learning to live with both knowledge and ignorance. They are shown into the workings of God's plan just as far as they need to be to fulfil their task and no further. They can never deceive themselves that they are co-designers of the plan. They simply announce what they have been told.

There is obviously some frustration involved in this annoying way of working. Because the prophet – and any other servant of God – does not know all the details of how things should be going, it is quite impossible to tell whether or not he is succeeding in his task. Most of the time, he is sure that he can't be, because there are no visible results at all.

But just as the prophet turns to God and says, 'I'm really sorry. I did my best, but I've failed. You know how hard I tried. I'm very sorry', at this point of despair, God suddenly reveals that the task is much bigger than the prophet ever dreamed. He thought he was being sent to his own people, Israel, but God says to him, 'Not just Israel, but the world.' It doesn't seem the best possible management practice to tell an employee who is already discouraged that actually his job is to get much harder.

24

But it is thanks to the prophet, and many others before and after him, who began to glimpse the enormity of God's salvation, that the Corinthians – and we – are part of the story at all. The Corinthians are not yet aware that God's personnel practices are strange, and that knowing your weakness is often the qualification that God chiefly looks for in his followers. But Paul is going to do his best to tell them. He starts cautiously, with well-judged praise. But even that is laced with phrases that should make the Corinthians pause. Paul tells them that they are called to be saints – but so are thousands of others who call on the name of Jesus. The Corinthians might have thought that they were special, but they are not. Anyone who calls on Jesus is the equal of the sophisticated and intellectual Corinthian believers. Paul acknowledges that they are, indeed, a very impressive bunch. They are doing brilliantly in their public witness, at least when it involves exciting speeches. Is there a hint that their lives are perhaps not quite such good missionary material (see 1 Corinthians 1.8)? The whole of the correspondence between Paul and the Corinthian church suggests that these are exuberant, confident Christians, who are slightly inclined to put their trust in themselves and in the outward signs of Christian power, rather than in God, or in each other.

One of the big changes between the prophet who speaks in Isaiah and the Corinthian Christians is the number of people who share in God's calling. The prophet experiences loneliness and misunderstanding, and his task is often a solitary one. But Christians are called to be witnesses together, and to learn from each other as well as from God. The thing that we are most apt to underrate or even despise – the Church – is the thing that the prophets would most have envied. So the first thing we see Jesus doing, as he emerges from the waters of baptism, is calling a group of people together. They have no idea how much they are to go through together, and how much they will need each other, or how much they will accomplish, and how their names will be revered down the centuries.

John the Baptist affirms that Jesus lives and moves in the power of God. And Jesus, the beloved Son, feeling the presence of the Holy Spirit, instantly begins to build a community that will be able to hold that knowledge for the world, and share it. Like Jesus, and thanks to Jesus, we too are beloved children of God, full of his Holy Spirit, called to share God's love with the world.

# The Third Sunday of Epiphany

——— ∾ ———

*Isaiah 9.1–4*
*1 Corinthians 1.10–18*
*Matthew 4.12–23*

Corinth in the first century was a busy, loud, exciting place. It had been a reasonably wealthy trading centre for a couple of centuries at least, and that had attracted people of many religions and races to settle there. The Jewish writer Philo tells us that there was a flourishing Jewish community in Corinth, and other classical writers detail temples to gods and goddesses of the Greek pantheon, possibly including Aphrodite. In other words, to be a Corinthian was to have grown up in a diverse, competitive, multicultural society. When Christian missionaries came to Corinth, they obviously found it difficult to change this basic ethos.

Acts 18 gives us one account of Paul's own missionary activity in Corinth, which clearly had its ups and downs, but was also highly successful. It also tells us, intriguingly, that Paul stayed in Corinth for eighteen months, which is quite a long time in his whirlwind career, suggesting that Paul not only saw enormous opportunities for the gospel, but also that he grew rather fond of the place. Certainly, in Acts and in the Corinthian correspondence itself, a lot of people are mentioned by name, so Paul not only kept in close touch with his converts, but also expected them to be known to the wider Christian community as people of substance.

But Paul was not the only one to see the potential in Corinth. Other missionaries, too, preached there. It is hard to tell if there was a spirit of rivalry among the different missionaries themselves, or whether this is just typical of Corinthians to pick up a good idea and turn it into something to argue about, but either way, the outcome is certainly a divided and contentious church.

Paul is not afraid of a bit of Christian infighting when he believes the truth is at stake – you might like to check out Galatians 2.11–14, to see Paul naming names in a big way when his mission to preach to the Gentiles is under threat. But here in Corinth, he is clear that the gospel is not just being undermined but is actually being fundamentally misunderstood because the Christian community is divided. Corinthian Christians are being fiercely loyal to whichever one of the missionaries it was that brought the gospel to their own particular group, and they are forgetting what the gospel is actually about. Whose death brought you salvation, Paul demands? In whose name do you accept the baptism that leads to new life? Is this about your teacher, or your God?

Paul knows very well that the gospel of Christ is rubbing against the grain, not just for Corinthians, but for most of us. The competitive instinct, the instinct to dominate, the instinct to define our own value by denying somebody else's is so basic, that Paul knows the gospel sounds like 'foolishness' to most of us, most of the time. As the Corinthians – and we – fight about who has the 'best' version of the gospel, they are turning their backs on the crucified God. What has the cross to do with the aggressive determination to be proved right? But it is the cross that is God's way in the world, and the demonstration of his power. The power to accept, create, recreate and save is so stunningly different from anything we understand as power that it is barely recognizable.

When Jesus walks beside the Sea of Galilee, what is it about him that the fishermen see? He is quite alone, as far as we can see. They do not know the stories of his birth, of how the mysterious travellers were taught a lesson about kingship. As far as Matthew knows, they were not present when the heavens opened and God proclaimed his love for his Son at Jordan. They do not know what Jesus has just been through in the wilderness, as he discovers what he must reject. All of this we, the readers, have just seen in Matthew's first four chapters. But Peter, Andrew, James and John come to it new, without the benefit of all these huge hints, and yet they drop their nets to follow Jesus. Jesus doesn't even offer them any very obvious inducements. There is no mention of fame, fortune, success, excitement. Instead, he offers them a mission, a chance to attract others, as they have just been attracted. Their acceptance starts the chain reaction that has never quite fizzled out, despite many wrong turns and shameful misunderstandings. We continue to preach the puzzling, spectacular, strange, unearned foolishness of God, who loves us and saves us. Christians have been as guilty as anyone else of wanting to be clever, successful and right, but if we keep preaching Christ crucified, maybe one day we will convert even ourselves.

# The Fourth Sunday of Epiphany

———— ❧ ————

*1 Kings 17.8–16*
*1 Corinthians 1.18–31*
*John 2.1–11*

Most of us think we would like the kind of communication with God that Elijah has. The narrator of 1 Kings tells us, very matter-of-factly, that God tells Elijah to do something, and Elijah goes off and does it. And, in return, God makes special provision for Elijah, to ensure that he is protected from the results of what he has to say on behalf of God. Immediately before the passage set for today, Elijah has gone to King Ahab and told him that the Lord has decreed that there will be a terrible drought. Then, as the land and its inhabitants begin to suffer, Elijah is given instructions by God, taking him first to one place and then to another where he will be able to find water.

How lovely, we think, to know exactly what God wants from us! If only God would be as clear in his directions to us, how we would love to be as obedient as Elijah! But if you look a little more closely at Elijah's life, I suspect you will find that you don't mean it. To go to the King and tell him that his land is about to suffer a human and economic tragedy, with the implication that this is the King's fault, because of his sinful lifestyle, is not an easy thing to do. And the relationship between Elijah and Ahab is not going to get any easier as the story unfolds over the next few chapters of 1 Kings. And then notice the fact that Elijah seems to have no home, and no friends. When the Lord says 'Jump', Elijah jumps, and that is not conducive to a happy and settled family life. What's more, although we know, and Elijah knew, that his message was from God, others around Elijah often doubted it. Elijah's calling is to solitude and uncertainty, and it requires enormous courage.

In today's passage, God tells Elijah that he has 'commanded a widow to feed you'. But when the widow actually comes on the scene, it is obvious that she has not heard the command, and is in total ignorance of her part. Nor has God actually yet given her anything with which she could feed Elijah. As always, it is Elijah who has to put into words what is to happen.

We are not told what the widow feels about it, when she does as Elijah tells her. It is hard to imagine that she is really enthusiastic about believing a total stranger to the point of giving him her last morsel. But the widow is almost as alone as Elijah, and much less powerful. She has few hopes or expectations for herself and her son, even before the drought comes and devastates the land. She is clearly in no position to argue, and you can hear her thinking to herself, 'Well, we are going to die anyway, so we may as well die with an empty stomach as a full one.' So she feeds Elijah, as the Lord had said she would, and thereby saves her household.

In one obvious sense, this story of God's miraculous provision clearly goes with today's Gospel reading about the exuberant production of wine for the wedding at Cana. Both are about God's care and generosity. But actually it goes even better with Paul's puzzling passage about the foolishness of God. Why is it only Elijah who can speak God's message to King Ahab? Why does God use the poor, desperate widow to nurture and be nurtured by his servant? With the power to supply endless provisions, Elijah would have been welcome anywhere, and could have picked a much cosier place to stay. Why does God choose the Corinthians, fractious, not very bright, of little social standing – a microcosm of what the Christian Church has always been, and still is? Why does he choose to come to us, as another human being, and suffer and die? As Paul points out, it just doesn't make sense, when you consider all the other options that God must have.

But what Paul is arguing is that it is absolutely vital to remember, all the time, that we do not understand God. God is, by definition, completely outside human possibilities. The minute we forget that, we are not talking about God any more. So ignorance and stupidity are basic to our calling – luckily for us! In us, as in the Corinthians, it is clear that 'wisdom, righteousness, sanctification and redemption' are not things we could manage for ourselves, so we know for sure that they are gifts from God. Knowing that, without God, we can hardly even be said to exist, that's the mark of the Christian, Paul tells us.

# Ordinary Time

# *Proper 1*

—— ≈ ——

Isaiah 58.1–12
1 Corinthians 2.1–16
Matthew 5.13–20

God is about to give you a present. You are very excited about this because, after all, a present from God is likely to be a particularly fine one. You also hope that God has been listening to the large hints you have been dropping. This present might at last be that thing you have been longing for. You unwrap it with shaking fingers, but when the paper falls away, you look at the object inside the parcel. You have no idea at all what it is. None of your friends has one. You have never seen anything like it.

Paul is saying that the Christian gospel is a bit like this. We think it is going to be something magnificent, something we have been longing for all our lives, but when we get it, we don't understand it at all.

What is it that we hope for and think we are getting from God? We are not completely stupid. We know it will be something 'religious'. Perhaps we hope for a sense of being at peace with ourselves. Perhaps we long to know that God is on our side. Perhaps we want the security and protection that the maker of the universe must surely be able to bestow on us. Perhaps, moving down the scale a bit, we want people to believe that we are good and religious, so God becomes a sort of status symbol for us. Perhaps we want to be part of a religious system that is clearly more powerful than any other and can put other people in their proper, subservient place. Most of us come to God with a mixture of these motives, and they are not all wholly bad. But they are all about us, and not about God.

The people to whom Isaiah writes might feel most indignant at his round condemnation of their religious practices. Here he is saying that the people seek God and delight in him, and that they strictly observe all the fast days, and wear sackcloth and lie down in the ashes out of their respect for God, and yet he says they are not acceptable to God. Whatever else can God possibly be expecting from them?

According to Isaiah, the answer is that God expects us to begin to see the world through his eyes, whereas we were rather hoping that he might see it through ours. In God's eyes, our little religious observances are like a kind of playacting. However well we do it, we turn straight from the play back to our ordinary, non-religious lives, as though the two were quite separate. But God wants us to be heart-broken with love and longing for the world, as he is. Our disciplines of hunger or self-denial are chosen, and we can pick them up and put them down at will. But there are many who have no such choice. For them, poverty, hunger, instability are their daily lot. Our religious disciplines should remind us that we and they are all human, all utterly dependent for life itself upon the God in whose image we are created. When we end our fasting, it is so that we can go out and share what we have with others. Our destiny lies together, because we are all equally dear to God. We cannot allow ourselves to be satisfied with having just our own needs met.

That's why Jesus says that his disciples are to be the salt of the earth and the light of the world. Their faith is not just – or even primarily – about themselves, but about their participation in God's work in the world. This is the fulfilment of the law, according to Jesus. The law is essentially a corporate thing. It is designed to build a people whose life together reflects the nature of God and so makes it more credible to others.

What, then, is this mysterious and unrecognizable present that God gives us? It is a gift that allows us to put others before ourselves. It allows us to care for the world as God does, so that we are incomplete while others suffer. Paul has found out how the gift works. It enables him, a proud man, to come in weakness and failure, and to trust in God. It helps him to rejoice at the faith of others, even if he gets no credit for it. It allows him to see and preach the crucified Christ as the measure of wisdom in the world. This gift does very little for our own personal comfort or sense of self-importance, and it will be sneered at and misunderstood by all who do not possess it. But it is a present that interprets the whole world, once you have the knack of it.

# Proper 2

———— ❦ ————

*Deuteronomy 30.15–20*
*1 Corinthians 3.1–9*
*Matthew 5.21–37*

This passage in Matthew decisively contradicts anyone who would like to see Jesus as a kind of well-meaning hippy, preaching an 'all you need is love' kind of gospel. It is terribly easy to assume that Jesus was into kindness and forgiveness and not judging anyone and letting everyone make their own path, and it was only later that the nasty old Church tried to introduce a whole set of rules and regulations. But, in that case, whatever is going on here in Matthew? In every single case, Jesus takes the prohibitions of the law and makes them even harder to obey.

The passage set for today covers murder, adultery, divorce and swearing, and it makes every one of us liable to extreme judgement, apparently. Jesus condemns not just the acts themselves but also the attitude that makes the acts possible. Anger leads to murder and lust leads to adultery, and Jesus seems to be suggesting that anger and lust are as culpable as the offences they lead to. He advocates the extreme measure of cutting out any part of the body that leads to temptation. All in all, this passage sounds like a fanatical rant, and it has been roundly ignored by almost all Christians ever since. Have you ever heard it suggested that anger is a sin that should debar people from ordination, for example? Yet in this passage, Jesus says that to be angry with a fellow Christian makes us liable for judgement.

This material is peculiar to Matthew – you might like to look at Luke 6.20–end to see how Luke's equivalent differs. But that doesn't mean that we can simply discount this hard and unsettling passage as Matthew's own invention. For one thing, Matthew hints at a context that we see again in some of Paul's writings. Are Christians actually still bound by Jewish law, or does grace replace it? All the Gospels are agreed that there were conflicts between Jesus and the Jewish authorities over the interpretation of the day-to-day regulations of the law. On food laws and sabbath laws, Jesus seems to have been rather lax, but on divorce and remarriage he seems to have been harsher than many of his rabbinic contemporaries. The earlier chapters of Acts reflect considerable confusion among his followers about whether or not they are still essentially a sub-division within Judaism, or not. Eventually, partly through Paul's pioneering missionary work, we have come to accept that although we will always have close family ties with Judaism, Christians do not have to be Jews too. But it would be a mistake to think that that conclusion was easily arrived at, and the confusion over the issue comes through Jesus's own teaching, as well as through later attempts to apply it in a situation of Gentile mission.

So here in Matthew, just before the passage set for today, Jesus says, 'Do not think that I have come to abolish the law or the prophets' (Matthew 5.17), suggesting that there were some who did think precisely that. And Paul's tortuous theology in Romans of how old and new covenants relate obviously led some of his readers to the same conclusion. 'Should we continue to sin in order that grace may abound?' someone seems to have asked him (see Romans 6.2). Some people have clearly heard Jesus's teaching, and the early Church's preaching of it, as liberation from all rules and laws. It doesn't matter what we do, because God loves us and forgives us. Rules and regulations are only for those blind fools who have not accepted Jesus as their personal Lord and saviour.

But what both Paul and Matthew are trying to suggest is that if you take that attitude, then you are still actually living in the same world as the world of the law. You are still living with the rules and regulations, even if you are reacting against them. Paul's image in 1 Corinthians is that of babies. Babies may throw their baby food about, but that doesn't mean that they are ready for solids. Similarly, Christians who spend all their time boasting about how the law doesn't apply to them simply demonstrate how much they still need it. They are still utterly preoccupied with what they are allowed to do and what they can get away with.

So perhaps the reading from Deuteronomy is actually the key to all three readings today. The commandments are given to Israel as a source of life, a source of knowledge of God, the life-giver. They teach God's people how to live in God's world. Deuteronomy assumes that after a while these laws will become second nature, so that we will be able to look only at their core and basis, which is our love for God and his for us.

# *Proper 3*

——— ❦ ———

*Leviticus 19.1–2, 9–18*
*1 Corinthians 3.10–11, 16–23*
*Matthew 5.38–48*

The passages from Leviticus and Matthew today are linked by the idea that our lives together as a community are designed to reflect our God. Matthew says we are to be perfect, as our heavenly Father is perfect, and Leviticus says we must be holy, because God is holy. These sayings are not abstract, but belong in the context of practical advice about how we are to do this job of showing the world what our God is like. But, all the same, they are frightening in the responsibility they assign to us.

Leviticus 19 has a lot in common with the Ten Commandments, often spelling out the implications of each clause. Its prescriptions sound odd to us, in that there are challenging and inspiring commandments about how to treat the poor, mixed together with detailed instructions about how long after being offered a sacrifice may be eaten. The lectionary chooses to leave out these verses in Leviticus 19.5–8, but that does lead to a certain loss of flavour. As far as the authors of Leviticus are concerned, the whole lot belongs together. No detail of the lives of God's people is more or less important. The steady beat of the refrain 'I am the LORD' (vv. 4, 10, 12, 14, 16, 18 etc.) is the heartbeat that keeps the blood flowing through the whole life of the people. It is the same heartbeat for the poor and the rich, the great and the small, the blind and the deaf, so that to attack any member of the community is suicidal – it is like cutting a vein.

This is not a message that any of us instinctively likes. Whatever we may know in theory, in practice we simply cannot help acting as though our needs are more important than the needs of others, and so we keep introducing malfunctions into our system, our life together. In today's reading from Matthew, Jesus is trying to get his listeners to compare their behaviour with God's. God gives life to everything, irrespective of whether or not it responds to its maker.

36

God 'makes the sun rise on the evil and on the good' (Matthew 5.45), whether they acknowledge this as his action or not. This is God's perfection that we are called to imitate. God does not see things divided into pieces, but whole, perfect, and that is what we have to learn to do. God sees that everything, whether it knows it or not, cares about it or not, is actually alive with the same life, which is his own. He sees the intricate tracery of the veins, carrying his blood throughout the body from his steadily beating heart that is the life-source of all that is. We may think of ourselves as separate, independent beings, but if we were to be detached from God's blood supply, we would soon find out how incapable we are of functioning without him.

Leviticus advises a strong, just community where all know that they will be fairly treated and so have no need to be selfish and self-protecting. You do not need to fight for your rights if they are being freely offered to you. But history clearly shows that such an ideal society is constantly being subverted by those who want more than just their rights. Greed and fear and selfishness so dominate our imaginations that we can never really believe that we have all that we need. We are convinced that if we are made to share fairly with the poor and the hungry we will not have enough for ourselves, despite all the evidence to the contrary.

So what Jesus offers in the Sermon on the Mount is a much more radical alternative. Those of us who know that we are children of our heavenly Father, and that our rights are guaranteed by him, need to be foolishly generous to others. We have to allow ourselves, Jesus suggests, to be treated unfairly by the greedy and the powerful and the anxious, because we know that nothing they can do can actually dispossess us. So Matthew 5.38–42 is a vision of how the justified are to live in an unjust world. Don't fight it, humour it. Play with it, give it even more than it asks for. Perhaps at last it will think to ask about where your own security comes from, and how you can afford to be so madly generous. Then we might have a chance to share this vision of a world that is whole, connected together by the loving life of God, where to diminish another is to damage ourselves.

Christians are as tempted to dismemberment as anyone else, as the reading today from 1 Corinthians shows. Think about what unites you, not what separates, Paul urges.

# The Second Sunday Before Lent

——— ∾ ———

*Genesis 1.1–23*
*Romans 8.18–25*
*Matthew 6.25–34*

Today's Gospel reading reminds us how important it is not simply to take all passages of Scripture and apply them directly to ourselves, as though they had no original context and no intervening history. Jesus tells his hearers that God will give them everything they need, if they only set their hearts on the kingdom of God, but many, many people have perished for lack of food, clothing and basic necessities. Are we to assume that they somehow failed to concentrate sufficiently on the Kingdom, and so were punished, whereas we, who have the good fortune to live comparatively sheltered lives, are also much better at keeping our hearts fixed on God? I think not.

Part of the discipline, then, of understanding what this text might mean is to try to imagine the people Jesus was speaking to. If you read the rest of the Sermon on the Mount (chapters 5—7), you begin to build up a picture of a fairly settled, law-abiding crowd. They are not so well off that they are cushioned from day-to-day worry entirely, but they have some savings and some education, and they are reasonably satisfied with their lives. Everything Jesus says to them is provocative and challenging to such a way of life, and with at least some part of themselves, they want to be provoked: otherwise what are they doing, following Jesus and listening to his teaching?

So instead of listening for the reassurance, we need to listen for the challenge – not what God promises, which this crowd already have, but what God asks. The radical, imaginative picture of discipleship that Jesus offers in the Sermon on the Mount is meant to shake us loose from the petty things and get us excited by the possibility of a new and adventurous attitude to life.

It is, perhaps, the kind of adventurousness that is found in God himself, in the first chapter of Genesis. This picture of God at work positively fizzes with excitement. The description is full of excess. As God talks – picture the three persons of the Trinity, shouting out to each other, 'Come and look at this!', 'Let's have another few hundred kinds of trees or animal. This is working so well!' – as God talks, roaming around in what is being made, colour and scent and noise spread out where once there had been nothing. And God just loves it. On any one of the 'days' of creation, he could have stopped, satisfied with what he had made, but instead he goes on and on, until at last he makes something that is as like himself as possible. And then what does he do, with all this glorious profusion he has made? He gives it away. He shares it with this, his final creature, because that is the whole point of it. The pleasure is not just for himself. A pleasure shared is a pleasure tripled – perhaps God the Trinity already knew that, long before creation.

In this image of God the creator, we see the essence of a joy that resists the worries and cares of tomorrow. In creating, God knows the risks he takes, and yet delights in what he has made. Up on the mountain, looking down at the puzzled and hopeful crowd, is Jesus trying to give them some sense of that kind of delight in life and creation?

Paul has certainly got the picture. It is an inspired idea to put Genesis 1 and Romans 8 together. Genesis lays out very clearly how things are meant to be, what joy each part of creation is meant to give the rest, and how all of it is there to love and be loved by the human creatures whom God makes to be sharers in his own pleasure. And in Romans we see the whole of the rest of creation waiting with agonized longing for human beings to catch up with the plot. 'How can they be so dense?' creation cries. 'Surely it is perfectly obvious?' 'Let's give them a few more clues,' suggests God. 'Let's show them some of the plot in advance.'

It is typical of Paul's realism to say that this knowledge, in the form of the presence of the Holy Spirit, is not there to make it easier for us. If God thought ease was the most important thing, he would hardly have risked creating. But the gift, the hint, the 'first fruits' of the Spirit do allow us to glimpse something of the glory of what God intends, it gives us that taste of the exhilaration of creation which might actually make us want to 'strive for the kingdom of God and his righteousness'.

# The Sunday Next Before Lent

—— ⁓ ——

Exodus 24.12–18
2 Peter 1.16–21
Matthew 17.1–9

What is the purpose of the transfiguration of Jesus? Is it supposed to reassure and confirm or baffle and alarm? And who is it for? Is it for Jesus himself, or for the disciples?

Matthew, like Luke, follows Mark in placing the transfiguration shortly after the disciples have admitted out loud that they believe Jesus to be the Messiah. So they have already made their decision about Jesus – it isn't prompted by what they see on the mountain. But if it is indeed God's confirmation of what they have already come to believe about Jesus, why are they not allowed to share it with anyone else? Peter, James and John are the only ones to have seen it, and they are specifically told that their news is embargoed until after the resurrection.

Certainly, by the time 2 Peter is being written, the apostles' eyewitness account is being used to give heart to a community that is beginning to doubt. They are beginning to suspect that they have been sold a line, no different from the stories that other cults put out. They had almost certainly converted to Christianity in the expectation that the world would soon end, and they would be on the winning side. But as the Second Coming delayed, so they began to wonder if they had backed the right horse, after all. In this context, the writer of the epistle is offering them the strongest possible proof that Christ is the one approved by God – he is offering them a witness, who speaks from his own experience.

In other words, in the context of this early Christian community, the witness to the events of the transfiguration is being used to back up what Christians already know of the nature and purpose of God. They know through the prophets and through the apostolic preaching of the gospel of Christ what kind of a God they are dealing with. Their temptation is to discouragement, and so they need to hear again the words from God, 'This *is* my Son, my Beloved' – you *have* made the right choice.

But in the Gospel context that is not how God's words would be heard by the first disciples. They are already struggling with Jesus's interpretation of his own mission. When, in the chapter immediately before today's Gospel, Jesus tries to explain to them that they are right to call him Messiah, but wrong in all their expectations of what a Messiah should be, their incomprehension is painful. The fact that only Peter tries to argue by no means suggests that the others are convinced.

So when they come to the mountain of transfiguration, how are they likely to hear God's words? Is there any chance at all that they are going to hear them as God's seal on all that Jesus has said? Or are they going to hear the words of love and approval as an endorsement of their own interpretation? Might they not think, if God loves Jesus so much, he will certainly make him victorious? The temptation to assume that God is on their side, and to discount the fearful picture of the mission of the Messiah that Jesus has been trying to paint must have been enormous.

After the crucifixion and the resurrection, of course, the story can be told. The disciples are not then in danger of thinking that Jesus's Messiahship can be simply glorious. They have seen with their own eyes how God works, and the experience of the transfiguration can be put into its proper perspective by the reality of Jesus's death and rising to life. They can understand that God does indeed love and approve of everything that Jesus is and has done, and they can see the pattern that their own mission must take, and that it must follow the hard path to life, not the easy path to success.

We are not told by the Gospel writers how the words affected Jesus. The Gospel writers are always very reserved in attributing thoughts and emotions to the Lord. But perhaps it is permissible to think that at a time when Jesus is very much alone, misunderstood by his disciples, alienated from his family and his people, and facing the terrible prospect of what is to come, he does long to know that he is loved by his Father, and that his sense of calling to the suffering of the cross is shared and approved by God.

When the Israelites see Moses disappearing into the fiery smoke, and when the disciples fall in fear at the voice of God, they demonstrate the fact that the presence of God is only reassuring if you actually trust the God you are faced with.

*Lent*

# The First Sunday of Lent

—— ≈ ——

*Genesis 2.15–17; 3.1–7*
*Romans 5.12–19*
*Matthew 4.1–11*

The devil, we are told, is the father of lies. Here, in the wilderness, or in Eden, what is on offer is nothing but lies.

Look at the cunning of the tempter. First of all, the really basic approach to a starving man: get yourself some bread. Notice that the devil does not offer to fetch the bread himself, or use his power to produce it – Jesus is to do all the work. And, after all, what harm can it do? It's just food. Jesus is intending to eat again sometime soon, why not now?

When that one fails, the devil moves on to something a little more subtle. All right, Jesus can manage without food for a bit longer, but what about love? All this time in the wilderness, Jesus has been pondering who he is and what he has to do, with God's words of love and affirmation at his baptism ringing in his ears. After all, says the devil, you already know that God loves you, that you are special to him, so you're not asking for a demonstration of anything new. God's already said the words, without any prompting from you. Why not a little action as well?

Finally, the devil moves on to power, and here I think he has misjudged his man, through arrogance and vexation. In this offer to Jesus, the devil is going on what he knows about human nature from all his previous dealings with people – they crave power. After all, it worked with Adam and Eve. They believed, with no other proof at all, that eating the apple would make them like God, and they believed it because that was what they wanted. They knew, with some part of themselves, that they were made to be like God, but they had this sneaking feeling that there was more to it than God was letting on to them. Surely just living in harmony with things and taking care of all that God had made couldn't be what it was really like to be God?

So when the devil offers Jesus all the kingdoms of the world and their splendour, he doesn't expect to have to make good his word. Do the kingdoms of this world actually belong to the devil? Are they within his gift? Who knows. Who cares, thinks the devil. All the things that the devil has offered are illusions, but such clever illusions, based on near-reality. Because Jesus does have the power to turn stones into bread, and he does know that he is God's beloved Son, just as Adam and Eve know that they are made in the image of God. What the devil offers they already have, but in their anxiety Adam and Eve do not notice that. Jesus, however, is too focused on the reality of God to be taken in by such an illusion.

When the devil offers Jesus power in exchange for worship, he doesn't realize how much of his own deepest desire he has betrayed. He longs to be God or, at least, to have what he imagines God has, because the strange irony is that the devil is as taken in by his own illusions as are Adam and Eve. He has not apparently noticed that God is not like that. The devil lives in his own world of illusions, longing to be what he is not, hating what he sees as his own incompleteness, just as he persuades Adam and Eve to hate theirs. Only Jesus is content to be what he is, God's beloved and obedient Son.

In Romans, Paul is talking about the pervasive and destructive effect of living in a world of illusions, and how what breaks through the web of deceit, through the anxiety and determination to have what we deserve, no more and no less, is God's self-gift. There is nothing in the fantasy world about giving away your rights out of love. And so here, Paul says, the illusion of sin can end. It is as though suddenly, in a room full of mirrors, we come across someone real.

'There comes a moment', C. S. Lewis writes in *Miracles*, 'when the children who have been playing at burglars hush suddenly: was that a **real** footstep in the hall? There comes a moment when people who have been dabbling in religion ('Man's search for God') suddenly draw back. Supposing we really found Him? We never meant it to come to **that**! Worse still, supposing He found us?'[1]

Letting go of illusions is hard. But when God, the gracious, self-giving God, finds us, then by amazing and wonderful irony we find that we are what we have longed to be: precious and made in his image.

---

[1] C. S. Lewis, *Miracles*, Geoffrey Bles, 1948, pp. 113–14.

# The Second Sunday of Lent

———— ❧ ————

*Genesis 12.1–4a*
*Romans 4.1–5, 13–17*
*John 3.1–17*

This passage from John's Gospel is one where we usually just concentrate on the edited highlights, like, for example, the wonderful statement about the freedom and power of the Holy Spirit, or verse 16, of course, 'God so loved the world . . .' But as you look in more detail at the whole encounter between Jesus and Nicodemus, it becomes more and more baffling. What exactly did Nicodemus come for, and why is Jesus teasing and testing him?

Nicodemus arrives, we are told, by night. So clearly he does not want his visit advertised. But, all the same, he is being quite brave. He is a 'leader of the Jews', and the conflict between Jesus and the religious leaders is already well under way. So Nicodemus comes to test the water. He has heard about the 'signs' Jesus has been performing, and he is impressed. What's more, he is impressed for the right reasons, not just because the signs are exciting, but because Nicodemus reads them for God's meaning and presence.

So here, you might think, is a chance for Jesus to carry his message into the heart of the Pharisees' camp. If he can get Nicodemus on his side, he will have inside influence. But this is not at all how Jesus is playing it. Instead, he starts the baffling conversation with Nicodemus about being born again. You can hear the irritation and frustration in Nicodemus's voice as he questions Jesus. This is not the treatment he was expecting. He thought that Jesus would be pleased and grateful for his interest, but instead Jesus seems to be mocking him. 'You're supposed to be a teacher of Israel, but you don't understand anything,' Jesus remarks. 'It would be better if you just started again, like a little child.'

Part of the problem is that Nicodemus arrives talking about 'signs'. The Gospels are very full of people who want Jesus to do 'signs', and John's Gospel has already, in the first couple of chapters, explored the bitter irony of the way in which we view 'signs'.

In the opening chapter, we see God's creative word going largely unrecognized in his own world, and then the stories of the calling of the first disciples, who believe and follow Jesus without the benefit of any 'signs'. Then there is the story of the 'sign' unwillingly performed – the wedding at Cana. Finally, immediately before poor Nicodemus walks in, the Pharisees have demanded a 'sign' from Jesus to justify his cleansing of the temple. And Jesus offers them the enigmatic sign of his own ministry. But no one can be bothered to try and interpret that sign. The only kinds of signs they care about are the miraculous healings that are such a strongly attested part of Jesus's ministry. But what are they supposed to be 'signs' of? Are the people really willing to look beyond the sign itself and try to work out what it might be pointing to? Or do they want the miracles as a quick fix, signalling, if you bother to think even this far, only that God will do as you want him to?

To be fair to Nicodemus, he has not come asking for a sign for himself. He has put some thought into the matter, and he has interpreted Jesus's actions as being connected, in some way, with the activity of God. So he has come by night to have his cake and eat it. He comes, rather smugly, offering approval and support to Jesus, but clearly not willing to jeopardize his position as a 'leader of the Jews' until he is clear which is the winning side.

The luxury of sitting on the sidelines and hedging your bets is not one that Jesus offers. Nicodemus thinks he is backing a potential winner without risking himself too much, but instead he is standing in the presence of his God. And he, a teacher of Israel, who thinks he knows enough about God to discern him at work in Jesus, does not know that he is seeing not a sign-worker, but God's own Son. Confronted with the Son, inexpensive goodwill really will not do.

Jesus is offering Nicodemus a chance to enter the real world, the one that God created through the Word. Suddenly, Jesus stops teasing, and spells it out. There is only one way to find out what God is like and what his purposes are for the world, and that is to commit yourself to the Son of Man, whose lifting up on the cross is to be the true sign of God's loving design. Nicodemus cannot go home pretending to be baffled by what Jesus has said. He has to decide.

# The Third Sunday of Lent

— ◈ —

Exodus 17.1–7
Romans 5.1–11
John 4.5–42

John is a masterly storyteller, and this story of Jesus and the woman at the well is one of his best. The Samaritan woman comes out of the page, cheeky, brave, vulnerable, and Jesus responds to her with warmth and humour, leading her skilfully into confidences, encouraging her to get beyond the superficial flirtatiousness that is obviously her natural conversational medium.

All through their talk, the woman is trying to keep Jesus at a distance and keep the talk between them jokey. She is good at the quick repartee, and to begin with, Jesus responds on that level. But everything he says has a serious point to it. The woman resists cleverly, turning the offer of the water of life into a joke, and swiftly engaging in theological argument when her own personal circumstances come into question. But Jesus will not let her get away with it. Every time she tries to turn the conversation away from the personal, Jesus forces it back. Finally, in desperation, she makes a faith statement: 'I know that the Messiah is coming.' But if she hopes that that will satisfy Jesus, she is sadly mistaken. Her belief in the coming of the Messiah is safe and impersonal; she doesn't expect it to have any immediate effect on her day-to-day life; it's something that belongs in a vague and unspecified future. Immediately, Jesus pounces. 'I am he.'

Now what is the woman to do? The moment she has been putting off all her life, the moment of truth about her faith, is now standing in front of her, demanding a response. So she runs away. She runs to get help, to find other people who will make the decision for her. 'He can't be the Messiah, can he?', she asks. Does she hope the answer will be yes or no? Either way, she has her moment of glory. For once in her life, she is the centre of respectful attention, and everyone is listening to her. It doesn't last long, as verse 42 makes brutally plain.

But what a very odd ending this is to the story. We know that through the woman's agency, many people come to faith in Christ, but we are not told if she did. Did her natural inclination to put off important decisions win, or was she convinced?

We presumably like to think that if we were faced, as she was, with Jesus in person, declaring 'I am the Messiah', we would not hesitate for an instant. We would not dither or postpone or offer Jesus a lukewarm reception. But there are an awful lot of warning stories in the Bible that suggest that dithering is one of the things we are best at.

The stories about the journey of Moses and his people through the desert are very full of dithering. Every so often, the people really make an effort, and manage to believe and trust long enough to take one huge step. Usually, it's only after all other avenues are closed to them, but even so, they did finally manage to follow Moses out of Egypt. God then performs a whole series of mighty acts to direct and protect his people, but their memories are notoriously short. After God has fed them regularly on manna, we now find them squabbling with Moses because they are thirsty. They seem to feel that their one great act of faith in following Moses out of Egypt is all that is necessary, and now Moses has to be responsible for everything else that is to happen to them.

Both the Israelites and the woman at the well are unwilling to believe what is put in front of them. It is almost as though the very ease of it makes it unreal. The Israelites cannot connect God's past actions for them with their present need. Every new challenge throws them into a panic, instead of reinforcing their understanding of their God – while the woman at the well cannot believe that her life is ever going to change, and that she is being offered salvation, just like that, in the course of a conversation. The very simplicity of it makes it enormous.

Paul has the clue. God's mercy is there, all around us, long before we even think to look. The hard part is not that we have to deserve it, because we don't. The hard part is just that we have to accept it. That's why John's ending to the story of the Samaritan woman is such a challenge – you decide the end. Did she allow the generous waves of God's grace to overwhelm her, or did she sit down in the desert and moan about being thirsty?

# The Fourth Sunday of Lent

———— ～ ————

1 Samuel 16.1–13
Ephesians 5.8–14
John 9.1–41

All the time we are called to try and find the difficult balance between faithfulness to God's known work in the past, and prophetic discernment of God's new work now. Faced with a completely new challenge, the hardest thing of all is to try to discern whether it is from God or not. When the challenge is past, and the new insights it brought are absorbed and become part of the 'tradition', it is hard to imagine the time when we were unsure. We look back, and we see that this new thing is absolutely in keeping with the character of the God we worship, as displayed in all his past interaction with us. How could we possibly have doubted it? But then the next new thing comes over the horizon, and we are left floundering again.

So it is easy to sympathize with Samuel. God used him to anoint Saul and support him in battle, to be committed to him, as God's way for his people. And so Samuel does what God asks. But when God then tells him to abandon Saul and anoint another in his place, Samuel cannot so quickly change his emotions. He grieves for Saul. And when, with a heavy heart, he sets out to do God's bidding, he is still, however unconsciously, looking for a direct replacement for Saul – another big, strong, handsome warrior, who will command the respect of the people. Only Samuel's prophetic gift from God enables him obediently to know David when at last he meets him.

But if we can sympathize with Samuel, can we also sympathize with the 'Jews' in today's Gospel reading? They – like most of us – don't have the advantage of direct prophetic communication from God, but they do have a profound, lifelong knowledge of the God of the Scriptures, the God of Moses. This God called his people to be holy, and to show his own character through their obedience. So the observance of the sabbath is not a detachable element, but a part of all they know of how to serve God.

50

Now, in retrospect it may seem clear to us that they had allowed the rules to take the place of a genuine seeking for God. They had assumed that it is enough to follow the law of Moses, and that no deeper confrontation with God is required. But it is easy to be wise after the event, and not easy to apply that wisdom to ourselves. What clues and hints did the 'Jews' have, that in Jesus God was making new, direct and personal claims upon their lives?

They are faced with a man who, they believe, was blind as a punishment for his sinfulness, and who has been healed on the sabbath. Is the healing itself enough of a sign of God's presence to counteract their fixed belief in what God does and does not want from his people? Over and over again, they question the man who was blind, and over and over again, doggedly, he tells his tale, though his exasperation increases throughout the story. He, at least, is in no doubt about what has happened and how to feel about it.

As a last resort, the 'Jews' try to direct the man's joy into more suitable channels. They have to accept that he was indeed blind, and now he can see, and that Jesus is somehow involved in this, but they try to make the man leave out Jesus and go straight to God with his thanks. But the man is not having it. To him it is clear that the two are connected. The power that healed him is the power of God, but the saliva and the hands that made the mud are Jesus's. 'What's the problem?' he demands.

The problem is not just that the 'Jews' cannot connect God's new work in Jesus with his previous work, but that they really don't want to. There is something about Jesus that they just long to escape from. They, Jesus, says grimly, are the blind ones, and their blindness, unlike the man's, is caused by sin, because it is their deliberate choice.

Ephesians is clear that trying 'to find out what is pleasing to the Lord' is the daily task of Christians. Everything must be laid out in the light of God, nothing must be taken for granted or left unexamined by that light. Even what we think we know about God must be brought constantly under that piercing scrutiny, because there is no other source of light, and no other possibility of recognizing the new acts of our unchanging God.

# The Fifth Sunday of Lent

—— ≈ ——

*Ezekiel 37.1–14*
*Romans 8.6–11*
*John 11.1–45*

There is a story that St Francis once got up to preach, looked down at the hushed, expectant faces below him and said, 'God has not given me anything to say to you.' And with that, he blessed the people, and got down again. Faced with today's readings from Ezekiel and John, I wish I had the courage to do that. The story of the dry bones and the story of the raising of Lazarus are so brilliantly and powerfully told that commentary on them seems like gilding the lily.

So let's start with the slightly less emotionally charged reading from Romans, which actually provides a useful key to the other two. Life, Paul suggests, is a symptom, not a cause. You are not alive because you have life in you, but because you have the Spirit of God in you. A life that is directed away from God is, whether it knows it or not, no life at all. It is not just that it misses the point, but that it is actively 'hostile', Paul says, to the point. The whole purpose of creation is to mirror God's creativity and love. So to try to live as though there is no God is to destroy the very thing for which we exist, and to drive ourselves further and further away from the source of our life, which is God.

In the Gospel reading for today, death is clearly subject to Jesus. But if the point of the story is to demonstrate beyond all possible doubt who Jesus is, through his mastery of that last great enemy, death, it also demonstrates that death is not negligible or cost-free, even for God incarnate. Jesus orchestrates this great miracle meticulously. He does not rush to rescue his ill friend. He wants it clear beyond any possible doubt that Lazarus is dead so that when they see life emerging from the stench of putrefaction, the onlookers cannot deceive themselves that this was just someone reviving from a faint. And then when Martha comes out to meet Jesus, he gives her an unambiguous statement of his power: 'I am the resurrection and the life', and Martha accepts it without hesitation.

But suddenly, what has seemed an unmoved, almost callous, opportunity to demonstrate his power changes and becomes charged with human emotion. As Jesus sees Mary and her comforters crying, the reality of what has happened hits him. Even though Jesus knows that he is the resurrection and the life, the tears and the loss affect him, and he weeps. This is one of those extraordinary moments when we see into the heart of the paradoxical things that Christianity says about God. Jesus is here to demonstrate God's absolute power of life over death, and yet he reacts as we all do to a life cut short, to the desolation of losing someone we love, and sharing the pain of others who mourn him, too.

And it is this Jesus, human, shaken, mourning, who goes to Lazarus's tomb and raises him from the dead. It is not an act of calm and majestic power, but an act of hope that love is stronger than death. Of course, after the resurrection, we know that to offer this hope is the purpose of the incarnation. We have chosen death, over and over again, as Paul reminds us, setting our hearts on our own needs as though their satisfaction could bring us life. But God offers us, in Jesus, a new way of being what we are meant to be, his children, made in his image. What we see in the raising of Lazarus is a foretaste of that hope that is offered to all through Jesus's own death and resurrection, the hope that God will not let us go out of the circle of his life and his love.

There is one more bit of irony in John's telling of this story. As Jesus goes out to demonstrate God's loving and life-giving power, he is, at the same time, setting the final seal on his own death. In going to Lazarus's home, Jesus is walking back into the full-blown hostility of 'the Jews'. Even as they sit, weeping professionally with Mary and Martha, they are waiting to see what Jesus will do. Will he risk coming back to visit his friend? How will he react to the death of someone he loves? Jesus's miracle and his words of liberation to Lazarus – 'Unbind him and let him go' – will lead directly to the decision to bring Jesus to his death. Lazarus's freedom and ours is bought by Jesus's imprisonment and death. We can only share in God's life because God is prepared to share in the death we chose for ourselves.

# Palm Sunday

—— ≈ ——

*Isaiah 50.4–9a*
*Philippians 2.5–11*
*Matthew 26.14—27.66*

Betrayal.

At the surface level of the narrative, it is Jesus who is betrayed, over and over again, by friend and enemy alike. First there is Judas who suddenly, inexplicably, has had enough. As he sits eating with Jesus, he has already betrayed him in his heart and is looking for a way to make that betrayal real. Then there are the three disciples who go with Jesus to Gethsemane to pray with him in his agony of indecision. But despite the tense scene at supper, despite sharing the cup that Jesus explicitly tells them represents his blood, they seem unaware of what must follow, how much Jesus needs them. Their sleep betrays him. When they wake to find themselves surrounded by an angry mob, these three and the rest of the disciples run away.

Peter has, at least, a little more courage than the others. He does follow Jesus as he is dragged away. But as the night wears on, and it becomes clear that there is to be no rescue for Jesus, from heaven or earth, Peter betrays Jesus again.

For the Jewish authorities, the crowd of shouting, sneering onlookers and the bandits crucified with Jesus, the betrayal is at least not personal. They do not know Jesus as a friend and their leader. But they do willingly collude with Roman injustice, as Pilate does, caught up in the frenzy of hatred and excitement.

But if this is all about the betrayal of Jesus, it is also about self-betrayal. Pilate is supposed to be the authority-figure, the one who symbolizes order, the one who stands above the petty infighting of the local people. But even with his wife's words ringing in his ears, Pilate betrays everything on which his career has been based, and gives in to the chief priests and the crowd. How was he to know that this was to be his only claim to fame for the rest of time?

The religious authorities let themselves down doubly. They know Pilate despises them and cares nothing for their religion, and yet they are prepared to use his hated authority for their own ends. And in doing so, they betray their God, because they prove conclusively that they do not trust God to give judgement on Jesus. Instead, they make their own judgement and engineer his end accordingly.

Peter's self-betrayal is so enormous that he can never be the same person again. Peter, the impetuous, the outspoken, the brave. Peter who never hesitates but always leaps in with both feet first. Peter has been at the heart of Jesus's ministry from the beginning. He was one of the first to believe, one of the most vociferous in declaring Jesus to be the Messiah. He has seen Jesus teaching, preaching, healing. He is one of Jesus's closest friends, in the inner circle, one of the few who has seen the transfiguration and heard the voice of God acclaiming Jesus. Peter is absolutely confident that under no circumstances will he ever betray Jesus. All right, he made a mistake by going to sleep at the vital moment in the garden, but he didn't run away when the others did. He followed Jesus all the way into the heart of the enemy camp. What is happening to Peter in the hours that follow? Why does his confidence and love begin to seep away? What brings him to that moment of terrible desolation when the cock crows, and he knows what he has done? Whatever it is, it makes Peter the man to whom Jesus commits his people. Without that moment of stark betrayal, of knowing what he actually is at his most basic level, could Peter ever have been the rock on whom the Church was built? In the end, as he weeps, Peter knows that Jesus is more precious even than his own safety. He believes he has come to that discovery too late.

And what about Judas whose name is to become synonymous with betrayal? The Gospels give us no insight into Judas's motives, but they do tell us that, when it was done, he could not live with himself. Like Peter, when he sees the truth of himself in this betrayal, he cannot bear it. But if Peter goes back to his friends, those others who have also betrayed Jesus, and who must all face their lives with that knowledge, Judas's self-betrayal is even deeper. He will not accept the reality of himself. He would rather die. Could Judas's story have been any different? Peter the betrayer became Peter the rock, and Paul the persecutor became Paul the great missionary. Judas's greatest betrayal was in believing that God's grace and pardon were too small for his terrible sin.

*Easter*

# Easter Sunday

—— ∾ ——

Jeremiah 31.1–6
Colossians 3.1–4
John 20.1–18

Real life is something so unusual that we can barely recognize it. Occasionally, we get a glimpse of it and it touches us with awe: the birth of a baby, for example, or listening to a perfectly performed piece of music, or a talk about the mathematics of infinity. All of these things have about them that combination of the ordinary and the completely mysterious that pings the chords of the mind and heart. In labour you know that what will come out will be a baby, but that tells you so little about the completely new character who is emerging. However much you may imagine what is growing inside you, or read all about the various stages of its development, or even see it, moving across the screen of the ultrasound scanner, the new-born child is still a complete surprise – utterly familiar and utterly strange.

The Gospel accounts of the risen Jesus suggest that when people encounter him, they do not immediately know him. On the whole, they are not terrified, they do not imagine themselves to be in the presence of an alien life-force, or anything like that. They recognize what is in front of them as a living human being, but not a familiar one. Even the people closest to him need help to connect the risen Jesus with the man they loved.

In today's reading from John's Gospel, you can, if you like, think of all kinds of reasons why Mary does not immediately see who Jesus is as he stands beside her in the garden. She is obviously in a terrible state, her eyes full of tears, and her imagination full of macabre visions of death and grave-robbers. She is utterly single-minded in her search for the dead body of her Lord, to the point where even a meeting with a pair of angels becomes uninteresting unless they can give her the one piece of information she wants.

But none of these seem real explanations of why she does not recognize Jesus. This is a woman whose whole mind is full of pictures of the man now standing beside her, and yet she does not know him. The simple explanation must be the true one – that real life is something we are poorly equipped to understand. So Jesus gives Mary the gift of sight, the gift of being able to connect the new life with the old. He says her name, and makes a bridge for her to see who he is, in all his extraordinary life.

By ourselves we do not have the power to see or understand God's vitality. By ourselves, we plod on, trying to be satisfied with the poor imitation that we call 'life', which is all about separation and death. But Jesus gives the gift of connection to the only true life, the life of the creator, which is about unity and sharing in the utterly real life of God. God's loving desire to share his life with us is implicit in everything he does, from creating us to redeeming us. Life is not 'natural' to us, but is a gift, reflecting the giver. Jeremiah puts into God's mouth the words 'I have loved you with an ever-lasting love, therefore I have continued my faithfulness to you' (v. 3), and that is the heart of it. We are loved into existence, and our continued existence is not our own doing but a demonstration of God's continuing commitment to us.

But for the moment we must be content with the sudden and fleeting reminders of God's eternal life that are available to us day by day. We have always before us the vision of the risen Christ, which helps us to recognize God's life where we see it. We have his voice, calling us by name so that, like Mary, we suddenly look up and see the Lord of life, standing beside us. And then, like Mary, we have to turn back to a world, utterly changed, yet devastatingly the same. We know this world now to be electric with the presence of God; we know our own lives now to be zinging with the resurrection life, and yet all of this is tantalizingly 'hidden with Christ in God' (Colossians 3.3). We are not called to cling to the presence of the risen Christ. Instead, like Mary, we are sent to shout out what we have seen. We are God's spies, now, searching for evidence of him in the robes of the gardener, listening for the familiar sound of the beloved voice of the Lord in the unrecognized strangers around us, helping to build the bridges of love that will enable others, too, to hear Jesus's voice and recognize the vast, free, unchanging, faithful love of God.

# The Second Sunday of Easter

—— ❧ ——

*Acts 2.14a, 22–32*
*1 Peter 1.3–9*
*John 20.19–31*

What makes people believe? Probably the reasons are as numerous as the people who give them. Today's readings provide just a few examples.

In the Gospel, we have two sets of responses. First of all, there are the disciples, gathered together, their misery and fear locking them in far more effectively than the door that they think is doing the job. They have heard some rumours, from Mary and from Peter and the beloved disciple. But Mary is the only one who claims to have seen the Lord, and even she has to admit that she didn't recognize him at first. Would you believe under those circumstances? But then Jesus comes to them, unmistakably Jesus, full of extraordinary and unpredictable life, free to come and go as he pleases, but Jesus, all the same. And they believe.

But Thomas is still sceptical. He'll trust nobody's evidence but his own. Even his best friends can't convince him. 'Unless I see the mark of the nails in his hands and put my finger in the mark of the nails, and my hand in his side, I will not believe.' He lays out very precisely what will constitute proof, in his case. And Jesus gives it to him, uncannily echoing his exact words. Only now, Thomas does not need to do it, after all. What he needed was for Jesus to hear and respond, and Thomas believes.

In Acts, the process is more complicated. Peter is offering his audience a mixture of reasons for believing. First, he is offering them a new way of seeing what they already know to be true. They have heard about Jesus and about the signs and wonders that he performed, and they know what happened to him. Now Peter shows them, through their own scriptures, that this man they thought dead is actually alive with the life of God. As evidence of this, Peter then offers them himself and the other disciples as eyewitnesses. 'Go on,' he urges, 'ask us anything you like.' But lastly, and powerfully, Peter offers them a way of acknowledging what they have done. '*You* crucified him', Peter tells them. No beating about the bush there. Who knows how many of the people listening to Peter were actually present at the crucifixion? But present or not, Peter has judged rightly in thinking that his listeners feel a sense of collective guilt. They know that they and their representatives invoked the ungodly power of Rome to carry out their dirty work, and that Jesus was killed for no good reason. Now they can confess, and hear that God's purpose was not deflected by their unfaithfulness. They can repent and believe.

Finally, in 1 Peter readers are offered two reasons for believing: hope and community. The hope is what brought them there in the first place, the wild, ridiculous hope that this talk of the resurrection of Jesus was true. Because if it is true, then perhaps there really is some point to this world, perhaps we are not born simply to suffer and to die, but are actually part of a dynamic movement towards the kingdom of God. And having accepted the hope, they have stepped into a community of others who have thrown caution to the wind and decided to live as though life matters. Together, they will hold on to their hope, whatever the opposition, and when one feels like giving up, the others will remind them why they are here.

So the reasons for believing are many and various, and all of them will, at various times, appear ridiculous to others, and even to ourselves. One man's proof is another man's sneer. But at the heart of all of these proofs stands the risen Jesus, breathing out his life-giving Spirit. Life begins to fill our lungs, as we breathe in, standing in his presence, inhaling the fragrance of God's own life. The longing that it might be true, the longing for more of that tantalizing scent of the life of God, is what Augustine described in the fourth century, as he speaks to God. 'You called me, you cried aloud to me, you broke my barrier of deafness. You shone upon me, your radiance enveloped me, you put my blindness to flight. You shed your fragrance about me; I drew breath and now I gasp for your sweet odour. I tasted you, and now I hunger and thirst for you. You touched me, and I am inflamed with love of your peace.'[1] God in his graciousness may well meet you at the point at which you think you need proof in order to believe, as he met Thomas. But then he will give you himself, and after that, you will need nothing more.

---

[1] Augustine, *Confessions*, Penguin Classics, 1961, Bk 10, ch. 27.

# The Third Sunday of Easter

———— ❧ ————

*Acts 2.14a, 36–41*
*1 Peter 1.17–23*
*Luke 24.13–35*

In his poem, 'The Lake Isle of Innisfree',[1] W. B. Yeats pictures a man so consumed with longing for home that even in the middle of a busy street, all he hears is the sound of the lake, more real than the shadowy place where he is actually standing.

What he longs for is the home of his imagination, on the Isle of Innisfree, where he will live in simplicity and peace. The slow beat of the poem's last line lets us see the man, standing stock still as the traffic flows around him, hearing the sound of the water of his dreams. Yeats did not, of course, abandon his literary life to live as a peasant by the lake at Innisfree, but the yearning that he expressed for a true home for his 'deep heart's core' is one that the readers of 1 Peter could easily understand. They, too, are standing in an alien land, longing for home.

But if they do not yet sit beside the lake, they are at least surrounded by their new family. 1 Peter reminds them that although they are living in exile, they know whose children they are, and so they know what is required of them. They can call God 'Father', with unimaginable intimacy, and although they come from many backgrounds and have had to be rescued from 'futile ways', they now know where they are going. For some unfathomable and utterly humbling reason, God's great plan for the salvation of the world waited for them, the ragbag of scraps from goodness knows how many cultures, to be ready, so that they could come home. They are bound together by that disproportionate gift that has made them a family, where before they were strangers, and set them on their path home, together.

Exactly the same thing is happening to the people who respond

---

[1] W. B. Yeats, 'The Lake Isle of Innisfree', *The New Oxford Book of English Verse*, OUP, 1972.

to Peter's speech in Acts. They are being made into a new family, with their loyalties changed, and their faces set in a new direction. Like the readers of 1 Peter, they know what it has cost to bring them here. In fact, their sense of the price paid for them is even stronger, because they recognize their own complicity in the death of Jesus. But that recognition is the start of the new life, and God's response to their contrition is overwhelming. They are to receive a share in his life, through the gift of the Holy Spirit. All around them, near and far, stretching away on every side, streaming into the future come the crowds of those who will now be their family, on the journey home together.

The disciples on the road to Emmaus do not know that theirs is a journey home. What are they doing, walking down that road with slow, distracted steps, talking as they go? Are they running away from the strange events in Jerusalem? If so, they are not very logical, because as soon as the stranger starts asking questions, they betray themselves as disciples of the recently crucified Jesus. If they are afraid, shouldn't they keep their mouths shut? Their most over-whelming need, greater even than their need for security, or space, or whatever it is that set them off on the road to Emmaus, is the need to talk. They have to find some sense in what is going on. They have talked themselves round in circles, unable to get to any sensible conclusion, and so they turn eagerly to the stranger, and the words pour out. They are past caring about whether he is a safe confidant.

At first they are angry with him. What luxury it is to be angry with a stranger! They must have been so angry with each other over the past few days, since the crucifixion. The only way to bear the guilt they all feel is to make sure they know it is shared. But here is some stupid idiot who seems not to know of the cataclysmic tragedy that has overturned all their hopes. But soon their anger is forgotten as they return again to their search. What is going on? What can it mean? They have asked themselves over and over again. All their hopes of Jesus confounded, and with them, all they had come to believe about God and his purposes. And then these strange rumours about the body being missing, about angels, about life. Oh, what can it mean? They turn to the stranger, too perplexed to realize how silly this ought to have been. How could he possibly answer?

Into their turmoil the stranger, who is no stranger, speaks his words of rough and humorous revelation. And suddenly the road to Emmaus is the road home, after all.

# The Fourth Sunday of Easter

—— ⌒ ——

*Acts 2.42–7*
*1 Peter 2.19–25*
*John 10.1–10*

It is easy to telescope these verses from St John's Gospel with verses 11–18. The second parable is also about sheep, and it is much clearer and more vivid, beginning as it does with Jesus's statement, 'I am the good shepherd'. But the parable we have today is more enigmatic, and repays careful study in its own right.

Picture a group of sheep. They are safe in their pen, which they know well, and they are keeping an eye on the only way in and out – the gate. A variety of people have been coming to that gate, and the sheep are all a little wary. They like it best when the shepherd comes. They know the shepherd, and he knows each one of them. He takes them out to places where they can get good pasture and feed safely. When he comes to the gate, they can abandon their watchfulness and just get on with eating, knowing that the shepherd will take care of them.

But when other people come to the gate, the sheep are in a quandary. Their instinct is to go out when the gate is open, because that is what they have always done. But they remember times when someone who wasn't the shepherd came and led them out, and they couldn't find the pasture, and didn't recognize his whistle, and some of them got lost. Ewes remember being separated from their lambs, and they all remember that the flock that made it home was smaller, less secure, and when they huddled together at night, they were not so warm and cosy.

Some of the sheep are recommending that they don't go out of the gate at all. That way, they know that they will be safe. But the other sheep point out that they will also starve to death if they don't go out to pasture. Poor bewildered sheep.

Clearly, this parable is at least partly a riddle. John tells us that its first hearers didn't understand it, and that Jesus had to explain that the point of the parable is not the shepherd, but the gate. A

64

closed gate functions to keep the sheep safely shut in, but the open gate is what this story is primarily interested in. It is the open gate that allows the shepherd to come in and it is the open gate that leads to the life-giving pastures. The strangers who confuse the sheep and the thieves who come to kill and rob all help to point to the one sure end. Sheep are always at risk, and they have to learn to value something more than safety. That something is what Jesus is offering them. The climax of the story is not security but abundant life.

At first glance, it might seem that the epistle of Peter has regressed in its interpretation of the sheep/shepherd motif, and gone back to putting the emphasis on safety again. It seems to be a very deeply held desire in us to see God as a kind of safety device, despite all the evidence to the contrary. We long to see God as the gate that keeps all danger out, instead of the gate that we go through into lush and exciting pasture. Isn't Peter just pandering to this desire, when he tells his readers that they have returned 'to the shepherd and guardian of your souls' (v. 25)?

But the only way that that phrase can be taken as superficial reassurance is if you detach it from its context. Otherwise what it says is that our shepherd and guardian, whom we must trust and emulate in all our doings, is the crucified Christ. Our gateway to life is made up of the wood of the cross. So in Christ we are indeed offered security, but on such a huge scale that it is almost frightening. What God gives us in Christ is the certainty that we are forgiven people, free to come and go in God's great pasture. For us sheep that is sometimes rather more than we might want. We might prefer a small mouthful of grass and then a quick scurry back into our reassuringly dull sheepfold. But that is too meagre a gift for God to offer.

So to 'return to the shepherd and guardian of your souls' is to step through the gateway of Christ's cross into an entirely new world, where we are no longer sheep, easily satisfied with small securities, but children of God, free to come and go in God's world. With that freedom comes responsibility, and a willingness to abandon our day-to-day security, as Jesus did, in order to gain the total security of being and doing what we are made for.

# The Fifth Sunday of Easter

———— ❧ ————

Acts 7.55–60
1 Peter 2.2–10
John 14.1–14

What are we Christians supposed to feel about the world we live in? All three of today's readings suggest that, at the very least, the world is not our home. Stephen dies as though death is irrelevant, with his eyes fixed on the heavenly vision; Peter's readers leave all their previous identity to be like newborn children in their new race; and Jesus holds out to the disciples the picture of his Father's roomy mansion, to which we are all invited. Is this world, then, just something to be endured until we can get to where we really want to be?

Peter's letter has a high theology of the people of God. Although there is, of course, some debate about the author and date of the letter, the consensus is that it is indeed primarily the work of the Apostle Peter, writing at an early stage of the life of the new Christian community. His audience is a diverse group of people, from a number of different races and faiths, and they are facing hard times. It is clear that they are, in fact, going to have to learn to live in this world for rather longer than they might have hoped. The expectation of the immediate return of Jesus to take believers to the kingdom of God is already fading and, to make matters worse, Christians in some areas are facing mob violence. What Peter is offering them is a vision of who they are, a vision of their value and status that will sustain them through what is to come.

New allegiance, new race, new family, new life – these are at the heart of Peter's theology of the people of God. Once they belonged nowhere and had no importance, but now they are God's own people, chosen, royal, holy (v. 9). When they stand together, this motley crew of unimportant people become a rich, magnificent temple, bearing witness to the grandeur of God. And at the heart of this temple is Jesus, the Cornerstone.

As Stephen looks up to heaven, feeling the hate and the stones battering at him, he too sees Jesus, and Jesus is standing next to God, part of his glory.

So Jesus is the key, the one who mediates an understanding of how we are to live in this world. In today's Gospel, it is easy to laugh at Thomas's stupidity as he asks what should have been obvious, but actually, he is asking the basic religious questions – what is God like, and how do we get to him? And Jesus's answer is the basic Christian answer – 'God is like Jesus, and can only be reached through Jesus, through following and imitating him.' A simple and utterly annoying answer. No system is given, no sets of rules, no course of study, with diplomas at the end, but a commitment to a person, whose life, death and resurrection reveal the world's creator and saviour.

In all the time that Thomas has been a follower of Jesus, he has known that Jesus's mission is about God. Thomas and the others have not always, or even often, understood what exactly is going on, but they have grasped that Jesus has the power to 'show us the Father'. They have felt the authority of Jesus, the strange, compelling novelty of his message about God, that yet makes sense of everything they already knew and had heard about God. Very occasionally, they seem to take the next step and realize that God cannot be understood independently of the witness of Jesus. Now, Jesus makes that explicit. 'I am the way, the truth and the life. No one comes to the Father except through me.'

So if Jesus is the way we follow, how does that way lead us through the world? Peter and Acts make it clear that Jesus's way is bound to involve suffering, but they do not suggest that we should hate the world, or count it as essentially unreal. As Stephen dies, gazing at the glory of God, the figure he sees is undoubtedly a human one. The humanity of Jesus, the incarnate God, is not accidental to God's relation to the world, but essential. God the creator makes a world and gives himself to it, without reservation, even to death. Our commitment to the world should be no less full. The result of God's self-giving in Jesus is the knowledge that every part of what is made, even death, can respond to its creator and be transformed. Peter urges his readers to come and be built into a temple where God can be joyfully praised and faithfully served. If Jesus chose to do that in this world, we, his followers, should be content to follow.

# The Sixth Sunday of Easter

———— ❦ ————

*Acts 17.22–31*
*1 Peter 3.13–22*
*John 14.15–21*

It is hard to tell if Paul's famous speech at the Areopagus is a triumph or a disaster of evangelism. He has done his preparation well – one of the basic rules of preaching. He has walked around the city and talked and listened and picked up on the concerns of the people to whom he is talking, and the kind of religious language they are used to. So he hasn't simply used a set speech, but is deliberately trying to tap into the world-view of his audience.

In the section before today's reading from Acts, we find Paul stuck in Athens, waiting for Silas and Timothy. Being Paul, he doesn't take a holiday, but immediately throws himself into the fray, arguing with anyone who will listen, in the synagogue and the market place. Clearly, this kind of argument is meat and drink to the Athenians, and Paul quickly gathers crowds who are more than happy to listen to and join in with religious debate. They liked nothing better than a new religion.

So when they invite him, politely and formally, to come and address them about his ideas, Paul starts cautiously, with compliments. He has noticed, he says, that they are a deeply religious people. The audience nod and preen themselves slightly. Indeed, Paul goes on, they seem to be prepared to worship almost anything, and put up altars to nothing in particular, just in case. The audience frown, wondering if that is still a compliment, or does it, in fact, contain a hint of criticism?

Throughout the speech, Paul does this subtle, sharp blending of flattery and criticism, first complimenting them on the array of altars they have set up, then telling them that altars are useless; or agreeing with them that all people share a common humanity and derive from God, and then telling them that they are not perfect, and will have to repent and be judged.

Paul is building towards his climax, which is the introduction of

68

Jesus. But the crowd are not ready for this. Paul has correctly identified their religious instincts. They like novelty, variety. They want to control God through the service they offer to him, and they think that is best done by keeping all their options open and performing sacrifices at as many altars as possible. They are aware that their lives are limited and transitory, and they seek to find their meaning by seeing themselves as part of the divine life. All of this Paul understands but ruthlessly confronts. Certainly, he tells them, your lives do have meaning. They will be seen, in their entirety, and judged by God in Jesus. But judgement was not what the Athenians were looking for. They wanted affirmation, not responsibility. In particular, they do not want to be judged by a God they can't buy with worship. They want to bind God to them with the power and scope of their religious service, but God is not to be bound, Paul reminds them: he is utterly free, and needs nothing. He does not need gifts, but is the ultimate source of all there is to give. So you cannot buy meaning and certainty by the rich variety of your religious observance.

So, having demolished their religious props, what is Paul offering instead? He is offering Jesus, the man appointed by God, and affirmed through the resurrection. He is asking them to swap their great profusion of ideas and hopes, all their sources of religious insurance, for faith in one man. He is telling them that there is no easy way, through religious observance, to security, but only a hard way, through repentance and an acceptance of limits. And he asks them to believe this because God has shown it to be the truth by raising Jesus from the dead.

But Paul gets no further. In fact, he doesn't even have time to introduce the name of Jesus. Just the mention of judgement and resurrection are enough. The crowd are bored and incredulous. What is it that so alienates them? Is it the very idea of resurrection that they find so incredible? Or is it the smallness and particularity of what Paul is offering them in exchange for their profusion of religious beliefs? What if another new and exciting religion comes along? Surely Paul doesn't expect them to stick with this gloomy religion even then?

To believe that God might focus all truth and meaning in one man, Jesus, is hard, but perhaps mostly because we, like the Athenians, like novelty more than commitment, like the idea of controlling God more than the idea of giving God control, like the idea of our lives having meaning, but not that the meaning is God's, not ours.

# The Seventh Sunday of Easter

—— ✑ ——

*Acts 1.6–14*
*1 Peter 4.12–14; 5.6–11*
*John 17.1–11*

Poor disciples. What they have been through over the last few weeks! What wild swings of emotion they have had to deal with. First of all the horrors of Good Friday, with the anguish they felt for Jesus, the fear for themselves, the guilt over what they had done, the confusion about their future now that Jesus's mission had apparently failed. Then the beginnings of the rumours that Jesus was alive, with all the hope and terror and sheer perplexity of that. And then, at last, normality again, though a much more wonderful normality than ever before, with Jesus back among them, talking, teaching, making them feel at the centre of God's world, as he always did.

It is very unclear from the Gospels and from Paul's writings how long this period between the resurrection and the ascension was. The Church's liturgical year suggests just a few weeks. In Matthew, it looks very short, while Paul seems to extend it to include the appearance to him on the Damascus road. John's account is the most vivid, with the details of significant meetings and memorable meals. But for sheer poignancy, these first few verses of Acts are hard to beat. In verse 6, the disciples are clearly imagining that life will now go on like it used to in the old days, only better. Jesus seems willing to concentrate only on them, with no preaching, teaching or healing outsiders, and he listens to them and answers their questions without the impatience and teasing that so often marked their relationship before. They have forgotten all their doubts about his mission, the terrible doubts that the crucifixion caused, and they are back to believing that Jesus is going to take over Israel, and that they will be part of the new ruling party.

And then suddenly they find that he is not going to stay, and that he expects them to carry on without him. As they trudge back to Jerusalem, back to the upper room again, the flatness of the descrip-

70

tion in Acts is striking. We hear nothing of their emotions – no fear, no despair, no joy. They are all out of feelings. Tiredly, they get on with things, waiting for whatever it was that Jesus said he would send to help them, though they are not sure that they will know it when it arrives.

So, one minute they are the inner circle, waiting to hear about the plans for the kingdom of Israel and their vital part in the matter, and the next minute, they are a leaderless, purposeless group of people. Jesus has refused, categorically (v. 7), to tell them what is going on, but instead has left them a job to do, and a very daunting one at that. They have to be his witnesses, all over the world, apparently. This Holy Spirit had better be good, whatever it is, if it is going to get this emotionally drained bunch of waifs and strays going again.

But they have at least learned two things through what they have all been through. They have learned to stick together – whatever happens this time, they all want to witness it together – and they have learned to keep praying. If the crucifixion did not mean the end of all they had understood about God, then God's purposes have to be deeper, wider and stranger than anything they could imagine, and their only chance of not getting it hopelessly wrong again is to keep praying. Perhaps they themselves hardly realize the significance of those two lessons learned, but sticking together and praying are to become two of the defining characteristics of the new Christian community that Acts is going to tell us about.

In today's Gospel, prayer and community are equally obvious. Jesus's prayer for the disciples is that they 'may be one as we are one' (v. 11). Christian unity bears witness to our understanding of God's unifying, reconciling work in Christ, which is not something he just chooses to do, but which demonstrates his own nature. (And, after such a statement, do you have to ask what Christian disunity bears witness to?)

Jesus's prayer for the disciples underpins what we have already seen in Acts. Jesus knows that the disciples may feel left behind, bereft, after the ascension. 'I am no longer in the world,' he says, 'but they are.' So he asks for protection for them. But not protection from fear, or persecution (as the reading from 1 Peter makes clear), or any of the things we might feel we want to be protected from. He asks for protection for his followers 'so that they may be one', and in their unity, demonstrate the loving unity of God.

# Day of Pentecost

——— ∾ ———

*Numbers 11.24–30*
*Acts 2.1–21*
*John 20.19–23*

It is typical of God's calling to us that on the day of Pentecost, instead of being allowed to dwell on what it feels like and means to have tongues of fire resting on you, the disciples have to go straight out and start preaching. The Acts account has got it just right. The description of the giving of the Holy Spirit is over in four verses, and the sermon takes most of the rest of the chapter. The first four verses are full of vivid detail – the wild wind rocking the whole house, the tongues of flame, and the strange speech – but we are not allowed to dwell on them. We don't even hear how the disciples got out of the house and into the crowd, but suddenly, that's where they are. And now that they have reached their destination, the narrative slows down, and there is time for dialogue, reaction, emotion. But not from the disciples. Instead, we are now focusing on the crowd, on their bewilderment, amazement, disbelief. 'What about the disciples?' you want to shout. 'Were they bewildered, amazed, disbelieving? Or were they filled with joy, certainty and power?' 'You don't need to know,' Acts tells us firmly.

And that makes it clear what the gift of the Holy Spirit to the Church is for. It is not designed to fill us with religious feelings, or give us unshakeable certainty, or impress others with our power, or even to form us into The Church, though it may have all those effects too. The gift is given primarily to allow the disciples, and us, to do what Jesus told us to, which is to be his witnesses 'in Jerusalem, in all Judea and Samaria, and to the ends of the earth' (Acts 1.8).

So when at last we hear directly from the disciples, it is Peter's voice, lifted in praise of God. He knows, with utter clarity, that what has happened to them is a sign of God's huge and faithful purpose. This is what God has always promised, through his prophets, and the point of it is our salvation. The verses that Peter quotes from Joel could be frightening, with their talk of the 'last days', the sun darkened and the moon turned to blood, but Peter is here to tell the crowd that God's presence is opportunity, not terror, salvation, not condemnation.

Peter's excitement and joy bubble through this speech. The immediate effect on Peter of the gift of the Spirit has been to make him wildly generous. He longs to share what has now become clear to him. He looks on the crowd around him, and he knows he is now responsible for them. He must, he absolutely must, make it clear to them what God is offering through faith in Christ.

That same dynamic is at work in the verses from John's Gospel. The Spirit is given as the disciples take up Jesus's mission, and its immediate effect is to send them out to take responsibility for the world. Throughout John's Gospel, the way in which people react to Jesus signals whether they will accept or reject God's forgiveness offered through him. Now the same thing is to happen to the disciples. Their mission, too, is to do with forgiveness and judgement. It sounds rather as though Jesus is giving the disciples a blank cheque when he says they now have the power to forgive sins or retain sins. But remember to whom this charge is given, and in what circumstances. This is a group of people who have just betrayed and deserted their leader, and now they have locked themselves in an upstairs room, fearing for their own lives. When Jesus comes to them, he shows them the marks of the nails, not just so that they can be sure who he really is, but so that the tremendous mission he is about to entrust to them can be founded in the reality of who they are too. These disciples know how much they have been forgiven. They are not going to take the power over sin lightly. The Christian mission starts in the knowledge of our own need.

The temptation is to see the gift of the Spirit as something for insiders, to be jealously guarded and enjoyed. But instead we need to share in Moses's generosity of vision, and long for the Spirit to come down on all of God's people. It is with that longing that Peter preaches, a longing that all should share in the forgiveness and new life that God has given to us. We receive in awed gratitude, and share because we know that God has given us what we do not deserve. Should we be more grudging than God?

*Ordinary Time*

# Trinity Sunday

———— ∾ ————

Isaiah 40.12–17, 27–31
2 Corinthians 13.11–13
Matthew 28.16–20

The people whom this second section of Isaiah is addressing are completely worn out. They have not even got the energy actively to reject God and seek other sources of comfort. Instead, they sit around and whine. Even the young are slumped wearily, unable to summon up enthusiasm for anything. They believe that they are utterly forgotten and of no value to anyone, particularly God, and this feeling of being despised and neglected fills them with terrible lethargy. If God doesn't care, why should they? To them, Second Isaiah offers a picture of a God of patience and diligence, who forgets nothing.

Underlying it all is Isaiah's insistence upon the utter freedom and omniscience of God. 'Who can claim to have taught God anything?' Isaiah demands. God didn't need to ask advice when he was making the world, and he doesn't need to be told what to do now. But although this could be read as a sweeping put-down for these depressed Israelites, it isn't. Instead, it is to be the source of their comfort and joy. Because the God who made the world, without help or guidance from any, is not a careless God, but one whose measurements are fiercely exact. You may not be able to measure every drop of water in the world, or weigh a mountain, but God can and has. Your very insignificance is, funnily enough, a reassurance. Although 'the nations are like a drop from a bucket' (v. 15), and nothing in the world can provide a sacrifice that is worthy of God, yet this majestic God is Israel's Lord, who cares for them, as he always has done. When they are too tired, bewildered and woebegone to find any way out of their plight, they can remember that their God is inexhaustible. They can remember, reach out and feel the potent, unending energy of God.

That God is both sovereign and free and at the same time utterly committed to us is at the heart of all the Bible tells us about God.

In creation, incarnation and Pentecost we see God at work, patiently, with infinite attention to detail, drawing us into his incomprehensible freedom and life. So when Matthew and Paul end their writings with references to the Trinity, they are not just paying lip-service to something they have inherited and feel they must mention, but are witnessing to the thing that motivates them, and that they believe can energize the hard-pressed and doubting congregations to whom they are writing.

What Paul wishes for the Corinthian Christians is about as comprehensive as you can get. He prays for them 'the grace of the Lord Jesus Christ, the love of God, and the communion of the Holy Spirit'. Such a familiar phrase, but with such far-reaching consequences. Jesus's grace allowed him to accept the will of the Father, and follow his way, even to death and the cross. God's love led him to create all that is, and to send his only Son to offer redemption and life to everything that is made. And the Holy Spirit offers to us the communion which is shared by Father, Son and Spirit, the absolute love and rejoicing of the life of God.

'The communion of the Holy Spirit' is a particularly baffling phrase, and one that it is easy to gloss over. Augustine, thinking deeply about the biblical writings about the Holy Spirit, called the Spirit 'the bond of love' between Father and Son. It is almost as though – unimaginable thought – Father and Son would be somehow separated without whatever it is that is represented by the Holy Spirit. So if we wish upon ourselves the 'communion' of the Holy Spirit, we are praying to be unified, as Father, Son and Spirit are unified. We do not pray to be made indistinguishable, but we do pray to be made inseparable, and to give and get meaning only in each other.

So when Paul writes to a divided and bickering church, this is what he wishes for them. They are to love the world as God, its creator, loves it. They are to give themselves wholly to God's will for the world, as God the Son did, and they are to find their true selves, their only real identity, in belonging together and together serving God, in the communion of the Holy Spirit.

Christian baptism in the name of Father, Son and Holy Spirit is very ancient. Matthew witnesses that the command to do this was given by Jesus himself. And if Christians do not always, conspicuously, demonstrate in our lives that we rejoice in the world and in each other as God does, Isaiah reminds us that, unlike us, God 'does not grow faint and weary'.

# Proper 4

——— ∾ ———

Deuteronomy 11.18–21, 26–28
Romans 1.16, 17; 3.22b–31
Matthew 7.21–29

These are frightening words from Jesus in today's Gospel reading. He imagines a group of people who truly believe they are his followers and yet are mistaken. These people perform mighty acts in the name of Jesus, but Jesus has no idea who they are. The people he knows and recognizes are the ones who act on what they have heard from Jesus and, since this comes at the end of the Sermon on the Mount, presumably Jesus is implying that they must act on what he has just been saying. The people Jesus is rejecting are only interested in 'religious' activity. They prophesy, cast out demons and do works of power in Jesus's name (Matthew 7.22), but when Jesus talks about 'religious' observance in Matthew 6, the contrast between his advice and the practices of these imaginary evil followers is quite striking. Jesus tells his disciples that the reward of genuine religious observance is the approval of God, not the admiration of the general public. The rest of the Sermon on the Mount is not really about what most people would recognize as 'religion' at all. It is about how we should live with each other in the presence of God.

But, of course, the whole of the Old Testament assumes that that is the heart of religion. God makes for himself a people who are to be instantly recognizable because of the way they treat each other. Their cultic and liturgical practices will simply be an extension of that life directed towards God. So Deuteronomy envisages God's commandments as the air that his people breathe. The outward symbols, bound on hand and head, will simply reflect the reality of the inward person, completely formed by the words of God, and forming the next generation in the same way, quite naturally. Jesus's words are to be like that for the people. They are to be so fully part of us that all our acts, whether we think of them as 'religious' or not, will speak of the Lord we follow.

But both Deuteronomy and Matthew recognize that people have a choice and that they do not always choose to bind the words of God into their very being. Jesus describes a man who builds his house on the sand, only to have it fall in the first storm. Deuteronomy is rather blunter – to choose to live against God's commandments is to bring down a curse on yourself. It is vital to keep this choice before us. It is the choice Jesus set before everyone he met, according to the Gospels. But in today's Gospel reading, as in so many of the encounters Jesus has, the choice doesn't look as clear as Deuteronomy seems to suggest. Over and over again, Jesus meets people who believe that they have made the right choice. They believe themselves to be following God's commandments, and many of them think that, as a matter of fact, they are being rather more obedient than Jesus is himself. And now Jesus is saying that his own followers are just as likely to deceive themselves, and believe that they have chosen obedience when they haven't at all.

And that's why, Paul says, we are always stupid to rely on ourselves. Rely instead on Jesus, he urges. Left to ourselves, we never quite manage to choose obedience, even when we think we have. We always manage to fasten on something irrelevant and make it the heart of our religion. So God, in his righteous mercy, gives us Jesus. Jesus is obedient as none of us can be, and generous too. Instead of using his obedience to show us up, he uses it to free us from our feeble attempts to get it right alone. Now all we need to know is that Jesus is the fulfilment of all that the law is trying to do. Jesus shows us the nature of God, and he draws around him a community of people who try to do the same, in the way we live together. We still need to try to live out God's commandments, since they do genuinely reflect what God desires for his people. And we will still fail, as people always have. But now we know that this isn't primarily about us, about how good or bad we are. We are not the central characters in this story. But the central players, Father, Son and Holy Spirit, draw us into their play. We cannot ruin it and we cannot run it, but we can enjoy it and make it clearer for the other new actors who come to take part. Some find it hard that they cannot be the stars, but most of us are only too delighted to share their reflected glory.

# Proper 5

———— ❧ ————

Hosea 5.15—6.6
Romans 4.13-25
Matthew 9.9-13, 18-26

'I knew the great Apostle Paul. Buy me a drink, and I'll tell you all about him. I used to act as his secretary, sometimes, which I knew, even then, was a great honour. Of course, I didn't realize quite how important he was going to be, but even in the early days, you could tell he was a man to watch. He had such energy, and he was always talking and thinking. It was quite hard to keep up with him when he was dictating. Sometimes I'm afraid I may have missed out a few words, or got a bit muddled. I hear now that his churches kept his letters, and read them out over and over again, and I do hope I didn't make it harder for them.

'I volunteered to help him, of course, because I'm quite proud of my writing, but also because, in a way, I owe my right to believe in the Lord Jesus to him. He fought hard for Gentiles like me to be included with the others, and he needn't have bothered about us because, after all, he was a Jew himself.

'I hoped I might get to know him better, working with him, but he was a hard man to know. I still don't understand, to this day, why he gave up his family and his own tradition to join the Christians. Going around with him, I heard lots of stories about Jesus. The ones I liked best were the ones where Jesus goes out of his way to help people that the respectable folk wouldn't touch with a bargepole. He used to eat with collaborators and prostitutes, so they say, and touch lepers and unclean women, and even I wouldn't want to do that, though I've had a varied life myself, and often been short of the next meal.

'It's easy to understand why people like that would want to follow Jesus. Or the people who came to him for healing, when everything else had failed. I heard a lovely story about how he cured a little girl when everyone else said she was dead. And her father was a leader of the synagogue, a respectable man, like Paul used to be. But then that father was desperate. So I can see why people who'd got nothing to lose would try Jesus. After all, if you're already an outcast, or if the person you love best is dying, then why not risk it?

'But Paul wasn't like that. He was really well educated, born and brought up a Jew, and put a lot of energy into becoming a real expert. He had a respectable trade, and a good reputation. He told me that when he first heard about the Christians, he hated them, because they seemed to be undermining all he'd worked for. He actually helped to persecute them, and when he first came to believe, they didn't trust him an inch, which is hardly surprising. Actually, I suspect that some of them are still not really sure about him.

'So what made him turn everything around, and give up his family and his comfortable life and start travelling all over the world, preaching about Jesus? More often than not, he got beaten up, or chucked out of the town, but he never gave up, and gradually the faith is spreading all over the world, thanks to him, and others like him.

'He spent quite a lot of time thinking about how his old religion and his new religion fitted together. I remember copying out passages about Abraham, and about how what's special about Abraham is that he trusted God, as though God was some kind of a friend he could rely on, rather than one of the old gods, whose whims you just had to put up with, or one who only cared if you'd done what you were told. Faith, that's what Paul kept going on about. Nobody can keep the law, he used to say, however hard they try, but anyone can get to know God and trust him, just like Abraham did.

'Of course, if all they say about Jesus is true, then there's good reason to trust, because Jesus's resurrection means life for all of us. But what if it's not true, I remember asking Paul once. I thought he would be angry with me, but he just smiled and said that he knew, better than anyone, how true it was, because he'd met the Risen Lord, and it had changed his life. He said that he hadn't realized how desperate he was. He thought his life was just fine, the way it used to be. But when he met Jesus, he knew that anything outside Jesus wasn't really life at all.'

# Proper 6

———— ～ ————

*Exodus 19.2–8a*
*Romans 5.1–8*
*Matthew 9.35—10.8*

Christians know that, through the work of God in Christ, made real to them by the Holy Spirit, the world is a different place. We are, to use Paul's characteristic phrase, 'justified by faith', through no merit or action on our part. But what does that feel like, and what does it mean?

In chapter 4, Paul has given a long and complex theological explanation of 'justification by faith', and how this is not a new departure in God's relations with us, but is characteristic of all God's dealings with us. Now Paul turns from abstract to concrete. So you are justified by faith. What does that feel like? According to Paul, it feels like the end of a war. We are now at peace with God. It is easy to think of peace as an inner state of quietude, but that can't be what Paul is talking about, if you read the next few verses, and if you know anything about his life. Peace, for Paul, is not a feeling, but an actual change in the world. He has known what it is like to be at war with God, fighting against what he knew, at some level, was God's work in Jesus. He has known what it was to be in an uneasy and mistrustful truce with God, when he tried to do God's will, but failed, over and over again. Peace with God is knowing that you are on the same side as God, for ever. God has sent his ambassador, Jesus, to grant you citizenship. Whatever you do or fail to do from now on, you have rights, a passport, that signals that you are at peace with God's kingdom.

So the characteristic of a justified Christian, according to Paul, is not a serene smile, but hope. Your passport is stamped 'nationality: Christian', and you know that that is more or less the equivalent of saying 'nationality: alive'. Everything that happens to you from now on proves where you belong. Everything is characteristically 'Christian'. So it may be 'British' never to talk to people on trains, and we have a kind of embarrassed pride in our reserve. Similarly, it is characteristically 'Christian' to suffer. This is not something we worry about, but something we see as a 'national' characteristic.

Hope is the beginning and end of our journey. We start out on it, our passport as justified citizens of God's kingdom clutched in our hands, because of what God has done for us and promised to us in Jesus. We trace with pride the way in which our national Spirit grows in us as we travel, our likeness to the archetypal 'Christian', Jesus himself, brought more and more to the fore by this Spirit of Christianity.

But this citizenship is not ours by right of birth or marriage or residence, but simply because the ruler of this nation goes out and searches for his people. We set out in hope, and the more we travel, the more we understand the nature of hope, God's great act of hope in Christ. God simply decides that we are his people. While we still think we are at war with God, he has already decided that we will carry his 'nationality'. But instead of conquering us to make us his own people, he allows us to conquer him. And when we find that we have no prison strong enough to hold him, whether that prison is made of hatred, or fear or death itself, God does not go free, mocking us for our efforts. Instead, he takes us with him into freedom.

But if we accept this passport, this citizenship into life, we must also accept the Spirit that goes with it. You cannot be citizens of God's kingdom without the Spirit of the kingdom, which is the Spirit of hope. God's hope is based on his unswerving love for us, which we can do nothing to alienate, which we do nothing to deserve. But once you accept that passport into freedom and life, you must accept that this Spirit of hope will increasingly form your being. This Spirit will begin to shape all your decisions, the way you respond to other people, the way you see life. You will not be able to do or be anything that does not proclaim your citizenship. Sometimes, admittedly, your fellow citizens may be ashamed of you, or see you as a failure, but that will not mean that you have forfeited the rights that the ruler gave you. You may even feel that you could share some of your rights, as the King did, by offering to end the wars you may be involved in. Not an uncostly business, but one full of God's hope.

# Proper 7

———— ⁓ ————

*Jeremiah 20.7–13*
*Romans 6.1b–11*
*Matthew 10.24–39*

The prophet Jeremiah lived through times of enormous political upheaval. His long career, lasting about 40 years, saw a good king, a couple of bad kings, a weak king and the forced deportation of all but the dregs of the population. Most of this Jeremiah warned his people about in advance, but his foresight won him no friends at all. He was increasingly isolated from the people he was born to serve, and at times his life was threatened by those who could not bear to hear that the truth was so different from what they wanted.

It was not as though Jeremiah had any choice about his calling. At the beginning of the book (1.5), we hear God telling Jeremiah that, even while he was a foetus, he was being prepared for the role of God's prophet. Perhaps he could have refused to pass on what God gave him to say – resisting a vocation is not unknown, after all – but in today's lament, Jeremiah cries out that not to speak is as painful as the fear and loneliness that follows after he has spoken. It burns him up, and the pain of holding it in becomes too much (v. 9). (Actually, it sounds a bit like childbirth – you don't want to push because it hurts too much, but the force is irresistible.) Nor does Jeremiah have any choice about what it is he has to say. God only gives him words of 'violence and destruction' (v. 8), however much he longs to speak love and reassurance.

So the words we hear from Jeremiah today are words of deep depression and despair. Jeremiah almost hates God, though he is at least honest about that. He accuses God of lying to him and forcing his words on him. The words are so strong that it is almost as though Jeremiah sees God's action as rape. All around him, he hears whispers, sees shadows, any one of which could mean his death, except that the God who assaults him is also the one who protects him from others.

And if verses 12 and 13 remind us that this horrible picture of

Jeremiah's relationship with God is only one side of the story, still it is a side we need to hear, while remembering that there is no hint of condemnation from God for what Jeremiah is feeling. Perhaps God recognizes something of the truth of the accusations Jeremiah is levelling against him. If Jeremiah's people had listened to the word of God, of course, Jeremiah's whole life could have been different. But at the moment it is not the stupid, self-serving people that Jeremiah hates, but the God who calls him to serve them, whether they will listen or not.

Christian disciples throughout the centuries have faced similar moments, as Jesus warned them they would. Like Jeremiah, they have to tell the people what they are given to tell, and most of the time their audience do not want to hear it, any more than the people of Judah did. Like Jeremiah, they cannot choose to soften the message if it is not to people's liking, not even if those people are their own families. Like Jeremiah, knowing that God protects them, and that they are 'of more value than many sparrows' (v. 31) to him, will not always be a great consolation. Sometimes, like him, they will long for ordinary friends, for family life, for simple pleasures, without the awful responsibility of being God's chosen ones. The life that God offers will seem very far away and unreal compared to the life they are obviously forfeiting.

That is why Paul is incredulous when he realizes that some people have heard his message of God's free grace as a signal that they can do what they like and get away with it. True, God's forgiveness is freely offered; it does not have to be earned, and it never can be. But accepting it means stepping out of one life into another, and there is only one way to do that. Stepping out of this life into the life of the crucified and risen Christ may seem like a good idea when you are wretched at your own sin and failure, but when you then have to follow in Christ's footsteps, you begin to wonder if you have made the right choice after all. 'Not peace, but a sword', 'our old self crucified', the Lord, a 'dread warrior', constantly beside you. Is this what you chose?

Hear God's silent acceptance of Jeremiah's scream of pain, see that the face of the 'dread warrior' is also the face of Jesus, and remember that the old life had moments like this too, but then they were meaningless. Now they are part of God's living purpose.

# Proper 8

—— ❧ ——

*Jeremiah 28.5–9*
*Romans 6.12–23*
*Matthew 10.40–42*

Ours is an age with a great deal of interest in 'spirituality'. We have rediscovered that 'spirituality' is good for us and, like exercise and a low-fat diet, we pursue it, but on the whole rather sporadically. It becomes another way of paying attention to ourselves, and trying to meet our own needs, but we do not allow it to make demands upon us or inconvenience us too much.

There is really remarkably little in the way of this kind of spirituality in the Bible. It may have been what Hananiah was offering. I see him as a kind of Californian guru, or a tele-evangelist. He looks at all the anxious, stressed people, and he wants to help them. And if, by some lucky accident, that leads to wealth and favour for himself, well, whoever said that God wants us to be miserable? That poor man Jeremiah really should get himself some therapy, and not lay his guilt trips on other people.

Perhaps Hananiah really did believe that he was speaking God's word into the situation, but he seems much more interested in the personal psychology of his listeners, their needs and fears. Jeremiah, on the other hand, is operating out of a different theology of spirituality and prophecy. For Jeremiah, the only imperative is God's. He, personally, would much prefer to be carrying Hananiah's message of victory and peace but, unfortunately, it doesn't happen to be true. Jeremiah expects his prophecy to have cash value – it will be proved. Does Hananiah expect that too? Or is that secondary to him? Is he really just going for the feel-good factor, and not expecting to be held to account for it? It is as though that woolly layer of living, in which most talk of 'spirituality' exists, is ripped away by Jeremiah. 'This is not about what we want,' he shouts, 'this is about what actually is.'

The same kind of horrible immediacy confronts us in Jesus's words in Matthew. We cannot just pursue what is good for us on and off. On the days where we lapse from our diets, or don't go to the gym, or don't get the feng shui of our houses quite right, we can always start again tomorrow. But every day, in everything we do, we are right up against God. Scarlett O'Hara's attitude – 'tomorrow is another day' – probably won't even work with diets. It does suggest a fundamental lack of commitment, even there. But if you are talking about missing opportunities to meet and serve your maker and redeemer, it becomes a little more serious. Jesus is putting it positively in this passage, speaking of opportunities taken, rather than missed; but you can't help thinking of the other side.

Paul, too, has no time for spirituality as a lifestyle choice. Choice is certainly involved, but Paul is clear that your choices shape you so completely that slavery is the only appropriate description of the relationship between you and what you have chosen. Most of us in the privileged West, most of the time, treat our choices as ephemeral – after all, we can always choose again. But Paul is arguing strongly against that kind of free-market spirituality and theology. Every time you choose in favour of one thing, you choose against another. You cannot have it all. What you choose today becomes your master. It directs and controls you, as surely as if you were branded and wore an iron hoop around your ankle. What you choose today will make it harder to choose differently tomorrow.

Luckily, Paul's gospel is the good news of God's redeeming work in Christ, which does indeed allow us to choose again, and which frees us from the power of all our other choices. The good news is that God chooses us. Intriguingly, Paul still calls this 'slavery'. Jeremiah could testify that to choose God is no less demanding than choosing self. But perhaps, too, Paul is saying something vital about the strength and passion of our choosing of God. It must at least equal the strength and passion with which we choose what we eat, what we wear, what we worry about, otherwise it will never prevail. So deeply are we enslaved to 'sin' that only a really strong and opposing enslavement can make any difference. This is what John Donne is talking about when he beseeches God to 'Batter my heart . . . Take me to you, imprison me, for I/ unless you enthrall me, never shall be free,/ nor ever chaste except you ravish me.'[1]

If it makes us uncomfortable to think of being God's slaves, that is perhaps because we seldom admit how much we are enslaved to other things already. Even 'spirituality' can enslave. Only slavery to God is freedom.

---

[1] John Donne, 'Holy Sonnets', *The Oxford Book of English Verse*, OUP, 1972, p. 198.

# Proper 9

——— ❧ ———

*Zechariah 9.9–12*
*Romans 7.15–25a*
*Matthew 11.16–19, 25–30*

The first half of chapter 11 of Matthew's Gospel is Jesus's tribute to John the Baptist. John is in prison, longing to know if he has stepped aside for nothing, aching to be reassured that he has truly listened to God. He gets the reassurance he needs and then Jesus turns to the crowd and says his public 'Thank yous' to John, the man who was prepared to be nothing so that Jesus could step into his rightful place.

But the crowd aren't really very interested. After all, John is yesterday's news. They have already moved on to the next sensation. The tabloids are full of Jesus, for the moment, until he puts a foot wrong, or something more interesting and less demanding turns up. They are getting restless with all this talk about John. They have come to hear about themselves, their needs, their hopes and fears. Who cares about that old has-been, John?

Jesus knows them well, as his ironic little parable shows. They are like selfish children, who will only play their own game, and even then, only if they can take the main part. When their fellow playmates, John and Jesus, try to initiate a game, the bored children won't play. 'I don't like that game,' they shout, 'I didn't make it up, and I don't like it. It's a silly game.' 'Your game is too sad,' they tell John, 'why can't we play a happy game? Someone's always dying in your game.' 'And your game is too noisy,' they tell Jesus, 'and I don't like that kind of cake, and you've got more squash than I have.'

But of course, the end result for these poor, cross, dissatisfied children is that they have no one to play with at all, and no idea of how or what to play on their own. They are alone, crying and grumpy, not knowing what they really want, only that they haven't got it.

But if the spoiled, tantrum-throwing child is one half of today's picture the other half is the excited, curious, wondering child of verses 25–7. This is the child who does not always need to be in charge, but who is happy to play the game by someone else's rules. This is the child who has not been left alone with only other children to try and sort things out by themselves, but whose Father is there to play too. His Father will not force the game; he will allow the child to take it in his own direction, but he will be there, sharing, enjoying, rejoicing in the imagination and creativity of his child.

The intimacy of these verses is very moving, with their repeated use of the child's voice calling on the 'Father'. When we move into the final few verses of this chapter of Matthew 11, what we hear is this voice again, but now grown up. It is the voice of the child who has been well fathered, who has known the love and support and delight of his father, and can now in turn care for others. Jesus, the child of the Father, turns to those spoiled lonely children from the earlier verses, and offers them rest. The burden of their discontent and frustration is too much. Can they learn to turn to the Son of the Father?

Paul is certainly tired of trying to play on his own, and is more than ready to accept the rest offered by Jesus. Paul could sympathize with those children who reject all the games they are offered, but then have nothing left to do. He understands perfectly well that the children are rejecting happiness. If only they could forget themselves and play, they would be happy, but some inner stupidity and pride won't let them. They know quite well what they want – they want to play with the other children, but only on their own terms. They know that they have deliberately cut themselves off from what they want. Nobody else made them do it; they chose to sulk and shout. They chose to be miserable when they wanted to be happy.

Paul has longed for the parent who would come and tease and laugh and start a new game that could persuade all the children to forget their pride and their grudges and play together. And now he has found what he was looking for all his life – a way to forget himself and so be what he wants to be. Julian of Norwich writes of this experience in her *Revelations of Divine Love*. 'God, of your goodness, give me yourself . . . If I ask for anything less, I shall always be in want. Only in you do I have all.'[1]

---

[1] Julian of Norwich, *Revelations of Divine Love*, Penguin, 1966, p. 68.

# Proper 10

—— ❧ ——

*Isaiah 55.10–13*
*Romans 8.1–11*
*Matthew 13.1–9, 18–23*

Why is God so profligate? With the second half of today's reading from Matthew, the emphasis switches from God's action to our response; but the first half of the story is all that the listening crowds get, and their reaction must have been one of incredulity. Jesus's audience may not all be farmers themselves, but they would all be much closer to the food-production cycle than most of us are. They would have known famine and shortage, and they would know that a sensible farmer does not just fling the seeds all over the place. He prepares the ground as well as he can in advance, precisely so that the seeds don't fall on rocky ground or among thorns. Whatever is this sower in the story up to?

No wonder the disciples need an explanation. The one that they got has provided generations of Sunday-school lessons, with the emphasis on how we receive the word of God, so generously scattered abroad. But it is still an immensely puzzling story. For one thing, it is hard to see what those who hear God's word are supposed to do about it. It isn't clear that any blame attaches to them. For instance, can it be entirely their own fault if they don't understand what is being said to them? I suppose the shallow people, and the ones who allow themselves to be distracted by 'the cares of the world and the lure of wealth' could be said to deserve what they get, up to a point.

But I still think the sower is really the key. It is the sower who starts the story, and the explanation is given to those who are going to be 'sowers'. God may be the primary sower, but the disciples have accepted the commission to join Jesus in spreading the word far and wide, so it is their duty to make sure that the soil is prepared, that the birds are scared away, that the thorns are uprooted, and that the seed does not fall where there is not enough soil to let it grow. The disciples are being given the key, not to make them feel superior, and to assure them of their status in the inner circle, but so that they can be responsible for those who have no other means of hearing the Word. This is not, then, primarily a parable for seed, which is, by its very nature, bound to grow or fail, depending where it is put. No, this is a parable for the sowers.

But if this sounds like too terrifying a responsibility, then take Isaiah and Romans to heart. Although for some inexplicable reason God chooses to involve us in his mission, and to give us real responsibility, he knows what we are. God's word will 'accomplish that which I purpose', says God through Isaiah, 'and succeed in the thing for which I sent it'. How very hard it is always to believe that. We long to take over from God, to bend him to our purposes. We are sure that we know best. We would not be the sower who flings the seed about without looking where it is going to land. We would make sure that the seed got only to the people like us, that we know can be trusted with it. How different our careful, defensive, well managed strategies are from God's wild randomness.

So when Paul says that there is 'now no condemnation for those who are in Christ Jesus', those of us who are trying so hard need to hear it, as much as anyone else. After all, people who don't care about the law at all are not the ones who fear breaking it inadvertently. It is those of us who are zealously law-abiding who need freedom. Both sets need forgiveness, but Jesus's ministry showed, over and over again, that it is those who are trying to be righteous who find it hardest to accept that forgiveness.

But if, on one level, this is reassuring for anxious sowers, on another, it is even more terrifying than the responsibility of sowing God's word. Because Paul also says that 'the mind that is set on the flesh is hostile to God'. He does not say that such minds have to be doing or thinking evil, but simply that they are, in themselves, hostile to God. All God's values are anathema to them. They cannot stand the generous profligacy of the Spirit.

So what must we wishful sowers do? Prepare the ground as much as we can, but then trust in the generous mercy of God, and sometimes throw caution to the wind, and watch with delight as God's word accomplishes what we could never have dreamed of.

# *Proper 11*

— ❧ —

*Isaiah 44.6–8*
*Romans 8.12–25*
*Matthew 13.24–30, 36–43*

This section of Romans is part of a long and not always lucid discussion of life and death, slavery and freedom. In chapter 6, Paul has been explaining that our Christian baptism means choosing Jesus's death and life rather than our own. On the whole, this choice is glorious for us. It means that we are no longer tied to sin and bound to do what sin tells us and pay the terrible price that follows. So it is freedom and life. But there are ongoing consequences from our previous life which sometimes make it hard for us to remember our new-found freedom. Sometimes we still act like slaves, rather than free people.

Then in chapter 7 Paul gives an illustration which is supposed to show what a good thing the death of the old life is. Once somebody is dead, the duties and debts you owed them are cancelled, Paul argues. So when you choose the death and life of Christ as your own, you are free of the things that bound you in your old life.

Finally, in chapter 8, Paul is looking at mechanisms – how does Jesus's death and life free us, and what does our freedom mean in practice? Paul's simple, compelling answer is that our freedom means life. When we 'belonged', body and soul, to the old life, that meant that we had to pay all the bills, fulfil all the demands of that life, and the final payment was our own death. But now we belong to God, body and soul, and God has a different way of demanding payment. Instead of asking us to pay, God gives us things. We thought we were being bought in the slave market by a new master, though admittedly one who would be nicer to us than the old. But instead we find that God has bought us so that he can make us his children, giving us equal shares in his property with his own Son. And what's more, the Son doesn't mind, and isn't jealous, but is actually the one who has gone out and done the buying, expressly so that he can share what should have been his.

Most of the time we can hardly believe it. We still keep looking over our shoulders, waiting for the beating. We still have the furtive, scared, selfish habits of the slave. But the third member of our new family is coaching us, gradually, teaching us the language of our new household, persuading us that it is really all right to speak to our owner as the Son does.

But if this is a wonderful new life for us – which it is – it does, unfortunately, carry some responsibilities with it. If we are going to talk like the Son, we also have to act like the Son. And until we do, the rest of the world cannot be free.

The problem is that when we set out to try to share our freedom with the world, we often revert to our old slave mentality. Isn't it interesting in the parable in Matthew that it is the slaves who want to uproot the weeds? The slaves have never owned anything themselves, but they are sure that if they did they could not stand to have it contaminated by weeds. The slaves would be prepared to put in any amount of back-breaking labour to uproot the weeds, even if it did mean damaging some of the crops at the same time. They are anxious, indignant, perhaps even a little fearful that the master will blame them for what has happened. In other words, they are acting like the slaves they are.

But the master's attitude is very different. The master's main concern is to preserve the crop. Separating out good and bad growth can more safely be done when the crop is fully grown. It's not that he doesn't mind about the weeds, or that he has any intention of pretending that they are anything else; it's just that he can take the long-term view, and the slaves can only worry. They are used to small, everyday tasks, with immediate results; they are not used to large, long-term responsibilities.

So what happens when the slaves suddenly become the children, and when the crop they are talking about is their own inheritance, and doesn't just belong to someone else? Will they panic and try to go for a completely weed-free field, whatever the cost? Or will they have lived with the master long enough to learn to think like him, and even to trust his strategies more than their own?

With creation still wrapped in the chains that we can still remember and feel around us, can we learn to act as children, not slaves?

# Proper 12

——— ∿ ———

*1 Kings 3.5–12*
*Romans 8.26–39*
*Matthew 13.31–33, 44–52*

With this piling up of images of the kingdom, I think you need first of all to listen to them and get an overall feel, and then to start trying to tease out some of the puzzles. After all, those who heard the stories in the first place could not have sat down and read and reread them, but a good story makes you go on thinking for ages afterwards. Clearly, the crowds who followed Jesus everywhere he went did so at least partly for the stories. Who knows how they told and retold them, for years afterwards, as we still do?

So, first impressions? Unpredictability and excitement. Small things, that only one or two people know about, that suddenly swell and take over the world. Beautiful and incredibly valuable things that you come across by accident and can't live without.

The two sets of parables seem initially to lead in slightly different directions. The mustard seed and the yeast are everyday miracles. Everyone knows how they work, and how extraordinary it is that something so small can have such an effect. But had you ever thought of the kingdom of heaven like that? Surely the kingdom of heaven is already huge and magnificent, not something tiny, working inconspicuously until suddenly you can't miss it any more? The surprise in these parables is not what the yeast and the mustard seed do, since we know about that already. The point is that other things, that you may not be so familiar with, may also behave like this. Don't discount small things until you know what they are capable of. Don't think about big things as though they can never have had small beginnings.

The parables of the treasure and the pearl, on the other hand, feed straight into the imagination. Who hasn't dreamed of finding treasure? But the odd thing about both of these lucky people is what they do with it. Most people's treasure dreams are dreams about wealth, but these two have dreamt of the beauty of the treasure

94

itself, and what it would feel like to know it was yours. Both of them seem to be reasonably well off already – they have things that they can sell in order to gain possession of the treasure, and there is absolutely no suggestion that they intend to sell what they have bought in order to get even richer. In fact, they might even appear to their neighbours to have lost their wealth. But little do the neighbours know.

(The parable about the fish seems to belong with the one about the crop sown with weeds, but it does serve to remind us, in this context, that treasure – or fish – are not always what they seem.)

What holds together the parables of sudden growth and the parables of treasure is the scribe in verse 52. He is the disciples and he is us. He is the one who has to use these stories to plant small ideas that will feed the world, he is the one who has to show that the treasure is so beautiful that it is worth selling all that we have to possess it. He has to ask people God's question to Solomon, 'What do you really want, more than anything else in the world?' Solomon's answer makes it clear that he already possesses, at least in part, what he has asked for.

Luckily, Paul tells us, so do we. Ours is not innate wisdom, but the presence of the Spirit, who can tell God what we meant to ask for, if only we had the sense to recognize our deepest longings. And what is this thing that we yearn for so deeply that we can hardly identify it, except to know that without it we are incomplete? It is, Paul tells us, to know that we are loved, completely, inalienably and for ever. God has had plans for us from the very beginning. He never intended his Son to be an only child. We are not an accident for whom sudden and unexpected alterations had to be made. God prepared his extensive nurseries from the beginning, and he knew that wipe-down surfaces would be necessary. We, with all that we entail, are God's choice. He knew what we would be like, and how expensive we would be, and he didn't care. God is prepared for everything that such parenthood involves.

So never listen to anyone who tells you that you are just adopted, and God wishes he hadn't done it. Don't believe a word if they try to say that God's love is conditional and might be forfeited. Don't see adversity as a sign that God has gone away. Simply stick with the Son, your brother.

# Proper 13

——— ❦ ———

*Isaiah 55.1–5*
*Romans 9.1–5*
*Matthew 14.13–21*

The pain in Paul's words is tangible, and made even more poignant by the victorious assurance of the end of chapter 8. Paul has just been asserting that nothing can 'separate us from the love of God in Christ Jesus our Lord', and now, suddenly, we move into this howl of lament. For one moment he allows himself to dwell on something that seems to contradict what he has just said, because something has separated his fellow Israelites from the love of God, apparently. How can these things be reconciled? Has Paul got it wrong, after all? He can only search the depth of his knowledge of Christ, confirmed, he believes, by the Holy Spirit. And remember his description of the Holy Spirit in chapter 8, as the one whose voice is increasingly heard in us, drawing us into true conversation with God. So when he now speaks of an inner confirmation from the Holy Spirit, he is not speaking simplistically of a 'personal conviction', but of the discipline born of the years in which he has tried, increasingly, to hear the conversation between God and God, going on in him and around him, to hear it, submit to it, and play his own part in it. This 'confirmation' comes as a result of the whole of Paul's Christian life, given to God, without counting the personal cost.

And yet, and yet . . . Paul cannot simply turn away from the love of his people. For all the years of his childhood and early manhood, until he was confronted by Jesus on the road to Damascus, love of his people and fierce pride in their role in God's purposes are what shaped Paul's life. There is no easy road from one allegiance to another. It makes it almost harder that Paul still retains deep respect for his former people. It might be simpler if he could just say, 'They're wrong and I'm right.' But he can't. He acknowledges the value of all that has been given to the Israelites. They are real gifts, not an illusion, and they really play their part in God's purposes, all leading up to that great moment when the Messiah comes. And that is the rub, because those great gifts should have prepared the people to recognize Jesus, but somehow the people mistook the signs for the reality.

The problem, as Paul works it out in the rest of this tortured chapter, did not stop with the Israelites. It remains a common human desire to tie God down. We may even be trying to make the knots out of real rope, made by God and given to us by him. But we are doomed to failure if we are relying on anything other than God himself. You have to trust in God, his generosity and mercy, not any righteousness you think you might have performed. Even if that righteousness is called out of you in response to what God has done, still you must trust the God who called it from you, not your own acts.

And if you do, Matthew and Isaiah suggest, then suddenly God's wild generosity bursts the banks of the little channel in which you thought you were sailing, and you are out on the huge, uncharted, enchanting seas of God's love for the world he has made. When the disciples come to Jesus and ask him to send the people away, they think that they are being thoughtful and kind. Jesus came out to be on his own, and he has been mobbed, so – first kind thought – let's carve out a bit of space for Jesus. Second kind thought: the people have come a long way, and they are going to start getting tired and hungry any minute now. For their sakes, too, it's time they went home. Notice the disciples carefully not mentioning their own needs.

At first it looks as though, in response to their kindness, Jesus is giving them an impossible task. 'You feed them,' he says. But actually, all he is asking is one small response – just five loaves and two fishes – and Jesus is the one who will make it bread for five thousand. 'You feed them' is only daunting if you don't trust in the generosity of God. 'Come and buy,' Isaiah shouts. You could look longingly at the things set out on God's stall and decide you can't afford them, count your few pennies and go and buy something inferior, or you could approach God, hold out your empty purse, your empty hands, and have them filled to overflowing. The stewards of God's stall must not spend their time bargaining, but instead give the goods away as fast as we can, knowing that they will always be replenished.

# *Proper 14*

—— ∾ ——

1 Kings 19.9–18
Romans 10.5–15
Matthew 14.22–33

There is something about us that is deeply resistant to the grace of
God. It's not that we don't believe in him, or wish to follow him, or
that we consciously reject him, but we simply cannot help reverting
to the belief that all of this is something 'we' do, something we have
to achieve with our own efforts. We act as though God is far away
and a hard taskmaster, who has to be won over by our grim
attempts to read his mind and so please him.

For once, in Romans 5, Paul is making a direct comparison
between the law and justification by faith. Usually he is at pains to
say that the law is not innately bad, it's just that we are not capable
of keeping it. But here he is comparing what he sees as the attitude
behind these two ways of approaching God. The law, he says, is
about doing things. It is about a kind of credit and debit account
that God keeps, so that you might, theoretically, end up in credit,
but the chances are strongly against it.

Faith, on the other hand, is an acceptance of what God has done,
in sending Jesus and raising him from the dead. All of that was done
without any effort or even consent on our part, and all we have to
do in response is recognize it as the activity of God. So Paul coun-
sels against turning faith into a new kind of strenuous pursuit,
where you have to search out God and grab him to you by force.
God is closer to you than your own breath and heartbeat.

But Peter shows how very hard it is to believe that. Chapter 14
marks a change of pace in Matthew's Gospel. Jesus's ministry is
about to come into the full public gaze, as it begins to really worry
both Herod and the Pharisees. Jesus is trying to carve out a little
space for himself, to pray and reflect and gird himself up for the
confrontations to come. Finally, after the feeding of the five thousand, he persuades the disciples to go off in the boat and leave him
alone. I wonder what the conversation was like in the boat that

night? They must all have been very excited by the miracle they had just been part of, and full of enthusiasm and hope. But as the storm begins to get up, and they are still hanging around waiting for Jesus, they begin to lose heart.

Typically, it is Peter whose enthusiasm returns immediately. As soon as he sees Jesus, he wants another dose of the high excitement of miracles, and Jesus indulges him. But out on the unstable water, with the wind even stronger without the protection of the boat around him, Peter panics. He had thought miracles were a kind of magic, that would make the waves feel like a road, and build a shield around him to keep the wind off. He had thought of Jesus's power as some kind of almost external force, to be tapped and used as he pleased. He had not realized that Jesus's power is not magic, but the absolute demonstration of nature responding to her maker. Peter had set out to do exactly what Paul was talking about – to try to get close to God's power by sheer force of will. Instead, he has to reach out his hand to Jesus, and recognize that he walks on the water as a disciple of Jesus, not by any other kind of power at all.

So the disciples' response is, at last, the right one. 'You are the Son of God,' they say to Jesus, as their boat rocks calmly on the friendly sea.

Christianity is not a system, which some people can use easily and some can't, and each person can only reap the rewards accordingly. Christianity is a relationship, offered by God, in which our place is opened up by Jesus, and in which we are constantly tutored and encouraged by the Holy Spirit. No one is 'good' at it, but that's all right, because entrance is not by exam, and places are not limited. The temptation is to go off looking for challenges to prove your worth to God, or seeking him in the terrifying power of the wind, the earthquake and the fire, because surely silence and the rhythm of your own heart are too small and mundane for God? Elijah, the disciples and Paul have all seen the spectacular power of God, but they all learn to be much more awed by God's offer of intimacy than by any other kind of demonstration. In the end, what more could we want?

# Proper 15

———— ∿ ————

*Isaiah 56.1, 6–8*
*Romans 11.1–2a, 29–32*
*Matthew 15.10–28*

This strange story of the Canaanite woman clearly scratches an itch for Matthew's readers. If you put this version and Mark's version side by side (Mark 7.24–30), you will see some subtle differences. Mark's version is, as usual, more abrupt, but both can be read on at least two levels.

The first level is the main strand of the story. Both Gospels put this interchange between Jesus and the foreign woman in the context of an increasingly angry and critical set of encounters with the Pharisees and scribes. The Pharisees are questioning Jesus's authority, and he in turn is challenging their understanding of the Law, and so of God. But although Jesus argues forcefully and with confidence, he is essentially arguing in terms that the Pharisees understand. This whole debate is conducted in the language of scriptural interpretation, with each side determined to make its case. Jesus is clear that his mission is continuous with God's great missionary enterprise in calling the people of Israel, and the Pharisees are determined to show him that he is mistaken. But this is still very much a family fight, however bitter and potentially bloody. Who has the right to interpret the Tradition?

But then the Canaanite woman comes and begins to skew this plane of the story. However much Jesus has criticized the way in which his people have tried to tie God down, he has still seen his calling as within the family. But the woman won't let him. She challenges Jesus to see the full implications of what he has been saying to his own people.

In Mark, Jesus seems less thrown by her challenge. It is as though he had already realized that his mission had universal application, but had thought that there was an order to be observed – children first, then dogs. But here in Matthew, Jesus at first cannot formulate an answer for the woman at all. But neither can he turn her away, because surely she is right: she is not asking for the children's bread, only the leftover crumbs. And we readers, who have just come from the feeding of the five thousand in the previous chapter, and are about to go on to another miraculous feeding, smile at her cleverness. After all, we have just seen how many crumbs are left over when God has finished feeding the children – twelve baskets, wasn't it?

So this first level of the story is about Jesus coming to a fuller realization of the scope of his mission, and how typical of him it is that he instantly praises the woman for her insight. 'Great is your faith!' he says to her.

But the second level of the story is the one that operates for the reader, and this is where today's Gospel really connects with Paul's painful struggle in Romans. The earliest Christians, too, had to find out the breadth of their calling. Clearly, in the church for which Matthew was written there are those who believe that Christianity is primarily for God's original people, not for everyone. This is a battle that Paul had to fight over and over again, in his certainty that he was called to be 'an apostle to the Gentiles'.

In the end, Paul's theological resolution of this problem – never a complete resolution, but one that he can live with – rests on the faithful love of God. God does not call people in order to dismiss them later, and he does not give gifts and then ask for them back. But when his people do not respond to the call or want the gift, that does not render them useless. Instead, God uses that refusal as an opportunity, not to take the gifts away from their original recipients, but to give them more widely, in the hope that when the first recipients see others enjoying God's presents, they will blow the dust off their own and start joining in.

Now, of course, the proper context of this is the relationship between Christians and Jews, and it is vital for each side to hear that God intends to include us all in his great plan for our salvation. But if Christians think that is the end of it, then perhaps we need a Canaanite woman to come and ask us impertinent questions. Because the simple truth of the matter is that Christians, too, often fail to see the scope of what God has intended and will bring to pass. God's call is what brings us into being, and his gift is to make that being real, by sharing with us his own life. Whenever we are tempted to make Christianity something small and anxious, we need reminding that even God's crumbs can satisfy us completely.

# Proper 16

———— ∾ ————

*Isaiah 51.1–6*
*Romans 12.1–8*
*Matthew 16.13–20*

There seems to be a bit of a break in the argument at this point in Romans. Chapters 9—11 are Paul's attempt to give some kind of coherent shape to God's activity in choosing first Israel and then all who believe through Christ. Now Paul is back to practical-sounding advice to the Christian community in Rome. Given the way in which ancient letters were written (dictated to a secretary) and preserved – read aloud and continually copied and recopied for wider distribution – it is hardly surprising that they don't always flow naturally from one paragraph to the next.

But actually the break is not complete. There is a logical progression from what Paul has been discussing in the last few chapters to this presentation of Christian ethics. The problem Paul identified with the law is that people put their trust in that rather than in God, and they believe that they can stand or fall by their own efforts. That attitude is not associated solely with the old covenant. On the contrary, it is the fall-back position of all humans in relation to God. 'Don't do it like that!' Paul begs his readers. 'Give yourself up, give yourself away, know that God is the active principle in all life, and dispense with the illusion that you are at the heart of everything.'

The great twentieth-century Protestant theologian, Karl Barth, calls Christian ethics 'the great disturbance'. In his commentary on Romans, Barth says that all human systems must inevitably be 'disturbed' by the thought of God.[1] God is not part of any of our systems, and none of them is capable of comprehending him. It is simply silly to think that we have the means of measuring and systematizing the creator of all that is.

Paul cuts straight through all the usual attempts to make moral systems that will allow us to continue our lives unchanged. Give your-

———————

[1] Karl Barth, *The Epistle to the Romans*, OUP, 1968, p. 424.

self to God, Paul says, and that 'self' is not some abstract, theoretical inner being, but your real, physical self. 'Present your bodies' is one of Paul's annoyingly inescapable orders. Discipleship is like belonging to the army. You can't have long involved discussions about whether there is a proper time for Christians to wake up. Instead, you get up when the order is given, and you march where you are told. Not a theory, then, but a practice – the practice of discipleship.

If abstraction is one of the main temptations of ethics, the other is to love systems that correct other people's failings and leave your own untouched. And again, Paul is having none of it. Look squarely at your own strengths and weaknesses, and thank God that they are balanced out in the Christian community. Thank God that we are called together, and can help each other out, rather than having to have all the virtues in our own individual person.

Peter and the other disciples have been subjected to 'the great disturbance' since they first met Jesus. They are constantly having to revise their opinions of themselves, others and God in the light of Jesus's unsettling presence. Now, suddenly, Jesus puts them to the test. He starts with the easy question, the question about other people's opinions. All the disciples are happy to chip in, expounding all the theories they have heard about Jesus. But then comes the crunch question. 'Who do *you* say that I am?'

It isn't really a fair question. After all, the disciples are demonstrating, by their very presence, by all that they have given up, what they believe about Jesus. Why is he pressing them now to formulate it? His response to Peter gives the answer. To know who Jesus is is vital. It is not enough to believe that he is very important. It is not enough to believe that he is like the other prophets and messengers of God. When Peter declares 'You are the Messiah', he is saying what has to be said. Jesus is the key to the whole of God's relationship with what he has made.

On the basis of his confession – and on no other 'ethical' basis at all – Peter is made the rock on whom the Church is built. This, then, is to be our defining characteristic, our knowledge of Jesus Christ, and with that knowledge, we can open the gates of Heaven, and be unafraid of Hades.

Does it seem an adequate foundation for the Church? Shouldn't there be more rules and ethical norms laid down? How odd that Peter's sole qualification for the job – apart from a big mouth – is that he can recognize the activity of God when he sees it. Funnily enough, that's what Paul is working for too. 'Be transformed', he says, 'so that you may discern what is the will of God.'

# Proper 17

———— ∾ ————

*Jeremiah 15.15–21*
*Romans 12.9–21*
*Matthew 16.21–8*

Oh dear. Now it's crunch time. Justification by grace through faith is fine. A theology of grace alone, which emphasizes our inability to achieve our own salvation, is central to Paul's faith, particularly as expressed in this letter to the Romans. But it cannot be taken as blanket permission never to change or strive. In today's passage, Paul moves on from what we are not capable of to what he seems to think we should be able to manage, and it is quite frightening.

The virtues Paul is asking the Christian community to exercise are not the dramatic, noticeable ones, like heroism or courage in battle, but the long-haul ones, for which we often get no praise, and which have to be practised every minute of every day – love, respect, patience, perseverance. But Paul knows that these are, in fact, often the hardest and most trying skills to acquire. You do get the impression, reading through his letters, that they didn't come naturally to him, either. So it is surely no accident that he uses emphatic and exaggerated language about these virtues. We are to love with a passion, and hate the opposite of love, with equal passion. We are to be competitively respectful, zealous in service, joyful in hope, and almost embarrassingly hospitable. Paul needs the Christian community really to understand that these qualities will not come by accident. They have to be worked at with all the dedication and energy that you would once have given to getting on in the world, or being the best at your chosen sport.

He also needs them to understand that they cannot expect to be loved and admired for their goodness. On the contrary, the better they are at exercising these Christian virtues, the more they will differ from the society around them, and the more they will be disliked and persecuted. They must not expect understanding. No one else will want to listen to their explanations of why they behave as they do, and no one else will know that they are in the right. And they simply have to put up with that. They must absolutely resist the temptation to take out full-page ads or hours of air time, telling the world 'we are right, and you are wrong'. No thought of getting their own back should ever enter their heads. This seems almost harder than anything else, to allow people to despise and dishonour us because we will not use their own weapons against them.

But we have it on very good authority that that is God's way. When the Son becomes incarnate, even the people he chooses as his closest friends do not understand him. Just before this passage from Matthew, Peter has made his enormous confession to Jesus – 'You are the Messiah,' he says, and Jesus blesses him. But his success seems rather to have gone to Peter's head. He seems to feel that he now has some kind of proprietary rights in Jesus's Messiahship, because here he is, telling Jesus off. 'No, no, you've got it wrong,' he says, 'a messiah doesn't lose. A messiah wins, and everybody worships him.' The savagery of Jesus's response just shows how very tempting it must have been. We assume that it was natural to Jesus to choose God's way, but the Gospels are full of suggestions that part of Jesus's identification with us is that, like us, he has to make his choice for God over and over again, every day. Of course he would have preferred to be Peter's kind of messiah. But unfortunately, that would simply have led to the perpetuation of violence and death. God's way is to bring life, but it can only be done by Jesus's completely unprecedented use of his power. He uses his power to love and to endure. So we know who our pattern is, when we come on to read Romans.

Listen to Jesus struggling to explain to his disciples why they must choose to follow his path. This is the way to life, the only way to life. Really, we do know this. We have only to look around at the history of a world governed by a different definition of power, and we see that the rulers are replaced by other rulers, that the governors die, just like the governed. No one can get their own way by force all the time. God's life is the only real and lasting life that there is, and he wishes to share it with us. At this point in Matthew, Peter has not got the point, but we know that he did, and that thanks to him and succeeding generations of Christians, we have a community that will help us to imitate Jesus.

# Proper 18

——— ❧ ———

*Ezekiel 33.7–11*
*Romans 13.8–14*
*Matthew 18.15–20*

I suppose we can take comfort from the fact that today's passage from Matthew needed to be written at all, because you don't need to give advice where it is already being followed; but there the comfort ends. Clearly, there has never been a perfect, harmonious Christian community that needed no guidelines about how to handle disputes but, equally clearly, having guidelines doesn't make you observe them.

What is laid out here is the proper procedure when individual Christians fall out with one another. It starts with the private word, moves on to a small meeting and ends up with one person being estranged from the community. It is told from the point of view of the person who is in the right, but at every stage of the matter, there is the other story to be told. For example, suppose you are not the offended person, but the offending one. When your fellow Christian comes to complain about your behaviour, how do you react? Perhaps you genuinely do not see their point of view, and are convinced of your own innocence. But when they come back with a couple of others, who also agree that you are in the wrong, what then? Do you pause, think again, and try to change, or do you shout that of course their friends would agree with them, and go off and find some of your friends, who will be on your side? That will, of course, escalate things, and lead to divisions and cliques in the church.

What about at stage two of the procedure? Suppose you are convinced that someone has done something wrong, but after a private word with them, they won't admit it. You go off and return with some other Christians who are not directly involved in the dispute. You expect, of course, that they will be on your side. But what if they are not, or not as whole-heartedly as you would like? What if they see how the other person might not have meant what you think they did? What if they suggest a compromise? Do you insist on total surrender, at the risk of splitting the church, or will you agree, even if you are not convinced?

And then, of course, there is the final stage, where you have been proved right at every turn, and it is now clear that your fellow Christian is wrong, and not willing to change. You are now allowed to treat them like 'a Gentile and a tax-gatherer'. But what kind of treatment is that? Those words cannot be accidental, in a Gospel that has detailed Jesus's constant care for just those groups of people. This ex-Christian, who has put herself outside the Christian community, must now be treated to all your evangelistic powers to bring them back in. You have to show them the love and the care that Jesus showed to 'Gentiles and tax-gatherers'. You don't have time to feel smug about being right, you have work to do.

We cannot always be united, though we could probably manage it more often than we do. We must sometimes hold out for what we think is truth against falsehood, though probably less often than we would like. But against that temptation and need to squabble, we have the vision of what our unity might do. 'If two of you agree on earth about anything you ask, it will be done for you by my Father in heaven,' we are told, 'and, incidentally,' Jesus adds, 'I'll be there too.' There is a terrible sarcasm in that phrase 'if even just two of you could agree about anything'. What we forfeit by our love of discord!

Romans broadens this practical advice to include our general conduct, both to other Christians and to the world in which we live. Paul sounds almost impatient. Surely, he implies, any fool knows what we ought to be doing. Any law promulgated by any government can be summed up by the phrase 'love your neighbour'. Unfortunately, most of us are so clueless about what that might involve, or so determined to concentrate on only loving ourselves, that we need that spelt out a bit more. Pick yourself a concrete example, and work it through. It will actually involve some work, I'm afraid, and you may not see any results for a long time. I'm afraid loving your neighbour might involve you in finding out something about them. Would you like to be 'loved' abstractly, as though you had no personal qualities of your own? I thought not.

For Paul, this is not something to get round to one day, but a matter of extreme urgency. Rather a lot depends upon it. Ezekiel seems to agree.

# Proper 19

————— ∼ —————

*Genesis 50.15–21*
*Romans 14.1–12*
*Matthew 18.21–35*

It is very annoying to think that God may have different standards of judgement from ours. All three of today's readings warn that the obvious surface reaction to one particular incident may turn out to be quite wrong, if you put it in the bigger context of what God is doing with the world.

Take the story of Joseph and his brothers, for example. There is no denying that his brothers treated him abominably, and even they do not try to excuse their behaviour. Even they realize that their reaction to an aggravating, spoiled little brother was completely out of proportion, and so they cannot quite believe in Joseph's forgiveness. Although they have been living safely and comfortably in Egypt for some time, under Joseph's influential protection, they still expect it to be withdrawn as soon as their father dies. They know what they have deserved from Joseph. But Joseph has seen the bigger picture. He has seen what God has done through the violent jealousy of the brothers, and he has seen that he was not the only one to benefit – all the Egyptian people who might have starved without Joseph's foresight can, in a strange way, plead for forgiveness for the people who unwittingly brought Joseph to Egypt.

In the parable that Jesus tells of the forgiven slave, again, you can see that the slave's mind was travelling in one direction, and he was forced to rethink. The slave sees the removal of the burden of debt as a chance to get his life straightened out. He will set all his financial affairs in order, and make sure that he never gets himself into that kind of debt again. Surely his master will approve of that? But his master's context was a bigger one. He was not thinking just about one slave and his money worries, but about the whole society of people he rules, whom he wishes to govern by example. He wanted the slave to see forgiveness in action and learn how to do it, so that more than one life could be put straight.

So both Joseph and the forgiven slave find out that what they initially thought was just about God and themselves turns out to have knock-on effects for many, many others. And that is what Paul is trying to say to the Romans. Of course there is an individual element to Christian obedience, but the point of it is not just to get our own life straight, but to demonstrate the power of the life of God in our midst.

Paul is writing this passage very carefully. Notice that he does not say that the 'weak' should wise up and start supplementing their vegetarian diet. Nor does he come down on one side or the other over days of observance. Each person must follow the path that God has given them, and they may actually be different yet equally obedient. It would be easy to read this passage as an endorsement of individualism and lazy liberalism. It really doesn't matter what you do, so long as you think it's all right. Love is all you need. But that isn't quite what Paul is saying. He is trying to get them to see the bigger context. This is not just about you and God, but about the sweep of God's saving activity in Christ. While you sit there, trying to force your own practices on other Christians, God is saving the world. Your small life will have ripples of consequences in God's great design. Will they be ripples flowing out from the huge impact of God's forgiving love in Christ, or just a very small eddy from a tiny, self-obsessed pebble, which has nothing to do with the tidal wave of God's love? Getting the big picture, that God in Christ wills to be 'Lord of both the dead and the living', does not necessarily make it easier to decide, day to day, how to live in obedience, but it does at least remind you why it matters.

At this time of year, inevitably, we are thinking about what happened in New York on September 11, 2001, and Paul's talk about forgiving a brother who won't eat meat seems irrelevant. But if we put these three passages together, in the bigger context they shout for, perhaps we in the West can see our society as one that is going to require a lot of forgiveness, and that might make us more careful in holding other cultures to account. What kind of reactions on our part might bring life out of death, might make an act of abominable violence a goad to the creation of a different society? How might we witness to our belief in the risen Lord of all?

# *Proper 20*

—— ～ ——

Jonah 3.10—4.11
Philippians 1.21-30
Matthew 20.1-16

Did Jonah ever get the point? The author deliberately chooses an open ending. Jonah knows his God quite well, but that doesn't mean he has to like him. He thinks God is ridiculously soft, but if God wants to make a fool of himself, that doesn't mean Jonah has to join in. As Jonah shouts at God, we finally find out why he ran away from God's commission in the first place: 'I know you, God,' Jonah shouts, 'I'll be preaching judgement, like you told me to, and then you'll go and forgive the people, and make me a look a fool.' And that is precisely what happens. In seconds, Jonah forgets how much he had relied on God's loving forgiveness to get him out of the belly of the whale or, if he doesn't forget, he doesn't see why these characteristics should not be reserved only for Jonah. Why does God have to be loving and forgiving to everyone?

Why does Jonah so hate the idea of God's forgiveness for others? It surely can't really be just about his own loss of face. After all, he has converted a whole great, sophisticated city to the way of the Lord. He must realize how he will be honoured and praised for it? So, no, this isn't really about Jonah's need to look big, but about his perception of justice. God should do what is just, and punish the wicked, otherwise who will ever take him – or his prophets – seriously again?

The people working in the vineyard, too, are a bit concerned about slipping standards. What this landowner is doing could create ill-feeling and unrest throughout the market place, with no one knowing what to expect. The people who had been working all day forget how glad they had been to see reinforcements, and how they had had to work less hard because of the extra help, and how the later workers had shared their food and drink, not having needed it themselves while they were standing around in the market place, waiting to be hired. They also forgot that they were still taking home a good day's wages to their families, and that the other workers had families too. Although they had got exactly what they bargained for, somehow it felt diminished because others also had it.

Like Jonah, the all-day workers forget that they needed first what God was now offering to others. In their case, they argue, it was their entitlement. But these others have not earned it, and should not have it. Jonah can't see a saved city, rejoicing in God and blessing the name of his prophet, because all he can concentrate on is what he thought God should have done instead. The all-day workers can't see the good day's wages, the well-picked vineyard, and the joy of the other workers at being able to feed their families, because they are too wrapped up with their own sense of grievance. Jonah could have dined out for months to come, fêted by the city he had saved, and the workers could all have gone to the pub together, and spent a little of what they'd earned, sharing a convivial evening, and telling stories about strange masters they'd worked for. But instead, they choose to be isolated and embittered. Philippians offers the alternative story, where people accept with gratitude what they are offered, and 'strive side by side'. Paul is not threatened because the Philippians are Christians too. On the contrary, he is thrilled. The Philippians are not angry about Paul's share of the limelight, but see him as an example, rather than a rival.

It is easy to see Jonah and the all-day workers as rather comic caricatures, responding as surely we never would to God's generosity to others. Which is why you have to take seriously not just their selfishness but also their concern about justice. Is Jonah not right to think that God will cheapen forgiveness, and will end up encouraging wrong-doing, because people can point out that God doesn't really seem to mind it much? Are the workers not right to suspect that the vineyard owner will have increasing trouble getting people to work for him all day, if they know they can turn up at the last moment and get a day's pay? In his brave and challenging book, *The Dignity of Difference*,[1] the Chief Rabbi, Jonathan Sacks, speaks, among other things, about what might happen if you dare to let go of the language of justice and rights, and speak instead in the language of 'covenant' and forgiveness. If God can bear to filter his justice through the lens of mercy, who are we to forget how much we have been forgiven, and demand harsh 'justice' for others?

---

[1] Jonathan Sacks, *The Dignity of Difference*, Continuum, 2002, pp. 202ff.

# Proper 21

———— ❧ ————

*Ezekiel 18.1–4, 25–32*
*Philippians 2.1–13*
*Matthew 21.23–32*

'Don't forget the bring-and-buy sale next week; the ladies' group will meet on Thursday to continue their excellent work on the worn-out hassocks; and by the way, don't forget that Jesus Christ is the Son of God and saviour of the world.'

That's not really a fair parody of what is happening in Philippians, because the verses before the glorious hymn on the nature of Christ are not as mundane as a list of church notices, but even so, the effect is extraordinary.

Paul's relationship with the church in Philippi is beset with drama and danger. Acts tells us about the founding of the church, and how it led to beatings and imprisonment for Paul and Silas (you might like to refresh your memory by reading Acts 16.11–40). By the time he is writing this letter, Paul is back in prison. It isn't completely clear which of his many spells in prison this is, but it must have been quite lengthy, because there has been time for an exchange of letters, for people to visit, and for the Philippians to send Paul things to make him more comfortable and to further his work (see 4.10ff.).

Typically, Paul has used his imprisonment as a missionary opportunity. He tells us in 1.12ff. that his imprisonment is widely talked about and that it has made other Christians bolder in their own witness. This is part of what is feeding the great theme in chapter 2. Paul has had time to reflect on the fact that his enforced absence is actually releasing gifts in others. Perhaps his followers had come to rely too heavily on him to do the primary outreach, and they are now having to shoulder some of that responsibility themselves. When Paul talks about Jesus's humility and obedience 'to the point of death', he is acknowledging that his own powerlessness may also be serving God's purposes.

It is a hard truth for any leader to have to face, that your absence may be the best gift you can give your followers. But if there is a degree of anxiety in today's exhortation to unity, there is also considerable confidence. Paul is sure that he founded the church in Philippi on Christ, not on himself, and so he reminds them that there is really no problem about transferring their obedience. 'You've always obeyed me,' he reminds them in verse 12, 'but that obedience was really always obedience to God. Now you will have to cut out the middle man, and acknowledge that it was God who made you a Christian, not me.'

But while Paul wants the Philippian Christians to take a responsibility for their own lives and witness, he wants to make sure that this does not lead to fragmentation in the community. If they can't rely on Paul's authority to keep them together, will they start to fall apart? Or will they remember to model themselves on Christ, and be willing to submit themselves to God and each other?

Verses 6–11 are almost certainly not composed by Paul, but are part of a hymn to Christ that may have been quite well known in early Christian circles. The theology of the song is profound. It suggests that the 'proof' of Jesus's divinity is that he is prepared to give it up, in order to share our life and death. What marks Jesus as God is not anything we would normally recognize as 'power', except when we begin to recognize that it is a 'power' completely outside our own experience and abilities – the power to be utterly given to God.

It is one of the striking things about the Gospel accounts of Jesus, that he seems to be completely uninterested in power. Instead of building himself an army of followers, he sends most of them away. Instead of laying out his manifesto and insisting that God is on his side, he so often just refuses to answer any questions about himself. In today's Gospel, he easily resists the temptation to talk about himself and his authority, and instead begins to probe his questioners. What was their real reason for asking? What would constitute an 'authority' that they would recognize? The ironic little story of the two brothers is Jesus's answer to them. They need to learn to be obedient to God, nothing else.

In the context of the letter to the Philippians, the hymn to Christ might seem to use a sledgehammer to crack a nut. But Paul knows that you can never underestimate the human will to power. This fundamental insight about the nature of Christ is alien to us all. We need to learn to recognize the authority of God, and we have absolutely no other pattern for it, except Jesus.

# Proper 22

—— ❧ ——

*Isaiah 5.1–7*
*Philippians 3.4b-14*
*Matthew 21.33–46*

The people listening to the story of the vineyard would have responded to it on a number of different levels. Some of them would have recognized this vineyard from Isaiah 5 and begun to make the connections from the beginning. The context in which Matthew puts this interchange assumes that the chief priests and Pharisees are a large part of the audience, and they would certainly be expected to hear the literary echoes. So they know, as soon as the story starts, that this is about God and Israel. But they are listening for the refinements, for the differences from the original, to see in which direction Jesus is taking the story. And they quickly spot the major difference, which is that this is not about what the vineyard has done wrong, as it is in Isaiah, but about the tenants. So, they guess, this is not going to be a story about judgement on the whole of Israel, but only some categories of people within it.

Others in the audience are listening to it with less educational baggage. They just want to find out what's happening in the actual story. To begin with, their sympathy is engaged with the landowner. They can imagine the hard, hot, back-breaking work that goes into clearing a piece of land and planting the vines. They can identify with the pleasure of the completed task. But then the landowner walks off, and the audience's sympathy begins to shift. All that work, and it turns out just to be a financial investment, they mutter. I wouldn't mind having so many vineyards that I could afford to let them out, they joke. Jesus's audience may not have been uniformly poverty-stricken, but the majority of them were probably more likely to have suffered from unpleasant landlords than unreliable tenants.

But these tenants are more than just a bit untrustworthy. They are mad. They are reacting with a violent and insane lack of logic, which culminates in their murder of the heir. Killing the slaves buys them a bit more time to enjoy the produce of the vineyard, so their mad calculations might just have led them to believe that there was some point to it. But their actions are completely oriented to the short-term. They don't stop to think about the increasingly heavy penalty they are earning for themselves. But their final act shows that long-term thinking is not within their capabilities at all. How can they ever have convinced themselves that killing the heir would make the vineyard theirs? Why is the owner suddenly going to make his son's murderers his heirs?

No, Jesus doesn't have to deliver the punchline to the story – all his audience know what is bound to happen.

But the reaction of the chief priests and Pharisees is extraordinary. Admittedly, their biblical knowledge would have helped them to the conclusion that they reach so quickly – that this is now a story about the leaders of the people – but, even so, you would expect them to reject Jesus's interpretation. 'We are not like that,' you would expect them to argue, 'that is a completely unfair characterization of us. We have always tried to give God his harvest. All our laws are set up to do just that. You're the one who is trying to keep the produce for yourself, not us.'

Would we so easily recognize ourselves as the villains of the piece? Admittedly this is not the vineyard story that Jesus would tell for us, exactly. The version of the story that we would hear might go like this. When the landlord sent to collect his produce, the tenants said, 'Of course, now, let's see, what is the correct procedure for this?' Or, 'We cannot agree about the best method for harvesting the grapes, and we cannot possibly work together until that is decided.' Or perhaps, 'Yes, indeed, but I'm afraid we had to sell all the grapes for the next twenty years in order to pay for the maintenance of the watch tower. As soon as that's under control, you shall have your produce.' Or, 'We're terribly sorry, but we couldn't get anyone to help us harvest the grapes, so they've all rotted on the vines. Could you just send us a few more helpers?'

Of course that is an unfair caricature, just as Jesus's story for the Pharisees was exaggerated and unfair. But Paul, at least, recognized enough truth in some such description of himself, and repented. All the credentials that he would once have trotted out as proof that he was the perfect tenant for God's vineyard he now realizes are worthless. There is only one thing he wants now, and that is to be more and more like Christ.

# Proper 23

—— ～ ——

*Isaiah 25.1–9*
*Philippians 4.1–9*
*Matthew 22.1–14*

This is an enigmatic little parable in Matthew. If you look at Luke's version of the story (Luke 14.15–24), you will see a much more straightforward narrative about the failure of those originally invited to realize the value of the invitation. The most striking difference between Matthew and Luke is the tone. Matthew's version of the story is full of urgency and bitter anger. It is only in Matthew that the banquet is completely ready and about to go to waste, and it is only in Matthew that the messengers are mistreated and vengeance exacted. And who is the mysterious guest without a wedding garment? He doesn't appear in Luke, but he adds an element of fear, so that there is no assurance of a happy ending, even for those who have made it to the banquet.

Part of the anger in the story is generated by the scene-setting opening verses. The King is throwing this party for his Son. The wedding banquet of the King's Son is a glorious and spectacular occasion for rejoicing, and most people would beg, borrow and steal to get themselves invited. But these strange people either don't care about the invitation at all, or else they treat it as a positive nuisance, to the point where they beat up the postman who brings the card. What should have been an occasion for national rejoicing is turned abruptly into a war zone.

There is bewilderment here – surely the people knew that the King's Son was about to get married? But there is also grief for the Son. Clearly, these people, his future subjects, don't care enough about him to want to share in his rejoicing. What's he got to do with us, they say? He won't make our businesses run. He won't generate an income for us. Their rejection of the Son is both personal and corporate. They reject not just him, but also their share in the future of the nation that he represents.

But the other source of anger in the story comes out of the sense of urgency. Twice (verses 4 and 8) the King says that everything is 'ready'. It cannot wait, it will not keep, it's now or never. Why don't the invited guests realize? They will never again get the chance to go to a royal wedding.

The three parables, from 21.28 to this one, are all about the way in which Jesus's audience are passing up their chance to share in the kingdom. The stories get more and more pointed, making it clearer and clearer that all of this focuses on Jesus. Jesus and the kingdom of God go together – to reject one is to reject the other. It is clear from the way that they react to all three of the stories that the Pharisees understand what is being said, and that it is directed towards them: it's just that they don't believe it. They do not believe that this ordinary human being, standing before them, taking liberties with the tradition that they alone understand and are authorized to interpret, has their lives in his hand. They do not believe that their reaction to him will decide their fates. Would you have done? Or are you, by any chance, the man without a wedding robe?

It is terribly hard to feel that this man is being treated fairly. After all, he didn't know he was going to be invited, and if the rest of the guests were picked up off the streets, how well dressed were any of them? You imagine this poor guest sitting there, eating as much as he can, filling up his cup steadily, not sure what he's doing there, but determined to make the most of it. Then all of a sudden, there's the King. The man is completely thrown. Perhaps he hadn't even realized where he was. He had just gone along with the crowd, eager for a free feed. He didn't know he was celebrating the Son's banquet. The King's initial question is quite friendly in tone. All kinds of possible responses might have allowed the man to stay at the banquet. He could have said, 'I could see how urgent it was, and I wanted to make sure I didn't miss it.' Or, 'I don't own a wedding gown, but I'd love to borrow one.' Instead, he is silent, and he loses his chance.

Like the people who rejected the initial invitation, this guest is not interested in his relationship with the King. He never expected or wanted to meet him or speak to him, and he doesn't care what the banquet is for. This is Matthew's sombre warning – unless we have come to rejoice with the Son, there is nothing for us here.

# Proper 24

———— ❧ ————

*Isaiah 45.1–7*
*1 Thessalonians 1.1–10*
*Matthew 22.15–22*

The question as weapon is one of the oldest techniques in controversy. You will hear it used to perfection most mornings on the radio. The art is to find the question to which there is no acceptable answer, so that any response simply digs the answerer into deeper and deeper trouble. This, of course, changes the whole nature and purpose of a question, since the point of most questions is to elicit an answer, with the assumption that the one asking the questions does not know the answer and is then, in some sense, dependent upon the one who does. But the point of the unanswerable question is to put the questioner in a position of power.

The Pharisees are confident that they have found the perfect question to ask Jesus. Whichever way he answers this, he will alienate some of his followers, and that is exactly what the Pharisees want: they want to erode Jesus's power base, without dirtying their own hands. So, they calculate, if Jesus replies that taxes should be paid to the illegal Roman usurper, he will anger those of his followers who hope and believe that he is the Messiah, the one who will reassert God's direct rule over his people, and get rid of the Romans. But if he tries to please that group by saying that taxes should be withheld, he will be liable for arrest by the civil powers, and he will frighten off the ordinary people, who want no trouble with the authorities, but who just come to Jesus to hear about God and to find consolation and healing. 'Got him!' the Pharisees chortle.

But if they think their weasel words of flattery will lull Jesus into a false sense of security, they are quickly proved very wrong. Within seconds, they are the ones scrabbling for an answer, with their careful strategy completely destroyed. Once again, as in all their dealings with Jesus, they are made to look like fools, who do not know their own business. They are supposed to be the religious

118

leaders, but they never thought to introduce the question of God's rights into the debate. It is Jesus who does that, as though he knows more about God than they do. And since that has always been the heart of their hatred for him, they go away with the situation completely unchanged, but their own anger growing to the point where it will not be contained for much longer.

It apparently does not occur to them that Jesus's answer is a real one, perhaps because their question was not real, and they didn't want an actual answer. But Matthew, through his careful placing of this story, and through the build-up of the question and answer, makes us pause. What does the answer mean? Commentators often dwell on the 'render to Caesar' part of the story, to abstract some kind of Christian response to a secularized authority. But it is not Caesar whom Jesus introduces into the conversation – he was put there by the Pharisees. The Pharisees are pretending to want guidance about our duty to 'Caesar', but they are patently refusing guidance from Jesus about our duty to God.

In Matthew's Gospel, this confrontation between Jesus and the Pharisees comes after a whole series of parables about people who refuse to give God his due, and who will not recognize and rejoice with his Son. So when the Son stands, now, in front of this group of religious leaders, and says, 'What do you think your duty to God might be?', the answer is plain. Their duty is to use all their supposed knowledge of God to recognize the Son, and allow others to do the same. But this is the one thing they are absolutely determined not to do.

Why? Why? Why? Why do they hate him so? What is it about Jesus that so challenges them? It is not enough to say that they thought he was a mad impostor. Jerusalem was full of mad religious impostors, but they did not require large conspiracies on the part of the Pharisees to remove them. No, the trouble with Jesus was precisely that they could not be sure that he was an impostor. It is hard to avoid the conclusion that they really did not want God to get that close. And they were right to fear. It would certainly be much easier if God were like Caesar, so that we knew for sure when we had paid our taxes. But if God is actually like Jesus, then we might need, painfully and humiliatingly, to recognize him over and over again, and give him everything, not just what we consider to be his share.

# The Last Sunday After Trinity

——— ❧ ———

*Leviticus 19.1–2, 15–18*
*1 Thessalonians 2.1–8*
*Matthew 22.34–46*

1 Thessalonians is almost certainly the oldest document in the New Testament. As in so many other things, Paul is a pioneer. It is hard for us to imagine ourselves back to a time when the Christian community had no 'writings' of their own. But one of the things that the epistles make clear is that there was, nonetheless, a remarkable degree of certainty about what constituted the heart of the Christian faith. It centred around the death and resurrection of Jesus, as the activity of God, at work to rescue his people (cf. 1 Thess. 1.10).

These earliest Christians had the Jewish scriptures, which might not be at all well known to those who were Gentile converts, and they had the stories of Jesus told to them by their founders, and then some, the lucky ones, had letters. How Paul's letters must have been treasured by his churches, longing for reassurance and sustenance in their new life. Very few of the epistles in the New Testament are formal theological treatises. The nearest Paul comes to that is in Romans. Most were personal, though clearly meant to be read several times, aloud, to the gathered Christian community.

There are all kinds of things about this letter that mark it out as something designed to be read in a way that we are no longer familiar with. We can flip back a few pages in the Bible and read Acts 16 and 17 for the story of how Paul came to found the church in Thessalonica, but these first readers do not have that luxury. So Paul reminds them. You can imagine that the person who was reading the letter aloud to the group of Christians gathered – in someone's house, perhaps, or outside under a tree? – would have had to pause at this point.

'I remember that,' someone would say. 'Poor old Paul and Silas. Their preaching caused a riot in Philippi, and they ended up in prison. Then when they finally got away, they couldn't find

120

anywhere else to settle for a bit. They were really exhausted when they landed up here.'

Christians who hadn't been present on that momentous visit would press for details. Some of them may even have become Christians after Paul had left, and they wanted to hear everything.

'Well, Paul stayed with Jason' – everyone turned to look at Jason, who went rather pink, but couldn't help being proud at the memory. 'And they started preaching round the synagogue, and lots of us realized that what they said made sense.'

'And lots of us,' chimed in the Gentile Christians. 'We'd always liked the sound of the Jewish God, but thought he wouldn't be interested in us. But now Paul told us that this Jesus showed us that God did want us too.'

'Well then,' continued the first speaker, 'some of the Jews didn't like the sound of what Paul was saying, and they came to get him.'

'Yes,' chuckled Jason. 'But they got me instead.'

'Good job you're rich, Jason,' teased one of the others. 'At least that way they only took your money.'

'Well, I got a good few bruises, as well,' retorted Jason. 'And then we managed to get Paul and Silas away.'

By this time, the gathered crowd of people are feeling glowing and pleased with themselves. They had believed when many hadn't, and they had helped to save their heroes. No wonder Paul was writing so warmly to them. Paul had put himself in danger to bring the gospel to them, and they had responded magnificently. He could absolutely rely on them.

This is a very clever tactic on Paul's part. There's nothing like a shared memory of triumph against adversity to bring a group closer together. How vital this kind of memory must have been for the small communities of the earliest Christians, facing hardship, struggling to maintain their distinctiveness. Only deep loyalty to Paul and to each other was going to keep their commitment to Christ going. How many times was this letter read by the Thessalonians, with every word and phrase being pondered and prayed over? How many times was it copied and recopied, over the years to come, so that it wouldn't wear out, so that it could be shared more widely, so that we, thousands of years later, could read the words of love and praise written by the Apostle Paul to the Christians in Thessalonica, within twenty years of the death and resurrection of Christ?

The Thessalonians were very aware of God's provision for them – he had sent them Paul, to preach the gospel. But even more, he sent his Son, the Word not just written, but incarnate.

*Sundays Before Advent*

# The Fourth Sunday Before Advent

———— ∾ ————

*Micah 3.5–12*
*1 Thessalonians 2.9–13*
*Matthew 24.1–14*


'That was a really depressing morning,' said one disciple to another, leaning back in the sparse shade of the olive tree to keep out of the midday sun.

'Yes,' agreed another. 'I'm thinking of packing it in. I can't see that he's ever going to show his hand and lead us all to power.'

'But that's just what he said would happen,' chipped in a third. 'He said that some of our hearts will grow cold, and that we'll stop being his followers.'

'He didn't mean *us*,' retorted the first disciple. 'As far as I could tell, he seems to think all of this could go on for generations, getting worse and worse.'

'And why does he have to keep annoying the Pharisees if he isn't going to take them on properly?' murmured the second disciple, discontentedly. 'He'll just get us all into trouble for no good reason.'

The little group sat back, hot and angry, contemplating the morning they had just had. First of all, Jesus had got into yet another slanging match with the Pharisees, one of the worst of the increasingly hostile encounters between them. Then, after they'd left the temple, followed by the buzz of furious and thrilled conversation, Jesus turned back and looked at the sacred beloved building, and said, 'It won't last much longer.'

Well, of course, that raised a lot of hopes. After all, the only way they could manage without the temple was if God was going to come and rule directly. So that meant that Jesus was at last ready to overthrow the Romans and the Jewish leaders who opposed him, and reign directly for God.

'When, when?' the disciples asked eagerly, hoping for an exact date, like 'next week', or 'at the Passover', or something definite.

But instead, what they got was a long list of things that had to happen first, all of them horrible, many of them painful to the very disciples who were ready to sacrifice everything for Jesus's cause.

Except, of course, they weren't ready. They might have been prepared to take up arms, if it came to it, though they were secretly hoping that enough of the people would come over to their side to make it unnecessary. But what Jesus seemed to be suggesting was that many of them would use up their lives, and die horrible deaths, and still see nothing. They also couldn't help noticing that Jesus kept saying things like 'They will hand *you* over', or '*You* will hear of wars', almost as though he wasn't going to be with them in it.

The only clue Jesus gave them about actual timing was that the end was linked to the spreading of the good news of the kingdom throughout the world. 'What good news?' they asked each other. 'I didn't hear any good news in what he just said.'

'Yes,' laughed one of them, going off into a parody of a popular preacher. 'Join my wonderful movement, and you might end up hating each other and getting killed. That message is going to catch on.'

And yet, amazingly, the good news of the kingdom of the crucified Messiah did catch on. Despite all temptations and occasional failures, most of those first disciples did endure to the end, and did persuade thousands of others that the kingdom of the risen Lord is the country that they have always longed for, a country where God directly rules his subjects, with justice and love held together.

When it is Paul's turn to preach this gospel, he gives us a little vignette of his methods in Thessalonica. He settles down with the people, earning his own living, trying to live out and embody that vision of a righteousness that is loving and converting. Above all, he doesn't want the Thessalonians to think of the gospel as something only he can give them. He is delighted that through his preaching they recognize God's greatness, not Paul's.

But if this is a brief pastoral idyll for Paul, there are many more scenes of violence and pain. Intrinsic to Jesus's message, as Paul and the disciples know so well, is the cost. The cost is borne first of all and supremely by Jesus himself, but this good news, of the direct reign of God, sweeping away all the false gods and false rulers we so busily build in God's place, can never be preached without warnings. If this costs you, will you still hear it as good news? Do you want the closeness of God more than anything? Only God can make this good news, because only God is supremely worth it. Our job is to get out of the way, so that we can become channels, like Paul, for God's word.

# The Third Sunday Before Advent

———— ∾ ————

*Amos 5.18–24*
*1 Thessalonians 4.13–18*
*Matthew 25.1–13*

These are odd Sundays, these ones before Advent. We are preparing to be prepared, getting ready to get ready, and all the readings are agreed that this is quite a sombre business. What is the best way to use this period of inaction, before the bustle really begins?

Matthew's Gospel suggests this is a good time to lay in provisions, and make sure that your oil supplies will last through any emergency. But perhaps verse 11 also suggests that this is a good time to familiarize yourself with what it is that you are looking forward to, so that you will recognize it when it comes, and, more importantly, it will recognize you. These flighty bridesmaids haven't bothered to get in enough oil for their lamps because they don't, at heart, care very much about the wedding they are going to. They don't seem to have paid visits to the couple and their family beforehand, or bought them an engagement present, or done anything suggesting that the bridegroom is actually a friend. They just want to turn up for the party. With better preparation, they might not have been treated as gatecrashers.

Amos, too, suggests that you should use as much of your time as possible familiarizing yourself with God, and not just looking forward to the party, without caring whose party it really is, or what kind of present he would really like.

Amos is talking to a group of his fellow-countrymen who have lost sight of what God is really like. They use religious language and rituals freely, and enjoy them, and they are confident that God is a chum of theirs. So they are quite looking forward, they think, to God's big party, the day of the Lord. They don't mind if it doesn't come too soon, since they are quite comfortable as they are, but they have no real worries about their relationship with God.

Into this well-off gentlemen's club kind of atmosphere Amos's words are hurled, and they scorch and burn everything they touch.

126

Amos reminds them that their primary purpose in life is to be God's covenant people, living a shared life that reflects what God really cares about. Sadly, the people have forgotten to do their regular checks on what God is really like. They have assumed that God must like what they would like, which is lots of attention and praise, and lavish ceremonies of which he is the centre. What God wants is a community of righteousness and justice, Amos thunders, where no one is performing easy religious ceremonies and going home to a large dinner, while other people starve.

Verse 24 is often sung as though it was something to look forward to, but read it carefully and what you see is the destructive violence of a huge torrent of water, sweeping away everything in its path. The puny little grain offerings and burnt offerings will vanish without trace, and the people will be left clinging helplessly to the mercy of the God they barely know any more.

The way the prophets of the Old Testament hammer home the message of God's fierce determination to shape a people of justice and righteousness should give us all pause. It is very unlikely that God has suddenly stopped caring about these things that have always been central to his communication with his people.

And if the reading from Thessalonians comes as a relief after all that doom and gloom, perhaps we should be careful to read it in context. The Thessalonians are, Paul tells us, people who have been preparing hard to be ready for the Lord. They have done everything they can to make sure that they recognize him and are recognized by him. They have accepted the gospel preached to them by Paul, and they have realized that it has implications for their life together. They are trying so hard to live in love and justice with one another. So to them, Paul can give some assurances. God is faithful, and for those who have shaped themselves according to his nature, the coming of God is good news. No doors will be slammed in their faces, and no floods will wash them away.

Preparing to be prepared involves looking back over God's dealings with us, so that we will know and be known. 'When our gratitude for the past is only partial, our hope for a new future can never be full ... If we are to be truly ready for a new task in the service of God, our entire past, gathered into the spaciousness of a converted heart, must become the source of energy that moves us toward the future', writes Henri Nouwen.[1]

---

[1] Henri Nouwen, 'All is Grace', *Weavings,* December 1992.

# The Second Sunday Before Advent

———— ∿ ————

*Zephaniah 1.7, 12–18*
*1 Thessalonians 5.1–11*
*Matthew 25.14–30*

The word 'gospel' means 'good news', and Christians believe that, in Jesus Christ, the whole world is offered the good news of God's love for them. But the New Testament also bears witness to the fact that not everyone receives God's love as 'good news'. Incredible as it may seem, some people look at Jesus and hate him and the God he represents. Some feel threatened, some feel bored, some hate the way he breaks their rules about God, and some simply do not recognize what is on offer. The passages that the lectionary gives us to reflect upon in these Sundays before Advent are all full of foreboding and warning. It is possible to reject the love of God, and so to reject your own life. It is possible to live in such a way that you do not recognize Life when it stands in front of you.

Zephaniah describes a people characterized by the word 'complacent' (v. 12). They believe that they have a good life because it is materially comfortable. They are well housed and well fed, and they believe that they can keep God at a safe distance. After all, their wealth has enabled them to keep all other uncomfortable things at bay so why not God too? It's not that they don't believe in God, it's just that they think they have bought his neutrality – he won't intervene, one way or another.

To them, God comes as a hostile and destructive army, taking away all their security and giving them only terror. There is no 'good news' for them, because the only good news they would recognize is no news. They don't want to hear anything about God at all. Unfortunately, in God's world, that is not an option.

The slave in Matthew's parable is not quite that far gone. He knows the master quite well, but he fears and dislikes him. We have no idea what has led to this state of affairs between master and slave. Obviously, the master is a bit of a maverick. Not many masters would give their slaves quantities of money, and go off for an unspecified period of time, to an unknown destination, leaving no instructions. He doesn't tell the slaves what they are expected to do with the property but, clearly, he knows them quite well, and they know him. They know that this is a test of some kind, and they approach it each in his own way.

The slave who is given one talent already believes that the master doesn't think much of him. There may be a longer history to this than we are told, but it is obvious to him that the master trusts him less than the others, because he gives him less. And this slave is both afraid and resentful. His resentment comes bubbling out when the master finally returns, and the slave finds himself pouring out what he really thinks of the master. He knows he's going to get into trouble, but he's determined to have his say first.

The master's response is interesting. He recognizes the slave's description of himself, but not why it led to that result. 'If you're so scared of me,' the master says, 'why didn't you try harder to please me?'

And to this, the slave has no answer. He had decided, long ago, that nothing he did would please his master, and he has given up trying.

To this man, God is not 'good news' because he is too obsessed with his own failure. He cannot see that all the other slaves are rewarded for their efforts, irrespective of whether they earned big profits or small. He has turned his own failure into a weapon. 'This is your fault, God,' he shouts, 'not mine.' He cannot recognize good news because he doesn't actually know himself at all. In order to hear good news, you have to have some idea of what would constitute good news for your situation. But this slave is only looking for the downside of everything. He doesn't want any good news, because he's sure there will be a drawback in it somewhere.

The Thessalonians want God's good news, though even they are slightly apprehensive about it. This good news is not something to take lightly. You have to be prepared for it, live your life in anticipation of it, stick together and help each other train for it.

Why should the 'good news' of the love of God be so alarming? Perhaps because few of us actually know how to be loved. We know how to be pampered, or to indulge ourselves, or to whine about being misunderstood. But to be loved with God's total, consuming, transforming and utterly perceptive love? Are we ready for that?

# Christic the King

——— ⁓ ———

*Ezekiel 34.11–16, 20–4*
*Ephesians 1.15–23*
*Matthew 25.31–46*

Matthew 25 is all about preparedness. First of all, there are the foolish bridesmaids, who ran out of oil and so missed the wedding; then there is the slave who wasted his chance of increasing his one talent while the master was away, and now we have the sheep and the goats. All of these people and groups are unprepared for what is about to happen, and they face terrible consequences, for the stories are not just about the importance of being ready, but also about judgement. The people in the stories make their judgements. The foolish bridesmaids decide there is no great rush. The slave with one talent decides to do nothing, and the 'goats' decide that some people are not worth bothering about. God then makes his judgement and, unfortunately, it is completely different from theirs.

All the people standing at the throne of glory are taken aback by God's judgement and, more particularly, by God's judge. They were not expecting to see the Son of Man up there on the throne, looking completely at home, with angels around him carrying on as if they thought he was God. As the people are separated into two groups, one on the right hand and one on the left of this awesome yet recognizable figure, it is clear that both groups are equally puzzled. They are both, you might say, unprepared for this standard of judgement. Neither group had lived their lives expecting to have them judged by this Man, in this way. As their sentences are handed down, both groups say, 'We didn't know we would be judged for *that*.'

The judge does not explain himself, but he could have pointed to both the law and the prophets, which make it clear what God expects. The reading from Ezekiel, for example, shows God himself looking for the lost sheep and longing to care for them. It also shows God's judgement on those 'fat sheep' who kept the pasture for themselves, and deliberately pushed away the hungry and the needy. Any well-brought-up Jew listening to Jesus's parable of the sheep and the goats would recognize the justice of the judgement handed out to the goats. No one could say that they were not warned about the nature of God.

So how did they – and how do we – manage so to be deceived? How did we manage to persuade ourselves that there would be no real consequences for the way we live? As we gorge ourselves to death, how come we do not realize that we are the fat sheep, pushing the starving millions away from our green fields?

That is what makes the Son of Man such a terrible judge. Judgement is not something alien and distant, but something that bears the human face of the neglected, the tortured, the crucified. God is not far away, and not easy to deceive, and we cannot plead that we did not know what he wanted of us. We know perfectly well what the hungry, thirsty, estranged, naked, sick and imprisoned people around us want. Jesus the Son of Man is to be our judge, and the human face he shows us is all too recognizable.

That is why Paul's prayer for the Ephesians is that they might come to know Jesus Christ. On the face of it, Ephesians and the parable of the sheep and the goats could not be more different. The parable has often been read as meaning that you don't need to be religious to please God. Although the Judge in the story is Jesus, the King, the Son of Man, it is certainly true that the sheep didn't think they recognized him in those whom they helped. They did their good deeds without any ulterior motives, looking for no recognition. Whereas the knowledge of God that the Ephesians have sounds like theoretical knowledge, issuing in no particular kind of behaviour, and with the obvious hope of rich reward in heaven.

But if you look more closely, that is far from the truth. This 'knowledge' is the knowledge that God's revelation is to be found in the crucified Jesus, and that this human, suffering figure is the one who rules for God, and to whom all creation is subject. When we, his Church, acknowledge him as our King, and become his body, we can have no illusions about what that body looks like. We believe in God's great power, at work in Jesus, to bring life out of death. And so we, his body, work to bring life out of the death all around us. We work to pay attention to the real human beings with whom God came to identify, and we look around us for the life that created and redeemed out of love.

# *YEAR B*

*Advent*

# The First Sunday of Advent

―― ∽ ――

*Isaiah 64.1–9*
*1 Corinthians 1.3–9*
*Mark 13.24–37*

A monk comes to his abbot, seeking enlightenment. He questions the abbot eagerly and impatiently, firing questions at him. But the abbot says, 'Just look.' The monk is very disappointed, 'I'm always looking,' he says sulkily. 'No, you're not,' says the abbot. 'In order to look at what is here, you have to be here, and you are mostly somewhere else.' Stories like this abound in monastic literature, and in the sayings of the Desert Fathers and Mothers. This particular one comes from the Benedictine tradition (you can read it in full in Joan Chittister's book, *The Rule of Benedict*).[1]

Advent is a time to start preparing to meet God, and most of the preparatory readings suggest that this is, at best, a sobering prospect and, at worst, a positively terrifying one. So it is terribly tempting to feel that we ought to be very busy, so that God will notice and be pleased. Probably for most of us it actually is a very busy time, whether we want it to be or not. Readings like the ones from Mark and Isaiah add to a general feeling of anxiety. There is something scary coming, and we're not quite sure what to do about it. Our instinct is to imitate Corporal Jones from *Dad's Army* and run around shouting 'Don't panic!' That must surely have been the reaction of Jesus's disciples as they listened to Jesus's description of the coming of the Son of Man. What he is describing is nothing less than cataclysmic, and who is this 'Son of Man'? They suspect that he is Jesus, or closely associated with Jesus, but they would much prefer it if Jesus made that clear. The impersonal way in which he talks about the Son of Man's judgement leaves them uncomfortable and uncertain about what their own position is. Are they among the elect or not?

---

[1] Joan Chittister, *The Rule of Benedict: Insight for the Ages*, Crossroad, 1992.

But then, when Jesus gets on to the practical advice, it is very much like that of the abbot to the impatient monk. 'Look, keep awake, be prepared.' Jesus does not recommend any particular kind of activity or busy-ness, just a tense, watchful preparedness, and a way of looking at the world that sees it as full of signs.

This is not an easy skill. It is much easier to look at the world and see it either as meaningless or actually as full of absences – places where God is not present, rather than places where, any moment now, he might be. The people in Isaiah have come to see the world as empty of God. God has withdrawn from them, they complain, so no wonder they sin. This is all God's fault. If only God would behave like God, like he used to in the old days, then the people would believe again. If only he would rain down fire, and make the mountains shake with awe, then of course people would serve him gladly. 'Do something, God!' the people shout, 'Let's have a bit of activity!'

Then, suddenly, in the midst of this rather melodramatic breast-beating and accusing of God, the people see themselves. It is as though someone has suddenly put a mirror in front of them, as they act out their rage and shame and shake their fists at God. And they suddenly realize that they are not in charge of this play, rather God is. They see themselves in this harsh mirror, as Wallace and Gromit-like clay figures, whose very existence is dependent upon God. And with this realization, the mirror fills with the reflection not of them-selves, but of God. They remember, suddenly, who this God is, their maker and their father. God has not hidden himself from them, but they have been too busy, being somewhere else, looking at everything but God. They need to learn to look again and see the world full of signs of God's mighty power and approaching pres-ence. Like the disciples waiting for the Son of Man, so with Isaiah's people waiting for the return of God: they cannot be sure that what is to come will be comforting, but they do at least know it will be real and not some illusion.

Only the Corinthians seem to be able to wait for the coming of Christ with anything like complacency. But that's because they have the sense to stay where they are and look at Christ. And what they see is the faithful God who, from our creation onwards, comes to us until we meet him as he is, in Christ.

So Advent is like a period of forced inactivity, where you have no choice but to sit still and look, learning to see the world as it actu-ally is, full of signs, joyful or terrifying, of the coming of God.

# The Second Sunday of Advent

———— ❧ ————

*Isaiah 40.1–11*
*2 Peter 3.8–15a*
*Mark 1.1–8*

The trouble is that we think we know the end of the story. We think that this time of waiting that we call Advent is all building up to the joyful time of Christmas. In fact, it can hardly be called a 'time of waiting' at all. The Christmas lights and Christmas decorations often precede Advent, and some people are well into their Christmas shopping. No shocks for us, we know what to expect. When we've celebrated the birth of the baby, everything will get back to normal again until next year.

So who is this strange, hairy man, striding out of the desert, shouting? Doesn't he know that this is a time for the family, not a time for unpleasantness? Why is he shouting about repentance? And he seems to have skipped all the bit about the angels and the shepherds, surely the real point of Christmas, and gone straight on to something about baptism and the Holy Spirit. That's not part of this story, is it? Doesn't that come in some other story, that we're not really very interested in? No thanks, let's get back to the baby.

Isaiah seems to be getting into the mood rather better. At least he's talking about comfort and tenderness. But no, there he goes too, ruining a perfectly nice message. He seems to think we only get to the comfort when we've faced the devastation. He's on about the wilderness as well. What's more, he seems to think that we are sitting in a desert because that's what we have made of our lives. He suggests that we've pulled up our roots, and turned away from our ground, our source of water, which is God. Now we are so weak and dry that we drift about aimlessly. For Isaiah, the coming God is not a sweet little baby that we can coo over and then ignore while we get on with our party. Instead, God is like a breath of fire on the dried grass of our lives. When he breathes on us, all that is left is the wilderness and God. When, at last, we have noticed that there is no life in us, then we will see the beginning of the extra-

4

ordinary transformation of the desert. Where there was the empty waste that we made, there will be paths, heralds, shouting, a huge crowd following the glorious king through the wilderness, and everywhere he goes life springs up, life that is directly dependent upon him, and knows it. The lambs don't go searching around for food, but turn directly to the Lord and are lifted up and fed. Oh yes, comfort and tenderness, all right, but only once we realize there is only one source. All the Christmas presents, tinsel and plastic reindeer are just a wilderness, without the life of God.

So perhaps the birth that comes at the end of Advent is not the end, but the beginning. That would make sense, after all. Most births are the beginning of something. When we have met this strange God at Christmas, then we don't pack everything away until next year, but start the journey with him, watching him grow, finding out what he is like, waiting to see the story unfold. Such a lot of waiting in the Christian story. Each time you get to a point that you think is the end, you find it is actually another beginning. After the birth, the ministry of Jesus, which seems to end at the cross. And then, suddenly, there is another beginning, in the resurrection, and things start up again, and end again, as Jesus ascends. This time, the new beginning is the Christian community, living by the Holy Spirit. The history of the Church's life has been a series of deaths, or near-deaths, and rebirths, each one unexpected and unpredictable.

2 Peter suggests that we should be grateful for this odd way of proceeding, grateful for the fact that each ending is actually another beginning, because each new beginning gives us a little longer before we have to face the final end. 'Be grateful for waiting,' Peter says. 'Stand in your wilderness and start to build a place "where righteousness is at home"' (v. 13). We are still a very long way from that dream. That's why Advent readings always contain the sombre note of warning. You think you want the coming of Christ? Are you sure you know what you are asking for? So make the most of this period of waiting, be grateful for Advent and use it, not just to prepare for the birth of the baby, but also to prepare a world where this baby, righteousness incarnate, will be at home.

# The Third Sunday of Advent

—— ∾ ——

*Isaiah 61.1–4, 8–11*
*1 Thessalonians 5.16–24*
*John 1.6–8, 19–28*

So at last, after weeks of foreboding, of warnings that the coming of the Lord is not something to take lightly or to meet with unprepared, now at last the excitement begins to mount.

First of all there is John. You could read his self-description as humble and self-effacing, but I'm not sure that it is. It rings with certainty. John knows exactly what he is and what he is not. He knows that he is a necessary part of God's unfolding plan, the first actor on the stage, the narrator who sets the scene and lets us know what is to come. There is barely suppressed excitement in his voice as he scans the crowd, waiting for the face that he knows he – and only he – will recognize. He does not mind that his work will be eclipsed. He understands the job of the herald, both its importance and that it is necessarily transitory. He has no hesitation in applying the words of scripture to himself. He knows that the prophets foretold his coming, and longed to see what he is about to see. John is hugely content to be where he is and what he is. Any part in God's coming is vital.

As soon as John opens his mouth, he brings with him the whole cloud of prophetic witness to what God has been preparing for so long. And although the readings of the last few weeks have reminded us that not everyone will be pleased to see God, or thrilled by what he has prepared for the world, today's reading from Isaiah is full of joy. It is a joy that John would have recognized and identified with, because it is the joy of the one whose news is for others. The joy of the anointed one is in seeing the faces of the oppressed, the captive, the bereaved as they hear the good news he brings. But even this, enormous as it is, is secondary. The real, uncontainable, wild excitement comes in Isaiah 61.10 and 11. The good news that the anointed one brings is the news that, at last, the earth is to see the full nature and glory of God. Righteousness, salvation, justice

6

and praise spring up all over the earth because now, finally, we see what God is like. Just as a garden cannot help growing what is planted in it, so the world cannot help but respond to the righteousness of God.

Does Thessalonians sound a little tame after Isaiah? It shouldn't. The Thessalonians are enjoying what the prophets longed for and John pointed to. And they know it, or if they don't, it's not Paul's fault. Paul is perfectly clear that joy is the natural condition of Christians, quite independent of the outward circumstances. Joy is the gift of the unquenchable Spirit, whose job it is to keep Christians connected at all times to the life of God, offered in Christ. It is the same bubbling spring of excitement found in John the Baptist and in Isaiah, the welling joy of those who have seen the nature of God, and the unfolding of his work. It is, perhaps, a reflection of the joy of God himself, looking on what he made and seeing its loveliness. Now the things that he has made can look at him, making again, recreating, and marvel at the beauty of the creator.

*The Shepherd of Hermas*, which was written in the second century and widely read and pondered on for generations, says: 'Put sadness away from you, for truly sadness is the sister of half-heartedness and bitterness . . . he that is sad always does wickedly, first because he makes sad the Holy Spirit that has been given to man for joy, and secondly he works lawlessness, in that he neither prays to God nor gives him thanks.'[1]

He might have been echoing Paul. This joy is not dependent upon prosperity, health, luck or anything external. It is based on the extraordinary gift that God the Spirit gives us, of being part of the life and work of God. So, like most of God's gifts, it has a purpose. In joy, we turn to the world God has made, and we become his heralds. Like John the Baptist, we shout aloud about the coming of Christ, who will bring joy to those who have never experienced it before in the whole of their lives. We shout about the faithfulness of God, creator, redeemer and bringer of joy. How extraordinary that Thessalonians says that the basis of our faithfulness to God is joy, and that to fulfil God's law we need to rejoice at what he has done. Now that really might get us into the Christmas Spirit.

---

[1] *The Shepherd of Hermas*, www.earlychristianwritings.com, Mandate 10.

# The Fourth Sunday of Advent

—— ∾ ——

2 Samuel 7.1–11, 16
Romans 16.25–27
Luke 1.26–38

How can we honour God? How can we show our gratitude for what he has done and promise our obedience for the future? Perhaps our offerings sometimes resemble the mauled mouse that the cat brings in and lays lovingly at our feet. You can see pride and joy in the cat's face, the knowledge that she has brought something valuable that she herself desires and so expects us to desire too. Is that what our offerings to God are sometimes like? Certainly David is offering God something out of the fullness of his own heart. At last the Kingdom is safe and settled and David has a home. The shepherd boy from the hills, who has lived an unpredictable and endangered life since first the Lord called him into his service is now a King, living in a proper house. No more tents and caves for him. A home no longer has to be something that you can pack up or leave behind at a moment's notice. This house represents safety, security, the fulfilment of a deep need for David. And so he assumes that God would like a house too.

David's desire to honour God is genuine, and he has thought carefully and lovingly about the best way to do it. But he has got it wrong. There is no anger in God's tone as he speaks to Nathan. You can hear the affectionate laughter in the words. But the simple fact of the matter is that although David's deepest need may be for security, God has no need of that at all. Is there some small, unacknowledged part of David that is actually trying to domesticate God? Does David think that if he builds a home for God he will know where God is and what he is up to? In the previous chapter, we have seen how awesome the ark, the place of God's presence, is and that David has hugely mixed emotions about it. He is both terrified and thrilled by it – quite rightly. So does he hope that a safely housed ark will represent a safely tamed God? If so, he soon learns what we all have to learn, that God cannot be tamed and

8

that recognizing what God wants might mean relearning the deepest desires of our own heart.

Patiently, God explains that it is not our job to make him a home, but his job – indeed his joy – to make this world a home for us. The great work is started at our creation, continued through calling his people away from Egypt and into a new community, and completed when God himself comes and makes a home with us. Patiently, the angel comes to negotiate with Mary for the kind of home that God is making. God, whom the whole world cannot contain, waits quietly while his angel talks to Mary. How gentle the angel is, as they talk. Mary is confused, bewildered, uncomprehending, but not afraid of this, God's messenger. How he must have muted himself so that she can ask what she needs to know.

Mary's one question is such a clue to her nature. She does not demand to know exactly what God is hoping to achieve; she does not ask what it will cost; she does not preen and demand praise because she is the one God is asking. All she asks is, 'Aren't I a bit of a problem? Are you sure I fulfil your requirements?' And when the angel replies, 'It's all taken care of,' then Mary says, 'Fine.'

Such an odd, almost low-key conversation to announce that God is coming to make the world his home, and so to make it our home too. Such sensible, manageable care for Mary, at this stage, putting her in touch with Elizabeth, who is the one person who will understand what has happened.

When David offers to make God a home, God explains that his home has always been with his people. He has gone with them, preparing things for them, making provision for them in ways that they never even noticed. He knows that they long for a home, but perhaps they do not realize that they can have no home without him. All the things that we long for, that we search for throughout the world, throughout our lives – love, security, peace, fulfilment, joy – all of these things are to be found in God, our only real home. So now, God is preparing, as Advent moves towards Christmas, to come to us, in our own place, in what we call 'home' and yet are never quite content with. He will make it, and us, his home, so that we can come to our true home, at last.

9

*Christmas*

# Christmas Day

—— ❧ ——

*Isaiah 62.6–12*
*Titus 3.4–7*
*Luke 2.1–20*

In these verses from Isaiah there is a great sense of subdued excitement, of restlessness, of purposeful movement a little distance away, as the dawn breaks. Actually, this would probably describe almost any household with children, on a Christmas morning. In both cases, it is anticipation that causes this stifled bustle.

In Isaiah, the watchmen who have been on night shift, straining their eyes in the dark, whispering to each other about what it is they are looking for, are about to be relieved. The day shift is coming on duty, but the ones who have been there all night are finding it hard to leave. Wouldn't it be awful if it all happened when they were asleep? Normally, watchmen live in the tension of knowing that if they do not see the slight movements of the enemy approaching, then the whole city will be in terrible danger. But these watchmen are not looking out, anticipating attack. They are waiting for salvation. Their excitement cannot be contained. Day and night they can be heard muttering, 'Come on, come on', and occasionally shouting it aloud, as though their impatience will communicate itself to the one they are waiting for.

All their lives, they have lived in garrison towns, watching all around them for the enemy, stockpiling food and necessities behind the walls, knowing that anything left outside the gates is liable to be forfeited to the enemy. But now, all of that is to change. The gates of the city are to be flung open, so that light and air can stream in. The rubble around the city wall is to be cleared away. You no longer need to try to make it hard to reach the city. Instead, all your efforts go into making it easy to reach, and highly visible. People are beginning to pour in and out, looking around them, laughing, shouting, rejoicing.

And then, the sudden hush, followed by a huge roar of sound. At last the Lord is coming! At last the city is a home, not a fortress. The Lord has come home.

This is the way it should be, when the great and conquering King returns, but Luke tells it another way. He shows us a King, laid in an animal feed trough, visited by shepherds. True, the watchmen – the angels – see him coming and announce it. But they do not tell the whole city, the whole world. Instead, with all their glorious joy, they go with their trumpets and banners to a group of shepherds. And where, in Isaiah, you see the whole town transformed, new buildings, new roads, clean, sparkling, waiting for the crowds to come and welcome the King, in Luke you see the shepherds scuttling along, mystified and stumbling, to see a child.

But perhaps the shepherds deserve more credit. The people crowded into the restored city are in no doubt about when the King arrives. They have the shouts of all the people around them, they have the sight of the King himself in all his magnificence. By the time the shepherds reach the child, the angels have gone, and all they see is a rough crib and a tired mother. But they recognize the King instantly, and straightaway take on their share of the herald's job. Just as the angels told them, so they now tell Mary, and anyone else who will listen, shouting their joy at what God has done.

And what is it that God has done? Both for the jubilant crowds in Isaiah's city, and for the shepherds and for us, God has brought freedom. The people of the city no longer have to live in fear, waiting for the enemy, never knowing which direction he will come from, or what the cost will be. They are free to live in their city as a home, safe and peaceful. They have not won any wars, they have not had to pay for their freedom with the lives of their soldiers. It has been given to them by the Lord. And the same is true for us, Titus tells us. We have done nothing to earn this freedom, and yet it is ours. We had been expecting to live all our lives in fear of the enemy, knowing that we might have to pay a terrible price to be free, a price that we were almost certainly incapable of paying. And suddenly the weight is lifted. We turn, expecting perhaps to be taken as slaves by the conquering King who has defeated our enemy, but instead he says we are his children, his heirs, and he pours his largesse over our uncomprehending heads, the richness of his Spirit, proclaiming that we are the freed children of God.

# The First Sunday of Christmas

---- ∾ ----

*Isaiah 61.10—62.3*
*Galatians 4.4–7*
*Luke 2.15–21*

Galatians is one of the most moving of all Paul's epistles. Paul is fighting for his calling in this epistle. The fight is partly for himself, because if he is wrong, and God has not called him to be an apostle to the Gentiles, then his whole life is wasted. But more importantly, it is for his converts, because if Paul has mistaken his vocation, then he has misled all those Gentiles who have given their lives to Christ through Paul's preaching. The argument is passionate, personal and convoluted. There are passages of personal history, interspersed with technical and not always transparent pieces of scriptural analysis. There are calm and carefully reasoned passages, side by side with passages that are almost libellous. But this section in chapter 4 is at the heart of the whole argument.

It is hard for us today to hear the real pain and joy in this passage about sonship, but it speaks powerfully of what Paul has given up, and why. All through his childhood and early adulthood, Paul would have believed that he was special, because of his relationship with God. This relationship was not anything he chose or opted into, but was his right, because he was a Jew. He was one of God's chosen people, an inheritor of the promises made to Abraham and David, automatically 'one of the family'.

Paul was clearly not alone in finding Jesus's preaching deeply threatening to that sense of being right with God. The Gospels show us that many of the religious leaders who met Jesus hated him, and rejected all that he said and demonstrated about God. Paul's own rejection of Jesus led him to help in a violent persecution of Jesus's followers, which only ended with his meeting with the risen Lord on the road to Damascus. When Paul accepts that his hostility towards Christians is a hostility towards God, he steps instantly out of his privileged insider's relationship with God.

14

So when, here in Galatians, he talks about our 'adoption' as God's children, there is a complicated and moving dynamic going on. Once, Paul would have assumed that he was a child of God, and heir to God's promises, simply because of who he was and where he was born. But now he accepts in gratitude from God's hands what he once thought was his by right. Yes, he says, we *are* children of God, but only because God chooses us, adopts us and makes us his own. We do not have any automatic right to call God 'Father', but God the Holy Spirit, in his mercy, comes to us, and teaches us how to be children of God. By ourselves, we do not even know the words that describe the relationship. Only God knows what this profound thing, 'sonship', is and only he can teach us its words and its meaning. What Paul preaches to the Gentiles is what he has learned himself, the hard way: you *can* be a child of God, but only if you accept it in gratitude, from God's own hand. If you think you already are a child of God, or that you don't need any teaching about how to be a child of God, or that God is bound to choose you as his child and reject others, then you have not begun to understand what only the Holy Spirit can teach.

Paul saw, in humility and joy, the huge shift that happens when God sends his only Son. Paul saw that all other relationships based on 'rights' have to be reworked, in the light of this relationship that we are offered, to which we respond in gratitude and obedience, or not at all. Mary begins to see it too. Mary watches the strange men who arrive at her son's cradle and demand a part in his birth. She listens as they shout about the child, telling everyone how special he is, boasting about how God sent messengers to them, explaining it all.

'But I thought God's messenger and God's meaning was a gift to *me*,' Mary thought, 'and now I find he has been telling half the world.' Before Mary has even started to be able to cling, to possess, to believe herself the only 'favoured one', the only one capable of helping God and interpreting God, already God begins to loosen her gripping fingers, and teach her that she must share what she has, or lose it. Quietly, 'treasuring these words and pondering them in her heart', Mary names her son. No family names, no names that make him part of her history or Joseph's, but the name the angelic messenger gave her. God does not belong even to us, who love him, and yet he is a gift that we can share.

# The Second Sunday of Christmas

—— ∾ ——

*Jeremiah 31.7–14*
*Ephesians 1.3–14*
*John 1.1–18*

At the heart of the Christian proclamation of God is the belief that before time, before creation, before the existence of anything but God, God is already love. God's very nature is the love that flows out and returns, that gives and receives, that multiplies and unites. God is generosity and delight so overflowing that it wishes to share its perfect joy with others. The first stage of this sharing is the creation of the world. John's Gospel radically restates the original biblical creation story in the light of the experience of Christ. We now know, John says, that that outgoing, creating, generating force that unleashes the world in the first place is the Son, the Word of God. The Son channels God's generous, overflowing love outward into the world.

But that is just the first stage. It is not in God's nature to make the world just as a kind of plaything, to be observed with detached amusement. Within his own nature, God knows the pleasure of union, of being together, of complete sharing. And that is what God wills for what he has made. He creates in order to share himself with what he has created. So the next stage is for God to give himself to his creation. Just as it is the Son who gives expression to creation in the first place, so it is the Son who goes out to bring creation home again. The Son brings God into the world that God has made, so that we can look at him and begin to long to share what we see.

'Come,' the Son calls. 'Come and enjoy the love of God, as I do. Come and express the generosity of God, as I do, come and display the glory of God, as I do. Come and be children of God, at home in God, resembling him in every way.'

What an offer. In Jeremiah, the people summon up the last remnants of their strength, and come stumbling and weeping towards this hope. They come from their isolation, terror, poverty, sickness,

16

into God's family. 'I will be your father,' God says to them. 'From now on, I will protect you and provide for you. You are no longer alone.' With incredulous joy, the people turn to God. Some dance and shout and sing, and some sit down, with their arms around each other, and experience safety and love for the first time. They are God's children, sharing all that God has. This is what they were made for, this is reality. All that has gone before is just a bad fantasy.

'That's right,' agrees Ephesians. 'This is what everything is for. God doesn't suddenly have a bright idea and think, "Today I'll adopt a few of those strange humans I made ages ago."' He makes us in order to share himself with us. Subtly, almost teasingly, the image of the Son is the template. 'I wonder when they'll notice,' God laughs to himself. 'I wonder when they'll realize that they are designed to fit?' Carefully, painfully, God works away at the encrusted dirt, the broken and torn limbs, the smashed faces of the creation. Everything that disguises the likeness between us and the Son is washed away until we, even we, can see what we are. But we are very weak. Our eyesight is not good. We look from our renewed selves to the glorious Son and we keep thinking that we must be imagining it. So the Holy Spirit puts God's trademark on us. 'Don't doubt, don't panic, don't worry,' the Holy Spirit says. 'Keep looking at me, and you will see the Son in yourselves more and more. You are children of God, you really are. You were made to share all that the Son is and has.'

But if we take our eyes off the Spirit, everything begins to blur again. John speaks with bitter irony of a world made by God, in God's likeness, through God's love and providence, in which God himself can go unrecognized. Busily, desperately, like lost children, we go running around in panicky circles, hoping to catch a glimpse of that desired and beloved figure. Stand still, John suggests, and look at the Son. You will never find God if you look anywhere else. As you look, the images will gradually coalesce. Through the Son you will see the Father, through the Spirit you will see the Son, through the Father you will see what you are meant to be – made in the image of the Son, to share in God's love and delight. God has made it as clear as he can, coming to live with us, sharing our life, so that we can share the life of the Father's only Son.

# *Epiphany*

# The Baptism of Christ
## (The First Sunday of Epiphany)

—— ∾ ——

Genesis 1.1–5
Acts 19.1–7
Mark 1.4–11

What is nothingness? We have no concept of it. Our image of it consists of the absence of things that we can picture and describe, which is very different from the nothingness before creation. Genesis struggles for the words to describe non-existence – 'formless', 'void', 'dark'. Although no words can actually describe nothing, Genesis is trying to convey a powerful sense of absence. Without God, there is *nothing*. Into this nothingness, God comes, and then there is, at once, something describable. God comes as wind, or breath, or Spirit, depending how you translate it, and before he does anything else, he speaks. 'Let there be light,' he says. At once, God begins to make sense out of the world. He begins to make it intelligible, imaginable, by using language. God brings the world out of nothingness into the light, speaking to it and making it part of his own language, his own communication. God talks to the world, as a mother talks to the unborn or newborn child, long before it can possibly understand what is said, because the act of talking signs the new child as part of the human community. So God's act of speech to his newborn world brings it into community with him and marks it, from the start, as destined to be part of God's family.

Just as at creation, so at Jesus's baptism: the Spirit, breath, or wind of God comes down to signal the presence of God and the promise of community with him. Just as at creation, so at this baptism: God's presence begins to make things imaginable, to build sense, to create images. Those watching see an ordinary man go down into the water, to receive baptism, as many others have before. But as Jesus comes out of the darkness of the river, into the light, we see the one whom God loves, and through whom he shares

20

his love with us. God's creating word, spoken at the dawn of the world, is spoken again, to draw us into his community. God's first act, at creation, is to create light, that symbol of understanding and clarity, that makes the world immediately intelligible. The beginning of the new creation is a new kind of symbol. We who have forgotten why the world was made – for loving communion with its maker – are given a new sign. God looks on the new creation, emerging out of the waters into the light, just like the first creation, and says to it, 'I love you.'

At the first creation, the Spirit is the intelligent, image-forming love of God at work. In the new creation in Christ, the Spirit makes the image even clearer. 'Perhaps you have forgotten,' the Spirit says, 'perhaps those first words God whispered into the world have been overlaid with other sounds, and you no longer remember the language of your making. So now, hear it again. God is speaking his Word, loud and clear, in flesh, living with you. This is the community that you belong to, the language you were born to understand, the language of God's love for the world, now shown to you again in the Son.' 'You are mine, I love you, you give me pleasure,' God speaks into the world, making and remaking it.

We plod through our lives, trying to live them as though they are bearable without those words of God. But without the words that give birth to the world, there is no point in it at all. If God does not love us and delight in us, we are pointless. There is no sense at all, in Acts, that the people Paul meets in Ephesus are doing anything wrong. They are earnest, well-intentioned, eager to be baptized and repent. But they don't know what they exist for. They know that they have sinned and must seek forgiveness, and then wait. That is what John the Baptist said, and that is what they have been doing. Paul knows instantly that they are still waiting to hear the Word of God, the word that brings the new life to creation. Repentance is necessary, but it is not the end in itself. We are made to hear God's Word, spoken to us in creation and redemption, the word of love that draws us into the world God has made, the real world, of light and image. God's Word instantly gives us a language, a home, a community. We hear it for the first time at our baptism, and yet it is as familiar to us as the long-forgotten voice of our mother, speaking to us in the womb. This is reality, light and love. This is God, Father, Son and Holy Spirit.

# The Second Sunday of Epiphany

—— ～ ——

*1 Samuel 3.1–10*
*Revelation 5.1–10*
*John 1.43–51*

The beginning of chapter 3 of 1 Samuel says, in a very matter-of-fact way, 'the word of the Lord was rare in those days.' 1 Samuel has already begun to paint a picture – centred round Eli and the once-famous shrine at Shiloh – of a society that does not automatically expect the presence of God. For example, when in chapter 1 Eli first meets Hannah, he does not immediately recognize the intensity of her expression as prayer. The fact that Eli assumes that Hannah has come to the shrine to drink rather than pray suggests what Eli's general experience has been. On the whole, apparently, he has not been used to people coming in off the streets to fall on their knees before the Lord. He has come to expect that the shrine will be used as a shelter from the sun, a place to sleep off a good party, or a place from which his sons will run their rackets. Eli does not expect people to turn to the shrine to seek the word of the Lord.

Eli almost certainly inherited his priestly role, as his sons are doing. They treat the temple at Shiloh as the family business, rather than any kind of vocation. But Eli, at least, has some vestiges of his training that rise to the surface under pressure. As soon as he is forced to recognize Hannah's real need, he responds, perhaps a little blandly and impersonally, but with the correct kind of priestly things. Almost certainly, that is the last he expects to hear of the matter. But again, when Hannah returns a few years later and expects Eli to remember, he knows how to react. To Hannah, at least, Eli's words were the words of the Lord that began the great change in her life.

And now things begin to gather pace for Eli. Casually, without really thinking about it, he invoked the name and power of the Lord for Hannah, and now the word of the Lord is streaming through that tiny, dry channel. In chapter 2, another 'man of God' comes to Eli with a message, and then, in chapter 3, the message

22

is repeated, through Samuel. There must be some part of Eli that longs for the old days, when the Lord kept quiet, and he didn't have to face the reality of the degradation that he and his sons have brought upon their profession and their family shrine. Even when he begins to suspect that Samuel is hearing the voice of God, Eli does not choose to go and wait with Samuel, in the hope that he too might hear the God whom, in theory, he has served all his life. Instead, Eli sends Samuel back alone, while he pulls the blankets up over his head. But at least Eli does not for one moment disbelieve the message of God. He knows its justice, and acknowledges that the judgement of God is true. He may not have heard the word of the Lord himself, but he does recognize it.

So we get the impression of Eli as a man, not wholly bad, but forgetful of his duty to the Lord. Although he is sorrowful and realistic about his sons, he does not send them away, or stop them ministering at Shiloh and using it as the base for their criminal activities. He has no idea what his perfunctory words of blessing to Hannah will unleash. If occasionally in the past he sat around after dinner and murmured nostalgically about the good old days when the word of the Lord was regularly heard by his people, he will soon live to see that the word of the Lord is not a safe plaything, or a nice merit award, but the terrible, dangerous proclamation of the justice of God.

Nathanael, too, will learn that the hard way. When he first meets Jesus, he is looking for a thrill. He is very prepared to find Jesus exciting, and to see everything he does as rather magical. We are not told how he responds to Jesus's drily deflating words or if and when he ever comes to understand the reference to Jesus as the ladder of the angels. When Nathanael runs eagerly up to Jesus, he has no idea at all about how God will choose to bring heaven and earth back into unity through the Son of Man.

The author of Revelation knows, of course. He recognizes the figure of the slaughtered Lamb, despite the fact that it has seven horns and seven eyes. But if he knows the cost of God's justice, still he longs for the time when the Word of the Lord, in all its terror and majesty, will be heard throughout the world.

# The Third Sunday of Epiphany

——— ❧ ———

*Genesis 14.17–20*
*Revelation 19.6–10*
*John 2.1–11*

We are created to praise God. We cannot truly find our existence in any other way, and neither can the created world, which longs to re-echo to the sound of human voices raised in songs of praise to their creator. So what Revelation is describing is the culmination of all the thousands of words that have gone before it in the Bible. It is describing the world shouting out in love, joy and praise.

In verse 5, a great voice issues from the throne, commanding God's servants to praise him. This is a command that God's people throughout the ages have tried to respond to as faithfully as possible. As the voice from the throne rings out, what sound do we expect to hear? Perhaps the reedy, distant voices of the small congregation somewhere near the back of the church. Perhaps the louder, more confident sound of a big, full church that still cannot help hearing the unheeding roar of the traffic outside. The worship of the churches, faithful throughout the centuries, has yet been marked, perhaps, by a sense of hoping against hope, a knowledge that our own fervent praise is met by a deafening silence or, worse, by real obscenity, from so many of God's human creatures. And if we are truthful, even our own praise of our creator has been marred by uncertainty and division, by inertia and weariness.

But now at last, in Revelation, when the call goes out for the world to praise God, the response is overwhelming. The prophet hears the praising voices all around him, far and near, in such quantities and with such volume that he can only describe it in terms of the sound of a huge waterfall or a massive storm. He has no experience of a human sound to match it, so enormous is the noise. All through the centuries, against such apparent odds, God's servants have declared that he is King, but now at last the prophet sees that the whole world acknowledges it. The Church that John has been describing is not one that can see any visible signs in the world around it of God's Kingship, and yet it has remained certain, under persecution, boredom, weariness, that God is indeed to be praised. As John stands, buffeted by the sound of the world roaring in joy to the King, how he must have thought of the small, struggling churches that he cares for, teaches and prays for. Can these little groups of ordinary people really have something to contribute to this mighty, confident Hallelujah? John knows that they can and do. The voices of all God's faithful servants go to make up the glorious sound. Each individual, however apparently insignificant, adds his or her voice. And suddenly this is not just a huge, joyful chorus in which individuals scarcely matter, and in which the God whom they are praising is, although utterly wonderful, also utterly distant. Instead, the angel comes to John, asking him to deliver wedding invitations to all God's personal friends. 'Tell them all they are welcome,' he says. 'Tell them that they are friends of God, and they have earned their place at this celebration.' Now the song of praise is not just a duty, not just the inevitable tribute paid by a subject to the King, but a song of beloved friends and family at a party or a wedding. This is our song, the song of God's friends, our duty as well as our joy.

But if we can feel, just for a few moments, the surge of love and joy that John is describing, much more of the time we are like the puzzled guests at the wedding in Cana. We are more than happy to drink the excellent glass of wine that God, in his goodness, has provided for us, but we quickly forget it and often fail to make the connection between this present gift and the duty of gratitude and praise that we owe to God for so much more than just this one moment of joy.

At this wedding, Jesus is the guest, and he adds a dimension of happiness that would otherwise be lacking. So when we are the guests at his wedding feast, what rejoicing we can expect.

Why does John say that this strange and irrelevant miracle 'revealed his glory'? Only Mary and the disciples know what has happened. Does it give them some insight into the kind of God they are serving? All of them will experience suffering, grief and loss as a result of their love of Jesus, but that is not what they were created for. They were created to share in the scene of wild rejoicing that Revelation describes. Drink this wine in remembrance.

# The Fourth Sunday of Epiphany

—— ≈ ——

*Deuteronomy 18.15–20*
*Revelation 12.1–5a*
*Mark 1.21–28*

'If I hear the voice of the Lord my God any more, or ever again see this great fire, I will die' (Deuteronomy 18.16). This, according to Deuteronomy, is the source of prophecy. The people of God have experienced the unmediated presence of God at Horeb, and they know that they cannot bear it again. Although in the garden of Eden Adam and Eve could walk side by side with God and talk to him in the cool of the evening, one of the results of the Fall is the loss of this intimacy. The people are no longer capable of being in the unveiled presence of God. From now on, they need to hear God's Word mediated through other human agencies, rather than direct from the mouth of God.

God shows no disappointment at this request on the part of his people. On the contrary, he acknowledges its justice. They are quite right to think that the presence of God could be fatal to our faulty senses, like a powerful electric current passing through a wrongly wired plug. So God makes alternative provision for his people, since it would be equally fatal for them to attempt to live their lives without hearing God's Word at all. God promises to raise up prophets for them, people who will be capable of receiving God's words and transmitting them faithfully.

But the people have to understand clearly that this is no soft option. They cannot use this as an excuse not to listen to God. They cannot say, 'We are not capable of being in God's presence and hearing his words, so we'll just have to get on with our lives as if he didn't exist.' On the contrary – they have asked for prophets, and they must take their prophets with the utmost seriousness. The whole people must take seriously their responsibility to weigh the words of prophecy and discern where God is genuinely speaking and where he is not. The failure to listen on the part of the people, or the misuse of the Word of God on the part of the prophet, will have equally serious consequences.

But of course the history of God's people, from that day to this, is full of instances of failures to listen and abuses of God's authority. The art of discerning whether or not the word is from God is one that has to be practised with great patience, and we are not a patient people. So by the time the Word of God comes in person, there is almost no tradition by which to measure him or listen to him. John's Gospel spells that out for us in its first chapter. 'He came to what was his own, and his own people did not accept him,' John tells us in 1.11. Mark makes the same point with understated irony. Here in chapter 1 it is only the mad man who recognizes Jesus. It is as though his illness has actually scraped away layers of blindness and insensitivity so that he is aware, as no one else is, of God's presence. Like the Israelites on Horeb, he is terrified by it. When Jesus heals him, there is a bitter irony in realizing that the man is being restored to the normality of the human community around him and, at the same time, losing his ability to discern the fearful presence of God. That is what is 'natural' to us now, not to be able to see God.

The lectionary-makers could have given us a reassuring third reading, reminding us that although we have unfitted ourselves for the presence of God, through our choices and the whole way in which we live our lives, as individuals and as communities, God himself has given us back the gift of discernment, the Holy Spirit. But instead they have given us the strange and frightening reading from Revelation. Perhaps they are right. Perhaps we pass over, too superficially, the terrible cost of our distance from God. Perhaps, too, we are too prone to accept God's self-gift and domesticate it, allowing ourselves to become cosy with God. But the Israelites knew themselves and their God well when they remembered how terrifying they had found it to meet him. Just because God has acted with graciousness and love to come to us and live with us, that does not mean that we should forget who and what he is. Revelation describes the cosmic consequences that follow from our sin and, although it reiterates, again and again, the triumph of God, perhaps it is right that we should remember what kind of a God it is who wins this victory for us.

*Ordinary Time*

# *Proper 1*

———— ❧ ————

*Isaiah 40.21–31*
*1 Corinthians 9.16–23*
*Mark 1.29–39*

There are two complicated, separate yet related themes running
through today's readings. The first is to do with proclamation – all
three passages talk about the ways in which God makes himself
known to us. The second is to do with the demands of that proclamation. To know God is to relinquish other 'rights' that might
conflict with what a relationship with God requires.

Isaiah's understanding of how God is proclaimed is fierce and
uncompromising. The whole world – its very existence – shouts out
the presence of God. The puny people who run around on the
surface of the earth, thinking themselves important, have only to
look up at the vastness of all there is and realize their mistake. Even
princes and rulers have no more claim to power over God's earth
than the grass that grows under their feet. All authority and power
belong to God alone. So when God's people start to grumble that
God doesn't seem to be paying enough attention to them, they need
to remember just who they are and, more importantly, who they
are not. God is not at their beck and call, and they cannot demand
that he explain himself to them.

The sheer, overwhelming force of the creation's witness to God
should remind his people that they do not have any 'rights' in relation to God. If, in his grace and mercy, he chooses to give them
gifts, they can never assume that they have deserved these things, or
earned them in any way. They cannot insist on having them, like
the payment of wages.

Paul agrees with that. It's one thing that does come clearly out
of this very complex and opaque passage of 1 Corinthians. Paul is
absolutely certain that being a minister of the gospel is not a 'job'
for which wages are due. Proclaiming the gospel is simply what he
has to do, like breathing. That is not to say that it goes unrewarded,
but the reward is the preaching itself – to share with others freely

30

the free gift that he has been given, through the gospel. Paul is no more to be commended for doing this than the creation is. Isaiah does not congratulate the created world on bearing witness to its creator – of course it must.

And just like the creation, Paul is not free to dictate the terms under which he proclaims God's message. He cannot insist that people accept it only in one particular kind of package. It almost sounds as though Paul is saying that he will sink to any kind of subterfuge to make himself acceptable to people, but that is to miss the sense of compulsion in Paul's description of his relationship to his calling. He is there to be used by others. Just as the creation has no other purpose than to bear witness to its creator, so Paul has no other purpose than to preach the gospel. He is as freely available to all as the witness of creation is. The Corinthians seem to think that being an Apostle might be a bit of a power trip, or at the very least an easy way to get other people to feed you and pay you, but Paul is trying to explain that to be a minister of the gospel is to be at God's disposal and the disposal of others, and to abandon yourself to the purposes of God.

That sense of the compulsion to preach the gospel is also there in Jesus's ministry. Others would obviously have liked to interpret his calling differently. He could have stayed at Simon Peter's house indefinitely, and all the sick for miles around would have come to him for healing. And surely that would have been a good thing, a ministry worth having? Simon clearly thought so. He was probably rather enjoying the glory of having the healer staying with him. Perhaps the crowd gathered outside his house are asking him to intercede on their behalf, to make sure that Jesus sees them. So when Simon goes looking for Jesus in the early morning, there is a slight sense of impatience in his voice. 'Why are you wasting your time out here in the desert, when there are people who need you?' Simon seems to say.

For answer, Simon gets swept up into the whirlwind of Jesus's real ministry, which is to travel round and talk about God, to anyone and everyone who will listen. That is what he is there for and, very soon, it is what Simon is there for too, as are we. We are bound to proclaim our God, just as the world he made is. We have no other purpose.

# Proper 2

—— ∼ ——

*2 Kings 5.1–14*
*1 Corinthians 9.24–27*
*Mark 1.40–45*

Mark's Gospel is almost certainly the oldest of the four Gospels. Matthew and Luke seem to know it and depend upon it for some of their information, though they do also have independent sources of their own. It is possible that, rather than Matthew and Luke having read Mark, all three of these Gospels have an earlier, perhaps unwritten, source in common. Scholars usually call this hypothetical Gospel 'Q'. The connections between the first three Gospels are fascinating, and it is always intriguing to read, for example, one of Jesus's parables as relayed in three slightly different forms. Oceans of ink have been expended by New Testament experts on arguing about why Matthew puts a parable in a different context from Luke, or why Luke changes the audience from Mark's version. This is what is called 'the Synoptic Problem', and any good commentary will give you some introduction to the main discussion. (John's tradition, by the way, is strikingly different in a number of ways from the first three Gospels.)

Mark's is the shortest of the Gospels, and its narrative is urgent, spare and driven. Nearly half the Gospel is directly concerned with the events leading up to Jesus's crucifixion. From Mark 8.27, where Peter declares Jesus to be the Messiah, the emphasis is on the preparation for death. But held in tension with this concentration on Jesus's fate is Mark's description of Jesus's power. Whether teaching, healing or simply moving around among the people, everyone reacts to Jesus. We have already seen how the fishermen give up their livelihood to follow him, how the unclean spirits fear him, how the sick and the desperate mob him wherever he goes. Mark is by no means portraying Jesus as a victim. On the contrary, the way in which he prepares for his death is part of his 'authority' – a word that Mark puts into the mouths of those who meet Jesus, for example in 1.27. Everything Jesus does, from beginning to end, is proclaiming the Kingdom of God, and Mark makes it clear that the way people react to Jesus is the way they react to God's reign. Jesus comes out of the wilderness proclaiming the Kingdom, and at his death the veil of the Temple is torn down, so that nothing protects the people from the direct presence of God again.

But while Mark constantly highlights Jesus's power, he does this by throwing the light on the stunned or angered faces of the audience, so that we cannot miss the effect Jesus is having. But at the same time he puts into Jesus's own mouth words of disclaimer. He wants you to see what Jesus has done, but every time you go to foreclose the discussion about who Jesus is, Mark says, 'Wait, think, there is more.' This is what is usually called the 'messianic secret' in Mark. Jesus seems to turn aside all attempts to identify him with the coming Messiah. But Mark certainly does not allow us to think that that is because Jesus was something less. On the contrary, the whole narrative demands that you ask more and more about Jesus.

But the leper in today's reading is asking no more questions – for the moment. He has the answer he needs, and is sharing it with everyone. He asked the one question he really wanted to ask, 'Can you be bothered with me?' It is not the standard request for help, but a genuine uncertainty about whether anyone could believe he deserved it, and we are told that his words moved Jesus. The other healings we have seen in this chapter do not mention Jesus's emotions, but something about this man's mixture of boldness and uncertainty touches Jesus. The man knows that Jesus is in control of his healing power, and can choose whether to heal or not.

When the healing is complete, Jesus sends the man straight off to register himself with the priest, so that he can be included again among his people. We are told that Jesus is 'stern' in his command that the man say nothing about the source of his healing. But the man cannot obey that command. It is simply beyond him. He is elated and uncontainable in his joy. We do not know quite what he told people, but whatever it was it results in such fame for Jesus that he cannot go into the town any more. Healing brings the leper back into his proper human community, but his witness to Jesus has the opposite effect. Jesus's power is already beginning to be costly, and to set him outside the community to whom he has come to proclaim the Kingdom of God.

# Proper 3

—— ∼ ——

*Isaiah 43.18–25*
*2 Corinthians 1.18–22*
*Mark 2.1–12*

Our capacity to respond wrongly to God is endless. All three of today's readings focus primarily on the generosity of God, but they also all have as a backdrop the stubborn stupidity of our response.

The miracle that Jesus performs in the reading from Mark's Gospel is a much loved story. What Sunday-school child hasn't drawn diagrams of the flat-roofed homes of Jesus's day, to illustrate how the friends of the paralysed man would have been able to lower him down in front of Jesus? And they had to resort to such methods because so many people had come to see and hear Jesus that they couldn't get through any other way. That already starts to make us wonder about the crowd. Jesus already, at this early stage of his ministry, has a reputation as a miracle worker. You might have expected the crowd to make room for the stretcher-bearers to get through, even if only in the hopes of seeing something magical. But no, the crowd are selfishly oblivious to the paralysed man and his need. They have come to see a spectacle, but at heart unconvinced, they are certainly not going to do anything to help Jesus prove himself.

So they are all ready to start arguing, as soon as Jesus begins to talk to the paralysed man, and although they seem temporarily convinced when the man gets up and walks away, we know that this is just the beginning. This group of people, who wouldn't let the man through to Jesus, who disputed Jesus's right to forgive sins, who are appeased for a few moments by something exciting – this group are the ones who will follow Jesus all through the gospel story, vacillating about their reaction to him. And in that respect, they are just like us. Jesus offers forgiveness and healing, and sometimes we think that's wonderful and sometimes we just can't be bothered.

Isaiah, too, has a mixed message for God's people. What God promises is a new start, where all the old bitter history of betrayal and sin is wiped away. The wilderness that the people have made of the promised land will suddenly be fertile and full of the sound of running water. From the dry throats, which had breath only to grumble and curse, will come again the praise for which they were designed. People will drink God's life-giving water and sing out their thanks.

But actually, of course, they don't. They drink the water all right, but the thanks? Instead of praise and gratitude, the people carry on as though this great new thing that God is doing simply hasn't happened at all. They take what they can and forget who has provided it.

The words that Isaiah puts into God's mouth are full of weariness and disappointment. They are the words that we would say if we were God, and they are the words that we should expect, because we have deserved them. But they are not God's own words, according to Paul. God's words to us are never just what we deserve; they are never what we, in our self-righteousness and anger, would say to each other. Instead, what God says to us is 'Yes'. Steadily and faithfully, God says 'Yes' to us, over and over again. Human nature might be changeable, and human plans might mean that a 'Yes' sometimes has to become a 'No', but God is not like that.

Jesus is God's great 'Yes' to us, Paul says. However often we say 'No, we are not God's creatures; No, we do not belong together; No, we don't even believe in God', Jesus simply says 'Yes'. 'Yes, God made you and loves you and shares his life with you and believes in you. Yes.' Jesus's 'Yes' is patient and inexorable. It does not shout down or drown out our 'No', it simply outlasts our feeble voices, so that all that remains is his 'Yes'.

So we need to recognize the fretful and changeable crowds who followed Jesus as ourselves. And we need to look back over the human centuries of avoiding God and his call and feel the weariness of the world at our stupidity. But we must never come to believe that our negative can be stronger than God's 'Yes'. There is a kind of fierce, baffled, shameful pride in thinking of our sins as so great that they can distort the purposes of God. It may take a great deal of humility to understand that even our most resounding 'No' is still only really like a child having a tantrum. God is not the kind of father who gives in to tantrums, because he knows we do not really know what we need. Jesus is what we need, God's great 'Yes'.

# The Second Sunday Before Lent

———— ⬦ ————

*Proverbs 8.1, 22–31*
*Colossians 1.15–20*
*John 1.1–14*

Recently, a lot of my letters and conversations have been with people who are really struggling to believe in the love of God in the face of personal and impersonal suffering. Some have come through an experience of watching someone die horribly, some have been overwhelmed by the weight of evidence of starvation and brutality from around the world. Some simply look at the world around them and see it primarily in terms of absence, rather than presence. They cannot see signs of an intelligent and loving purpose, rather a completely random and meaningless set of occurrences.

The Sunday lectionary readings do, on the whole, allow us to focus on the central Christian belief that God does all things out of love towards his creation. Even when the readings focus on the suffering of, for example, Paul or the Christian community, this pain is held securely in a circle of belief about its value and meaning. For those who are already so deeply committed to the purposes of God that they see everything, whether good or bad, as part of that, it is sometimes hard to hear the seriousness and indeed the religiousness of this question about God and suffering. Those who ask the question long with passion to see a world in which they could believe in the goodness of God, but they just can't.

Today's readings do affirm the goodness of creation and of its God, but they do so in a way that requires us to take seriously religious questioning. And that is because at the heart of what is being said today is the statement that God's creative intelligence has something about it that we should recognize. Proverbs calls it Wisdom, John calls it the Word, and John and Paul both call it Jesus. Jesus is the language in which the Creator speaks to us, a language which we at least partly know, and which we can learn if we try, with a lot of help.

Proverbs speaks of Wisdom as sharing in making creation habitable for people. As God measures things, as he makes the earth firm and confines the sea, as he creates water and fixes up the sky, there beside him is Wisdom, working with him. Together they plan all the delightful treats they have in store for their new creation. God looks at Wisdom and thinks, 'Soon there will be others to share in this, as Wisdom does.' Wisdom looks at God and thinks, 'Soon there will be others who will understand and love God's wonderful ideas, as I do.'

John, too, describes God's creative work as being shaped in a way that is, in principle, comprehensible to us. God speaks the Word, and the Word is, by definition, a means of communication. Indeed, it is one of the characteristics of human beings. For John, God's whole purpose, from beginning to end, is to communicate with us and allow us to begin to enter into that communication, begin to learn to speak God's Word. But John introduces a cautionary note, which is also bitterly ironic. God speaks to us in a language that we were designed to understand, and comes to us in a form that is utterly familiar to us, and yet some of us still manage not to recognize him. John can only see the stupidity and waste of those who cannot hear when God speaks to them in their own language.

Colossians, too, is aware that not everyone has seen what God is doing through Christ, in creation and redemption. But in today's passage, we have the stunning image of the ongoing synthesizing work of God. God reaches out to his estranged creation, to bring it back into communication with him, to re-establish the language that allows us to see the purposes of God.

So when we call out to God in anger at so much evil and suffering, we are demanding that God explain the world to us, as he himself seems to promise he will, by creation through 'Wisdom', 'the Word', 'the image of the invisible God'. We are demanding that God be God. God's answer is the Word, Jesus. It is, in one sense, no answer because it does not take away the suffering and injustice that we cannot bear to see in God's world. But Jesus suggests God's anger and love in the face of suffering. He also suggests a way of living that confronts injustice, that has compassion for suffering, that brings the vitality of God into everything. And he suggests a way of dying that might hold, contain and transform evil and suffering.

Is that enough? If not, honour God by demanding to see the 'image of the invisible God', through whom all things have been created and who makes God known to us.

# The Sunday Next Before Lent

———— ∼ ————

*2 Kings 2.1–12*
*2 Corinthians 4.3–6*
*Mark 9.2–9*

Elijah is taking part in his own funeral procession. Everywhere he goes, people come out to watch him, the coffin, go past. The people do not speak to him. It's almost as though they think that he has already lost the power of speech and hearing. They talk instead to Elisha, the next of kin, checking how he is feeling about his impending bereavement, but also, of course, pointing out their credentials as prophets. Prophets are supposed to know this kind of thing, and could certainly never hold their heads up again if they could not predict the death of Elijah, the Father of all the prophets. They slightly hope that they are telling that upstart, Elisha, something he didn't know. But no such luck. And he's quite rude to them, basically telling them to shut up when they try to talk to him.

What is Elisha feeling? The prophets are treating him like Elijah's servant. That's certainly what they call him, and they seem determined to demonstrate their own prophetic powers, as though to point out the fact that Elisha was just a ploughman before Elijah inexplicably called him into service (see 1 Kings 19.19f. for the story). They are adding to the great feeling of uncertainty that is filling Elisha as he doggedly follows his master. Elijah isn't really helping. He seems to be trying to get rid of Elisha, constantly suggesting that he might like to stay behind, first saying he's just going to Bethel, then to Jericho, then to the Jordan. If Elisha had waited in Gilgal, as Elijah originally suggested, he wouldn't even have known where his master was when the Lord took him. Elisha has given up his family and his livelihood to follow Elijah, and he has, at present, no idea of what will happen to him when Elijah is taken away.

But his faith is to be rewarded. At last he is alone with Elijah on the other side of the river, and at last Elijah turns to him. When Elijah asks what Elisha wants, the answer comes out so slickly that it's clear Elisha has been thinking it over for some time. He wants to be a prophet of the Lord and he wants to be not just as good, but better than his master.

The vision that he sees is one that reinforces his belief in the importance of the prophet. All the chariots and horsemen of Israel come to meet Elijah, and Elisha is overwhelmed. What's more, although he may not be able to take it in at the time, the vision is entirely for his benefit. No one else witnesses it. It is a gift for him, a confirmation of his calling. When Elisha returns to the other prophets, no one is in any doubt about the fact that he is Elijah's successor.

Is this the function served by the Transfiguration? Is it a confirmation for Peter, James and John of their calling? They are the only witnesses to the extraordinary sight of Moses and Elijah deferring to Jesus. They hear God's voice, telling them that Jesus speaks for him. What wonderful assurance for these men who have given up everything to follow Jesus.

Well, perhaps it would have been if Jesus himself didn't keep confusing the issue. Peter must be tempted to turn to Jesus and say, 'See, I told you you were the Messiah. Why won't you let us tell everyone else what we now know for sure?' But the problem is, that although God has now left them in no doubt about who Jesus is, he has also said that they are to listen to Jesus, and Jesus has just been explaining to them exactly how he sees his own calling. Both before and after the Transfiguration, Jesus talks about suffering and death. How are the disciples to put together what they have just seen and what Jesus is telling them? How are they to be faithful to the vision and the command of God, which seem to point in different directions? The vision tells them how important Jesus is, and the command tells them to listen to him while he stresses how he must suffer and die.

Poor disciples. How they must have envied Elisha, picking up his mantle of power in the certainty of his calling. All they can now be certain about is that they must follow Jesus and, somehow or other, try to hear his baffling words as the words of God. Paul would sympathize with them. He knows that Jesus's gospel is still 'baffling' to many, but nothing will prevent him from preaching it. He is going to proclaim Jesus and trust to God to do the rest.

*Lent*

# The First Sunday of Lent

—— ❧ ——

*Genesis 9.8–17*
*1 Peter 3.18–22*
*Mark 1.9–15*

When God makes his covenant with creation after the flood, it is a covenant not just with Noah and his family, or even with all future human beings, but with 'every living creature that is with you' (v. 10). What's more, God goes on to emphasize this, by detailing all the creatures who are to be involved in this new covenant. Every time the covenant is mentioned, the living creatures are deliberately included (see Genesis 9.12, 15, 16, 17). It is as though Noah's action then binds human and animal destiny together for ever.

But, of course, Genesis has already suggested, in its first creation story, that that was always God's intention. When God makes human beings in chapter 1, he does so expressly saying that human beings are to be responsible for 'every creeping thing that creeps upon the earth' (Genesis 1.26). According to Genesis, human beings have always been closely bound up with the rest of the created order, so when Noah takes animals into the ark to preserve them, he is exercising the proper stewardship for which people were created. It is his duty and his joy to care for what God has made. So when God tells Noah that the new covenant is to include the rest of creation too, God could not have paid him a higher compliment. 'Thank you, Noah,' he is saying, 'You are helping the world to be the way it should be.'

This intimate and necessary connection between the human creation and the rest of what God has made is part of what Lent is supposed to help us rediscover. So much of our human lives is constructed around the premise that we can isolate and protect ourselves from the forces that beset the rest of the world. We build houses to shield ourselves from the elements, we generate electricity to keep out the dark and make night and day bend to our will, we develop medicines to keep death at bay – the list is endless. And when the forces of nature break through and we have to submit to them, we are outraged.

Lent challenges us to remove some of our safety nets. Most of us do that in very small ways. We give up alcohol, or chocolate or (my own vice) coffee, and it is frightening how hard it is to manage without these inessential luxuries. Many human beings, of course, manage daily without such cushions. But Lent is not just an exercise in breast-beating and self-testing. Its basic questions are: 'What are you for?' 'What do you depend on?' 'Where do you get your self-definition?'

The story of Noah is perfectly clear about the proper answers to that. All life is utterly dependent upon God. If God did not choose to preserve it, it would not be. If you depart from that basic fact, then you have lost the possibility of finding out your purpose.

The first three Gospels all bear witness to a turning point in Jesus's ministry, where he had to go into the desert to find out what he was for. Matthew and Luke spell this out quite compellingly. (John, as so often, has a different pattern entirely, and does not mention the wilderness experience.) Mark is, as usual, brief to the point of curtness. But this Gospel does include a detail that the other two do not. Mark says that Jesus was 'with the wild beasts'. At his baptism, God speaks with a love that is to compel everything that follows in Jesus's ministry, and Jesus's response is to go into the desert, with the wild beasts. I do not wish to romanticize animals. It may be that Mark only wants us to see Jesus's vulnerability. But it is tempting to see more in this phrase. It is tempting to read it in the context of the stories of Creation and Flood, and to see Jesus accepting his destiny as the one who is to fulfil the Creator's intention. The wild beasts do not try to protect themselves from God, or from the effects of our Fall. They accept death and disease, and they do not fight against their mortality. It is as though they are one kind of paradigm of acceptance. They accept that they have no control over their fate.

But Jesus is another kind of paradigm. He too is about to accept his part, and to relinquish control, so as to acknowledge dependence upon God alone. But his is the acceptance that is to bring God and humanity together again, as at the beginning.

Our Lenten discipline cannot bring us back to Adam's state, or even Noah's, but it can help us to accept, with gratitude, our creation and re-creation in Christ.

# The Second Sunday of Lent

———— ≈ ————

*Genesis 17.1–7, 15, 16*
*Romans 4.13–25*
*Mark 8.31–38*

The Old Testament readings for Lent this year are encouraging us to think about covenants. Last week we had the covenant with Noah, this week we have Abraham, and next week – let me give you a sneak preview – we get the Ten Commandments. On a superficial reading, covenants are a good choice for Lent, because they remind us about obligations, about promises made between two parties, about duty. But actually, both the covenant with Noah and the one with Abraham seem to undermine that serious, disciplined note, because it is not until we come on to next week's reading that we start to hear about our side of the bargain – be sure not to miss next week's thrilling episode.

But as God speaks both to Noah and to Abraham, the duties are all on one side – God's. God promises huge things to both of them, and asks almost nothing in return. In verse 1 of today's reading from Genesis 17, Abraham is told to walk before God 'and be blameless', but there is no suggestion in the promise that follows that the covenant is dependent upon Abraham's behaviour. The command to 'walk blameless' is not attached to the promises but to God's statement about himself. 'I am God Almighty. Walk before me and be blameless.' Both Abraham's status and the fulfilment of the promises being made are wholly dependent upon the nature of God, not upon Abraham.

This is certainly the interpretation that Paul puts upon the matter. He is absolutely clear that Abraham does not receive from God because he has kept his side of the bargain and God must do the same. Abraham has not earned the fulfilment of God's promise, and it is not dependent upon him. The promise to Abraham is fulfilled because the one who makes the promise is God, 'who gives life to the dead and calls into existence the things that do not exist' (Romans 4.17). It is the nature of God the giver that guarantees the gift, not the nature or acts of Abraham, the receiver. The only thing Abraham does is to recognize what God is like and trust him to be able to fulfil the promises he makes.

God's covenant with Abraham comes as a series of steps, all of them leading Abraham into a deeper and deeper exploration of the trustworthiness of God. And, of course, he can only test God's trustworthiness by trusting. By the time we come to chapter 17, Abraham has already left his homeland and been through a great many vicissitudes, following God's command, and so far he has more reason to trust than to distrust. He is alive, well and prosperous. But the thing that set Abraham off on this great adventure was actually not a desire for God, or even wealth, but a longing for a son. And although God has been hinting at this all along (see 12.2, 13.16, 15.4), he has yet to deliver on this promise. In fact, by chapter 16 Abraham and Sarah have decided to take matters into their own hands, and bypass God.

This covenant in chapter 17 marks a new phase, which is symbolized by a change of name for both Abraham and Sarah (see 17.5, 15). The journey so far has led them a long way into trusting God, but now they are to see that God is to be trusted beyond their wildest dreams. And just as the covenant with Noah is both a fulfilment of what God promised Noah and a promise for the rest of the world, so is the covenant with Abraham. Abraham and Sarah are to have the child that they long for, but they are also to be 'ancestors of a multitude of nations' in a way that they could never have anticipated. Paul spells it out for us – God's promise to Abraham is a promise to us all.

Lent is a good time for taking small steps in trusting God, and these steps are not about making ourselves feel better and holier, but about allowing ourselves to explore the trustworthiness of God. But the reading from Mark does sound a necessary sombre note. You will only find God trustworthy if you want what God is offering. Abraham could trust because he wanted a son more than comfort or safety. Jesus's challenge to his disciples throughout the ages is the same. God's promise to the followers of Jesus is that they, like Abraham, will have the chance to be parents to millions, bringing them into the family and the life of God. If I am honest, that is not my deepest desire. Peter speaks for many of us when he rebukes Jesus's interpretation of God's promise. But he got another chance to learn to trust God for what he is actually promising.

# The Third Sunday of Lent

—— ❦ ——

*Exodus 20.1–17*
*1 Corinthians 1.18–25*
*John 2.13–22*

Are Exodus and 1 Corinthians in direct conflict with each other? Do they give wholly irreconcilable pictures of the nature of God and our response to it? The God of the Ten Commandments is, surely, a God who loves order and rules and rational systems. In order to please this God, we have just to follow his rules. The God of 1 Corinthians, on the other hand, is anarchic and incomprehensible, and the only way of pleasing him is to abandon your own rational concepts of hierarchy and order and preach 'Christ crucified' as the defining picture of God.

At this point in Lent, some of us would like to take the 1 Corinthians reading of the nature of God completely out of its context and allow ourselves to give up on rules and discipline. 'God's not like that,' we tell ourselves, comfortably, as we sip our first glass of wine for a couple of weeks, 'he's interested in grace, not law.' But I'm sorry to have to tell you that there is a strong strand of the Christian ascetical tradition that sees this kind of Lenten discipline as responding precisely to that anarchic and unpredictable streak in God. After all, unless you are really addicted to coffee or wine or chocolate biscuits, there is no particularly sensible reason for giving them up. Lent is simply a time for reminding ourselves that the world may not be quite what it seems. Lent nudges us into thinking about what we are here for, which is more than just living comfortable lives with as little unpleasantness as possible. The desert fathers and mothers of the early Christian centuries went out into the wilderness partly at least as a challenge to the increasing wealth and stability of the cities they left behind. 'Don't forget', their lives shouted, 'that God is unpredictable. We are being fed here in the desert with food far more fitted to our needs than all of the dishes that are spread on your groaning tables.' And if most of us are not called into the desert, all of us need to allow God to surprise us from time to time, by leaving our routines and our comforts behind, at least for a while.

But if you think the Ten Commandments are the other side of God, the safe side that you can get back to when you have dipped your toe adventurously into Lent, think again. The Ten Commandments aim to create a society that can recognize the strange, irrational work of God, and be ready to preach 'Christ crucified'. If we have made them into tame, safe rules it is only because we have a genius for dumbing God down, to the point where we can't hear him too clearly – after all, we manage to wear crucifixes as jewellery.

If you forget what you thought you knew about the Ten Commandments and read them again, it is clear that God is asking something extraordinary of his people. He is asking them to throw away all their other comforts and securities and rely on him alone. He is asking them to forget all the normal rules of power and dominance and build a society that will reflect God's own strange preference for the poor and the powerless. The Israelites are, rightly, terrified. From the top of a mountain wreathed in smoke and fire, too holy even for the priests to approach without the utmost caution, comes this picture of how the people of God should live. Above all, they are to believe that only this God is real and holy. No other back-ups are allowed. You can't believe in God and carry on propitiating other kinds of gods. As the hot ash fell on them, and the thunder deafened them, that may have been obvious to the Israelites, but people are good at forgetting. The rules that follow are equally hard and strange. Why waste one whole day resting? You can't even choose which day, and you can't make your slaves work on that day either, or even give them a different day off. One whole day when you have to remember that the world is not just there for your use. And as if that isn't weird enough, you then have a set of rules designed to prevent people from using their natural advantages to their own ends. The strong cannot take what they want, the clever cannot lie their way out of things, the sexy cannot go off with whoever they fancy.

These commandments are not the rational system anyone would come up with. They are the 'foolishness' of the same God who demonstrates his holy might on the cross. If we have forgotten it, like the moneychangers in the Temple, be reminded by Jesus's reaction.

# The Fourth Sunday of Lent

—— ∽ ——

*Numbers 21.4–9*
*Ephesians 2.1–10*
*John 3.14–21*

The imagination nourished by the Bible immediately springs into action at the mention of snakes.

In Numbers, they may be real rather than metaphorical, but that does not prevent them from carrying heavy symbolic baggage. The Israelites have been wandering around in the desert for quite a while. All kinds of exciting and terrifying things have happened to them, and given them proof, over and over again, that God goes with them to save them – in the first three verses of chapter 4 he has just helped them to victory over a formidable foe. But now the wanderers have hit a stagnant phase, where they just have to trudge along through the inhospitable terrain and they are, frankly, bored. They sound like spoiled children, cross and illogical: 'We're starving. There's no food, except the food we hate.'

At this point, we are told, God sends poisonous snakes to bite them – something with which many parents of spoiled toddlers at teatime may feel a sneaking sympathy. But the people have not wasted their years in captivity and their dark evenings round the camp fire in the wilderness. They know the creation stories, and they instantly recognize these snakes. The people recognize that they have given in to temptation, just as Adam and Eve did, and they quickly run to Moses to confess. And God gives Moses the strange remedy of a bronze snake to cure the fatal bite of the tempter.

How intriguing, then, Jesus's use of this bronze serpent is. John puts it in Jesus's conversation with Nicodemus, who is 'a teacher of Israel' yet does 'not understand these things'. Nicodemus should surely recognize Jesus as God's cure for the venom of the devil, but apparently he doesn't. Even the childish and grumbly children of Israel instantly spotted what God was up to, but not Nicodemus.

This whole conversation is about new life, being born again. The old life is the one that comes about through human sinfulness, and it leads inevitably to death. But the new life of the Spirit in Christ is the cure for everything associated with that ancient serpent in the garden, and it leads to life eternal. Jesus's death will be the cure for death, just as Moses's serpent was the cure for snake bites. Were there people in the company of the Israelites who were too stupid to run to the bronze serpent when they were bitten by a snake? Surely not. But there are those too blind to notice the healing sign lifted up in the cross.

Ephesians does not mention snakes, but it does further elucidate old lives and new. The old life led so inexorably to death that Ephesians just cuts out the middle bit, where you might temporarily believe yourself to be 'alive', and calls the whole thing 'death'. In that non-life it is as though we are all born with the fatal snake bite, and that's all there is to it. But God again provides the remedy, which is to cling to the cross of Christ and so to be raised from our death by Christ's death and resurrection. There is no medicine that we can manufacture to cure the old life. This passage is utterly emphatic about that. It cannot say often enough that this is entirely the work of God, his gift to us. And what he does is to give us a new life instead of the old one. We are created again, in Christ, and this time we will be able to do 'good works' (Ephesians 2.10), with no serpent to tempt us otherwise and fill us full of venom and death again.

But the problem with all of this talk of 'new life', wonderful though it is, is to find out what it means day to day. At the moment of conversion, and at moments of crisis or special meeting with God, you can feel an absolute clarity and certainty that this is, indeed, a new life, and that the old life has lost its hold upon you for ever, through the work of Christ. But in ordinary life, the old habits and failures and doubts reassert themselves time and time again, as if mocking any hope of real renewal. What Ephesians seems to be saying is that your situation is, as a matter of fact, now completely different, thanks to God, whether you always feel it or not. Wandering in the wilderness, the Israelites are no longer slaves, but they still grumble. Their status has changed, but their nature has to learn to respond. So with us. God has brought us into freedom and life – that is simply the case. The rest of our lives are about learning to live in our lively freedom.

# The Fifth Sunday of Lent

——— ❧ ———

*Jeremiah 31.31–34*
*Hebrews 5.5–10*
*John 12.20–33*

At last a nice easy covenant. At last, Jeremiah seems to be suggesting, God will give up trying to teach us things and just zap us, changing us so that it becomes natural to us to know God. We won't need to be taught, we won't need to ask others, or experiment or learn about God through rehearsing past history. God will be part of us, written on our hearts. But I'm sorry to have to tell you that it isn't that simple. Although the emotion that is uppermost in this passage is longing – for the time when God and his people will be united – there is also anger and despair. The words that Jeremiah is speaking to his people on behalf of God are very hard to hear. For one thing, he is saying that the covenant that constituted them as God's people in the first place has been broken. The story of the Exodus is a foundational story for the people, and they base all their identity and their claims on God on that covenant. But Jeremiah says, very baldly, 'You broke that covenant. It's dead and gone.' He is also implying that the people are actually incapable of faithfulness and love of God. This new covenant, written on their hearts, may sound wonderful but it is actually a last resort. God has to do it this way because his people are incapable of keeping any other kind of covenant. Only by wiping the slate clean and starting again can God achieve what he set out to do when first he created people.

But if Jeremiah correctly describes failure and longing and hope, he does not yet know how God will fulfil this promise of a new covenant. Hebrews and John tell us the answer. The new covenant, carved on the human heart, is the promise God makes to us in Jesus. And suddenly the words 'written on the human heart' become not a comforting and painless metaphor but a terrible and searing reality. The cost of God keeping his promise to us, despite our inability to keep our side of it, is written on the human heart,

50

the human life and death of Jesus. The way God does what we cannot and will not do is to come himself as one of us, and keep both sides of the promise himself.

Hebrews and John both make clear that the undertone of anger and pain in Jeremiah's words of comfort is a proper echo. Hebrews's picture of Jesus crying and begging is hard for us to face, but it is the inevitable cost of the failure that Jeremiah highlights. Today's passage from John follows directly on from the triumphant entry into Jerusalem. Jesus's opponents are furious, and expect him to be more idolized and sought after than ever – and how right they are. The minute they've said it, in John 12.19, we're told in verse 20 that some Greeks come in search of Jesus. But at this moment, at the height of his fame and 'glory', Jesus starts to talk again about a different kind of glory altogether. The Greeks want to see Jesus, do they? Well, they and all the world will see him, lifted up in glory, all eyes upon him as he forces other rulers into submission. But the place of this triumph is the cross.

So when, in Jeremiah, God promises his people that they shall know him intimately, this is what he means. He is not talking about taking away our human nature and replacing it with something that will respond automatically to him, something that will recognize him not with love and fear and gratitude but as a computer recognizes a password. No, we will recognize him because he is one of us. We will see his struggle and his pain and his costly obedience and recognize it as the truth about our own humanity. Just as God promises in Jeremiah, Jesus is not our example – we are no more capable of copying him than Jeremiah's people were of keeping the covenant. In Jesus, God does both sides of the covenant – he makes the promise and faithfully keeps it on our behalf.

But if we begin to respond in awe to this new freedom, what might our response look like? Might it perhaps look a little like God's own response to our need? Sister Frances Dominica writes, 'If we really pray we take a big risk because by doing so we are saying, "Here I am, send me". God may take us at our word.'[1] If God's own way is one of costly involvement, perhaps we might need to risk that ourselves.

---

[1] Sister Frances Dominica in *Tradition and Unity*, ed. Dan Cohn-Sherbok, Bellew, 1991.

# Palm Sunday

———— ～ ————

*Isaiah 50.4–9a*
*Philippians 2.5–11*
*Mark 14.1—15.47*

It is as though there are any number of parallel stories in Mark's account of the trial and death of Jesus. The characters in each story are largely unaware of the others, though they may interact with each other to some extent. But each story believes it is the main story, carrying the meaning and purpose of the whole thing. The characters in each story seem to live in parallel time zones in which their decisions and actions make and remake history. They are the ones whose heroic lives and selfless decisions will be taught to generations of people to come as *the* history of the period, the only possible narrative. But the impact of Jesus's death is about to fuse all of these characters and these stories into something much bigger.

The first set of characters who believe themselves to be central are the people who oppose Jesus. The story they tell themselves is one in which they stand up for God against imposters and false prophets. Other people may be deceived by Jesus, but they are not. By their steadfastness and their willingness to take tough decisions they stand up for the purity of their religion and bring the people back to God. They know that their story is coming to a successful climax when the people they have been trying to lead towards God finally turn against Jesus and shout for his death. 'This is our story,' they say, 'the story of people who remained faithful to God.' But when their story merges into Jesus's, the faithfulness that they had so prided themselves on is judged to be utterly misguided.

Then there are the Roman authorities, represented by Pilate. The story Pilate tells himself is the one where he, a powerful and resourceful Roman governor, helps to uphold the Empire in this remote and troublesome spot. Pilate thinks this is the story of the Roman Empire, the most successful and civilized force ever. He knows that this incident in Palestine is a minor matter that will hardly be remembered in the history books at all, except as an

52

example of his own strength and loyalty to the main story of the world. But when his narrative takes its place in Jesus's story, it turns out that he will chiefly be remembered as the man who put the hero to death.

What story does Judas tell himself, to justify his action and make himself believe that he is the one who truly knows where the plot is going? Is it a story in which he holds Jesus's fate and the fate of the other disciples in his hand? Is he convincing himself that he, Judas, is the one around whom all of this really revolves? The authorities need me, he tells himself. But he will not let himself see that they don't need him at all. They just want him to take the blame from them. They know perfectly well who Jesus is; they don't need Judas to show them. But they want to be able to say that Jesus was handed over to them, betrayed by his own followers. All through the last supper, Judas lives out his fantasy of himself in the centre, playing a clever double game as a secret agent. But in the end Judas sees where the real story was going, and sees his own shameful part in it.

Peter, too, gets a chance to see the real story and to put his own fantasy into its proper perspective. In his own story, Peter is Jesus's best friend, the one who has been with him at all the most exciting points of the ministry. He is the one who will finally persuade Jesus that his mission is really to throw out the Romans and proclaim the Kingdom of God. Jesus has some strange ideas at present about needing to die, but Peter is confident that he can talk him out of it. Talking has always been his strong point. But when he has talked himself into desertion and betrayal, that's when he gets a chance to be part of the main story, and even to take the plot on himself, after the resurrection, once he knows what the story is really about.

All of these stories suddenly coalesce and collide with reality around the cross of Christ. Suddenly it is clear that these are not short stories, with different possible endings, but one huge story, which is the story begun at the creation and not finished until Jesus returns to judge all the other stories about the world. This is the true story – the only true story – of God's faithful love for what he has made. All our stories are about how we journey into that one great story of creation and redemption.

*Easter*

# Easter Day

— ∽ —

*Isaiah 25.6–9*
*1 Corinthians 15.1–11*
*Mark 16.1–8*

After all the horror, and the crowds and the noise of the day of Jesus's crucifixion, this chapter of Mark's Gospel starts quietly. We have already seen these women at the crucifixion scene, but we hardly noticed them there. Some of them were standing at 'a distance' (Mark 15.40–41), watching the terrible death of the man they had followed and supported. They made it their business to keep an eye on the body of Jesus, as it was taken down from the cross and laid – with kindness and courtesy, but without the reverence they knew it deserved – in the tomb. But although we are told their names, it is not until this final chapter that the women spring sharply into focus. Clearly, they had a strategy, unlike the male disciples. The disciples whose names we have heard all through the Gospel accounts of Jesus's ministry had a plan that led only to victory. The terrible end of all their hopes leaves them in disarray. They are notable by their absence in the whole of chapter 15 of Mark's account.

But the women have obviously got together and decided that, whatever happens, they will not lose sight of Jesus, and they will make it their business to treat him as their King, right up to the end. Perhaps things are easier for them because they are women. Perhaps their gender acts as a kind of cloak of anonymity to protect them from the kind of attack that Peter and the other disciples fear. Perhaps the very fact that they have decided what to do is giving them a kind of strength and fearlessness.

Their plan does have holes in it. They have bought all the spices they need to give the precious body its royal anointing. They could not have bought them on the Sabbath, surely? Does that mean that they, unlike the other disciples, had listened to Jesus and were actually expecting his death? Anyway, that part of the plan is in hand, and they know where they are going. But there is one big problem that they must have anticipated, which is the stone over the entrance to the tomb. In the original plan, had they expected at least one or two of the male disciples to be around to help? If so, it is now obvious either that the women have no idea where the men have run to, or that the men won't help. But the women are not going to let that stop them, although their whole plan stands or falls on being able to get to the body of Jesus. A kind of reckless determination has set in, and they will not acknowledge the possibility of failure. 'Someone will help us,' they tell each other. And if they think, 'But who will be around at this time in the morning, and who would be willing to help us anoint the body of a condemned criminal?' they don't say it out loud.

But then, as it happens, their plan, forged in fierce love, bravery and despair, hits a rather bigger plan. If the other disciples are thrown into terror and confusion by Jesus's death, these women are utterly confounded by his resurrection. The young man in white, who has so helpfully rolled the stone away, is saying things to them that they just cannot take in. They were not afraid of death, or of handling the dead body of the beloved master, but they are afraid of the empty tomb and the words of astonishing hope that are spoken to them. They had heard and understood Jesus talking about his own death, but apparently they had blocked out what he told them about the resurrection.

Why should hope and promise be harder to bear than death and despair? Why is it so hard to believe, now as then, that life and transformation and joy are as much part of the world and its maker as death and disintegration? The Christian hope of new life is not based on a kind of blind and meaningless optimism. On the contrary, all our hope is scarred with the wounds of the cross, and it is only hope because of that. It is the hope that God is indeed God. God is the creator, the source of all life, and nothing can make him not God. Our active, malignant sin that desires and makes death and destruction cannot force God into nothingness, and neither can our passive, despairing sin, that colludes with death and destruction because it can see no alternative.

So when the angel speaks the words of life and joy to us, let us believe them, and go and tell them, make them real and credible to others, show them the scars that are the source of life, not its end.

# The Second Sunday of Easter

———— ∾ ————

*Acts 4.32–35*
*1 John 1.1—2.2*
*John 20.19–31*

The recent popularity of *The Lord of the Rings* has helpfully given new vitality to the word 'fellowship'. The people who make up the 'fellowship of the ring' are not natural allies. They have little in common, and they join the fellowship with different personal priorities. But they are held together by the overriding need to save their countries from the menace of evil. They have to learn to trust one another, to rely on one another's skills and judgement, and allow for one another's particular weaknesses. This sense of struggle and adventure is a useful import into the rather debased Christian usage of 'fellowship', which is often used to mean little more than being temporarily nice to each other. We need to remember the sense of a continuing commitment and interdependence, and the reason why this fellowship is so vital. The world urgently needs it from us.

In the writings that we have under the name of 'John', 'fellowship' is rather more than an expedient device in the face of a particular threat. Entering into fellowship with each other is entering into the nature of God, and our failures in fellowship will obscure our witness to God. This is particularly striking in the talks that Jesus gives to his disciples at the Last Supper in John's Gospel (see, for example, John 17), but is very evident in the epistles of John too.

This opening section of 1 John echoes the beginning of the Gospel in its insistence that the witness to the particular life, death and resurrection of Jesus is a witness to the way the world is in its entirety. The life that pours out to those in fellowship with Jesus is the same vital source that gives life and breath and being to all that is. The world starts with the fellowship of God, Father, Son and Holy Spirit. Creation exists because God chose to share that fellowship.

58

This fellowship of ours, through which the world will begin to glimpse what God is like, can tolerate weakness and failure. The epistle is liberatingly clear that sin does not cease just because we have joined the fellowship of Jesus. What it cannot tolerate is lies. In the struggle to which we now commit ourselves, we have really to know our own and each other's strengths and weaknesses, and so the cause will be harmed if we are not truthful or if we lead ourselves or others to rely on us in areas where we cannot be reliable. It is, in any case, simply stupid to try to hide things from God, who is searing light, penetrating all darkness and deceit.

But both the Gospel and the epistle for today show God's enormous gentleness with us. God is not interested in guilt, but in a truthfulness that will build this vital fellowship. Isn't it moving that when Jesus comes to his frightened disciples, locked away in what they hope will be a safe house, he says not one word of condemnation to them? To these, his closest friends, who have betrayed and abandoned him to his horrible death, his first words are 'Peace be with you'. He must have said it with enormous conviction, because not one of the disciples tries to apologize or justify himself. They are all filled instantly with joy. That, they realize, is the only necessary response to the risen Christ. Even Thomas, the doubter who speaks for so many of us, is not greeted with any kind of impatience. Although there is certainly a teasing note in Jesus's voice as he speaks to Thomas, he knows what is needed to convince him, and he is happy to provide it.

The task that Jesus gives his disciples is an awesome one. He sends them out to build a fellowship that is strong through its truthfulness. They know that they lied about their own capabilities. They said they would never abandon Jesus, that they would follow him and stick with him through anything, and they know that their lies led to the disintegration of the fellowship at the cross of Christ. Now the new fellowship must be different. It must be based not on any foolish and unrealistic estimates of their own strength but on the vision of the searching and gentle God who has called them. It must give people a chance to glimpse what genuine fellowship, the life of Father, Son and Holy Spirit, might be like.

Very occasionally the Christian community can mirror that life, as in Acts 4, but more often it can only bear witness to the fact that the fellowship is made up of people who know their own weaknesses, and have needed and continue to need the forgiveness of God in Christ.

# The Third Sunday of Easter

—— ❧ ——

*Acts 3.12–19*
*1 John 3.1–7*
*Luke 24.36b–48*

A puzzled seeker writes:

I've been interested in this Jesus movement for years, but I'm no closer to understanding it now that I'm an old man than I was all those years ago in Jerusalem. It started when my uncle took me on a business trip with him, to give me a chance to see the world, and to see if I'd like to go into the trade with him, since he'd got no sons of his own. Now I send my sons and grandsons, and just sit at home and reminisce. They tell me I've earned that right, after all these years, but I notice they don't listen to my stories!

Anyway, that first trip to Jerusalem, I was more interested to see the Temple than anything else. We weren't the most religious family in the world, but we knew that our people are special in God's eyes, and we did what we had to do to make sure God kept remembering that. So I pestered my uncle, and that's how we happened to be in the Temple the afternoon a lame man got healed. My uncle insisted it was a fraud, but he didn't see the expression on the man's face. He was shocked, more than anything. Of course, everyone came running, hoping for a show, but the two men who'd healed him acted as though it was the kind of thing that happened every day. They said that if we believed in Jesus, our sins would be forgiven and we'd be able to do things like that too.

My uncle didn't want to hang around, wasting valuable trading time, but he let me go out in the evenings and sniff around. I found out quite a lot more about these Jesus people. Their Jesus had been killed by the Romans, though they seemed to blame us for it, saying that if our people had read the scriptures properly, we'd know that Jesus was the Messiah. They were causing quite a stir in the city, with their preaching and healing, and they'd

60

made quite a lot of converts. I liked them. They seemed kind, and they talked a lot about God loving us and forgiving us, if we believed in Jesus. I thought it would be good to be forgiven. Us traders are always breaking the Law, in little ways. You can't get a boat to stop on the Sabbath, and you can't be too choosy about what you eat when you're sealing a deal. So we've got no hope of being righteous that way.

Even after we went home, I never entirely forgot about the Jesus people, and it wasn't long before they'd spread to my part of the world. So obviously I wasn't the only one who thought they were making a kind of sense. I used to sneak out to their meetings sometimes and try to find out more. The main thing they were saying was that you can only find out about God through this Jesus. They said that Jesus showed us what God is like, and that Jesus came to die to take away our sins, and that he rose from the dead and is alive now. Apparently, some of the people had met people who'd met Jesus after he rose again, so they knew it was true.

That was all very interesting, but that main question kept niggling at me. What do I have to do to know that I'm right with God? Now that I'm old and I know I can't live for ever, it's become the most important question in my life. I haven't been a bad person, but I haven't been a good one either. Is it enough just to believe in Jesus? Some of these Christians seem to say that's all there is. But some of them say that if you do believe, it will change the way you live, and you will be good and loving. If so, I can't say that I've seen any proof of it. These Christians are as good at hating each other as anyone else. There are at least two different lots of them just in my town, not speaking to each other. How can I believe what they say about us being the children of God, free and forgiven, if they can't even forgive each other? They're good at blaming others, like my people, or the Romans, or some other leader who doesn't say things their way. Perhaps they should try blaming themselves for a change. If they were to say, 'We crucified Jesus, and we keep doing it, but he still forgives us and trusts us,' then I might be able to believe that he'll forgive me too.

# The Fourth Sunday of Easter

—— ≈ ——

*Acts 4.5–12*
*1 John 3.16–24*
*John 10.11–18*

Today's readings are deeply challenging. Christian mission has some-times been done as though determined to prove that we are right and everyone else is wrong, whereas all of today's writers think that Christians must preach and show Jesus Christ because that is actu-ally how the world is.

In Acts, Peter and John have been arrested. They healed a lame man and then preached to the astonished crowds that gathered. But whatever the ostensible reason for the arrest, the question that the religious authorities ask is a telling one. 'How did you do it, and whose side are you on?' is what it boils down to. The Temple com-mittee are already a bit suspicious of this new movement but, on the other hand, the healing did take place in the Temple, so it's possible that they are hoping to make religious capital out of it for themselves. If Peter and John are amenable, and say that they work through the power and in the name of God, then perhaps a happy compromise for all can be reached.

But Peter and John are not in the business of compromise. They are filled with the courage of the Holy Spirit, the life-giver, and they answer the question with alarming forthrightness. There is only one name, Peter says, that connects heaven and earth, that expresses the way in which God relates to us, and that assures us of God's powerful and saving love for us: Jesus.

Peter's certainty may sound embarrassingly harsh. Interestingly, several of the commentaries I checked chose not to say anything at all about this verse. The claims that Christians make on behalf of Christ just are demanding and exclusive of other descriptions of the world, and there is no getting away from that. But if you look at them in the light of today's other two readings, the strong impres-sion emerges that Christians can only make these claims about Christ by living them.

## Year B: Easter

In the Gospel reading, Jesus describes his ministry as that of the shepherd. This metaphor is one that has inspired countless sermons and pictures, but I haven't seen one where the frightened sheep have our human faces, watching our shepherd, Jesus, fighting off a pack of wolves. Our instinct is to run, scatter, and thereby make ourselves easier targets for being picked off by the wolves. The shepherd is fighting, desperately, to keep us together, to keep the whole flock safe. It is only our trust in him that enables us to stay there, shivering but together. Even so, every so often one of us makes a panicky break for it, but then the well-loved voice of the shepherd calls that one by name and brings it back to its senses.

Love, cost and purpose are the themes of the description that Jesus highlights, but purpose is the one that often gets left out. One flock, one shepherd, Jesus says, that's the goal. The flock will come really to know the voice of Jesus, and the love of Jesus, which is also the voice and the love of God.

The sheep come to know the voice of the shepherd because it is the voice that they have learned to associate with care, safety, warmth, food. In a crisis they will trust the shepherd because he has proved himself trustworthy before, in providing for their basic needs. The sheep would not have come to trust the shepherd if he had come out and given them a sermon a day. His voice would not be the one they loved and believed if they had not experienced it first as the voice of practical care.

This is certainly the point being made in 1 John. 'Let us love not in word or speech but in truth and action,' the epistle urges. The words are the easy bit. They cost the speaker very little, but equally they yield very little. The sheep wander off, unfed and unprotected, because they do not recognize this unfamiliar voice. It has never done anything for them. Christian shepherds, like Jesus, have to build up the trust of the sheep, and be prepared to redeem it at great personal cost, if necessary. We have to live in the world as though we really did believe that Jesus, the good shepherd who lays down his life to save us, is the way of God. We have to live together, one flock with one shepherd, as though we knew that this is what we were made for. Any other way of living is out of tune with the whole purpose of the universe. Luckily, the voice of the good shepherd is still heard in the Holy Spirit, since we still need to learn how to be shepherds ourselves.

# The Fifth Sunday of Easter

―― ～ ――

Acts 8.26–40
1 John 4.7–21
John 15.1–8

The writings of John, both in the Gospel and the epistles, are bafflingly determined not to come down on one side or the other of the 'chicken or egg' question. Which comes first, love of God or love of our neighbour? Which is more important, being or doing? Are we saved by grace or by works? Instinctively, temperamentally, most people come down on one side or another, and hear only those parts of the good news of Jesus Christ that seem to reinforce what is natural to us. Some people instinctively hear the message contained in Jesus's first public statement in Luke's Gospel: 'good news to the poor, release to the captives, sight to the blind, freedom for the oppressed' (Luke 4.18–19). Surely this is the heart of Jesus's message, they argue, and Christian witness to Christ is most faithful when it is actively doing things to improve life for society. Other people instinctively see that all of Jesus's activity arises out of his times of silence and prayer. His ministry starts not as he stands up and speaks, but as he wrestles alone in the desert.

The problem is that today's Gospel and epistle, like most of the New Testament, do not let you see that as an either/or. Instead, they argue, it is always both. Both epistle and Gospel are talking about the nature of God, which we contemplate with awe, but which we are also drawn into. 1 John talks about love as the fundamental nature and sign of God. Where you see love, you know the presence of God. Out of love, God the Son comes to die, so that we can be drawn back into the love of Father, Son and Holy Spirit. In God, then, love is not an abstract quality, but one that we experience very directly as *activity*. God *acts* lovingly towards us, and that is how we know that he is indeed love. In God, being and doing are not separate – he is love and acts lovingly. For us, that is not always the case because, unlike God, we are not yet complete.

64

The people to whom 1 John is addressed are presumably people who have accepted the saving love of God with gratitude, but who are still able to act without love to one another because in them, as in us, love has a beginning and a finite end. The great aim of our life is to make the beginning and the end of love get further and further apart in us, so that there is more and more room, more and more things we can love. In God love has no beginning and no end. As the great seventeenth-century poet John Donne said in one of his Christmas sermons, God's love is like a circle – endless.

The Gospel is talking about another one of God's inalienable characteristics, which is life. 1 John's language about love can sound a bit repetitive and soft-edged, despite the urgency of what is being said, but if you put it alongside today's Gospel, the reason for the urgency becomes clearer. God is the only source of life. If you pick flowers, they die. If you take people away from God, they die. It is not that this is a punishment, exactly; it is more that it is just a fact of life. So only branches grafted into the true vine can live and bear fruit. That is why this choice between being and doing is a false one. You are either alive with the life of God, the life in which there is no distinction between what God is and what he does, or you are not alive at all.

Many of us would quite like to rely on the life-giving love of God for ourselves without having to change too much. Philip, in today's story from Acts, wouldn't understand the question 'Should I spend time in prayer or should I go out and preach?' He has allowed himself to be very directly grafted into the life of God, so that everyone he meets is an opportunity waiting to be shown the love of God. An Ethiopian eunuch, miles from home, reading the Bible? When did you last expect to find someone like that waiting for you? Most of us wouldn't know such an opportunity if it passed us by, not even in a golden carriage full of treasure, and so we miss the chance that Philip seized to work with God. And on his way home, 'as he happened to be passing through the region' of Azotus, he preached there too. 'What, travel through a whole region without showing people the love of God?' Philip asks. 'Are you mad?'

# The Sixth Sunday of Easter

—— ❧ ——

*Acts 10.44–48*
*1 John 5.1–6*
*John 15.9–17*

The desire for certainty goes very deep, and all of today's readings look at that longing with sympathy, though the answers they give are as challenging as they are reassuring.

In the Gospel, Jesus is at last giving his disciples 'commandments'. If the disciples have been listening to Jesus throughout the weeks and months before this, they must have some inkling already about how Jesus interprets God's commandments to his people. Underlying the great commandments given by God to Moses is the imperative that his people should show by their lives what their God is like. This commandment Jesus has fulfilled utterly. Through all his life he has kept the commandment to love God, be loved by God and to show God's love, and that is the commandment that he now passes on to his disciples.

If the commandments given to Moses have proved difficult to interpret and fulfil, then Jesus's retelling of them has proved even harder. How do we know if we have fulfilled this great command to love one another? The example that Jesus gives, of his own willingness to die for his friends, is not a comforting one. Is that, then, to be the measure of love? Well, the Gospel suggests, it may need to be sometimes. But the verses that directly follow the giving of this commandment suggest that there are other interim measures too. One is the insistent changing of roles that is so characteristic of Jesus's teaching. 'I have called you friends', he says, 'because I have made known to you everything that I heard from my Father.' The sharing that characterizes Father and Son is extended to us. We are not simply issued with instructions that we must follow without needing to understand them. Instead we are invited to God's table, to eat and discuss and share in his great plan for the world. So one mark of our 'love' for one another and God will presumably be our willingness to extend this invitation to others. 'Come and join us at

God's table, come and help us to work out with God what to do next.' If God makes friends, not servants, so should Christians.

The second measure of our success at 'loving' that these verses suggest is 'bearing fruit'. Bringing others to share in the life and love of God will make us more loving. Anyone who has had any experience in Christian evangelism, whether in word or deed or both, would I think agree with that. It is deeply challenging and enlarging to see the word of God at work in the lives of others, and to see that before you and your feeble attempt at love got anywhere near the situation, God's love was already at work.

That is certainly the experience of Peter and his hearers as they watch Cornelius and his household respond to the love of God. They hear these strangers praising God long before they have gone through all the proper forms, and they realize that their own love for the Gentiles has been much smaller than God's. If they were looking for certainty about the next step in relation to the Gentiles, then they are given it abundantly. They see the Holy Spirit poured out with unmistakable power – and notice that that power is proved not just by the use of tongues, but by the praise of God. Of course, the certainty experienced by these witnesses is not easily transmitted to those who weren't present, as you will discover if you read the next chapter of Acts or Paul's letter to the Galatians.

1 John combines both love and the Holy Spirit in its explanation of Christian certainty. Like the Gospel, 1 John suggests that the commandment we are given – the thing we have to do to know that we are in the right – is to love God and love each other. Like Acts, it suggests that it is the Holy Spirit rather than our own innate discernment that leads us to spot the love of God at work. 1 John also reintroduces the sombre note of suffering sounded by the Gospel. The cross of Christ is not a past thing that has been superseded by the praise, joy and certainty of the Spirit. The Spirit witnesses constantly to the truth of the life, death and resurrection of Jesus which, in its totality, is the way of God's victory in the world.

Today's readings imply that certainty comes through sharing our faith, praising God and loving one another. Each one of those activities makes the others more and more possible and natural, and brings us closer and closer to the life of God, Father, Son and Holy Spirit.

# The Seventh Sunday of Easter

———  ∼  ———

Acts 1.15–17, 21–26
1 John 5.9–13
John 17.6–19

What would you like people to pray for on your behalf? What is your most usual – truthful – prayer request? Does Jesus's prayer for his disciples match your expectations in any way?

This prayer comes as Jesus prepares to leave his disciples and, although the context here is the preparation for the crucifixion, it is a good prayer to think about in connection with the ascension as well. At the heart of it is Jesus's love for the disciples, but also his certainty that the Father, too, loves these people who have recognized and cared for the Son. More than that, even, Jesus's prayer reveals to the disciples that God the Father actually gave them to the Son, to be his companions and witnesses. They may have thought that they chose Jesus or, if they were feeling very humble, that Jesus chose them, but now they discover that God himself chose them for Jesus because he loved them. This prayer is in the nature of an account-giving, as Jesus explains to the Father what he has done with the people the Father entrusted to him.

But now that that phase of Jesus's ministry is past, Jesus moves on to direct prayer for these people he has come to love. What does he pray for? Well, he does pray for protection, which must be high on most people's wish list, but perhaps not all of us wish to be protected so that we may be one (v. 11). Yet this is the central force of this extraordinary prayer, and it reveals something of the purpose of Jesus's own ministry. All those who accept Jesus know that they are in the active, dynamic presence of the will of God. Where Jesus is, there God's purpose is being fulfilled. This is the quality that Jesus now thanks his Father for in the disciples. They have believed that fundamental fact about Jesus – that he was sent by the Father – and so they have been able to share in the unity between Father and Son. As they proclaim the presence of God in Jesus, they themselves step into that place, or that way of being, where God's

68

will is done. This is to be their 'joy' (v. 13), as it has been Jesus's joy, to do the will of the Father, and so to be part of the spread of the Kingdom of God.

So Jesus prays for his disciples that they will be protected from the 'evil one', whose purpose, it seems, is to destroy Christian unity and so destroy Christian witness to the unity of Father and Son. And he prays that they may have joy. Unfortunately, just as the description of protection may not be the most common one, nor is the description of joy. Christian 'joy' involves being hated and rejected by a world that does not recognize the unity of Father and Son. It involves witnessing to the truth of the incarnation by holding on to each other under all circumstances, and never allowing the world's scepticism or hostility to divide us, just as it did not divide Father and Son in Jesus's earthly ministry.

This prayer of Jesus's is a very revealing bit of doctrinal theology, and it intimately connects the being of God and the being of the Church. It is at the heart of the Christian proclamation of God that the Father is most fully revealed in the Son and the Son in the Spirit. Trinitarian theology insists that 'unity' is an active concept, shown forth in dynamic interdependence and self-giving. It would hardly need to be called 'unity' at all if God were one in a simple and undifferentiated way.

So we are used to the idea that implicit in the whole of Jesus's earthly ministry is the unity of Father and Son. Everything Jesus does and is, he does and is in obedience to the Father and to demonstrate and exercise the will of the Father. But we may not be so used to the next step that the author of St John's Gospel takes in today's readings. Jesus comes to bring the active, redeeming presence of God into our human situation. We are called to bear witness to that. Jesus does this because he is one with the Father. We can only do our witnessing job if we are one with Jesus. We cannot be one with Jesus while clearly at odds with each other. How can witnesses who squabble about the truth possibly bear witness to the unity of Father, Son and Spirit?

As Jesus ascends to the Father, the Christian community is given the particular responsibility of witnessing to what we have learned about the unity of Father, Son and Holy Spirit.

# Day of Pentecost

——— ❧ ———

Acts 2.1–21
Romans 8.22–27
John 15.26–27; 16.4b–15

The Holy Spirit has been in danger in recent years of becoming the soppy one of the Trinity. Think about it for a bit – the Holy Spirit doesn't go off and do uncomfortable and challenging things like getting crucified. The Holy Spirit gives spectacular gifts that add a distinct touch of excitement to what could otherwise become rather dreary religious lives. The Holy Spirit can be described as the 'comforter', which sounds just lovely. The Holy Spirit is very politically correct and not at all gender-specific. The Holy Spirit likes to leave things to the last minute, like us, and works best if you stand up unprepared and allow the Spirit to take over. S/he really hates to be called upon by untrusting people who fussily want to prepare several days in advance. All in all, the Holy Spirit is the acceptable face of the Trinity.

Unfortunately, this picture of the Holy Spirit bears no resemblance at all to the Holy Spirit as depicted in the New Testament. Today's reading from Acts does sound, initially, rather exciting. We might feel, a shade wistfully, that if we had had tongues of fire resting on our heads then we might be able to match the sudden boldness of the disciples as they stand up and witness to Jesus. But when Peter begins to talk, fuelled by the power of the Holy Spirit, what he is led to talk about is judgement. The coming of the Holy Spirit emphasizes the finality and totality of what God has done in Jesus Christ. The way in which people react to Jesus seals their fate just as surely as if the world had indeed come to an end with 'portents in the heaven above and signs on the earth below' (v. 19). And if Peter's words today ring with excitement and conviction, he is to spend the rest of his days witnessing to this truth he once denied, and he is to pay for it with his life.

The Gospel reading also talks about the Holy Spirit in terms of judgement. With exactly the same theological force as in Acts, John

70

says that the work of the Holy Spirit is to point out the consequences of how we respond to Jesus. The Holy Spirit comes to prove conclusively that the world has got most of its judgements skewed. The world judged Jesus to be mad and dangerous, and it condemned him to death, thereby proving that it didn't know right from wrong. The Holy Spirit comes to reverse that judgement, and turn the tables. Those who convicted Jesus of sin are now shown to be the deluded sinners. The Holy Spirit comes to prove that Jesus is the one who knows the truth, and that is because Jesus's judgements are the same as God's. The Spirit of truth comes to bear witness to the unity of Father and Son and to empower us to do the same.

Romans 8 speaks quite graphically of the work of the Spirit in terms of childbirth. Not the happy, sanitized version, where the cleaned-up baby smiles up at its well-rested parents, but the real version where there is far too much groaning and pain and blood. This is a good metaphor, Paul suggests, because the point of all that anguish is the child that is to be born. In the middle of labour it is possible almost to forget that it will ever end and that there will be an outcome. But the Holy Spirit, like the midwife, keeps the world straining and pushing. 'Come on, you're nearly there, I can see the head now,' the Holy Spirit shouts, reminding us constantly why we are doing this.

The Holy Spirit knows how to interpret the anguish of the world. The Holy Spirit has seen the image of Jesus forming more and more clearly in so many people that, in the midst of our cries we can hear the words, 'It's all right. This is how it is supposed to be. Nothing has gone wrong. Keep hoping, keep working. The end is in sight.' Hope is one of the hallmarks of the Holy Spirit, according to Romans 8, and this is no mindless self-deceiving hope but the truthful hope of one who knows the will of God.

All of these readings suggest that the work of the Holy Spirit is to bear witness to the truth of Jesus Christ, and to enable our witness to that same truth. Sometimes that will be accompanied by gratifying gifts of power and sometimes it will involve a complete surrender of human power, to the point of death. But wherever the Holy Spirit witnesses, there is judgement. 'Do you choose for or against God?' the Holy Spirit asks, echoing the life and work of Jesus.

*Ordinary Time*

# Trinity Sunday

———— ∾ ————

Isaiah 6.1–8
Romans 8.12–17
John 3.1–17

John Donne, the great seventeenth-century Anglican poet, said in his *Litanie* that the doctrine of the Trinity is 'Bones to Philosophy, but milk to faith'.[1] Bones and milk are both provided by today's readings.

The belief that God is Trinity is the foundation for the belief that God is also love. If God were not Trinity, the most we could say with absolute confidence would be that God occasionally – or even regularly – chooses to act lovingly, but not that he is, in himself, love. Belief in God the Trinity says that before there was anything external to God towards which God could act lovingly, God's being was still expressed in the love between Father, Son and Spirit. This 'love' of God is not an abstract quality, unrecognizable by the usual marks of what we humans would call love. It is personal, dynamic and creative. It is full of delight and generosity. It longs for the rest of the world to see the loveliness of the beloved. We, God's creation, come to be out of the exuberance and sheer vitality of that love, and we are designed to share in it, to be drawn more and more into the reality of the loving God.

That is why verse 16 is the climax of the odd, teasing conversation between Jesus and Nicodemus. 'This is the point of it all,' Jesus says, 'that God's beloved people may live with us for ever.'

Does Nicodemus understand that? It is very hard to tell, just as it is hard to tell what he is doing there at all, creeping about in the dead of night like a young revolutionary rather than a weighty religious leader of a people who have made a sensible compromise with their irreligious rulers.

---

[1] John Donne, 'A litanie' in *John Donne: Selections from Divine Poems, Sermons, Devotions, and Prayers*, ed. John Booty, The Classics of Western Spirituality, Paulist Press, 1990, p. 87.

From his opening words, Jesus wrong-foots Nicodemus. Nicodemus has rehearsed what he is going to say to open the conversation. He pays tribute to Jesus's ministry, while at the same time making understated claims for his own credentials. 'I'm someone who can recognize the activity of God,' he says in effect, 'and you're really doing very well, old chap.' To which Jesus answers, in effect, 'How would you know?' All through the sharp-edged conversation, Nicodemus is trying to get things back on track, back into normal conversational and debating mode, and Jesus won't let him. The activity of God cannot be ordered by your little checklists, he says to Nicodemus. You have to tear them up and be prepared to start again.

Nicodemus, like all religious people throughout the ages, believes to some extent that God is love. But he believes that God's love is measured and sensible, and follows a set of rules. He believes that Jesus's healings are, largely, consonant with the activity of God, but he has some worries about them, which is presumably why he is here, to get Jesus to fill in the proper forms. And he does deserve some credit for this – many of his colleagues couldn't or wouldn't see even this far into the love of God. But it is not far enough, because all Jesus's replies to Nicodemus suggest that Nicodemus has to let go of all the measures that he has been using, and launch out into the unfathomable reality of the totality of God's love. God does not love when we have met the requirements, or when we have changed enough to be lovable, or when we were lucky enough to be born in one race or sex. God just loves. And trying to measure the love of God is like trying to control the wind. God will do anything for this world he loves, including coming himself, the Son, to die for it. To understand this is to be, in Jesus's words, born again, to start the world again, learning to walk and speak and think and grow in a world where the love of God is the breath that we breathe, so that our every response to the world around is informed by that love.

So don't try to measure the wind of God's love, Paul argues, just go with it, let it breathe through you and power you – God's Spirit, a totally renewable power source. To be filled with the vitality of God's love is to share in God's relationship with God and to know ourselves beloved. It is also to share in God's wild love for the world. Send us! we exclaim with Isaiah. Paul and John both warn us that our love must be as insane as God's. No reintroducing the checklists, no loving on our terms only. God the Son preferred to go to the cross rather than force his creation into a dutiful, fearful obedience to the Father, so that must be our choice also, if necessary.

# Proper 4

—— ～ ——

*Deuteronomy 5.12–15*
*2 Corinthians 4.5–12*
*Mark 2.23—3.6*

Today's passages send out an alarmingly confusing set of messages. On the one hand, Deuteronomy tells us how vital it is to keep the Sabbath, while Jesus seems to suggest that we can sit a bit more lightly to that in certain circumstances. The Pharisees are obeying the scriptures and Jesus, apparently, is not. Next confusion: Jesus is acting with authority and power, and that makes his message incredible to those around him, while Paul is weak and vulnerable and that seems to prove to the Corinthians that he can't really be God's messenger.

So let's start with the confusion over the Sabbath, since that is probably slightly more easily resolved. Jesus's words cannot be taken as validating the state of affairs that we have now reached in Britain, where there is no recognizable, shared culture of rest and relaxation, no protected time for families to spend together, no obvious evening where people sit down and talk to each other and remind themselves of what is really important in life. Sharing Friday evening Sabbath meals with Jewish friends has been a revelation to me of what we have lightly lost. In eating, talking, remembering and sharing, all in the context of prayer, it is not just a family that is being built up, but also a whole society. This is where we might remember what we value, what we were made for.

So when Jesus picks food and heals the sick on the Sabbath, he is not saying, I think, that it's OK to go to Tesco seven days a week, but reminding his listeners of what the Sabbath does. The Sabbath recreates us as more than just people who live to work. It recreates us as images of God. There is no record of Jesus being criticized for doing trivial and irrelevant things on the Sabbath, things that could easily be done any other time. Instead, he is being criticized by those who have forgotten the real meaning of the Sabbath, and its witness to the creative God, who delights in what he has made and wants that delight to have time to flourish in others. If the hungry and the sick are to be able to share God's joy, they need to be fed or healed. But the bored and the overworked and overfed need to rediscover the Sabbath.

What makes Jesus's use of his authority so unacceptable to his listeners in this context is that he is reasserting the claim of God on their lives, whereas they had been assuming that the commandments are there so that we can assert our rights over God. 'See, God,' we say, 'we have kept our part, now behave properly towards us.' While Jesus is saying, 'Come and live in God's world and his life, come and be recreated in his image and delight in his world.'

In all of what he does, Jesus offers two pictures of life, only one of which is real. We either live with God's life or we don't actually live at all. And that is exactly what Paul is saying. The creative power of the God who said 'Let there be light' is alive through Christ, and we are privileged to share in it. This is not a power that is innate to us. By ourselves, we are 'clay jars', just as, by himself, Adam was a clay figure until God breathed life into him. The life is God's, not ours. That means that a lot of the self-perpetuating myth of life with which we live for most of the time has to be relinquished. This myth says that being properly alive means being well, rich, happy and – preferably – sexually fulfilled. It is a myth that says that immediate gratification is the goal of human life. But Paul argues that real life, the life that flows from God, returns to God, and that knows how to live in the world that God has made, looks like Jesus. We have no other model of a human being fully alive, only Jesus. And that makes authentic Christian life a little harder to spot. It might not always be as tough as Paul's life was, but it can't automatically be measured by other definitions of 'success'. Jesus's brief life ends in a horrible death and a failure, apparently, to impose his understanding of God on even his closest followers. And yet Jesus was so fully alive and vital with God's own life that even death could not extinguish him, but is forced to serve God's resurrection life, and become the source of life for the world. Paul's life is a true response to the boundless life of Jesus because, like Jesus's life, it brings others into the life of God. It is life because it is life-giving for others.

# Proper 5

——— ❧ ———

*Genesis 3.8–15*
*2 Corinthians 4.13—5.1*
*Mark 3.20–35*

Things are moving at a relentless pace for Jesus in these early chapters of Mark's Gospel. Already he is being followed everywhere he goes by large crowds of people. Already he has made bitter enemies out of the local clergy. Some of the people who follow him are just hoping to be in on the action, and they don't much care if it is a healing or a pitched battle that they witness. But some of the crowd can already be called 'disciples' (see Mark 3.7), and they would no doubt believe that they are following Jesus out of conviction. From them, Jesus has just chosen the twelve, who are to be particularly closely identified with his mission throughout their lives.

And now he goes home, Mark tells us, and even here the crowd press around him so thickly that his family begin to get rather peeved. His antics are annoying the neighbours and getting the family a bad reputation. Perhaps they had thought that Jesus's healing and teaching was like a job – he could go out to do it by day and come back to a normal family life in the evenings. This great heaving, struggling mass of people, with their noise and their litter and their complete lack of concern for any other part of Jesus's life is not at all what they expected. They begin to be rather afraid that the experts from Jerusalem are right, and Jesus has gone mad. After all, no one in their right mind would want to be the centre of such scenes, would they?

But if the anger and bewilderment of Jesus's family is comprehensible, the scribes are up to something a bit more sinister. Jesus's family are reacting much as any other family might whose brother or son has catapulted to superstardom overnight. They knew he was something special, but they hadn't anticipated it having this kind of effect on all their lives. But the scribes are not bewildered and overwhelmed – they are appalled. They cannot allow all this huge crowd of people to believe in Jesus, and perhaps even pass on

78

their belief to yet more people, because Jesus is not singing from their hymn sheet. He has already made it perfectly clear that he will not dutifully follow the rules, and the scribes are afraid of losing control of large proportions of the population. Perhaps they are not just cynically thinking of their own prestige and pockets. Perhaps they are genuinely devout students of scripture, and are shocked at what they have heard about Jesus forgiving sins and healing on the Sabbath. He is not obeying the clear word of scripture, so he must be wrong, whatever the crowds think, and however commendable his healings appear to be. They see his power and they know only two sources of such power – God or the devil. It can't come from God, because God can only work according to the scripture, so it must come from the devil.

Jesus's answer asks them to look not just at the theory of God, but also at the reality. The simple fact of the matter is that everything Jesus has done is good. It has resulted in the restoration of the children of God to the human community. Everywhere he goes, madness, evil and sickness are banished. The voices of the demon-possessed call out to Jesus throughout these first chapters of Mark, and they call out in fear, in longing, and in recognition of the power of God, so alien to the small, mad, dark power that tries to control them but is nowhere near strong enough to blind them to the reality of God. In St Luke's Gospel, Jesus begins his public ministry by saying in scriptural words what we are about to see: good news is brought to the poor, the captives are released, the blind see and the oppressed go free (Luke 4.18). But here in Mark's Gospel, Jesus simply does God's word; he performs it in action, rather than proclaiming it in words. Those who read God's word should surely recognize it in action. Evil does not work against itself, Jesus says. Recognize the strong, liberating might of God, come to put an end to all captivity. Do not dare to confuse the action of God to free his people with the action of the enslaving enemy.

This, Jesus says, is the 'blasphemy against the Holy Spirit'. It is the willingness to confuse God's living, liberating Spirit with the death-dealing, imprisoning spirit of evil. You cannot confuse them by accident. You can only do it if you wilfully reject God, and prefer to be bound yourself and see others in chains than accept God's redemption in Christ.

# Proper 6

———— ❧ ————

*Ezekiel 17.22–24*
*2 Corinthians 5.6–17*
*Mark 4.26–34*

Paul's argument in this section of 2 Corinthians is complex and far-reaching. He is putting forward a whole new theory of reality and knowledge. Christians, he argues, carry their own reality system around with them, and they have to learn how to make judgements based on that reality and not be fooled by the virtual reality that other people still live in. There will sometimes be some very uncomfortable dissonance between the two 'realities', which can confuse and alarm Christians, and Paul is trying to give the Corinthian church some pointers, to help them to judge wisely.

One of the things that makes negotiating this new Christian world particularly difficult is that our bodies are obstinately stuck in the old reality. They will insist on seeing the world with old eyes, and on wanting the kind of comfort and security that they were always used to seeking. Interestingly, Paul does not say that our bodily needs are wicked. There is no simplistic dualism between body and spirit, wrong and right. Instead, he just says, 'Don't worry'. What we increasingly have to learn is that these old bodies are not our home. Although we are not urged to try to shed them too quickly, we still have to learn not to trust their judgements about the world.

So, for example, we have to learn not simply to trust what we see. Our old way of seeing things may suggest that we are walking into danger or, at the very least, discomfort, and try to stop us. But we have to remember that we are now walking with a different map. 'We walk by faith, not by sight,' Paul says (2 Corinthians 5.7). It is not any longer our main aim to please ourselves and keep ourselves safe. Now we are working to please God.

That is going to affect the way we judge other people too. It sounds, from verses 11–13, as though the Corinthian church has been judging Paul by other kinds of standards and finding him wanting. There seems to be a suggestion that they would like Paul to stop giving them sensible instructions and telling them off. Other religious leaders, they say, fall into ecstatic fits, and lead worshippers into exciting frenzies of adoration. You just keep writing us letters, they complain. I could concentrate on charismatic devotions, Paul says, but it wouldn't do you any good. My worship of God is between God and me, but my job in relation to you is to teach you about the love of God in Christ, and to teach you how to see the world in the light of that reality.

Paul knows that what he is describing is difficult. He himself has had to learn how to judge differently and by completely different criteria. After all, he made his own independent judgement about Jesus, and it led him to persecute Christians. He used all his old standards of knowledge and judgement, and decided that Jesus and his followers were enemies of God. His conversion turned all his own knowledge and understanding completely on its head.

Paul had obviously believed that his primary religious role, in the old days, was to keep people out, by force if necessary. If they did not agree with him then they had to go. Now, through the eyes of Christ, he sees the world very differently. Now he sees that God in Christ seeks to bring people in, not keep them out, and so those of us who try to walk by faith, not sight, have to do the same. Every single Christian is given the opportunity to become part of God's reconciling work in Christ. We can become his ambassadors, Paul says (v. 20). Where we are is God's country, God's reality, where the main currency is forgiveness. It is not our job any longer to make judgements according to any other criteria. All the criteria that Paul had available to him previously led him to believe that Jesus, who died a criminal's death on the cross, was a sinner, and just look how wrong he was. All we can do now is affirm, loudly and constantly, that if we walk in Jesus's reality, then we are forgiven and brought into God's home.

To change our standards of judgement so completely is very hard. But we make it, perhaps, even more difficult than we need to by assuming that what is called for is something huge. It needn't be, Jesus suggests. It might be just getting up day by day and doing what has to be done. Walking by faith, as Paul calls it, might just be a matter of putting one foot in front of the other, and moving imperceptibly into God's reality.

# Proper 7

———— ∽ ————

*Job 38.1–11*
*2 Corinthians 6.1–13*
*Mark 4.35–41*

In today's readings we have two different, and potentially incompatible, views of how God works.

The reading from Job and the reading from the Gospel seem to have one vision, which is of the colossal and unquestionable power of God. In Job, God finally rounds on Job's so-called friends, with their endless quasi-theological advice about what has caused Job's sufferings. At last, God speaks for himself. He does not deign to explain himself, since it is clear that his hearers are too stupid to understand, even if it was God's concern to make himself comprehensible. Instead, God sets about pointing out exactly why Job, his friends – and we – are unfit to question the Lord. 'What exactly *do* you understand?' God asks, and the implication is obviously 'nothing'. Nothing about how the world functions is either understood or controlled by us, and yet we are indignant that God does not lay his plans before us. We are like tone-deaf concert-goers sitting and grumpily complaining that we don't understand this thing called 'music'.

As Jesus stills the storm in today's Gospel reading we see again the awesome power of God. The unpredictable and merciless forces of nature suddenly respond like obedient children to the voice of Jesus, and the disciples are amazed. They were already terrified by the storm, but they are almost equally terrified by its sudden cessation at Jesus's command. When Jesus asks them, 'Why are you afraid, have you no faith?' the Gospel is deliberately unclear about which fear he means.

These statements of the inexorable power of God need to be heard, perhaps today more than ever, when a debilitating theology of the 'niceness' of God can all too easily portray him as utterly ineffectual. But we have to be careful to allow God to define power, and not to impose our own longed-for definitions on him. Otherwise what Paul is saying in 2 Corinthians looks simply contradictory. Paul is talking about the power of God at work in his ministers as they suffer 'beatings, imprisonments, riots' and all manner of other sufferings (2 Corinthians 6.5). And the Jesus who commands the storm is soon to be forced on to the cross. So what is God's power like?

The strange thing about God's response to Job and his friends is that it is almost exactly what Job's friend Elihu has been saying since chapter 36. 'Don't expect to understand God,' Elihu says, 'just fear him' (37.24). But the problem is that he isn't following his own advice. He is still trying to give a neat, pre-packaged theory about God, rather than facing the enormity of God himself. And Jesus's disciples are as afraid of the end of the storm as of the storm itself, because it has brought them up sharply against God. The Corinthians, Paul says, have reservations about him and his ministry. Is it because they do not like the raw, unavoidable presence of God in the preaching of Paul?

'Give us the theory,' human beings cry out to God, 'but don't give us yourself. That's more than we want.' This then, is the power of God, the huge generosity that fills our little outstretched begging bowls so full that the bowl is utterly swept away in the torrent. Is that more than you bargained for?

In his beautifully honest and humble book *Basil in Blunderland* the late Cardinal Hume says that for years he lived with a concept of God as a kind of gigantic teacher or policeman, who would know if you sneaked into the larder and took an apple, and would make sure you paid for it. 'Now many years later', he writes, 'I have an idea that God would have said to the small boy, "Take two ...".'[1]

So the end of the story of Job is that Job – the devout and lifelong servant of God – says to him, 'I had no idea. I had only heard about you before, but now I've seen you, I know I can only throw myself on your mercy' (42.5, 6). The disciples, too, have to learn to trust God for what God is and gives and not for what they would like. As they argue with Jesus and try to dissuade him from the road to the cross, do their hearts cling to that moment when he stilled the storm? 'More of that,' they cry, forgetting that they were afraid of it when they saw it. This is a lesson that Paul has amply learned – the thrilling, mad power of God, recklessly throwing out apples, and bread to the starving. Will the Corinthians open their hearts to it, or we ours? Or do we actually feel safer with a world that will stingily dole out one apple and make sure we pay for it?

---

[1] *Basil in Blunderland*, DLT, 1997.

# Proper 8

———— ∾ ————

*Wisdom of Solomon 1.13–15; 2.23, 24*
*2 Corinthians 8.7–15*
*Mark 5.21–43*

'Do not fear, only believe,' Jesus says to Jairus. It's easier said than done, of course, with his daughter dead and the house full of the sound of wailing mourners. It's also quite ironic, in that it is fear of just this moment that has driven Jairus to Jesus in the first place.

Both of the people Jesus encounters in today's Gospel reading are driven by one kind of fear so strongly that it overcomes all kinds of other fears that they might be expected to feel. Jairus's overwhelming fear is that his daughter will die. Mark's storytelling never wastes words, but he doesn't need to describe how much Jairus loves his daughter. His actions make it crystal clear. He is risking the disapproval of his community, in which he is a leading figure; he is pushing aside his own inevitable doubts and uncertainties about who Jesus is and by what power he performs healings. He is prepared to risk everything for the faint hope of life for his daughter. So he elbows his way to the front of the whispering, nudging crowd, and makes his demand of Jesus. And Jesus goes with him. No words said, no questions asked.

The nameless woman, too, has one fierce fear that puts all the others in the shade. Her fear is that she will never be well again, she will always be bone-tired, pale, thin, listless and in pain. But also, she will always be alone, never fully part of the community, no one to help her bear her condition more cheerfully. So she braves the fear of discovery and rejection by the crowd, the fear of painful, embarrassing exposure if the bandages and extra clothes she has bound around herself do not hold, the fear that she will not reach Jesus through the crowds, or that if she does, it will be useless.

You can tell that her driving fear is long-term, that she has lived with it for so long that it has changed her character completely. Once, presumably, she was reasonably well-off – comfortable enough, at any rate, to afford a lot of doctors, and confident enough to go on spending her money in expectation of a cure. But now she is poor and cowed and tired. She is not like Jairus who, even in the extremity of his fear, is a man of authority who expects to be heard and to get his own way. This woman is not even intending to ask for what she needs because she is sure the answer would be no. But she has just enough desperation left to try to steal it.

Her chance comes as the crowd begins to move. Jesus and Jairus are walking fast to get to the sick child, and the crowd is streaming around them, thinner in some places where people are not hurrying to be at the front. The woman seizes her chance, while the important men are concentrating on their important things. She reaches out her hand and brushes Jesus's clothes as they blow out behind him with the speed of his walking. She had meant to turn away at once and hobble off home and wait and hope, but she is shocked into stillness by her body's reaction. How long is it since she felt well? So long that she can hardly recognize the feeling. And in that one awed moment, the crowd stops moving and she hears the dreadful question, 'Who touched me?'

She could have stood silent, but part of her needs the crowd to see what has happened to her, to make it real, to assure her that she isn't imagining it, even if she gets into terrible trouble. It is strange to have all those eyes on her, when she has spent years with eyes that avoided her or slid away from her fast. Most of the eyes are not friendly. She is just a distraction, kneeling there, abject and shaking. The crowd wants to get on to Jairus's house to see the real drama unfold. They expect Jesus to push her away, perhaps even to make her ill again. Instead, he tells her that she has done right, and that her health is what she deserves and has won for herself.

Jairus must be in an agony of impatience while all of this is going on. He knows that every second counts and, sure enough, when they get home at last, it is too late. Even in the midst of his terrible grief, he can spare a little hatred for the insignificant woman whose healing has cost him his daughter.

Don't be afraid, Jesus says. God's love is not that small. There is enough for the woman and your daughter. There is enough for all.

# *Proper 9*

—— ∽ ——

*Ezekiel 2.1–5*
*2 Corinthians 12.2–10*
*Mark 6.1–13*

This passage of 2 Corinthians has caused enormous speculation down the ages. It is tantalisingly full of hints about Paul, which may have made sense to his readers but which we can only fill out with hyperactive imaginings, which can never be proved or disproved. It seems pretty certain that Paul is talking about his own spiritual experience in the first half of chapter 12. The convoluted language and the use of the third person shows how reluctant he is to do so, but he is driven to it by the theological point he has to make. For some people, this kind of mystical experience is a 'natural' result of meeting with God. It clearly was for Paul, as his encounter with Jesus on the road to Damascus shows. And does Galatians hint at a prolonged period of spiritual experience, in the three years after Paul's conversion, before his Gentile ministry begins (Galatians 1.17–18)? But the point Paul is making to the Corinthians is that these experiences are irrelevant – it is the meeting with God that matters, not the form it takes. The Corinthians are rather keen on exciting experiences, and they have clearly been intrigued by 'super-apostles' (2 Corinthians 11.5), who have, presumably, been pandering to their love of spectacle. So Paul needs to make it clear that he is not talking out of envy of those who have experiences that he doesn't. He could match them in every way. But his calling as an apostle is not to gather crowds of admiring followers who gasp at his spiritual prowess. His calling is to witness to Christ.

But if we long, like the Corinthians, to know exactly what Paul means by being 'caught up into Paradise', we also long, tabloid readers that we are, to know what his 'thorn in the flesh' was. We want to know the highs and the lows. Some commentators have assumed that Paul's 'thorn' was a physical defect of some kind. But the context makes it just as likely that the 'thorn' is actually someone who is opposing and undermining Paul's work. These 'super-apostles' have been bringing out the worst in Paul, making him defensive, aggressive, boastful, suggesting that his gospel is not the real one, dividing the community he loves and has struggled over. He has begged God three times to remove this obstacle, but God has said no.

If that is a correct interpretation of the situation, then God's 'No' to Paul is a very hard thing to hear. God's 'No' means that Paul must live without God's public vindication of his apostleship. It also means that Paul has to hear God's deeper challenge. 'Do you want to be proved right for my sake, or for your own?' We can all too easily convince ourselves that unless we are publicly proved right, God will be miserable. But that is simply not true. God does not need popular acclamation to know that he is right. He is not dependent upon the world's good opinion. That is our problem. God is our God and our saviour, whatever opinion polls may say, and he knows it. We don't actually need to worry about God. So whatever Paul's thorn in the flesh is, it is something that reminds him of that basic fact. It is something that, at least in Paul's own view, makes him less plausible and authoritative for God. But that is why it is God's gift to him, because it reminds him that Paul is dependent upon God, not vice versa.

It is not wrong to long for love and support and understanding. But those things, like mystical experiences, are the occasional luxuries, rather than the staple fare of Christians. When Jesus goes home, with his disciples, does he hope to be able to relax among people who love and trust him? If so, he is sorely disappointed. His people resent his authority, his reputation, his followers. They want to pull him back down to their level. They don't want to face the challenge and the opportunity that he brings. They spend all their efforts on looking for reasons not to pay attention to him. The question, 'Who does he think he is?' frees them from the responsibility of hearing what he is saying. But if Jesus is shocked by them, and if they reinforce his sense of loneliness and isolation, that does not deter him from doing the will of the Father. Instinctively, at a time when his own authority is called into question by the disbelief of his townspeople, he looks around for another way, and sends his disciples out to preach. That is the vital thing for him – not that people love and honour him, but that God's word is heard and his will is done.

# Proper 10

—— ～ ——

Amos 7.7–15
Ephesians 1.3–14
Mark 6.14–29

The letter to the Ephesians sets the life of the Christian Church in the context of the cosmic plan of God. The letter will go on to give quite detailed advice about how Christians should live together, day to day, but it is important that that advice should be seen in its proper setting. Christianity is not, at its heart, about living a decent and moral life. It is about living the life we were created for, in tune with the God who made us. That is why Christians are right to agonize over the way our lives bear witness to the God we seek and serve. We are trying to brush away the dust and dirt that cover the beloved features, not bury them even deeper. Luckily, our frantic but ineffectual efforts are not the only force at work. Behind them all is the awesome majesty of God, whose purposes will not be thwarted, even though, dog-like, our digging obscures more than it reveals.

So Ephesians begins right at the very beginning, reminding the reader of our dependence upon God, and how much we already have to thank him for. In Christ, God has always chosen to be our God. Even before we existed, and certainly before we consciously turned towards God, God chooses that we are to be 'in Christ', and share that relationship between Father and Son. It is the nature of God the Son to go out and show the love of the Father, so that Son and Spirit can gather everything that is made back into the life of the maker (v. 10). This is what we are made for. We are designed to be part of the ceaseless flow of love between Father, Son and Holy Spirit.

Christians, then, live as people who know God's plan for the world. We know that God has made us to be part of his glorious life and love. We carry in our very blood the serum, the antidote to the belief that life is pointless and that evil always triumphs. Our baptism, you might say, injects us with the Holy Spirit so that now, inseparably linked with our own weary, bored, unbelieving life-blood is the life-blood of God, who creates, sustains and redeems all things. And the life of God is irresistible, as Jesus's resurrection shows.

We do need to make it our solemn and binding duty never to forget the Christian calling to joy and hope, to praising and glorifying our God. We do need to hold always before us the knowledge that the world and its fate are in God's hands, and he who has held it in love from its birth is not going to drop it now. Knowing the huge and final plan of God does not always help us to see where we are going every day. Many, many days and weeks and months can pass without any sign that they are furthering the final goal of gathering the world into Christ. Most of our own plans are all too clearly human and lead, if we are lucky, into the dust and, if we are not so lucky, into apparent disaster.

As John the Baptist waited to have his head chopped off, did he believe that things were still on track and leading to God's goals? It can't have been at all obvious. He'd been sitting in prison for some time, visited regularly by Herod. Perhaps John believed that he was beginning to get through to Herod, beginning to make him see that he was leading a life that was contrary to the will of God. And then one rash promise from Herod, and John is dead, and the opportunity gone. If, as Mark suggests, Herod continued to feel guilty about John's death, still it had no visible effect upon his future behaviour. We readers of the Gospel know the central role John the Baptist plays as God's herald to the coming Son, and so we also need to note that John did exactly what he was supposed to do, and yet it did not bring him fame, fortune and friends. John fulfils his role by standing aside, making room for the Son, and continuing to bear faithful witness right up to his strange and tragic end.

To praise and glorify God, and to live in the truthful knowledge of the overriding purposes of God will not necessarily make our lives easy. As followers of Christ, the crucified and risen Lord, the image of the invisible God and the fulfilment of all of God's plans, we should perhaps not be surprised by that.

# Proper 11

—— ～ ——

Jeremiah 23.1–6
Ephesians 2.11–22
Mark 6.30–34, 53–56

In today's reading from Mark's Gospel, we get a strong sense of the enormous pressure Jesus and the disciples were under at this point in his ministry. Jesus is at the height of his popularity and although his conflict with the religious authorities has begun, as chapters 2 and 3 make clear, it has not yet escalated into full public confrontation. To the crowds who follow him everywhere he goes, Jesus is still a teacher and healer, not primarily a political player. Jesus knows this about them. He knows that they come to him for immediate gratification and to satisfy their pressing need. Just like sheep, they have no long-term plans. Sheep don't worry about what will happen when they have eaten all the grass in their field, or when winter comes. That's the job of the shepherd. In the same way, the people who flock round Jesus have come either just for entertainment or for healing, but without any idea that what Jesus is offering has more long-term consequences than either of those things. That's what he sees, as he looks at them: he sees sheep with no shepherd and, we are told, he 'began to teach them many things' – not make decisions for them, like their shepherd, but teach them things so that they can be human beings, not sheep any more.

What makes Jesus's compassion and understanding for the crowds even more striking are the circumstances in which all of this is taking place. His disciples have just come back from a groundbreaking independent mission and are longing to tell him all about it. They are all tired out, every conversation they have is interrupted, they are recognized and tracked wherever they go, they are not eating or sleeping properly. All of them must be aware that they are living on their nerves and their instincts. Clearly, in that utterly defenceless state, Jesus's instincts are to put others and their needs first. We rightly concentrate on the cross when we are thinking about what Jesus suffered in order to bring about our salvation, but this passage reminds us that Jesus's bodily existence does not begin and end on the cross. Many of us who hope and pray that we will never be called upon to suffer as he did on the cross can remember that he also suffered from hunger, weariness, stress and all the more common symptoms of embodied living.

Is it accidental that Ephesians puts so much emphasis on the bodiliness of the way in which our salvation was achieved? Ephesians 2.14 does not say, as you might expect, that Jesus's physical suffering on the cross wins our salvation. Instead, it says that his 'fleshliness', in and of itself, unites the divided and breaks down the walls of hostility. All the metaphors of belonging and wholeness that are used in verses 19–22 depend on this work done by Jesus in the flesh. Because Jesus came in the flesh, we are now familiar and beloved to each other, instead of unrecognized and untrustworthy. Because Jesus came in the flesh, we are now part of God's family. Because Jesus came in the flesh, we can, together, be built up into the place where God lives on earth, where he may be visited and worshipped and known. Because Jesus came in the flesh, our bodies are familiar with the Holy Spirit and, through him, with the Father.

It is so tempting to spiritualize salvation, but the Christian gospel of incarnation absolutely militates against that. God himself has made our bodiliness central to salvation. If we will not be saved in and through our actual, physical lives, we will not be saved by Christ at all. That is why this terrible, painful, costly debate that is going on in the Anglican Church now about the proper use of sexuality is, at least in its subject matter, necessary. It does matter what we do with our bodies. We are right to sense, however inarticulately, that something vital is at issue here. We may be wrong to think that it all hinges on our bodies seen in sexual terms. We may be wilfully ignoring the other facts about being embodied creatures, like the fact that many of us struggle with obesity while others starve, or the fact that bodies with different coloured skins are treated differently, or the fact that all bodies are born to die. All of these are truths about being creatures whose embodied existence Jesus chose to share in order to break down walls of hostility between us. The only way in which these our bodies can be built up into the temple of God is if we will hold hands and stand, body to body, together.

# Proper 12

—— ～ ——

*2 Kings 4.42–44*
*Ephesians 3.14–21*
*John 6.1–21*

The story of the feeding of the five thousand is found in all four Gospels, making it one of the best attested of Jesus's miracles. John's Gospel sometimes uses memories and stories that clearly come from different sources from the ones used by the other three Gospels. So this episode of miraculous feeding must be one that was told in pretty well all the early Christian witness to Jesus. It might very well have been regularly retold in a eucharistic setting, as the way Jesus breaks the bread and gives thanks would be a good way into teaching about the eucharistic meal, and Jesus's self-breaking on the cross. But there are also details that are particular and superfluous to that teaching use, that make it clear that this is a real memory of an extraordinary event. For example, the little boy and his fish – I can't help feeling that the boy may have had some role in keeping the story fresh. We aren't told who he was, but it is slightly odd that in such a huge crowd of people, the disciples knew he was there and that he had his picnic with him. Perhaps he was even the son of one of the disciples, or one of Jesus's regular followers. Or perhaps he was just a very loud and ubiquitous boy, the sort you can't help noticing in any crowd. Either way, I'm sure he was often called upon in later life to tell the story of what happened when Jesus took his sandwiches.

St John, always the theologian, and clearly with high expectations of the intelligence of his readership, puts the feeding miracle in the context of Passover. What God is doing in Jesus is similar to the divine action that brought the people of Israel safely out of Egypt. But he also expects his readers to understand that God's new act of power is only prefigured in the feeding of the five thousand. It is to come to its full fruition in the cross, when Jesus breaks himself to nourish the whole world. So John's readers should groan with despair as they hear that people respond to this miracle by trying to make Jesus King. The crowds are already obsessed with Jesus's miracles. They have followed him to see healings and signs, and now they have been rewarded for their persistence by another demonstration of magic. The conclusions they draw are both truthful and perverse. They assume, rightly, that here is God's chosen Messiah, but they have no idea how the Messiah will bring God's salvation. They have seen the power and wholly misunderstood it while we, thanks to John, can see its real meaning. That they are correct in their assumptions about who Jesus is is immediately reinforced by the story of the stilling of the storm and the walking on the water. Jesus is, indeed, the one who brings the power and presence of God. The creation obeys him through whom it was made – unlike us.

Learning to respond to our creator is what this passage in Ephesians is all about. To be 'rooted and grounded' (v. 17) in the love of Christ is to come back to the source of our life. It is God who makes us, with care and individuality, not just in a great and indiscriminate creative splurge, but each one given its name, its particularity. As we gradually learn to breathe the air of the Holy Spirit, filling our lungs with it, so we learn what the wind and the waves knew instinctively: that we are made to respond to God. Everywhere we look, we see the power of God at work, in all that he has made and remade and in all that he has done and is doing.

Christian praying and believing can be very small and unimaginative, as though we don't really think God can manage more than the three wishes of so many fairy tales. We need to hoard our wishes, and make sure we only ask for what we really want and don't waste the magical power. But Ephesians says, 'Don't be so silly.' It constantly widens the frame, so that our lives are put in the context of God the creator and redeemer of the world. Part of us is terrified of that power, as the disciples were terrified when they saw Jesus walking towards them on the water. If that creative power, the power of God's unimaginable love, is unleashed on the world and, even more frighteningly, is at work in us, then we are adrift beyond our limits. If we have to see the world with that shatteringly generous love, then we, and the world, will be irrevocably changed. It is not ours to control, but we could co-operate.

# Proper 13

—— ❧ ——

*Exodus 16.2–4, 9–15*
*Ephesians 4.1–16*
*John 6.24–35*

This is a very revealing set of questions and answers between Jesus and the people following him. It tells us a lot about what the people thought they were looking for in Jesus, and gives us one of Jesus's own central definitions of his work.

The theme is food, which is not surprising, considering the conversation follows very closely on the feeding of the five thousand. At the beginning of chapter 6, we are told that the people following Jesus are hoping for more healing miracles, but now, after being fed by him, they are hoping never to go without a meal again. They are quite indignant with him for slipping away, and very relieved to have caught up with him again.

We don't know very much about the people who followed Jesus. They can't have had steady nine-to-five kind of jobs, because some of them obviously followed him around for days. Perhaps they were very largely from the strand of society where the source of the next meal is a continual worry. Jesus doesn't seem to be angry with them, but he is definitely trying to make them look beyond lunch time. For many of them, this conversation is to be a turning point. Up to now they have been largely spectators and recipients, but Jesus is forcing them to think and make choices. They have followed, watched, eaten and had a really exciting time, and most of them hope it will continue. But now they are confronted with the annoying question of meaning. What do Jesus's signs and miracles tell us? By the end of this chapter of the Gospel, quite a lot of the crowd will have gone home, unwilling or unable to answer that question satisfactorily.

To begin with, they humour Jesus, though carefully skirting round the central issue. Although Jesus challenges them not to waste time on things that have no lasting value, he instantly ties that in with his own mission. 'Oh, right,' they say, 'we're on to religion. OK, so tell us about your idea of God, then.' They have sort of noticed that Jesus means them to ask about who this 'Son of Man' is, but they're not sure that they want to know the answer. But Jesus presses again. This is no abstract theological discussion from which everyone can go home with their ideas unchanged. This requires a commitment, now, to Jesus.

The people try to wriggle out of it. 'Do another miracle to help us believe,' they say. And remember, these are people who have just the day before seen Jesus feed five thousand people with five loaves and two fishes. This request could hardly be more cheeky. But Jesus will not let them pretend that they have not understood. He will not let them go home and talk only about the amazing things they have seen. Jesus's mission is not a spectator sport. 'I am the bread of life,' he says bluntly. 'Do you want it, or not?' He completely cuts across all their attempts to stop him from demanding a decision.

Isn't it strange that they don't know how to answer? When they could persuade themselves that Jesus was only talking about actual food, they knew the answer quickly enough. 'Give it to us always!' they say. But now, when it is clear what Jesus is really talking about, the crowd go quiet. They know they don't want to go hungry again, but they don't know if they want salvation.

It is terribly important to know that, about our deepest needs and desires, we can be remarkably stupid. According to Ephesians, it is one of the functions of the Church to minimize that stupidity. There is always the hope that if we stick together, somebody else will know what you don't and vice versa. Otherwise you are in danger of being as stupid as a single arm, out there on its own, thinking it can function fully. This metaphor of the Church as a body is not the only description in the New Testament of the nature of the Christian community, though it is one of the most vivid. Pretty well all the descriptions, though, have unity as one of their central themes. Unfortunately, we don't seem to have taken that in. Our natural stupidity, that doesn't know any more than that we need lunch for today and tomorrow, reasserts itself. If our salvation depends upon being one body, indwelled by the Holy Spirit, activated by Christ the head, do we want it or not? Or would we rather be the perfect arm, utterly divorced from the body, therefore utterly useless, but nonetheless proudly uncompromised by trying to live with people who are different? If Ephesians is right, that's the choice. Take it or leave it.

# Proper 14

——— ∾ ———

*1 Kings 19.4–8*
*Ephesians 4.25—5.2*
*John 6.35, 41–51*

On the grounds that there is no point in telling someone to do something if they are already doing it, the Ephesian community must be quite like a church you know well. It is interesting how much of this section is concerned with *talk*. There is a rather perfunctory mention, in verse 28, that thieving is wrong, but even that is condemned, in this context, because it is an activity destructive of community, rather than because it is innately wrong. (It clearly is, I hasten to add, but that is not the point that is being made here.)

So, apparently, the chief threat to the internal harmony of the Ephesian community is talk. Lying and anger are the main forms of talk that are destabilizing the Ephesian church, and verse 31 details the different forms that these emotions can have, while verse 32 suggests countermeasures.

But the real point of the section comes in the last verse of chapter 4 and the first two verses of chapter 5. The well-being of the Christian community is not just important because it will make us happier, or better able to market our brand product because of our excellent record for keeping our employees happy. It's more that, if we cannot build strong community, there is no point in us at all. We demonstrate that we do not understand God, and so completely undermine our witness to him, Ephesians suggests. We are called together to live as 'imitators of God'. We have come, through the gracious and costly work of God the Son, to know the Father, and to know that we are his children too. Our life together shows our family likeness, and so enables others to begin to see what God is like. That is why actions of ours that damage our common life 'grieve the Holy Spirit', whose task and goal it is to build us into the likeness of the Son, so that we too can love the Father.

Ephesians does not tell us what we are to do in cases of deep and genuine disagreement. But given this very high theology of Christian community, it is unlikely that it would take schism as anything but the most serious possible failure. What else is said to 'grieve the Holy Spirit'? To give ourselves up for one another marks us as imitators of Christ, and Christ certainly managed to do this without needing everyone to agree with him first, and admit he was right.

Although the reference in Ephesians to Christ's self-giving almost certainly refers to the cross, John's Gospel makes it poignantly clear how much else, day to day, was involved in that whole movement of self-giving, through incarnation to death and resurrection. Living constantly with those who misunderstand and misjudge is part of the daily fate of the incarnate Son of God. Here in chapter 6, Jesus is speaking vividly and with force about what he has come for, and yet people misunderstand him. It is more than honest perplexity, in some cases. It is almost as though there is a wilful determination not to understand. 'Who does he think he is?' is basically what people are asking.

Patiently, Jesus tries to explain, as he does so often in John's Gospel, that he is not making claims for himself, but simply building on what they already should know about God. God has been working, Father, Son and Holy Spirit, from our creation, to make our hearts warm to the Son incarnate, just as God has been working, from our creation, to bring us to share in his life. What Jesus is offering is something that we should instinctively recognize, which is the source of our true life.

But built into Jesus's glorious offer of himself as the bread of life is the knowledge that we will not recognize it, that we will turn away from it and choose dust and ashes and death. There is bitter irony in these words 'bread', 'life', 'flesh'. Since, wilfully and stubbornly, we choose death, rather than the life that we were made for, Jesus, with painful but irrepressible creativity, chooses death too. He chooses to be in our death, so that even as we choose death, we choose him. There is no illusion in Jesus's choice to be the bread of our life.

Why does God make this extraordinary choice? Why does he give us the power to crucify the Son, to continue, even after the death and resurrection, to grieve the Holy Spirit by our obtuse unwillingness to acknowledge our dependence upon God and upon each other? God does not need us, since he is complete in himself, Father, Son and Spirit. But perhaps it is this sheer gratuity and grace that we find most incomprehensible about God.

# Proper 15

—— ~ ——

*Proverbs 9.1–6*
*Ephesians 5.15–20*
*John 6.51–58*

'You are what you eat', so the saying goes. Our modern western culture is wise to the fact that food is not all the same, and will not all be good for you. We are now very anxious about food additives, very aware of possible allergies to food that might normally be thought nutritious. We spend a lot of time worrying, rather literally, about where the next meal is coming from. Was it organically grown? Did it start life too near a motorway? Will its deceptive rosiness mask the slow pollutants it contains? Not all cultures have quite that luxury. Our children have food fads, sometimes encouraged by us, in case of allergic reactions, but some children suck helplessly at empty paps, or scavenge the streets for almost anything that will fill the aching void in their bellies. Their version might be, 'You are *if* you eat.' We who pick and choose and read every detail of our supermarket labels still showed a tendency to be shocked when an African country recently refused food aid if it had been genetically modified. In every culture and at every time, food has been one of the main obsessions of human beings, though we might be unusual in the West in being a culture obsessed with not eating, rather than eating.

The Jewish culture into which Jesus spoke was particularly sensitive to issues of food. They already knew that their God was very interested in food. This was shown not just by the rituals and taboos surrounding food preparation, but also by a whole host of other things. The people of Israel knew that God had himself provided food for them in the desert, when they were about to starve. They knew that for certain of his servants, like Elijah the Tishbite, God sent his creatures to bring them food. They knew that food had been the cause of their separation from God, as Adam and Eve ate the apple, and that food, as symbolized by the Passover meal,

98

set them apart as the people whom God himself chose and brought out of slavery.

Jesus's eating habits were already causing some comment. He was not an ascetic like John the Baptist, and he was known to be a little indiscriminating in who he ate with (Mark 2.15ff., for example). For a people like this, the teaching of a religious leader about food would be part of how they assessed his message. So their suspicions are already slightly raised before Jesus says this particularly disgusting and outrageous thing. We who are used to reading Jesus's words as reference to the eucharist may not hear the full and shocking impact of what he says. But John's Gospel makes it completely clear that his words caused major ripples, and lost him some followers.

Their disgust and bewilderment are understandable, if you read the words as though you did not know the future history of the Church. It sounds as though Jesus is talking about violent cannibalism. Indeed, early Christians were, half-seriously, accused of cannibalism in later years, by those who heard that their central ritual involved eating flesh and drinking blood.

Unquestionably, Jesus intended to shock. The violence of his words is calculated. Throughout this chapter he has been involved in conversations with people who do not want to see what he is talking about. They are happy with his miracles. They are quite intrigued by some of his teaching, but they are still assuming that, basically, they choose. They decide whether or not he is religiously interesting and important. They tack on the bits of his teaching that they like to the system that they already live with. They come and listen when it suits them, and go back to their ordinary lives when they need to. But Jesus is not an optional extra. Jesus is life, the only possible source of it. Feeding on Jesus is our only hope. The world in which we depend upon other kinds of food is not the real world. The real world is fed only by Jesus, created in him, redeemed by him and sustained through him alone. We live wholly dependent upon the life of Jesus, which is the life of God, the source of all life.

How can Jesus make the people understand this, when they persist in seeing him as one of a number of possible options? His words are meant to force a reaction, then and now. We may be Christians, but do we actually believe, any more than Jesus's original hearers did, that 'unless you eat the flesh of the Son of Man and drink his blood, you have no life in you'? Or do we persist in choosing the bread which can only sustain the illusion of life?

# *Proper 16*

—— ∾ ——

Joshua 24.1–2a, 14–18
Ephesians 6.10–20
John 6.56–69

Peter's tale:

That's about the only time I ever remember being sure that I'd
got it right. Oh, I don't mean that I had doubts about what came
out of my mouth when I was preaching to people after the Lord
had risen. But those words never really felt like mine. I remember
Jesus saying that the Spirit would come and give us the words,
and that has certainly been my experience. When I stand up to
witness to what I have seen and heard, I know I am doing it
through a power that isn't my own. That doesn't mean that I
always get it right, or even that I always make myself clear, but
I do get the sense that the responsibility lies elsewhere. I have to
do my best, and then leave the consequences up to the Lord.

And I don't mean to be all modest when I say that's the only
time I got it right on my own. I've never been shy, and I don't
mind making a fool of myself. My mother said I started talking
almost as soon as I got out of the womb, and I haven't stopped
since! When I'm nervous or excited or happy or sad or drunk or
sober – I talk. All the others used to rely on me to start the ball
rolling. I'd say something daft to Jesus, and then they could come
in sounding judicious and sensible when they'd had a chance to
see how he reacted to what I said. I didn't mind. Every group
needs someone like me, and even if people do sometimes think
I'm an idiot, they usually like me too. Jesus did tell me off once or
twice, when I was really crass, but on the whole he was pleased
that I wasn't too scared to risk things. The others never liked to
ask him what he was doing, or what his mission was, but I just
jumped in with both feet and told him straight out that I thought
he was the Messiah. I knew all the others wanted to find out
whether or not he was, but didn't dare ask. Of course, I realize

100

now how little I understood what it means to be God's Messiah, but I was sort of right about Jesus anyway, wasn't I?

But the time I'm trying to tell you about was odd. We'd had a real rollercoaster few days. Jesus was doing the kind of miracles that make your hair stand up on the nape of your neck with a mixture of excitement and fear. He was healing people, and feeding thousands of people with hardly anything, and then there was that time when he came walking to us across the water – I'll never forget it, and I still can't describe, to this day, what it looked like, to see him *walking* on the water towards us. We hardly had any time together to talk things over because hordes of wildly excited people were following us everywhere, begging for more.

But then, suddenly, they started turning nasty. Jesus tried to talk to them, and explain what he was up to and who he was, and they hated it. They didn't understand – well, to be honest, neither did we. He kept telling us that he had to die and we had to eat him if we were to live with him in the life of God. That sounded mad and thoroughly disgusting as well. We all felt that he wasn't explaining himself at all well, and that he was deliberately putting people off, just when he was getting a real following. I still wonder if that was actually part of what he was trying to do. Perhaps he actually wanted to get rid of all those people who were determined to believe he was what they wanted him to be, and weren't prepared to listen and find out what he thought he was himself.

Anyway, that was certainly the effect he had. Lots of people stopped travelling with us that day, and stopped thinking of themselves as followers of Jesus. He'd made it just too hard for them. But even if that was what he'd expected, he was sad. I remember he turned to those of us who were left and said, 'Do you want to go, too? It isn't going to get any easier, you know. In fact, it's going to get much harder. If you think this is difficult to understand, you just wait. Why don't you go now, while the going's good?'

And that's when I said it.

'Where else could we go? You're the only one who can speak the words of life.'

I knew I was right, as I said the words, and I know it to this day.

# Proper 17

———— ~ ————

*Deuteronomy 4.1–2, 6–9*
*James 1.17–27*
*Mark 7.1–8, 14, 15, 21–23*

We rather value versatility and unpredictability in people. To say that someone is predictable is to imply that they are boring and hidebound. I suspect that this actually reflects the comparative security and dependability of a lot of our lives in the West. Most of us know where our next meal is coming from, when our next holiday will be, even quite accurately when our next baby will be born. We can afford the luxury of finding predictability boring. But that is still not the case for most of the world. Unpredictable weather can spell death, and an unplanned pregnancy starvation. No wonder that many cultures value God's immutability so highly. Even we, who think we like variety, may actually be unexpectedly hurt by friends or partners who leave us for someone new and more exciting. We say that they have acted out of character, when before we might have thought we found their whimsicality appealing. Or we travel in search of novelty and then recreate our own home wherever we go. Perhaps we are not entirely truthful with ourselves in thinking that stability is tedious. 'Yesterday, today, for ever, Jesus is the same. All may change, but Jesus never, glory to his name,' runs the chorus that has comforted many for years.

These verses from James are verses in praise of unchangingness. In God there is no change. Things from outside him cannot make God react uncharacteristically. Light does not force strange shadows from him, making him appear what he is not. God does not have to return to the drawing board each morning with his design and alter it to fit unpredicted events, and we cannot force God's hand by shouting at him.

But if this kind of language quickly degenerates into a description of God's master plan which seems to leave no space for genuine human freedom, read the rest of what James says in this chapter. He is not saying that God has a kind of gigantic crystal ball in which he has already seen everything that will ever be. Nor is he saying that we are just pieces on a celestial chessboard, destined to move only according to the rules. What he is actually saying is that nothing – nothing – nothing can make God act in a way that is not characteristic. God is so completely himself, at home with himself, at ease with himself, that he has the genuine freedom to be who he is, always. He is not trying to change to get affection or a laugh or more power. God is wholly, dynamically content. And if that sounds like a contradiction in terms, just think of the one or two genuinely happy people you know. The late, great, Metropolitan Anthony of Sourozh, for example, radiated a kind of energetic contentment that made everyone he was with feel more content to be themselves, and more determined to be better. Could that be, perhaps, a pale reflection of the nature of God?

Much modern Christian writing has misunderstood what is meant by the immutability of God, and has assumed that it makes God less loving, less personal, less like Jesus. But perhaps, in fact, God's unchangingness is a sign that God does not need to waste time worrying about himself at all, and so is wholly available, wholly present for us, in a way that no human being can ever be; because for us, some part of our own worry or insecurity always impinges, to a greater or lesser degree.

James is here exhorting us to imitate God in knowing what we are like. Unlike God, we may need to change, but even this cannot be done if we do not really know ourselves in the first place. We can, he says, know ourselves in a completely superficial way, so that we might recognize ourselves if glimpsed in a mirror, without having any idea of how we behave, or how others perceive us. Instead of looking into the mirror, we have to look, James suggests, into the steadfast nature of God, and begin to see ourselves truly. Slowly, slowly, as we get to know ourselves through God's eyes, our lives will become consistent with the great and liberating consistency of God. We will not have to vow each morning to behave with love and charity because love and charity will be what we are. At the moment they are still attributes that we can sometimes summon up and sometimes not, depending what kind of mood we are in. We need to work towards that perfect state that we see in the nature of God, where doing and being are never separated.

# Proper 18

―――― ～ ――――

*Isaiah 35.4–7a*
*James 2.1–17*
*Mark 7.24–37*

I suppose it's comforting, in an Eeyore-ish kind of way, to know that ours is not the only generation of Christians to think that belief is simply a matter of the words you use, and that it doesn't need to affect ordinary life in any way. James is writing to a Christian church that is, apparently, just like ours. The people who go to James's church are convinced enough of the claims of the gospel to call themselves Christians, and to meet regularly with others. But they don't see this as a matter that affects their fundamental understanding of the structuring of the universe. James finds this almost incredible.

His readers seem to be viewing faith as a kind of insurance policy: you probably need it as part of a sensible attempt to keep unpleasant reality at bay; in case of sickness or accident, it's nice to know that God is on your side. And surely part of the point of an insurance policy is that it allows you to carry on your normal life without any worries about the consequences of your actions? So James's congregation still like rich people better than poor people, clean people better than dirty people, well people better than sick people because, after all, who doesn't?

God doesn't, is James's alarming answer. God doesn't have favourites. God is shockingly blind to the normal measures of society. He doesn't seem to notice accents, or cost out people's clothes and treat them accordingly. He has absolutely no need to keep in with the rich and famous, or to find favour with the influential. After all, he is God.

One of the worrying consequences of this is the possibility that God doesn't realize where he belongs in our carefully planned life. He might not be aware that he is a fail-safe mechanism, to be invoked when we are up against something that we can't cope with on our own. He might, indeed, believe that he is the way, the truth and the life, and that our attempts to make him fit our way, our truth and our life are at best touchingly misplaced and at worst completely absurd.

Faith changes the way you live, James says, in that obnoxiously black and white way of his. You might feel tempted, at this point, to turn to that nice St Paul, who really understands about the importance of faith, and doesn't go droning on about having to do things as well. Dream on. Try reading Romans 6. There is no escaping the New Testament conviction that faith is a commitment to a changed way of life, because it is a commitment to trying to see the world with the eyes of God. This has enormous benefits for us personally, since God is understanding and forgiving beyond what we could ever expect or deserve. But the downside is that he is equally concerned about others. We are not his favourites. We must try to see as we are seen, James says in verse 13. We cannot expect God to use one standard of judgement on us if that is not the standard of judgement that we are using on anyone else.

Probably, however, we should give ourselves permission not always to be certain of God's standards. There are some fairly consistent clues in the New Testament and, sadly, suspicion of the lure of wealth is one of them. But there is also the fascinating story we have in Mark's Gospel, of Jesus's own vision being enlarged by his encounter with the Syro-Phoenician woman. It feels shocking to say that this woman, in her insistent need, reminded the Son of the scope of the Father's love. But the very least the story demands is to see Jesus deeply moved by the depths of the woman's faith. She is certain that God does not have favourites, and that there is always enough in his provision to go round. It is we who are stingy, not God.

Over and over again the Gospels show us Jesus interacting with those whom most societies consider marginal. Today it might be a woman who is also a gentile, and a deaf man who cannot communicate, but most of the stories are the same. They suggest that there is something about being an insider, comfortable in the world you live in, that actually makes it harder to hear God. If the world is basically treating you quite benignly, then you tend to forget that its standards may not be God's. Why would you want to be reminded of something that might end up making your life more uncomfortable?

When James says, 'beware of a faith that has not visibly changed your life', he is speaking words we have to hear, but seldom want to.

# Proper 19

———— ≈ ————

*Isaiah 50.4–9a*
*James 3.1–12*
*Mark 8.27–38*

The disciples are quite enjoying the discussion, to begin with. Everywhere they've been with Jesus, they have heard speculation. People must have asked them, over and over again, 'Who is your master? Where does he get his power from? What's he really up to?' The disciples are very tactful. They only pass on the repeatable theories they have heard. They don't say, 'Some people think you're mad, and some people think you're demon-possessed, and some people think you're a revolutionary.' No, they stick to the complimentary and religious options. They do this partly to be kind to Jesus, but partly also for their own sakes. After all, if they're his followers, they are going to be tarred with the same brush as him.

It's very easy, passing on the gossip. Lots of voices are raised with contributions to the conversation. But when Jesus asks the next question, there is sudden silence. The next question is going to commit the one who answers it. It might make him look stupid, if he gets it wrong; it might make him look overcommitted or undercommitted to Jesus. Suppose they say they think he is just a prophet, and then he tells them that he is really the great prophet Elijah, returned from the dead? Or suppose they say he's the Messiah, and he laughs and says, 'Don't be silly, I'm just a minor prophet'?

So, as usual, it is only Peter who has the courage of his convictions. He knows who he hopes Jesus is, and he doesn't care if saying it makes him look silly. His answer is right, of course, but he still looks silly.

Words are terribly important. Peter uses the word 'Messiah', and even though he has no idea at all what it means, the word is to become his whole vocation. As Jesus describes what Peter has actually said, the word, which has already shaped Jesus, is beginning to shape Peter too. He doesn't know it, but he has already accepted the definition that that word will give to his life – and death.

We don't usually believe that words have that kind of power. 'You are what you eat,' we say, but what about, 'You will be what you say'? What if our increasingly wordy and foul-mouthed world is actually choosing its destiny, with every word it utters? What if we are making ourselves vile, crude and debased, with no belief in the truth or the bindingness of words any more? As all our media sit increasingly lightly to the truth of what they report, they make truth something that we are no longer sure we can recognize. Distrust breeds. As more and more of us casually use disgusting language, we increasingly believe that others are the dirty and worthless things we say they are, and treat them accordingly.

That is what James suggests. The community to which he writes has a bad word problem. It is full of people who don't really think that words matter. You can say religious words without them affecting your lifestyle, and you can say horrible things and still call yourself a Christian, they think. But James says that your words are the things that guide your whole life. Whether you know it or not, you are judged by your words. Whether you know it or not, your words shape your future. James uses the illustration of a stream – it either gives good water or bad. It cannot do both. Words can contaminate the stream of life.

This concept of communication is so basic because God himself is the great communicator. The reading from Isaiah today pictures somebody whose ear is really attuned to the voice of God, so that he can 'sustain the weary with a word' (Isaiah 50.4). But those who constantly misuse words, and divorce them from their starting place in God, will eventually not recognize God's words – or his Word – at all. In Jesus, God's spoken word is lived and God's lived word is spoken, because in God there is never any separation between word and act. But the people around Jesus are reluctant to allow him to remake or recreate their speech. They try to make God's Word conform to their own language. When Peter speaks the word 'Messiah', he thinks he is defining Jesus. But really Jesus, the creative Word of God, is taking our words and remaking them into a language that we can again share with God. The process is painful and costly, as all three readings agree, but vital. Unless we give our language back to God, and allow him to retranslate all our ideas, we will continue to move further and further away from the truth that sets us free to communicate in God's language.

# Proper 20

—— ∾ ——

*Jeremiah 11.18–20*
*James 3.13—4.3, 7–8a*
*Mark 9.30–37*

What an emotional roller-coaster ride the disciples are on by this
stage of Jesus's ministry. Not that life with Jesus had ever been
boring, exactly, but at least they had known what they were doing.
Or they had thought they did, anyway. Whereas now, Jesus seems
to be trying to undermine everything they thought they were following him for. They should have been on an emotional high. In
Mark's Gospel, this episode is set immediately after the Transfiguration and the spectacular healing of a dramatically ill child. But
instead of building on this, Jesus takes his disciples away and makes
another attempt to explain his mission to them.

How can they possibly understand? After all, we who know the
end of the story still do not really believe that Jesus is God's way
with the world. We may say that we do, but we certainly don't act
as though we do. Instead, we act just like the disciples. We nod
wisely and bow our heads piously to the notion of the cross, and
then we go away and argue about which of us is the most important. Like the disciples, we absolutely cannot see the connection
between the power of God and the suffering and death of Jesus and,
like them, we are afraid to ask because we don't want to know the
answer. We want to get back to our interesting discussions about
real power.

It is quite easy to see why the disciples, at this point in the story,
might be arguing about which of them is the greatest. The three
who witnessed the Transfiguration might well feel superior to the
others, who had not only been left at the bottom of the mountain
but had also failed to heal the sick boy while Peter, James and John
were witnessing Jesus talking with Moses and Elijah. 'I expect we
could have healed him,' you can hear Peter saying. 'But you don't
pray any more than we do,' the others would protest.

In the middle of all these rivalries, and with the power that they have seen whizzing all around Jesus, which they long to be able to tap, how can they possibly pay attention to what Jesus is saying? How can they avoid being offended by the implication that some child they don't even know is more important to Jesus than they, who have followed him faithfully and given up so much to be his disciples?

Our society may pay lip-service to the importance of children, but they are still the ones on whom decisions are imposed, the ones who have to do as they are told. In Jesus's times, children would have had even less freedom and importance than we accord them. Jesus is deliberately choosing as his example someone with no status and no power. 'This is me,' he says, pointing to the anonymous child. 'If you want to be powerful, you won't be able to welcome someone like me.'

This is the part of Jesus's message that we – I – have most defended ourselves – myself – against. Instinctively we turn away from the belief that in this weakness and vulnerability, as in the rest of his life, Jesus is showing us the nature of God. In his healings, in his authoritative teaching, in his resurrection, we agree – there we see God's power. But in the form of a helpless child? Surely not! But the Christmas story tells us that that is precisely the route God chose to our salvation. So if we are called to be followers of Christ we, like the disciples, need to start trying to follow this path too. We might need to start by approaching unexpected people with caution and awe. The tramp, the cleaning lady, the checkout assistant, the bus conductor, the kind of people who are generally almost invisible in our lives – might they be the ones in whom we welcome Christ?

But if this is frightening and hard, it is also liberating and easy. We do not need to earn our place any more. We do not need to struggle to be 'best', to be important, to be greatest. We do not have to be at the centre of everything, frantically trying to prove that we are interesting. In the world of God's strange mercy, the minute we let go of this desperate obsession with ourselves, we are where we should be – beloved, chosen and free. No effort of ours can do it, but it doesn't need to. God has done all that needs doing, through the death and life of the Son. The Father welcomes us, helpless children, as though we were that other child, the Son. All we need to do is practise doing the same for others.

# Proper 21

—— ❧ ——

*Numbers 11.4–6, 10–16, 24–29*
*James 5.13–20*
*Mark 9.38–50*

Moses has had enough of the people. He has led them out of slavery, and they have been saved and protected by God's strength throughout. They have seen the waters of the sea part just for them, they have seen water springing from the rock, just for them, and they have had food provided in the middle of the desert, simply because God is their protector. But still they whine. Now they don't like the kind of food God is giving them. They choose to forget that they were slaves in Egypt, and prefer instead to remember all the delicious meals that they had. They don't look around the barren, lifeless desert and praise God that they are alive at all. Instead they dream up menus, and blame Moses because they have tantalized themselves into a bad temper.

In other words, they are still living as slaves. They do not expect to make decisions or provisions for themselves. They look to Moses as to their former masters, without love or loyalty or thought of his feelings. They simply expect him to tell them what to do, and to provide for them, and when he fails, instead of taking any initiative themselves, they grumble.

So what happens now is the next stage in their liberation. They are physically no longer slaves, but mentally little has changed. Now God and Moses are going to make them take some responsibility for themselves. Now God takes some of the task he had given to Moses and shares it among the 70 elders of the people. From now on, they are to share Moses's responsibility for God's people, and begin to equip themselves for the freedom to which God has called them. With freedom goes power, but also responsibility. You cannot prophesy and heal one moment, sharing in the glorious power and purpose of God, and go off and sin the next, and pretend that the one is your responsibility and the other not.

110

Both Jesus and James make this connection. The two sections of today's Gospel reading don't seem immediately related, unless this is the key. In the first section, some people who are not immediately part of Jesus's circle have discovered the power of his name. They have accepted a share in the power of God, and Jesus says that a lot more goes with that, whether they know it or not. They have proved that through Jesus, God acts, and so they have become part of God's mission in Christ. They cannot step in when they want the buzz and excitement of power, and step out again when it comes to Jesus's teaching and his demands upon their whole lives. Either God does act in power through Jesus, or he doesn't. You can't have one bit without the other.

If these people who were healing in Jesus's name were doing it lightly, thinking they would just try it out for fun, then the second section of today's reading would have terrified them. In stepping into partnership with the power of God in Christ, they have stepped into one vision of the world and its purpose. And its demands are fierce and overriding. Nothing must ever tempt you to imagine a different course for yourself or the world. By exercising the power of God, you have become free, adult sharers in his mission, and have accepted responsibility for God's people.

These are sombre words for all those who try out God's power, intending to remain as slaves or children, intending always to run to someone else, or give up, or whine when things go wrong. If you accept God's protection and provision, you enmesh yourself immediately with God's people, with care for them and responsibility for them.

James speaks of the joyful power given to Christians in the name of Jesus. We have been given a share of God's saving and healing power, every one of us. This is not something to be reserved for heroes and saints, like Moses or Elijah, but is poured on us all, through Christ and the Spirit. But that immediately makes us all 'elders'. It's no longer somebody else's job to care for the sick, or to notice the lost, it is ours. But if this is burdensome, it also has its satisfactions. Perhaps it feels most irksome when we just sit and worry about it, instead of getting out there and doing it. James suggests that when you pray for the sick, search for the lost, live in close and truthful community with God's people, then you know what you are doing and why. You are sharing in God's great mission to bring his people out of the slavery of sin and death, and into his glorious kingdom.

# Proper 22

—— ～ ——

*Genesis 2.18–24*
*Hebrews 1.14; 2.5–12*
*Mark 10.2–16*

It is very tempting to go straight for the second half of the passage from Mark's Gospel set for today, and just speculate, if possible with some sentimentality, about what Jesus meant by 'theirs is the Kingdom of Heaven'. After all, the two halves of today's reading may not be very directly related – it may just be that the author thought, 'A saying about marriage and a saying about children go well together.' And it *is* endlessly fascinating to think about what particular quality children have that makes them such suitable inheritors of the Kingdom. But I think the two paragraphs may have more of a common theme than immediately emerges.

The question about marriage has obviously taken a lot of hard and cunning work to formulate and, interestingly, it seems to assume that the questioners did know that Jesus had rather a hard line about divorce. So they design a question to get Jesus into trouble, preferably with both religious and national institutions. Deuteronomy 24 assumes that divorce is bound to happen, and the Herod family were notorious for their broken marriages. (They try the same kind of tactics again in Mark 12. You can't help feeling that there was a minor industry in thinking up questions to trap Jesus.)

What Jesus does with the question is to open it up into a broader discussion of what scripture says about the purpose of creation. He does not say that Moses was wrong in allowing divorce, but he does say that the kind of technical discussions that focus on when divorce is acceptable and when it's not miss the point. He asks his questioners to look back to the Genesis creation story and remember that marriage is a gift from God. In all the glorious profusion of the new creation, with animals all around, still God sees that the creature God has made is lonely. It is very tempting to read this passage from Genesis 2 in terms of the slightly different narrative of

Genesis 1, and to add in the Christian belief in God as Trinity, and also to say that the creature on its own was not yet in God's image. To be in God's image, it needed to be distinct but united.

At the very least, Jesus is saying that human marriage is deep in the purposes of God, and that something of what God is trying to do in creating is lost in Moses's reluctant allowing of divorce in some circumstances.

To allow divorce because our hearts have become too hard to recognize God the Trinity at work in our relations is certainly not the only way in which we fail to understand why God created us. Jesus, who comes to ransom the world with his life because it can no longer find its own way back to God, surely knows this. But over and over again he tries to incite and excite people with a vision of the reality of God. Human religiousness is, instinctively, an attempt to harness God. What we long for from God is security and certainty. But the problem is that we look for that in places that are actually not God. Our security lies in the fact that we are utterly beloved by God, and that he wills for us to share his life, in his image. But we are constantly trying to bargain with God. 'If I do this, this and this, will you promise me a long and happy life?' What Jesus is saying is that negotiating about when God will allow us to break his image in us without minding too much is stupid. Of course we will break it, over and over again, as we crucified the Son. But if we can catch something of the vision of the nature of God and his purpose for us then the whole debate can be conducted on different grounds. It will no longer be our aim to justify ourselves in God's eyes, but to see how we can bring him our broken lives for healing.

And what does this have to do with the children? The disciples are treating the children as a problem. They are anxious to stop them from pestering Jesus. He is in the middle of a serious debate that may have ongoing consequences, the disciples themselves are uneasy about his teaching on divorce, and now these children come barging in. But Jesus sees the children as a gift. Is it too simplistic to say that they will inherit the Kingdom because it never occurs to them that they won't? They don't expect to earn it, but they have sensed that they give Jesus joy.

# Proper 23

—— ◇ ——

*Amos 5.6–7, 10–15*
*Hebrews 4.12–16*
*Mark 10.17–31*

Is it just me, or are the readings actually getting harder at this time of year? Not only more difficult to understand, but also more sombre? Certainly, today's reading from Hebrews has taken large quantities of caffeine, and even so I'm not sure that I've got to the bottom of it. So if anyone out there has the key, I'd love to hear it.

The first half, Hebrews 4.12 and 13, is part of the argument that has been going on from the start of chapter 3. You can tell this because it is regularly punctuated by the phrase 'Today, if you hear his voice, do not harden your hearts' (cf. 3.7, 13, 15; 4.7). That is a quotation from Psalm 95, and in the Psalm it is clearly talking about the years of whining in the wilderness. It contains an underlying warning – that it is possible to see the wonderful works of God and yet not really believe in them as saving. How could the people whom God had liberated ever forget the parting of the waters, the pillar of cloud and of fire, the water and the manna? How could they ever believe that those were just passing phases in God's mercy, and convince themselves that God had lost interest and gone off and left them? But they did manage it, according to Deuteronomy and Numbers. Hebrews is arguing that if Moses was great and performed great deeds in God's name, then Jesus is even greater. We mustn't be tempted to lack of trust, like our forefathers.

So then, at the start of the passage set for today, the warning that has been fairly safely anchored in the past, in stories of our foolish ancestors, suddenly comes home. The rather rambling style of the previous chapter and a half, with its clauses, sub-clauses and quotations, suddenly flashes into life like the sword it describes.

What is this sharp, 'two-edged sword' that can pierce through things that you thought were completely welded together, and see through to a reality even you didn't know you were concealing from yourself? The verses that follow make it clear that this living, active word is primarily Jesus, our great High Priest. But I think it also requires us to hear that in this particular context of perceptive, eagle-eyed judgement, it is Jesus speaking the word 'Today'. 'Today, if you will hear his voice' has been the refrain running through the last chapter and a half. It is a word requiring immediate response. It cannot take its time and talk about yesterday, and it cannot say, 'Hang on, let's see what happens tomorrow.' 'Today' is now or never.

And then the second half of this reading from Hebrews becomes less comforting, rather than more. Usually we read it as saying that Jesus understands our weaknesses and so he'll overlook them more easily. But notice it is also saying that, yes, he does understand our weaknesses, but he didn't give into them. The Israelites in the wilderness could just about argue that God didn't know what it was like to be hungry, thirsty and frightened, otherwise he might be a bit more understanding about their complaining. We have no such excuse.

It is interesting to see Jesus, the sharp two-edged sword, discerning exactly where the knife must go into the man who asks what he must do to inherit eternal life. Jesus looks at him and says 'Today' to the one thing the man cannot bear to do today. This is a man who is, by all standards, good, and he truly believed that there was no space between soul and spirit, joint and marrow where the sword of judgement could go in. But Jesus sees it, and says 'Today'. And the man goes away, shocked and grieving.

But notice that although Jesus has found the place of deceit in this man, he has done it with love (Mark 10.21). He does not let the disciples mock him, and he makes it clear that he knows how hard a thing he has asked. So much so that the disciples begin to panic about their own position. This man goes away by himself, either to accept or reject that 'Today'. But Hebrews suggests that we turn to the Word and ask for help. There is no point in trying to pretend in front of this living, active judge, but if 'Today' is the day of testing, it is also the day of mercy. There is no possibility of persuading the judge to let you in on your own merits, because for every one of us there was a 'Today' that we turned away from, and heard it as 'next week', 'next month', 'never'. So Hebrews recommends the bold approach – no concealment, relying only on the great High Priest.

# Proper 24

—— ∾ ——

*Isaiah 53.4–12*
*Hebrews 5.1–10*
*Mark 10.35–45*

There is an extraordinary consistency in what the New Testament tells us about the mission of Jesus Christ. At the heart of all the great biblical accounts of why the Son comes and how he saves us is the cross. No New Testament writer is tempted to underplay the suffering of Jesus and concentrate only on his teaching and his resurrection. Our human religious needs remain deeply suspicious of this strange way God has chosen to operate. We long to jump straight to the security and joy that we think God is supposed to be there to provide.

So James and John's request to Jesus is a natural one, and has rather better motives than many of ours. After all, they are taking it for granted that Jesus will, indeed, be reigning in glory one day soon; they are aware that there may well be some kind of a struggle and they are happy to play their part. They answer with confidence that, yes, of course they can share Jesus's cup and baptism. They'll fight by him with the best. But their main focus is the future, when all the nasty stuff will be over, and they will be on the winning side. Their concept of 'the winning side' has not been influenced at all by the conversation they have just had (Mark 10.32–35), in which Jesus tries to tell them what must happen to him.

The other disciples are indignant with James and John, so that Jesus has to sit them all down and tell them, in very simple language, what the values of a Christian disciple are to be. So what James, John and any other Christian disciple asks of Jesus, if we ask to share in his glory, is a life of service and suffering. However plain Jesus's language, you get the impression that the disciples didn't take it on board, but hurried on, saying, 'Yes, yes, but *after* that we get the reward, right?'

116

But according to Hebrews, the service and suffering *are* the reward. This is how God rewards the Son for his obedience, by putting him at the service of human beings for ever.

Hebrews takes us through this slowly and carefully, because it is a hard idea, and one we don't like the sound of. 'It's like this,' Hebrews says. 'You know what high priests do, don't you?'

A priest, according to Hebrews, is someone chosen – and the implication seems to be that the choice is made both by God and by us – to handle the relationship between God and people. The fact that he or she is chosen is the main qualification, the other one being that a priest is not essentially different from other human beings. Priestly work is done as much on the priest's own behalf as for others. So there is no particular merit in being chosen to be a mediator.

When Jesus takes on this role for us, Hebrews says, he knows that. He does not expect to be honoured for his priestly task, but simply responds in obedience to the call, as all human priests do. Jesus, like all priests, knows human need and human dependence upon God for salvation because he, like all others, knows weakness and human frailty. Although Hebrews is unequivocal about the fact that, unlike all other human beings, Jesus does not actually fall into sin (cf. 4.15), it is equally clear that he could have done. Such a possibility is not ruled out in advance by Jesus's divine and human nature, but is learned through struggle. Jesus learns the will of God, just like us, only better. So while ordinary human priesthood learns where God keeps the sticking plaster, Jesus's priesthood becomes the source of complete healing. It makes room not just for little drips of God's mercy but for the whole raging torrent of God's creative salvation. All the little devices which we have, up to now, thought of as 'priestly', devices that are to keep us more or less in God's favour without changing too much, all of these now become obsolete. 'Priesthood' tries to bring God and humanity close enough to come to some kind of understanding, but Jesus brings God and humanity together in dynamic unity, so that God's salvation can never be misunderstood again. This is Jesus's 'reward' – his 'priesthood', learned in suffering and obedience, will last for ever. Perhaps that was not the kind of glory that James and John had in mind, but through the eternal priesthood of Christ we too can offer the fruits of his priesthood to a hungry world.

# Proper 25

———— ∾ ————

*Jeremiah 31.7–9*
*Hebrews 7.23–28*
*Mark 10.46–52*

Some theologies sound a bit vague about what happens to Jesus after the resurrection. His work is completed, once for all, on the cross, he is vindicated by the Father through the resurrection, and that's that. Then, depending on your point of view, either the Holy Spirit takes over or the Bible does or else human morality does, with pious references to the Jesus who is now conveniently not there to be checked with. (I am, of course, exaggerating, but bear with me.) The Holy Spirit knows about the cross but that's all in the past now, and the present job of believers is to tap into the power that the Holy Spirit has to offer, and not to talk about that nasty old cross too much. The Bible, too, knows about the cross, since it tells about it at great length, but its present role is to give to believers a certainty and power that is not at all unlike that delivered by the Holy Spirit, though without the choruses. Human morality expects our own will-power to deliver the goods. It talks about the cross as something that really could have been and should be avoided, if only we will follow Jesus's example and be thoroughly nice to each other and non-judgemental.

As I said, I am exaggerating and caricaturing. No one I know actually espouses any of the post-Jesus theologies I have just outlined, though they do sometimes come quite close. But the basic thing that all these caricatures share, which is an ever-present danger, is to forget, imaginatively, that Jesus is not an aberration, but our only real clue to the nature of God. All these unreal theologies assume that Jesus is basically in the past. They may pay theoretical lip-service to him, but their view of God has not been fundamentally altered by the life, death and resurrection of Jesus. Fundamentally, we continue to believe that God is there to deliver what we need.

And, of course, that is true. God is indeed there to deliver what we need. The only problem is that we don't know what that is, and we constantly confuse what we want with what we need.

Does the blind man in Mark 10 *need* to see? Many blind people would argue not. Being blind is a way of life, different from that of the sighted, but not worse, certainly not in religious terms. What is it that Bartimaeus *needs* from this encounter with Jesus? Does it perhaps lie in that last verse of today's reading? Jesus tells him that his faith has made him well, and Bartimaeus responds by following Jesus. The need Jesus sees in him is his need to be a faithful disciple, a need that he doesn't believe he can ever fulfil and hasn't even voiced to himself. He is lucky enough to find that what he wants and what he needs coincide. The thing he is prepared to admit that he wants – his sight – leads into what he needs, which is a certainty that he is worthy and able to follow Jesus, that his faith is up to the task. Actually, there was no particular reason why he shouldn't, as a blind person, be a disciple, but he couldn't believe that. Jesus gives him charge of his own choices, and he instantly chooses to follow.

Hebrews argues that that discernment, which we see over and over again in the earthly Jesus, continues to be his vocation for ever, as it always was and always will be. Hebrews calls it 'priesthood', and links it for ever to our salvation. Jesus's work, completed once for all on the cross, makes him the means by which we can approach God in our need for ever. Just as the earthly Jesus looked at people, called them and challenged them to recognize their true need, so Jesus our intercessor continues to do. This is not passive passing-on of superficial requests to a rather bored God, but a genuine gateway between what we think we need and what God calls us into.

'It is fitting', Hebrews 7.26 says, 'that we should have such a high priest.' Why is it? What is so fitting about this Son of God, who has done what none of us, priest or otherwise, is capable of doing, and offered perfect obedience to God in our human form? What is fitting about that? It is fitting because that is what we need. We need to be what we are made to be and called to be, which is God's children, sharing the love of Father, Son and Holy Spirit. 'What do you want?' Jesus asks, and keeps asking, until we see that what we need is to follow him.

*Sundays Before Advent*

# The Fourth Sunday Before Advent

—— ⁓ ——

*Deuteronomy 6.1–9*
*Hebrews 9.11–14*
*Mark 12.28–34*

Person A:

Do I love God? Well, why should I? What's God ever done for me? I've worked hard all my life and nobody's ever given me a thing. There are people out there born with everything they'll ever need – they can love God if they like. They can sing songs to God as though he was their boyfriend, and weep with joy at how good it makes them feel. God's for people who don't need to fight and cheat just to stay alive. Is it right that some people never have to do a hand's turn and are surrounded by people who love and admire them, while some of us can barely keep ourselves alive by working twenty-four hours a day, and everybody despises us? The law's there, like God, to protect the people who have.

I was doing quite a good day's work, picking pockets in the crowd the other day. They were all gathered round this man, Jesus. I've made quite a good living out of him, because he draws a crowd wherever he goes, and they forget to keep their hands on their wallets. Well, I nearly got caught because I got too interested in the discussion. They were talking about the law and about loving God, and they seemed to think that if you love God and you love your neighbour, then you've kept the law. I must remember that one, next time I'm up in front of the magistrate. So I said to this snooty-looking woman, standing listening to them, 'Give us a kiss, show how much you love God.' She gave me a really dirty look, but some people laughed. I felt quite pleased with myself, till I realized I'd made them turn and look at me, which isn't professional, for a pickpocket. I had to scarper. But as I walked home, I got quite angry, thinking about the discussion. When people start giving me their wallets before I take them, I'll believe they love God and their neighbours, not before. I can't start being all soppy to other people first, or what would I live on?

122

Person B:

I was just doing the shopping when I saw a crowd of people standing round Jesus, listening to him talking to some scribe. I stopped to have a look. I've heard Jesus before, and although I don't agree with him, I find him quite interesting. I mean, he was saying today that all you have to do is love God and love your neighbour and you can forget the rest. Well, obviously that's nonsense, isn't it? I mean, naturally I love God, though I find it a bit embarrassing to have such words bandied about. After all, that's rather personal, isn't it? I know I've always tried to do what is right, and have often consulted my minister about exactly what is and what isn't allowed on the Sabbath. But surely that's far more important than all this nonsense about 'love'? And I hope I've always been a good neighbour. I keep my house and yard clean and quiet, and I give charity to the real poor. Obviously, you can't let yourself be put upon and exploited by people, like that nasty, dirty chap who tried to get a laugh by asking me to kiss him, to show my love. People like that can't be loved, they don't understand the meaning of the word. No, I'm confident that I've done my best by living a decent life and keeping myself to myself. All that nonsense about love is just a way of ducking out of our responsibilities.

Person C:

I don't know what made me agree with Jesus. I think I just felt he could do with a kind word. People had been questioning him and tricking him and arguing with him all day. When I asked my question about what's the most important commandment, I could see he thought I was doing the same. But I wanted everyone listening to think about what they were doing. They weren't trying to please God, they were just trying to make Jesus's life a misery. His answer was exactly right. From what I've heard, that's just what he tries to do. He tries to get people to see God as a loving God, worth loving in return, and he tries to get people to treat each other with forgiveness and care. I don't know why that makes them all so mad. But he looked so tired, that I just said, 'You *are* right, you know. Don't ever let them make you doubt it.' I'll never forget how he looked at me. Such gratitude, for such a small thing. I felt really warmed, as though God's sun had suddenly shone right on me.

# The Third Sunday Before Advent

—— ≈ ——

*Jonah 3.1–5, 10*
*Hebrews 9.24–28*
*Mark 1.14–20*

Hebrews is convinced that the work of Jesus is completed in the cross. And not just the work of the Son of God, but the whole providential work of God in creating us in the first place. The cross of Christ is 'the end of the age'. Nothing more can ever happen that will change what God has done for us, or replace our triumphant and suffering judge with some other. Remember how this letter starts, like the Gospel of John, with the big picture. Before all else, the Son is with the Father in creating and sustaining the world. He is 'the reflection of God's glory and the exact imprint of God's very being' (Hebrews 1.3). It is vital to remember this setting in all that Hebrews goes on to say about the High Priesthood of Christ. Christ's dealings with us are part of God's eternal creative design, and the glory and imprint of God is as much to be found in the cross as in the worship of the angels. The cross of Christ is the denouement, it is where God intended to lay bare the plot. Any careful reader, Hebrews argues, could see all the clues and be prepared. There is a great urgency in Hebrews, as the author pulls images and quotations from the Jewish scriptures and from the religious practices that his readers would have been familiar with, and tries to show that each is a hint, a shadow, a preparation, however poor, for God's great work of salvation.

The same kind of urgency rings through today's other readings. Jonah gets up, obedient at last, to walk across the great city of Nineveh and warn of God's judgement; and Simon, Andrew, James and John throw in their lot with Jesus, little knowing what consequences it will have.

There is, of course, a huge difference in what Jonah proclaims and in what makes the disciples follow Jesus. Jonah is proclaiming judgement. 'It's too late!' he shouts, 'You are going to pay for your wicked lives. You and your city will be destroyed!' You can hear both the relish and the uncertainty in what he was saying. This is what he hopes will happen, but will it?

Jesus, on the other hand, is offering an alternative. Jonah wants people to suffer for their sins, but Jesus apparently wants them to change and hear 'good news'. According to Mark, there are two elements to this good news – the general and the particular. The general is that 'the Kingdom of God has come near', and the particular is that specific invitation to the disciples, 'You, come and make it come near for others.'

In a way, Jonah too is saying, 'The Kingdom of God has come near', but for him God's rule is punitive, and there is nothing that anyone can do about it. Much to his annoyance, he turns out to be wrong in that. God, the King, makes room for the second, specific invitation that Jonah leaves out. 'Make a difference,' God adds, in effect. He leaves room, as Jonah doesn't, for the people of Nineveh to change.

Hebrews is not saying 'The kingdom of God has come near.' It is saying, 'God is ruling, now.' But although completeness and finality are central to Hebrews' theology of the cross, it is clear that there is still an expectation that we will join in – that like the people of Nineveh, we will repent, and like the disciples, we will become fishers of men.

But if the work of God is done and completed in Christ, why must we still do it? I suppose the answer lies partly in Jonah. We still do not, in our heart of hearts, think that God knows what he is up to, and so we are still in the process of repentance. Jonah longs for God to judge with his own standards of judgement, which are perfectly good and learned from good religious sources. But he wants God to be just and to preserve his honour and greatness – not just Jonah's but God's own. That's what we just do not understand, that God's honour and greatness lie in his total faithfulness to what he has always been and always will be – the God who made us for himself. Jonah would have been horrified at the idea of God dying on the cross, and Jonah has never been alone in this. But if God is really the maker and ruler of the world, then he alone knows how it works. This is how it is done, Hebrews says. Nothing else works, only this. It is not God who has to change until he learns to leave out the cross. We have to repent until we hear it as good news.

# The Second Sunday Before Advent

——— ❧ ———

*Daniel 12.1–3*
*Hebrews 10.11–25*
*Mark 13.1–8*

All of today's readings are set against the background of a disintegrating world, and all see that as something joyful. Daniel and Mark seem to be talking about the future, though there is no indication about how far away that future is – certainly close enough to impact on present behaviour. Pretty well every historical era has read the descriptions in Daniel and Mark as closely describing its own circumstances, and pretty well every era has then given in to the temptation of second-guessing God's judgement. But that is precisely what all the passages deplore.

Daniel speaks of the time of deliverance as accompanied by 'anguish' – such a strong word, yet certainly describing the lives of many in our time, living and dying with poverty, war, disease, torture and manifold injustices. To long for a prince and protector is natural, just as natural as it is to assume that the role of such a person is to condemn our enemies, those who have made our lives such anguish. But what Daniel longs for is a time when wisdom and righteousness will be visible. With utter profundity and simplicity, he identifies the missing ingredients that make it possible for us to inflict anguish on one another. We do not recognize wisdom and righteousness. They do not blaze across our skies. People argue with one another about what is right or wise, and bury wisdom and righteousness deeper and deeper underground. Daniel's vision of deliverance is of a time when wisdom and righteousness are the lights in the sky, by which we make our every movement, wholly clear and unarguable. Under those lights, we will not need to condemn or praise one another, because the light itself will make the judgement clear. Daniel does not long primarily to be justified and to see his enemies suffer, but he longs to know what is right and good.

What the disciples long to know is 'When?' But they don't get an answer. If you notice, the disciples very often have their eyes fixed on the future. They are aware that they are part of something important, but a lot of the time it doesn't feel important in a way that they can identify. Now, finally, Jesus seems to be talking about revolutionary change. 'At last,' they say. 'So, when's it going to happen, and how can we be sure that we're ready for action when the time comes? What will the signal be?'

Frustratingly, Jesus simply describes to them the world that they, and we, have to live in. And as in Daniel's time of anguish, what is missing is any way of being really sure where the truth lies. Many different factions will be claiming to represent the work of Christ, and every side in every conflict will be sure that right is on their side only. Simple realism suggests that Christian disciples will not always get it right. Some of us will be 'led astray', and we will not always be able to resist being alarmed. You have to read the rest of chapter 13 to find out what strategy Jesus recommends, but I will give you a clue. It is a really difficult one, and it involves an alert restfulness and concentration on the figure of Jesus that has certainly not always characterized the Christian Church, and generally doesn't today. We are still much more prone to shout 'When? When will you come, Lord, and show the rest of the world that I'm right and they're wrong?'

But Hebrews recommends the exact same strategy as Mark. Concentrate on Jesus. In the work of Jesus, everything is already accomplished. We may not always see and feel that, caught as we are in the middle of the anguish, and Hebrews does not want immunity from reality for us. It says we must step into Jesus, into the suffering, torn flesh that is our hope and our reality. The assurance that we have in Christ Jesus is not an assurance of protection or tranquillity, nor even a fail-safe method for discerning wisdom and righteousness, but just a total dependence upon the faithfulness of God. The judgement is not ours. It will not fail if we are not at the centre of it. The work we are given is almost insultingly small, and yet we are quite incapable of doing even that much. Hebrews says we have to learn to live together, even with those we have not chosen, in love and kindness, 'encouraging one another' (Hebrews 10.24–5). We would much rather charge around, wielding judgement in God's name, but remember that in Mark, Jesus says that is just what imposters do. Christian disciples work at living together in Christ.

# Christk the King

—— ❧ ——

*Daniel 7.9–10, 13, 14*
*Revelation 1.4b–8*
*John 18.33–37*

Philip Pullman's brilliant *His Dark Materials* trilogy ends with the words 'and then we'll build . . . The republic of heaven.' This is the vision that Lyra holds out to us after all she has learned and suffered – that human beings must and can learn to live wisely and unselfishly and build worlds that help others to do the same. There is no place for God in Lyra's picture, because a concept of God would, according to what Lyra has seen, automatically undermine her vision of a human republic of heaven. Throughout the trilogy it has become clear that 'God' is a cipher that power-hungry people use to justify violence and to impose their will on others. 'God's' followers never have to give an account of themselves, or answer to others for their actions, because they are all justified in the name of their service to God, the ruler.

This is a critique that all Christians should take seriously. Do we, indeed, use the notion of God's rule actually to impose our own? Do we demand, in God's name, the power and respect that we long for ourselves? Do we impose our understanding of the world on those weaker than ourselves, and tell them that it is God's understanding? I'm afraid that in the past the answer has often been 'Yes', and still is. The readings for today focus on Christ as King, and they are a severe challenge, to Christians first and foremost. They suggest that this most vital and central fact about Jesus, whom we believe to be 'the image of the invisible God', is one that we have not taken into our hearts and minds at all. It is the most counter-intuitive thing about the Christian concept of God, and our systems of belief and behaviour and organization barely reflect it in any way.

The reading from Daniel starts off with a picture of power that is reasonably in line with our undisturbed non-Christian understanding of power. Perhaps, nowadays, we would prefer our ruler not to be called 'the Ancient One', but at least there are thrones and fire and innumerable bowing servants. But then what happens? An ordinary human being, who looks very like the rest of us, comes to the awesome throne, and instantly the fire and throne and bowing crowds fade, and we wait to see how they will be manifested in this unprepossessing human figure.

So then the reading from Revelation takes up the story. Now we have seen how this human figure was to exercise dominion. He came to love us and die for us. His dying, Revelation says, has made us free people, who can exercise our freedom to act as he did, in service.

The reading from St John's Gospel makes the point even more graphically, because it has two pictures of power face to face. Pilate's power we recognize. Pilate exercises power over these squabbling people, whom he really can't be bothered to understand. They have brought a man to him and, although Pilate knows the charges are trumped up, that is not his concern. He goes straight to the only point that is of interest to him: 'Are you challenging my power?' And he reads Jesus's answer – rightly – as a 'Yes'. He is too impatient to hear exactly why, but he is surely right to pounce on that central word, 'King'. If Jesus is King, then Pilate is not.

If Pilate had really listened to the nuances of what Jesus was saying, would it have changed his mind? Jesus's kingship, after all, has left Pilate's kind apparently largely untouched. Jesus himself points out that his followers are hardly acting like revolutionaries, bent on setting up their own king. But when Jesus offers to explain to Pilate exactly what his kingship is, Pilate doesn't care. He is obsessed with the one word, 'King'. To him, it means only one thing, and that is a thing that he longs for and would commit any perjury and injustice for – power.

But what Jesus is offering as a description of his own kingship is truth – reality, you might say. Revelation calls it 'the Alpha and Omega, who was and is and is to come'. If the actual reality of the world, from its creation to its end, is like Jesus, then this strange human obsession with power is an aberration. It has no ability to create, to redeem or to sanctify. Jesus's challenge to Pilate's kind of power is too slow and subtle for many of us, who long to use the weapons of worldly power to force victory for God. But if Jesus is the truth, then any other way is falsehood, and will fail. Reality, as it was and is and is to come, is shaped by a different kingship.

*YEAR C*

*Advent*

# The First Sunday of Advent

—— ≈ ——

*Jeremiah 33.14–16*
*1 Thessalonians 3.9–13*
*Luke 21.25–36*

Intelligent waiting seems to be the theme of these three readings – not a bad theme for the start of Advent, but definitely to be distinguished from Aunt Juley in Forster's *Howard's End*, who goes through life overprepared. The point of Advent is to learn God's characteristics so as to recognize him when he comes, not to be so armoured against life that we never really experience anything.

It is hard to believe that today's reading comes from Jeremiah. From Jeremiah, the prophet of doom, one of the most depressing reads in the Bible, comes this lyrical piece, full of hope and trust. Jeremiah has spent the whole of his life telling Israel things they did not want to hear, and watching the destruction of the nation and the division of the people. In the first chapter of Jeremiah, we are told that he was aware of his prophetic calling as pre-dating his earliest memories. We are also told that the only way that he will be able to speak God's terrible judgement on his people is to become 'an iron pillar and a bronze wall' (Jeremiah 1.18) – God will protect him, but at the cost of separating him from the love and companionship of his own people. In today's reading, Jeremiah has been imprisoned by his own King for being right. The enemies of Jerusalem are besieging the city, as Jeremiah had said they would, and suddenly he is filled with hope. At last Jeremiah is allowed to tell people that God's judgement does not undo his earlier promise to Israel. If they wait, watch, endure, and try to see the hand of God at work, they will be preparing themselves and the people for the time when 'Judah will be saved and Jerusalem will live in safety' (v. 16). Did people hear the word of hope from the prophet of doom? Find out for yourselves.

The passage from Thessalonians is a passage full of relief. For once

Paul, the man full of the white-hot confidence of the convert, has been uncertain about his mission. Did it work? Did the Thessalonians remember what he taught them? Were they still constant? Paul had got so edgy that he had finally sent Timothy to find out, and Timothy has come back with good news. So now Paul can relax – as far as Paul ever does – and express his joy in these new Christians. But Paul is never one to give praise and leave it at that. His prayer for the Thessalonians is that they will use their time to prepare for their final meeting with God. There is no time for complacency, every minute is vital. In fact, Paul seems to have given his readers such a jolt of urgency that they seem, from the later correspondence with them, to have given up everything else in order to concentrate on Jesus' second coming. Paul has to write again later to tell them that they do have to get on with their normal lives while they prepare for God's arrival.

Luke seems to have taken on Jeremiah's normal tone. Normally, we associate Luke with heart-warming stories of women and children. It is Luke who tells us about John the Baptist's mother, and who gives us the Magnificat. It is Luke who provides the shepherds and sheep, the stable and the manger, so many of the props of the nativity play. But those who only see the picturesque side of Luke need to read a little more carefully.

The fig tree is the key to all three of today's passages. Just as we know how to watch for the signs that mark the changing of the seasons, so we have to train to be people who can recognize the signs of the coming redemption. Luke also has the wonderfully vivid picture of the Christian standing up like a dog sniffing the air for the familiar smell of the master, even in the middle of distress and confusion. The irony of this is, of course, that Jesus is talking to his disciples just a short time before his arrest and death, an event that they were wholly unprepared for, so the Gospel writers tell us. Interpreting the signs of the times is not an easy task.

Jeremiah and Luke are both talking about seeing the signs in times of turmoil, but Paul is talking into a situation of growth and joy, and trying to keep the note of urgency. So how do we wait intelligently, noting the signs, sniffing the air, yet also preparing ourselves to wait it out? Well, the three passages suggest that the key is to know what you are preparing *for*. In Advent, we are waiting for God's arrival, so our task is to make sure we will recognize him when he comes.

# *The Second Sunday of Advent*

———— ∾ ————

*Malachi 3.1–4*
*Philippians 1.3–11*
*Luke 3.1–6*

The passage from Malachi and the passage from Luke go together well. At first glance, the alternative reading from Baruch (5.1–9) matches the Luke passage even better, since Luke and Baruch both seem to be quoting the same passage from Isaiah but, in fact, the contexts of the Malachi passage and the verses from Luke are more thought-provoking.

In Malachi, there is an argument going on between God and his people. At the end of chapter 2, Malachi says that the people have wearied God, and they ask indignantly what they have done. Malachi replies that they have called into question God's justice, and so God's very character. They have said, 'All who do evil are good in the sight of the LORD. Where is the God of justice?'

In this context, the verses set for today's reading are in the nature of a threat. It is hard to hear them like that, because generations of us can hear them only with Handel's music behind them, sounding very jolly and Christmassy. But if you look at them carefully, they are answering the people's scornful question. God is a righteous God and his will ensures that righteousness prevails.

So God will send his messenger and the people may well live to regret it. They are looking for the Lord, full of their own grievances, wanting to hold him to account, but they may find that it is they who are to be judged, not God. They are to be purified and refined by fire until they recognize righteousness again. It is not God who has changed but the people, and they must learn again, the hard way, that God is a God of justice.

The point of the passage in Luke is to tell us who John the Baptist is and, more importantly, who he is not. He is the messenger, but he is not the message. The message of God to his people is Jesus Christ, and John's work is to prepare people to receive him. Both Malachi's audience and John's audience have made themselves unable to recognize God, because they are trying to make him meet *their* standards, rather than trying themselves to meet *his*. Malachi's hearers have questioned the justice of God, and John's audience are going to fail to see God's justice in Jesus.

But another thing that Malachi and John the Baptist have in common is that they are there to be superseded. Malachi may not even have left his name to posterity, since *malachi* comes from the Hebrew for 'messenger' and, once his message is given, he himself fades into obscurity. Similarly with John: although we do know his name, we are told that his mission is to be no more than a 'voice', and we know that even that must be silenced when Jesus starts to preach.

It is worth noticing that although Malachi was written at a particular moment for a particular audience, without the commentaries beside you, you cannot now tell what that moment was. But Luke gives a detailed and circumstantial account of exactly when and where John the Baptist appears. God's message through Malachi could have applied to his people at a great many different points in their history, but John's preparatory work is directly tied to the coming of Jesus. *This* moment, and no other, is the moment at which all the paths to God are suddenly made straight, there are no more valleys to be trudged through, no more hills to be climbed, no more winding lanes to take us out of our way. At *this* particular historical moment, God's salvation comes to us as a gift, not by our own effort.

And Philippians? The verses in Philippians, too, are about facing God's presence. Malachi warns that the people will be able to restore their old relationship with God only after a long and terrifying process of trial, whereas the words that Paul writes to the Philippians exude a quiet confidence and joy. Despite the fact that Paul is writing from prison to a people who have suffered for the gospel, he is sure that they have already come through to the place that Malachi longs for. But there is still an element of caution. Until the 'day of Christ', Christians have to live in a world that is partly the kingdom and partly not.

Paul's prison cell must have been a busy place, with messengers and scribes flying about. Paul seems to have taken enforced rest as a chance to catch up with correspondence and to pray for all his churches. So when he tells the Philippians to use their time well, he has practised what he preaches.

# The Third Sunday of Advent

—— ∼ ——

*Zephaniah 3.14–20*
*Philippians 4.4–7*
*Luke 3.7–18*

The book of Zephaniah is not, on the whole, cheerful reading, and almost everything about it is disputed by the various commentaries on it. No one is absolutely sure when it was written, despite its firm placing of itself in 1.1 in the days of King Josiah, and no one is quite sure how much it has been edited and patched together from different sources. The lovely verses set for today's readings are so uncharacteristic of the rest of it that they are generally thought to have been a later editor's attempt to give a happy ending to an otherwise totally gloomy book. Certainly, it moves from a condemnation of Jerusalem, through dire warnings to most of the neighbouring states, to this sudden passage that could have come straight out of Isaiah. But even if it has been added on, it has a certain logic to it. In verses 12–13, the only people left are 'a people humble and lowly', and to them God comes. At last, God chooses to come and live in Jerusalem and his presence makes it home. There is a sudden change in verse 18 from the third person to the first; this is no longer reporting what God will do, but God himself promising to bring his people back.

Isn't the word 'home' an emotive one? Think of all the things that have been done in the name of protecting this idea of 'home'. To think of 'home' and 'Jerusalem' in the same breath is almost unbearably ironic just at present. Who has a right to call Jerusalem 'home'? But Zephaniah suggests that Jerusalem can only be 'home' when God is there himself. Home – not so much where the heart is, as where God is.

The trick, then, is to train your heart to feel at home only where God is. Augustine wrote, 'Our hearts are restless till they find their rest in thee', but the problem is that that is not often true, or at least that we don't know that it is true. We may know that they are restless, but until

6

they do find their home, they don't know what they are looking for. The final verse of one of G. K. Chesterton's Christmas poems goes like this:

To an open house in the evening
Home shall all men come,
To an older place than Eden
And a taller town than Rome.
To the end of the way of the wandering star,
To the things that cannot be and that are,
To the place where God was homeless
And all men are at home.

It is God's willingness to be homeless to bring us home that we celebrate at Christmas, and that we spend Advent trying to imagine and prepare ourselves for. But the passage from Luke, like Zephaniah, warns us that dispossession is the only preparation for possession. In today's passage from Luke, John the Baptist is warning his hearers, in no uncertain terms, that they have placed their faith in the wrong things. They are trusting to the fact that they are Abraham's children to get them into God's home. Or, even more insidiously, they have actually demonstrated that their security lies in having two coats, more than enough food and money, the strength to make others do what you want them to. They have clearly made their 'home' here, where they are comfortable and secure.

And almost incredibly John does not fall into his own trap. He does not make the people's response to his preaching into his own 'home'. He is strikingly successful, and people come to him, asking advice, and speculating about who he is, even wondering if he is the Messiah. The temptation to believe in his own centrality to God's work must have been enormous. But John is clear that he is no more than a 'voice crying out in the wilderness', and that he will only succeed in what he has been sent to do when he is redundant.

Traditionally we are told that John the Baptist stands on the cusp of salvation-history, between the old covenant and the new, not really belonging to either. In that sense, he is the perfect person to prepare the way for the homeless God, since he himself was prepared to belong nowhere for the sake of God's calling.

And in the background to these Advent readings we can see the hugely pregnant figure of Mary, waiting, close to her time now. She is to give birth to a child in a stable; her son will reject the home and the mothering that she offers; she will have to repent and be converted, and enter God's 'open house' and, like us, learn to be at home only where God is.

# The Fourth Sunday of Advent

—— ∽ ——

*Micah 5.2–5a*
*Hebrews 10.5–10*
*Luke 1.39–45*

The readings from Micah and Hebrews are so dauntingly obscure that it is tempting simply to concentrate on the lovely passage from Luke. Luke's is the only Gospel that has any of John the Baptist's biography before his adult entrance into the story as the messenger who prepares the way for Jesus. And what Luke tells us makes John's willingness to be only the messenger even more moving. We are told that John's birth is meticulously prepared for, as is Jesus' own. His parents have given up hope of having children – like Abraham and Sarah – and his father, Zechariah, is visited by an angel, who announces what is to come. If you read Luke 1.8–17, you will see that the role John is to play is really built up by the angel. The child is to be a source of gladness, he is to be filled with the power of the Holy Spirit, from birth, and he will bring many of his own people back to the Lord. While the angel does mention the fact that John is to prepare the people for the Lord, there is really nothing in what he says to make a proud parent feel that their son is to play second fiddle in God's orchestra. If Zechariah really remembered everything that was said to him and reported it back to Elizabeth, then surely they must have begun secretly to wonder if their son was to be the One, the Messiah, who would prepare the world for the direct rule of God.

But if Elizabeth ever had any such illusions, it seems that the child in the womb – full of the Holy Spirit as the angel had promised – had none. As soon as Mary steps into the room, the baby John leaps. And without a second thought, Elizabeth recognizes what her child is conveying to her and accepts their secondary role as a privilege. When she calls down a blessing on Mary for her obedience to the

Lord, she hardly seems to notice that she, too, has earned the blessing of one who 'believed ... what was spoken to her by the Lord'.

What must it have been like for Mary at last to be recognized as faithful and obedient? She has been surrounded by suspicion, hard words and looks, and her swollen belly has been seen as a symbol of her faithlessness to the covenant, not its fulfilment. But now, Elizabeth and John see her for what she really is, the Ark of the Covenant, and John dances in the womb, just as David danced before the Ark, rejoicing in the presence of the Lord.

But when you put this lovely story into the context of today's other two readings, what you get is the long view. You see God carefully, slowly, patiently preparing for the revelation of his Son. In Micah, we see a prophet picking up the significance of Bethlehem. As far as Micah knows, its task has already been fulfilled. It has been the source of David, the great king of Israel. But he is given this strange prophecy that seems to suggest that Bethlehem's task is not yet over. Hebrews, too, makes the Davidic connection by putting words into the Messiah's mouth that were originally ascribed to David in Psalm 40. And here again, the sacrificial system which was thought to be the goal of God's plan is seen to be just one step on the way. It is now to be replaced by another kind of sacrifice, one that never needs to be made again, one that God performs for us rather than we for him.

When you see Jesus, the end-result of God's great plan, it is easy to discount all the steps that it took to get there. But today's readings suggest that would be fatal. The final fulfilment of God's plan involved all those other steps – David dancing before the Ark of the Lord, Elizabeth and John accepting their second place, Mary believing what the Lord said to her – and many, many more small, even unknown events in which people say yes to God. God has deliberately made his plan out of this long chain with many links, each one of them fragile, each one of them necessary. Who knows how many times the links were broken as people rejected their place in the plan? God is never thwarted, but he does not change his plan or his methods; he simply waits and works until the chain can be mended. In Advent, we accept our place, however small, in God's great and purposive chain of salvation, and we dance with joy that we are privileged to be part of it.

# *Christmas*

# Christmas Day/Christmas Eve

———— ∼ ————

*Isaiah 52.7–10*
*Hebrews 1.1–4*
*John 1.1–14*

What difference would it make if the Christmas story were not true? If God had not come to be born, live and die as a human being? Today's readings shout out that the Christmas story is the key to what the world is all about, from beginning to end.

Hebrews tells us that the incarnation is the climax of God's continuous, creative, communicating love. God's love, Hebrews says, is always 'son-shaped'. Through God the Son, the world comes into being; through God the Son it is sustained in being; and God the Son will bring it to fulfilment when he, the 'heir', rounds everything up. All the other ways in which God has chosen to communicate with the world he made and loves are interpreted by this great event that we celebrate at Christmas. The incarnation tells us that that is what we are here for – to be drawn into dialogue with God, hearing his word and responding to it.

The majestic language of these opening sentences in Hebrews should not blind us to the reality of the way God chooses to come to us. Hebrews piles up radiance upon radiance. The Son is 'the reflection of God's glory', the 'imprint of God's very being'. He is no mere messenger, but the actual presence of God. And what does this dazzling reflection of God look like? A small baby.

St John's great prologue makes that point perfectly clear. Like Hebrews, John's opening scene is the creation of the world through the same power of God that makes the incarnation possible. The Word of God, the Son of God, is the overflowing, incarnating, life-making power of God the Trinity. Our understanding of God as Trinity brings with it the belief that God's very being is relational love, and that that love pours out into the world to bring us, too, into God's love.

Although the incarnation is an extraordinary overturning of every-thing that we thought we knew about God, both John and Hebrews suggest that it is, at the same time, consistent with the nature of the God who chooses to create the world in the first place.

But John takes that one stage further. Yes, God is consistent in creating, in becoming incarnate, in redeeming. And part of that con-sistency is that it does not force a response. John says, with terrible irony, 'the world came into being through him; yet the world did not know him.' The way in which God chooses to create and redeem us allows us the option of ignorance about the very purpose of our existence. The incarnation, which Hebrews describes in such grandilo-quent terms, still comes down to this, the child in the manger. You have to suspect that 'sensible' is not a word in God's vocabulary!

So here at the beginning of the Gospel John sets out what is to be one of his themes throughout – *you have to choose*. You can turn away from the light and choose the darkness, the darkness that represents not only evil but also ultimately unbeing. It is the darkness that was over everything before God created. It is formlessness, hopelessness, ignorance of the purpose of our existence.

Or you can choose light. To choose the light, according to John, is to step into our proper created place, as God's children, alive in his love. God is the only source of life, John tells us, and this life is offered to us in the incarnation.

But the choice is ours. What we see now is the child, a symbol of life, but so vulnerable. To choose that life, to choose to nurture it and celebrate it is to choose God's kind of life, since it is the only kind on offer. To choose something without the ambiguities and uncertainties of Jesus' life is to choose the dark and that, says John, is actually not life at all. To recognize the life-giving power of the Creator in the baby Jesus, in his life, his cross and his resurrection, is the study of the Christian. Can we see 'the glory of the Father', here, at Christmas?

Would Isaiah have recognized this baby as the triumphant act of God that he longs for? In the incarnation, God does indeed bare his arm, but not to lead his armies to victory, but to show us the flesh. Isaiah proclaims the time when God will be 'in plain sight' (Isaiah 52.8) and, indeed, what could be more visible than another human being, just like us? What kind of a victory is this? It is the victory of God's consistent and unchanging nature, that cannot be deflected from its original purpose, which is to share his life – his life, and no second-hand, trumped-up copies – with us.

# The First Sunday of Christmas

—— ∾ ——

*1 Samuel 2.18–20, 26*
*Colossians 3.12–17*
*Luke 2.41–52*

To get the full picture of what is going on in the reading from 1 Samuel, we really need the verses that the lectionary chooses to leave out. The story is actually about different kinds of sonship. The contrast is between Samuel, who is not Eli's own son, but who is growing up to reverence Eli, the temple and God, and the men who *are* Eli's own sons, but who see the whole religious cult as something to be exploited for their own benefit. These 'natural' sons will die, but Samuel, the son by grace, will grow up to serve God's purpose for his whole people.

The passage from Luke, too, is about different kinds of sonship. Jesus' parents are expecting one kind of behaviour, due to them as his parents, but he has chosen another road, that reflects his true parentage, and he is amazed that Mary and Joseph have not noticed whose 'son' he is. We are told of Jesus, as of Samuel, that he increased in 'divine and human favour', both flourishing in their new 'families'. This tension between the family of birth and the family of God's grace is a significant undercurrent in Jesus' message, and those who live in a world where it is culturally acceptable, if a bit uncool, to be a Christian, should remember those many Christians throughout the world who still have to make the choice between being children of God and children of their parents.

You could see today's readings as a kind of saga of mistaken identities, of the true heir going unrecognized, in which case, the verses from Colossians add another twist. Samuel is the heir whom God has chosen, but who has no birth claim. Jesus is the one that no one thought of as the heir, but who proves to be the Son of the King. And we are the ones, Colossians tells us, who are to put on the heir's clothes and stand in the place that he has made for us in his family.

14

There is a story of a corrupt young man, who has lived all his life for pleasure and profligacy, but who at last falls deeply and genuinely in love. The problem is that his beloved is a young and innocent girl, who will undoubtedly be disgusted not only by his past life, but also by the marks of dissipation that it has left upon his face and body. So he decides to wear a mask, to make himself look like a handsome and unclouded young man while he woos the girl. All goes well, until someone from his former life threatens to unmask him to the girl. Aghast, the man realizes that he cannot keep up the deception for ever, and he confesses all to the girl, and tears off his mask. He expects to see loathing on her face, but all he sees is bewilderment, for the face is exactly the same with or without the mask. His great love for the girl has transformed him into what he longed to be for her.

It is striking that we are told in Colossians to 'clothe' ourselves with all the virtues. We are not told that we have to become naturally good, all at once, but that we have to learn to put on goodness, as a deliberate choice, out of love. And the love that makes us want to do it is given to us as a gift to enable us to do it. If we are to act this part with any success, we have to study the true heir, Jesus, learn what he is like, copy his gestures, let his word 'dwell' in us 'richly', and 'do everything' in his name.

These 'clothes' that we are to put on are a bit like the robe that Hannah brings for Samuel on her annual visit to the temple. The thought of Hannah, year by year, remembering how big her son had been last time, making a robe a bit bigger, and allowing room for another year's growth, is one of those little understated stories that you just can't forget. She has sacrificed this first son, Samuel, so that she can have others, but he is still her son. Now what does that remind you of?

We are the ones who can come into the family because of the sacrifice of the Son, but God has clothes for us, too. The clothes that God makes for us to wear allow plenty of room for growth. None of us is big enough to fit into them properly, yet, because they are the clothes of the Son. But perhaps if we put them on, resolutely and with all the help God offers, they will eventually transform us into his likeness.

# The Second Sunday of Christmas

—— ～ ——

*Jeremiah 31.7–14*
*Ephesians 1.3–14*
*John 1.10–18*

What is grace? Both John and Ephesians have the word more than once. It's a word that we use quite frequently in Christian circles. Most meetings I go to, you know when they've ended because someone says the Grace. We say Grace before meals. But what does it mean? Its Christian use seems very divorced from the everyday use of the word – we know what a graceful dancer is, or what it is to have a few weeks of grace in which to finish a piece of work. The latter seems to be a bit closer to the Christian understanding of grace, but all of today's passages suggest that the loveliness, the sense of 'rightness', in the former use of the word 'grace' needs to come into it, too.

In Ephesians, grace is something that belongs to God, but that he lavishes upon us (Ephesians 1.8). God has designed his world as a great dance of grace and life, with parts written in for us from the beginning. These parts we are to learn by watching and imitating Christ, the principal dancer. We are not, initially, very good dancers. We are quite clumsy, and we can't hear the music very well. But that's all right, because God has designed the dance to accommodate us, and varied the music, so that there are whole sequences that are appropriately danced by lumbering creatures and toddlers, like ourselves. The music and the choreography is designed to make us look natural and graceful, in the right place at the right time, even if we ourselves have only the haziest notion of what we are supposed to be doing. The principal dancer works around us, weaving our well-meaning efforts into the whole, drawing us out and responding to us, making us look good with his own gloriously graceful dancing. Gradually, our confidence builds, and we begin to invite others from the audience to join in. We give them our understanding of the shape and flow of the

16

dance, and encourage them to experiment, as we have, to respond to the music and the principal dancer and begin to build their own style into the dance.

It is perfectly clear that the whole conception and execution of the dance stands or falls with the choreographer, the musician and the principal dancer. Without them, there would be nothing. But their enjoyment comes from our participation. We can carry the Spirit of the music around in our hearts and our heads and as we hear it, we begin to see the magnificent design of the whole dance, and to know and trust in our own part in it. We become graceful with God's own grace, because he has specifically designed the dance to suit our abilities and enhance them.

John's picture is slightly more sombre, because he is looking not just at the experience of those who have joined in the joyful dance, but also at the great crowd of people all around the stage. Some of them are watching the dance, some puzzled but intrigued, some openly sneering at the failings of the dancers. Others are not looking at all, and haven't even noticed the dance going on. Yet others think that the principal dancer is doing it all wrong and is deliberately ruining an old traditional dance, and they try hard to discourage people from joining in the dance at all.

But those who do join in soon find that they are working, for the first time in their lives, with a dancer who can really teach them how to be graceful. He is endlessly patient, and he seems to know exactly what each person is capable of and how to bring out the best in each one. Instead of hogging the limelight himself, with his own superb dancing, he puts all his energies into helping all the dancers to look wonderful. Some of them have been trying all their lives to dance, but never had anyone to show them how, before Christ came. He is the only one who has ever been able to show them how to move gracefully and respond to the music.

God adores our dance. He has designed it from the beginning specifically for us. Father, Son and Spirit – choreographer, dancer, music maker – have worked out a dance that is utterly appropriate for us, in which we will be graceful. Dancing together, watching the Son, listening to and moving with the Spirit, we find our own freedom and gracefulness for the first time. We never thought we had it in us, and to begin with we have to accept it as a gift, but soon it becomes so utterly natural to us. We are doing what we were born to do, and giving joy to God as we do it.

*Epiphany*

# The Epiphany

——— ❦ ———

*Isaiah 60.1–6*
*Ephesians 3.1–12*
*Matthew 2.1–12*

The wise men have always had enormous appeal. Everything about them has been elaborated in poetry and story. They have become kings; they have been depicted as representing youth, maturity and old age; they have been given the features of different races; they have been named. They function as our representatives; all of us Gentiles were not actually there.

That is the connection that runs through these three passages, and forms the theme for today. It is the theme of God's great self-revelation to the world.

In Isaiah, the scene is in darkness. The figure might be asleep, or might be prostrate with grief. Suddenly an incandescent light shines, illuminating the central figure and emphasizing the darkness all around. Behind the figure, the light gathers, brighter and brighter, forming into a clear, majestic shape, made of brilliance. Gradually other shapes come on to the stage, drawn by the light, shuffling out of the darkness. The whole stage erupts into a party, as the light spreads further and further. The one who was alone and in darkness is now surrounded by light and laughter. Bit by bit, through the happy sounds, the central character's voice is heard, singing a hymn. Gradually other voices pick it up, until the whole stage coalesces into one song, a song of praise to the Light.

This is how Isaiah sees God's revelation. It is to be a time of vindication for his people, but in their triumph they are generous. They are thrilled not only by the wealth and honour that recognition brings, but also by the fact that the nations can now share in their worship of God. The culmination of today's passage is the picture of community united to 'proclaim the praise of the LORD' (Isaiah 60.6).

This is how Ephesians sees it, too. The point of God's epiphany is that everyone should be drawn to him. Huge claims are made for Paul – and, by implication, for all Christians – in this passage. In Ephesians 3.2–3 it is said that the 'mystery' of God's inclusive call waits upon Paul's conversion and commission. To Paul and, it is rather grudgingly admitted, to 'the holy apostles and prophets', is entrusted the revelation that all can share in the gospel. The enormity of this claim is clear – God's original plan for his whole creation, thus far 'hidden ... in God', is now entrusted to the Church. The 'rulers and authorities in the heavenly places' (v. 10), who may have felt that they had rights over the Gentiles at least, are shown a community drawn from all races and owing allegiance only to God. Perhaps the church you attend Sunday by Sunday does not always remind you of 'the wisdom of God in its rich variety', but it should.

But again, as with the passage in Isaiah, the purpose of this self-gift of God to his people is not to elevate believers above others, but to enable worship. We can now approach God, knowing that we are called, loved, wanted.

What strange messengers God chooses for his gospel – the dark, mourning figure in Isaiah; the difficult, touchy apostle Paul, whose mission often lands him in prison; the infantile, squabbling Christian Church. And that brings us full circle to the wise men, again. If you actually read the passage in Matthew, trying to forget the preconceptions you bring to it, you will see that they are very odd figures. We don't know where they come from, just that it is 'the East'; we don't know how many of them there are, just how many presents they bring; we don't know their status, though they do have the confidence to call at Herod's palace. What they saw, in the end, cannot have been what they were expecting. They were tracking a king, so they looked for him in a palace, and brought presents that must have looked singularly out of place to Mary and the child Jesus. Not for them the direct visitation of the angels, with clear instructions on how to find the baby – that is reserved for the shepherds. The wise men follow the bright, enigmatic star, using their intelligence to calculate its path, making assumptions in their visit to Herod – and with what fatal consequences.

So the real story of the wise men seems to be about the challenge of God's coming. God's kingship is not what you might expect, and his revelation is blindingly unpredictable. But at least the wise men do recognize their journey's end when they see it. We are told that they are 'overwhelmed with joy'. They leave their strange presents and go home satisfied. Let us hope that in that, at least, they are our representatives.

# The First Sunday of Epiphany

— ∾ —

*Isaiah 43.1–7*
*Acts 8.14–17*
*Luke 3.15–17, 21–2*

The first three Gospels all have the story of Jesus' baptism by John in very similar words. John's version of events, as so often, is slightly different – you might like to go and have a look at it in John 1.29–34. But all four Gospels are agreed that this is a moment of confirmation, when God declares his love for Jesus.

What is so moving is that this is before the start of Jesus' full ministry. He has yet to embark upon the painful and costly path that will lead to the cross. The love of the Father is not just because of what the Son does, but because of who he is. The hectic, exhilarating and terrifying ministry of Jesus is set in motion by this affirmation – 'You are my Son, the Beloved; with you I am well pleased' (Luke 2.22). It is because Jesus is loved that he is obedient.

This passage in Luke also continues the story of John the Baptist. Here he is, at the height of his powers, with the crowd hanging on his every word. They have no interest in Jesus, yet. He is just one of the many coming for baptism. Their whole attention is fixed on John. 'Who is he?' they ask. 'Surely he must be the chosen one of God?' It is a symptom of the drivenness of John's calling that he is not distracted by the flattering and tempting voices all around him. He knows what he has to do, and he knows his limits.

But what of John's assessment of the ministry of the One who is to come? John's preaching has been fiery and full of anger. He has preached repentance with a ferocity that has obviously got through everyone's defensive barriers. He is sure that the Messiah will confirm everything he has said, and add to it. He waits for the Messiah to bring devastating judgement. He may be prepared to submit his own ministry to that of the Messiah, but is he prepared to have his clear message of hellfire and destruction reinterpreted? Later stories of John the Baptist suggest that he did learn that Jesus' message was not his, and accepted that. But that is not to suggest that judgement is absent from Jesus' preaching. On the contrary, it is a sombre and continuous note. People's reaction to Jesus is their reaction to God, and since to hate God is to hate life, people choose their own judgement as they react to God's beloved Son.

But John's preaching is a sub-plot in today's readings. You have to remember it, because it will come back later in the story. But for the moment, the emphasis is somewhere else. It is on the loving interaction of the Trinity.

In the Gospel reading, the love of the Father for the Son is made visible by the Holy Spirit, descending like a dove, descending 'in bodily form', verse 22 says. What the Son does for us, which is to make God's love incarnate, the Holy Spirit does for the earthly Jesus. The Holy Spirit gives Jesus the confirmation that he is, indeed, the Beloved Son of the Father. Is it heretical to think that Jesus might need such a confirmation as he embarks upon his mission, or is it yet another part of his saving identification with us?

Acts gives us a further elaboration of the way in which a relational, Trinitarian God works. This is actually a very odd little passage. It is easy to get distracted by the intriguing question of what was missing when the good people of Samaria were baptized only in the name of Jesus. What dramatic gifting did Peter and John convey with their prayers and their laying on of hands? But the 'magic' is a fatal distraction, as the verses immediately after today's set reading make clear. The point of it is that Jesus' ministry is not about himself: it is about the Father who has sent him, and the Holy Spirit who keeps the love of the Father an ever-present reality. Christian baptism is baptism into the loving community of God.

This, then, is what we are called to: to hear God say to us, as to Jesus, that he loves us and is pleased with us. The resounding joy of today's reading from Isaiah is what we are promised in Jesus' baptism, as he takes up his mission for us. We are created by God, Isaiah says, for his glory, and that is why he chooses to redeem us. Not because we are worthy but because, inexplicably, he loves us.

# The Second Sunday of Epiphany

——— ∾ ———

*Isaiah 62.1–5*
*1 Corinthians 12.1–11*
*John 2.1–11*

The story of the wedding at Cana is an intriguing one. The dynamic between Jesus and his mother is fascinating, as is the nature of the miracle.

The Gospels that emerged in the first few Christian centuries, under the guidance of God, as the 'canonical' ones are very reticent about Jesus' childhood. John and Mark don't mention it at all; Matthew goes straight from the Christmas stories to the baptism of Jesus; and Luke has one story of the 12-year-old boy in the temple. Some of the other writings that were circulating among Christians in the early centuries are not so restrained. They tell stories of a miraculous boyhood, of a child whittling a bird out of wood and then giving it life to fly away. Considering the human temptation to biographies, it is very interesting that the common mind of the Church rejected these stories as not essential to our faith. There are all kinds of reasons for this, but one thing that is noticeable about the four Gospels that we base our lives on is their drivenness – they tell a story that leads inexorably to the cross, and nothing is included that is not vital to that story.

But the interaction between Jesus and his mother in this first miracle story in John's Gospel does suggest that Jesus' childhood was not completely ordinary. Why did Mary expect Jesus to be able to do anything about the empty wine jars? What did she know about him? John's Gospel does not tell us.

What it does show us is a gradual building of Jesus' ministry. John's description, in the previous chapter, of the calling of the first disciples shows Jesus as an attractive, teasing, compelling figure. People are drawn to him, and when they are with him, they know they are at the heart of something wonderful.

And then comes this lovely, happy wedding story. Jesus is there with his friends, who are already, John implies, a recognized group, invited together to the wedding. Mary, the bossy, affectionate mother takes no notice at all of Jesus' attempt to avoid doing a sign. 'My hour has not yet come,' he tells her, but Mary clearly feels it is *her* place to decide when his hour had come, not his. She treats him almost like a sulky boy, who just needs humouring and cajoling into performing.

And perform he does. Why does he do it? Only Mary, the servants and the disciples know what has happened. Does it set up all kinds of false impressions in the minds of those closest to Jesus? Does Mary expect to continue to control his ministry? Do the disciples congratulate themselves on throwing in their lot with someone who is going to give them such a good time? If there is any such implied uncertainty in John's narrative, then the shock of the cleansing of the temple, which immediately follows this story, is even greater. The picture of happiness and harmony is shattered as Jesus comes face to face with the reality of his mission and we, the readers, begin to sense the escalation of tension, the beginnings of the mighty conflict between darkness and light.

John tells us that this miracle at Cana was a revelation and a confirmation of faith for the disciples. They saw the exuberant, creative power of God at work in bringing uncomplicated human enjoyment to this wedding. Through the rest of their time with Jesus they had to learn many other kinds of things about God's power, not all of them palatable, but this streak of anarchic joy is characteristic of God as we encounter him through Jesus.

It is the point that is made for us by the reading from 1 Corinthians. God works in a wild variety of ways, and does not always follow our rules. Although there is an inherent consistency in our encounters with God, we will see it only if what we are looking for is the shape of Jesus. The point of our faith is to enable us to say, and live, 'Jesus is Lord'. Sometimes, Paul tells us, this will be accompanied by very satisfying gifts of power, but they are not the point. The point is to build a worshipping community, made up of people whose lives are directed to God. This community will rejoice in the exercise of gifts that help it to grow, but they won't care who has the power to speak, or heal or work miracles, so long as the community as a whole is learning to say, 'Jesus is Lord'. To see the Holy Spirit at work, building a people to praise and worship, to recognize this power, that is the true spiritual gift, one that we are all called to exercise.

# The Third Sunday of Epiphany

—— ∼ ——

*Nehemiah 8.1–3, 5–6, 8–10*
*1 Corinthians 12.12–31a*
*Luke 4.14–21*

The book of Nehemiah is an exciting and inspiring story. It is written in the first person, and its narrative is vivid and action-packed. Nehemiah, one of the many Jews carried away into exile, is working as a cupbearer for King Artaxerxes when he is overcome by such a strong sense of shame at the plight of his people that he cannot forget it. He is ashamed partly because he knows that his people have deserved their punishment, and he includes himself among those who have sinned against God and forgotten the law of Moses. But he is also partly ashamed on God's behalf, because the plight of the people of Israel seems to call into question God's faithfulness to his promise. (You can see all of this in Nehemiah 1.)

So he gets permission from the king, though he can hardly believe it, to return to Jerusalem and rebuild the city. In the months that follow, despite opposition, ridicule and constant danger, Jerusalem is rebuilt. But that is the easy bit. The next task is to rebuild a people fit to live in Jerusalem and be God's covenant people.

It is at this point in the story that today's reading comes. The people of the rebuilt Jerusalem are a very mixed bag. Some of them are the dregs of the population who were left behind in Jerusalem during the successive waves of invasion. They were not thought worth the effort of taking into captivity, even. Some are Jews who have chosen to return, many of them wealthy and independent, who have done well in their exile. Some may have continued to be as faithful to God as was possible under the circumstances, but some have clearly forgotten even the most basic things about their God. Some have wives and families of other nations and religions, and their loyalties are severely divided.

And in front of these people, Ezra stands up and begins to read

26

'from the book of the law of Moses, which the LORD had given to Israel' (8.1). The people have to learn again about their God, and it is utterly characteristic that they must do so by learning to live together as a society that is obedient to God. Their knowledge of God is not abstract, but utterly practical. So great is their desire to remember and to be themselves again, that we are told they stand from early morning until midday, listening as Ezra reads, and with trained people going through the crowds to make sure that people can really understand what is being said to them and asked of them.

So why do the crowds weep as they listen? Is it with a nostalgic longing for the past, the great days of Moses? Is it with shame because they have forgotten so much of what they now hear, and have failed to keep the holy laws of God? Or is it with joy that at last they can enter again into their proper heritage? Whatever it is, they are told to turn their emotion in two directions – they are to remember to feed the poor, and they are to worship God.

The reading from 1 Corinthians, too, is about trying to build a new people. The more you read the Bible the more inescapable is the conclusion that *community* is basic to any human attempt to understand God. You can get only so far with personal, private knowledge of God. The test of it will come in the way you interact with others. The Corinthians are a very attractive lot, from what we glean about them in Paul's letters. They are enthusiastic, gifted, clever, determined. But they are infantile in their ability to live together in love. (Does that sound anything like a church near you?) This whole section is an impassioned plea for an attempt to think in a completely new way. Instead of thinking always about themselves and their individual needs and rights, instead of always battling to be the most important and gifted person in any gathering, the Corinthians have to learn to think of themselves as one entity, one body, whose health and whose very life depends upon co-operation and connection. And we cannot pretend that that is a lesson we have now learned.

And so, finally, to Jesus' chosen description of his mission. Isn't it interesting that this declaration of intent is not about teaching us a better spirituality, but about doing God's justice, and creating God's community? The Christian body that Paul is pleading for will be recognizable by the way it treats others. To be the body of Christ, we have to do as he did.

# The Fourth Sunday of Epiphany

—— ～ ——

*Ezekiel 43.27—44.4*
*1 Corinthians 13.1–13*
*Luke 2.22–40*

Today's reading from Ezekiel is chosen, presumably, because it connects well to the account in Luke of Jesus' presentation in the temple. Both talk about the proper fulfilment of the law, and the verse before our reading from Luke uses the phrase 'eight days', as does Ezekiel. 'Eight days' seems to be a complete cycle, in terms of the requirements of the temple, after which things can move into a new phase.

The passage from Ezekiel is part of the long tour that Ezekiel is taken on of the rebuilding of the perfect temple, the temple in which true and acceptable worship will be offered. At the beginning of chapter 40, Ezekiel tells us that he was brought out of his exile, in visions, into the land of Israel, and that a man 'whose appearance shone like bronze' (Ezekiel 40.3) conducts him on a tour of the temple, measuring as he goes. The measurements are all given to us, in great detail. I, at least, cannot begin to imagine the finished product from those measurements, but the detail builds up, piece by piece, into an overwhelming sense of how important this is, how much it matters to get it right.

In particular, what strikes home is the mixture of intimacy and awe in Ezekiel's account. The sheer practical detail of the measurements, the decorations, what must be washed, what must be offered and where – all of this is, in a sense, mundane. It is architects' and builders' plans, with some post-ordination training for priests thrown in. And yet, as a result of that attention to detail, God comes to the temple and fills it with his glory (44.4). Ezekiel's response is the only one possible.

Intimacy and awe characterize the reading from Luke, too. This is just a family, doing the usual things after a child is born. Probably there are several other couples there, doing the same thing. Even the two,

28

strange, old people could be part of the family picture, like having grandparents present, perhaps? But they, like Ezekiel, are witnessing the glory of the Lord coming to the temple.

Ezekiel sees the glory of the Lord in what he clearly knows to be a vision, though it is one for whose fulfilment he longs, and for which he has sacrificed all shreds of normality. Anna and Simeon, too, have anticipated this moment for so long. Luke gives us only hints about them, but they are enough to suggest a long period of faithful waiting, and being guided in prayer and patience to the point where they can recognize the glory of God in the child they see. We, the readers, have had all the fanfare of the angels and the shepherds, as well as Luke's own narrative instruction. We would have to be stupid not to know who this child is going to be. But Anna and Simeon have been shaped into truth the hard way.

It would be easy to think that Ezekiel, Anna and Simeon arrive at this point by sheer gift, and to forget the drivenness and the longing that has kept them looking for the Lord. They are not concerned that people should see they were right; they only want, with desperation, to see God glorified.

'Is that what you want, above all else?' Paul is asking the Corinthians. And the answer is clearly, 'No'. They have confused the accidental trappings with the reality, the gifts with the glory. They have become so enchanted with the things that they can now do, thanks to God, that they have lost track of God himself.

Paul's description of love, in verses 4–7, might be a description of Simeon or Anna, but it is, above all, a description of God. And that is utterly extraordinary. If *God* does not insist on his own way, then we are hardly in a position to do so. If *Jesus* bears all things and endures all things, then our impatient need for instant gratification looks very petty.

This 'love' that Paul is talking about is not a romantic and flowery thing, but a compound of exactly that intimacy and awe that we have seen in all of today's readings. We are called into a family, sharing homely, mundane, daily lives, and yet those lives are taken up into the life of God the Creator. We can see God's glory, day by day, in our Christian lives together. Will it be enough? Will we know it and fall on our faces, with Ezekiel, at the privilege that has been extended to us? Or will we be like the Corinthians, and prefer the shadow to the substance?

*Ordinary Time*

# *Proper 1*

——— ⌇ ———

*Isaiah 6.1–8 (9–13)*
*1 Corinthians 15.1–11*
*Luke 5.1–11*

The question of the correct posture for worship – should we sit or should we kneel – is a perennial one. Well, if anything can make us less sedentary, it should be today's readings. They are none of them conducive to sitting about.

Isaiah is telling us about his calling. It is as though he is attending a perfectly ordinary service, and suddenly everything in front of him slides away, to make space for this vision of the heavenly court. As a result of what he sees, Isaiah is called to be God's prophet, to speak for the Lord – to speak, but seldom to be either listened to or understood. The angel's burning coal brings Isaiah the knowledge that he is worthy to serve God, but he is pretty quickly disabused of any illusions of grandeur that might follow. His mission is to speak to a people who are totally immune to his words. This overwhelming vision brings with it the knowledge that his people will be all but destroyed, and that he is perhaps the only one who will understand what God is doing.

Peter's response in the reading from Luke is uncannily similar to Isaiah's, though the setting could hardly be more different. Instead of the temple and the glimpse of worship in heaven, we have a straightforward work setting. Fishing is what Peter and his friends do from nine to five on Mondays to Fridays, as it were, and at the moment, they are not doing it at all well. In the middle of that, they are called. Peter's first reaction, like Isaiah's, is to know that he is in the presence of something that he is wholly unprepared for. He does not expect it to last, it must be a mistake, he urgently needs reassurance – 'Go away!' he shouts.

Peter, like Isaiah, is given the confidence he needs by the fact that he is asked to do something. God must trust him a little, or he would not

32

give him a job. In Isaiah, the irony is spelled out for us – working for God may not be a bed of roses. In Luke, the irony unfolds over the story that is to come.

The same kind of dynamic is at work in 1 Corinthians 15. Paul is talking about the world-transforming knowledge of the resurrection that he has received, and that he has passed on to his converts as something worth basing their lives on. Just like Peter and Ezekiel, Paul knows that he has not been given God's work to do because he is clearly the best person for the job. Knowing you can't do it seems to be high on God's checklist for applicants.

But surely I am missing the point of these readings? Aren't they about God's grandeur, his miraculous power? Aren't Isaiah's vision and the miracle that Peter witnesses a tiny ripple of the tidal wave of creative power that we see in the resurrection? Of course that is true. If you do not believe that God creates the world out of sheer exuberant power, that he holds it in the palm of his hand and wills its transformation with the same energy and love with which he brought it into being then, as Paul says, don't waste your time, 'you have come to believe in vain'.

But these stories come close enough to Christmas for us, even us, still to remember that we have a lot to learn about God's power. He chooses to redeem us by coming to live with us as one of us. He chooses to give himself – and so the whole of creation – into our hands. The temptation is to think that God could make better use of his power. The temptation is to join the people who entirely failed to understand Isaiah, who put Peter and Paul to death, like their master, and who continue to find the resurrection laughably improbable.

The proper response to God's action, when we are privileged to witness it, is the one that all three of our heroes today demonstrate. They know they have nothing to offer, and they accept the task that God gives them. They do not attempt to bargain about terms, conditions, outcomes. They see God, and are grateful to be allowed to be involved in his work. Perhaps we think that if only God would reveal himself in his power as he did to Isaiah, so that we saw him with the angels praising his glory; or as he did to Paul, on the Damascus road; or even as he did to Peter, filling the empty nets with abundance – then we too could trust and do what God has called us to. But I suspect Isaiah, Peter and Paul would look with envy on what we have seen of God's power in two millennia and wonder at our lack of faith.

# *Proper 2*

—— ∼ ——

Jeremiah 17.5–10
1 Corinthians 15.12–20
Luke 6.17–26

Paul's discussion of the resurrection in 1 Corinthians 15 has fascinated scholars and Christians alike. It shows clearly that the earliest preaching of the gospel contained the witness to the risen Christ. This is, as Paul has said earlier in this chapter, something that the Corinthian Christians heard as 'good news' when Paul first came to them.

Clearly, there has been some debate going on in Corinth about the nature and reality of the resurrection. From the insistent and slightly impatient tone of this chapter, you get the impression that Paul views these discussions as typical of the Corinthians' ability to concentrate on inessentials. There is a kind of 'let's sort this out once for all' tone about chapter 15. Paul suspects that the Corinthians have been sitting about, having late night arguments about exactly what form Christ's resurrection body took, and whether and in what order Christians will be raised, and getting themselves and others in a great state about it.

So, in the first part of the chapter, Paul reminds them – yet again, he implies – of the proofs of Jesus' resurrection. In the section we are looking at now, he goes on to demonstrate the theological centrality of the resurrection. The resurrection of Christ is not an additional extra, which can be debated as though it left the rest untouched. Paul says, in no uncertain terms, that this is about the doctrine of God, and about our salvation.

If Jesus was not raised from the dead, then everything that Paul has taught the Corinthians about the nature and purpose of God is called into question. The resurrection is not only God's affirmation of Jesus' life and teaching, but it is also God's demonstration that he is 'Christ-like, and in him is no unChristlikeness at all', to borrow a phrase from Michael Ramsey. The power that raised Jesus from the dead is the power that offers us redemption and the power that made us in the first place. It is all of a piece. It cannot be a matter for idle debate and speculation, Paul insists. If it is not true, then we have no foundation on which to put our trust in God.

The picture of God that Jesus builds up, through his life and his teaching, his ministry and his death, has strong, consistent elements. They are not wholly new. Many of them can be found in the great prophets and lawmakers of the Old Testament, as you would expect, if this is all the work of God. The Beatitudes in Luke follow a pattern that this Gospel makes particularly clear for us. The themes that fill Mary's mouth in the Magnificat and that, strikingly, Jesus chooses from Isaiah to announce the beginning of his ministry, are picked up here (see Luke 1.46ff.; 4.18ff.). Luke paints a vivid picture. Jesus is standing surrounded by people who are hungry to benefit from the power that streams from him, and he announces, both through his healings and through his words, God's care for the poor, the hungry and the suffering. The power of God is a power that is used to comfort and renew, and it is the power that will work, through the cross and resurrection, to comfort and renew the world. But it is not a power that we instinctively recognize or trust, unless we are utterly powerless ourselves.

It is instructive to compare Luke's Beatitudes with Matthew's, in chapter 5 of his Gospel. Although some of the characteristic concerns of each Gospel writer come through in their reworking of the material, the essential message about God's values is the same.

Unlike Matthew, Luke has woes as well as blessings. This, like 1 Corinthians 15, is a passage about where you put your trust. Those who have nothing else in life to trust in, and so have to fall back on God, are the ones who are blessed, Luke tells us. The rest of us have had our blessing from what we chose to put our trust in.

Trust in God is at the heart of Jeremiah's message, too. His people have gradually come to trust in other things, in themselves, in novel religious rituals, in wealth, in pretty well anything but God, and they are paying a terrible price. They have chosen to rely on things that are not the source of life. Jeremiah uses water as his image of God. God is as essential to life as water is, and to choose to live without him is as stupid as it would be to choose to live without water.

Choosing to trust the God of the resurrection is not without risk. But in the end it is the only thing that makes any sense.

# *Proper 3*

— ∾ —

*Genesis 45.3–11, 15*
*1 Corinthians 15.35–8*
*Luke 6.27–38*

These verses in Luke mark a shift in tone from the preceding verses. The 'blessings and woes' section that comes immediately before this passage is about what is 'now', it is about results. But now Jesus moves from this alarming prophetic tone to a no less alarming explanatory one. If you want to deserve the blessings, rather than the woes, this is what you have to do.

It is just about possible to read these verses as a call to passivity, if you don't think about them too hard, or imagine yourself doing them. But if you start thinking about how people might react to such tactics, you realize that what Jesus is recommending is creative, cheeky, even provocative. It is to lay yourself completely open to abuse, but not to abandon your wit and your control. If somebody is taking from you only what you are prepared to give, then you remain the victor. Very few people, let alone communities or states, are ever prepared to take the risk of winning by not caring if they lose. Instead, most of us, most of the time, engage in conflict by retaliation with exactly the same means that were used against us, only more so, which ensures that nothing will ever change. Whichever one of us loses will go away and build up our armoury, while the one who wins will have to strive to protect what they have won.

Whereas what Jesus is suggesting is a change in ground rules. Don't do it the way everybody else does it, do it God's way instead. God loves all that he has made, even if it doesn't love him. Jesus is, of course, the living – and dying – proof of that. And when Jesus accepts the violence done to him, without retaliation, he creates a completely new situation, in which all hostility to God, all separation from God, is accepted and reconciled. We have done our worst, and it didn't change God's

36

feelings about us, so now we have to admit that God's love is stronger than any hate we can muster.

Joseph is demonstrating the power to turn things around by an unexpected response. What his brothers expect is retaliation – after all, it's what they would do, in Joseph's place. Instead, Joseph tells them that their betrayal of him had wonderful results. Their action enabled Joseph to save the lives of many Egyptians during the famine, and is now going to make it possible for him to save them, too. In fact, Joseph tells them, your action could be said to have been God-given. No wonder the brothers are dumbfounded. They have lived, every day of their lives since that fateful day, with the dreadful knowledge of what they have done, and now here is Joseph telling them that it was just what God needed them to do. And the result of Joseph's action is reconciliation and life, for himself and his brothers. Because he did not triumph over them, and rub their noses in what they had done, the brothers are able to accept forgiveness and become a family again.

This creativity of response, illustrated by Joseph, but supremely by Jesus, is something that the Corinthians have no innate sympathy with. They are strongly concerned with cause and effect, with proper explanations. Throughout the whole of 1 Corinthians 15, you can hear the impatience in Paul's tone, but now he finally loses it altogether. 'You fools!' he shouts. What is it about their seemingly innocent query that so provokes Paul? Is it so unreasonable for the Corinthians to ask for a bit more detail about the resurrection body? After all, their questions are still around now. 'What do you mean by a physical resurrection? If something is physical, how come we can't see it and feel it? And where exactly is it?' It's possible that part of Paul's exasperation is that these are questions he – and we – can't answer. But throughout the chapter, what Paul is really defending is the doctrine of God. The Corinthians are constantly trying to make God too small; they seem constantly to assume that God can only do things if we can understand them. Now Paul is pointing out that we actually understand almost nothing. We don't understand why life comes in so many different forms, and how any one form – say a seed – turns into another – like a plant. But we forget that this is miraculous, because we see it every day. Do we really think that God's creative power is limited by the scope of what we can see every day? Think again, Paul says.

The only thing you know for sure about God is that he will constantly surprise you, and that his surprises are life-giving.

# The Second Sunday Before Lent

——— ∼ ———

*Genesis 2.4b–9, 15–25*
*Revelation 4*
*Luke 8.22–5*

If you go straight from today's Genesis reading to the reading from Revelation, you could almost imagine that the history of God's relations with people had been one of unbroken communion. From the intimacy of the Garden of Eden to the glad worship of the heavenly court, human beings were made to live in the presence of God. But there are some subtle differences that suggest the reality of what lies between these two 'times' in our story with God.

In Genesis 2 we have the second story of how God made people. In Genesis 1, God makes humanity as the culmination of his labours, a kind of completion. Genesis 2, which has a much fuller and more narrative style, also sees humanity as central, but here, man is made first, and everything else is then made to keep him company. As God makes all the living creatures, we are told that he brings them to Adam, to see what he will call them (Genesis 2.19). This picture of God and Adam playing together sets the tone of this stage of the story. There is an unimaginable closeness between God and the man that he has made out of nothing.

But already the masterly story-teller has put in hints of what is to come. All the lushness of the garden is there just for Adam to enjoy, except the one tree 'of the knowledge of good and evil' (v. 17). (In the interests of good feminist exegesis, I must just point out that the command not to eat from the tree was given to Adam on his own, before the creation of Eve, which makes the tradition of blaming Eve for what follows even more unfair!)

And the other dark note comes in God's understanding that Adam is lonely. Although it is hard to believe that anyone who can talk and play with God could be lonely, it is a measure of God's generosity and

38

understanding that he creates a companion for Adam. In other words, this act acknowledges what is basic to God's creativity, which is that it creates something genuinely new, 'other'. God's artistry is such that he can make something that is genuinely different from himself.

We, the readers, know what will happen as a result of disobedience to God's command, and how that innate separation between God and his creation will become a huge rift. But in this reading, all we get is the peace and closeness that exist between God, Adam and Eve. Notice that they do not need, explicitly, to worship their God, here in Eden; they just need to live with him.

In Revelation 4 that natural, quiet closeness has gone, and has instead been replaced by the vision of God's splendour and our proper worship of it. This chapter, like most of Revelation, is full of allusions to the Old Testament. Echoes of the visions of Isaiah and Ezekiel are unmistakable, and it is hard not to compare the living creatures in Revelation with the beasts in Daniel, though there are very significant differences, both in their appearances and in their characters. But like Isaiah 6 and Ezekiel 1, Revelation's description of the heavenly court is meant as much to mystify as to clarify. What is seen must be described, but in terms that show that it is beyond any human imagination.

So in this chapter, the one seated on the throne is not described in personal terms. The images that come to the author's mind as he describes his vision are those of jewels and the rainbow – an impression of brightness and glorious light. The creatures around the throne do not fit into any ordinary earthly categories. But the 24 elders who sit around the indescribable throne are recognizable human figures, and the worship that they and the strange creatures offer can be put into words, with the assumption that we the readers can share in that, at least.

So between Genesis and Revelation, a distance has opened up between human beings and God. The familiarity and ease of the relationship between God and Adam is replaced by the awe and the knowledge of our created dependence with which this chapter of Revelation ends. But that gap can be bridged by our worship. In worshipping God, Revelation implies, heaven and earth are united, and we are again in our proper relationship, knowing who made us, and who wills our existence.

And, of course, what makes that bridging possible is Jesus. In Luke's story, we see Jesus acting like the Creator, bringing order out of chaos, commanding the waters. The human Jesus holds together Creator and created as he stands in the boat and stills the storm.

# The Sunday Next Before Lent

— ∿ —

*Exodus 34.29–35*
*2 Corinthians 3.12—4.2*
*Luke 9.28–36*

Today's lectionary readings give us the rare chance to see one biblical author doing a thorough exegesis of another. In the passage from 2 Corinthians, Paul is referring directly to today's reading from Exodus. But his take on the story is eccentric in the extreme. In Exodus, there is no suggestion that the people of Israel are to be blamed for the veiling of Moses' face. It is natural that the after-effect of an encounter with God should be so dazzling. But Paul implies that the veil is a sign of the Israelites' determination not to see what is offered to them. He suggests that they deliberately choose to put a barrier between God and themselves, and that that barrier remains until Jesus removes it.

Paul does not choose to dwell on the figure of Moses, which has a certain poignancy in the Exodus account. As a result of his meeting with God, Moses is able to give his people the law, which shows them the nature of God, and how to be his people. But Moses also pays a price. He can now be himself only in God's presence. With everyone else, he must be veiled. Gift and cost go together.

Instead, Paul wants to home in on other images of 'veiling'. In particular, he is exhorting his readers not to copy the Israelites by choosing to 'veil' things. Christians, he urges, have had the veil removed by the Lord, the Spirit, and must now learn to live and speak openly. Subterfuge and deceit are 'veiled' things. Christians live with the open truth. Is it too much to believe that Paul also has in mind the veil of the temple, torn in two at the crucifixion? If he has, then he is interpreting the Exodus story in a way that has at least some things in common with today's reading from Luke.

Luke is reflecting on the same passage from Exodus, but he is not interested in the concept of veiling, except insofar as the meaning of

40

the event is veiled to the disciples until later. Instead, Luke concentrates on the 'transfiguration' – the dazzling sign of an encounter with God. But his account is also a dense and evocative study of the connection between Jesus' transfiguration and his death.

Like a number of other vital occurrences in Luke's account, the transfiguration happens after prayer. You might like to compare this section with the choosing of the disciples in Luke 6.12ff., and notice that they both happen on the mountain.

Luke's use of the Exodus passage is less direct than Paul's, though the allusion is unmistakable. But although we are meant to recognize the parallel in the transfigured faces of Moses and Jesus, Moses is actually here with Elijah as representative figures – the great lawgiver and the great prophet, symbols of God's covenant relationship with his people.

The transfiguration comes at a pivotal moment in Jesus' mission. Moses and Elijah talk to Jesus about his 'departure' (the word is *exodus*, of course). This might mean nothing more than that he is soon to leave for Jerusalem, but if you put the word together with the fact that the disciples are wrestling with sleep, just as they will in Gethsemane, you see where Luke is pointing us.

Peter, James and John have no idea how to interpret what they have seen but again, Luke gives us, the readers, the clues. The voice from the terrifying cloud echoes the words that were heard at Jesus' baptism. Just as his baptism is a confirmation of his ministry, so his transfiguration is a confirmation of the next, terrible stage of the journey. After this, Jesus begins to try to prepare himself and his followers for what will happen in Jerusalem. But the words spoken by God – words of acceptance, reassurance and commissioning – are also echoed in the jeering words of the crowd at the cross. 'Let him save himself if he is the Messiah of God, his chosen one', Luke writes in 23.35, for it is exactly this certainty of who Jesus is in God's eyes that seems called into question by his death on the cross.

Luke tells us that Peter, James and John did not understand, 'in those days' (9.36), what had happened on the mountain of transfiguration, but he implies that they had been given a key that they would learn to use after Jesus' death and resurrection. They will have the guide to help them see that to be the chosen One of God, the One who fulfils the law and the prophets, is not incompatible with death on the cross.

*Lent*

# The First Sunday of Lent

———— ∾ ————

Deuteronomy 26.1–11
Romans 10.8b–13
Luke 4.1–13

Proust's great theme is that without memory there is no character or understanding. One of the things that is so appealing about his work is that the small memories are at least as significant as the huge ones; indeed, the meaning of the huge is sometimes only apparent through the memory of small details.

Today's reading from Deuteronomy brings us the 'remembrance of time past', mediated in small ways. Here is a ritual for remembering what God did for his people in bringing them out of Egypt. Slavery is remembered, as is God's 'terrifying display of power' (Deuteronomy 26.8), all the pain and the glory that have led to what is now pictured as a settled domestic state. At harvest time, those who have arrived at the luxury of the time of the fulfilment of God's promises are to remember. They are to fill a basket with the best of their crop, go to the appropriate place, and tell again the story of their salvation. Their action is small, easy and apparently banal, but its significance lies in the act of recitation and memory. After the ritual, there is to be a party for all the people who live in the land that God once promised and has now delivered to his people. But the party is for *everyone*, not just the people to whom the promise was made.

Romans, too, is about small things that stand for bigger ones. It comes in the middle of Paul's long and tortuous explanation of how the old and the new covenant fit together, and how the memory of the old can enrich and channel the new. But what is striking about this passage is the apparent *smallness* of what Paul is asking of his readers. They are asked to pay attention only to what is in their hearts and on their lips. For the moment, all that Paul is asking of the Romans is that they remember what brought them to belief in the first place, and that they make that memory available to others by talking about it. Just before the passage set for today, Paul outlines the temptations to complication, to pursue theological issues beyond the reaches of knowledge and memory. We know enough of Paul as a theologian to be sure that he does not always consider these questions to be inappropriate. But it is central to all of his teaching that we can question God only on the basis of our memory of what he has already done. As this particular passage goes on, the picture grows bigger and bigger. Although we are to start only with what is in our hearts and on our lips, that will lead us to the knowledge that our memory of how God acts to save us is, in principle, a shared memory. All who start with that small memory, of Jesus as the risen Lord, can share in God's massive salvific work. Deuteronomy and Romans both know that God's generosity is not limited to those who remember. The point of their remembering is to bring others into the story of their memory.

Luke's account of Jesus' temptation in the wilderness does not connect as obviously as Matthew's might with the theme of memory. While Matthew 4.2 would make any clued-up reader connect Jesus' experience with the Exodus, Luke's references are much more subtle. But the passage is actually full of references to Deuteronomy. Every time Jesus quotes Scripture to the devil, the passage chosen comes from Deuteronomy, and Luke 4.4, 'one does not live by bread alone', refers to Deuteronomy 8.3, which is a direct instruction to remember how God fed his people in the wilderness.

Notice where Luke puts this passage – after God's word of affirmation to Jesus at his baptism, and after Luke's own genealogy, firmly establishing the proper place of Jesus in our memory of God's dealings with the world. Notice also, the ending of this particular passage: we are to look forward as well as back, and remember where in the story the tempter returns. This is a pivotal moment in Luke's story, a moment in which Jesus understands and accepts his calling by rejecting the false paths the devil offers to him.

These passages are all about remembering, accepting and re-enacting who you are. Memory on its own can be debilitating. It can be a memory of what you once were, or might have become. Accepting what your history has made you can be a passive thing, undermining your individuality and choice. But all of these passages are about a dynamic acceptance of the meaning that self-knowledge might offer, not just to you who remember, but to those with whom you choose to share the liberating memory.

# The Second Sunday of Lent

—— ∾ ——

*Genesis 15.1–12, 17–18*
*Philippians 3.17—4.1*
*Luke 13.31–5*

Conversations between God and Abraham are always worth listening to. You can't help noticing that God likes Abraham, and talks to him, man to man, and that Abraham talks freely, even cheekily to God. That is not to say that Abraham forgets his place – when God seems to ask for the sacrifice of Isaac, on whom all the fulfilment of God's promises hangs, Abraham prepares the altar. But the ability to whinge at God, or even to question God, is one that Christian piety has rather bred out of us.

Here, Abram (for he has yet to become Abraham) is devastatingly honest with God about what he really wants. He could have fallen on his knees in worship, and proclaimed his gratitude that God condescended to have any kind of dealings with him. But that would not have been honest. What Abram wants, more than anything, is a son to be his heir. And God does not try to fob him off with anything else, even if the 'anything else' is the much greater reward of intimacy with his Maker. The enormous compassion of God in responding to what Abram desperately wants is matched only by Abram's trust that God will deliver it. God sees his trust and 'reckoned it to him as righteousness' (Genesis 15.6). Apparently, this willingness on the part of God to accept our trust in him as the equivalent of actual goodness is an abiding characteristic of God. We see it over and over again, not least in Jesus' response to the penitent thief on the cross.

There then follows one of those extraordinary Old Testament ceremonies that make your hair stand on end with a mixture of horror and sheer power. Abram watches over and defends the corpses of the animals he has cut up until the symbols of God pass between the bodies, binding God to his promise to Abram. Jeremiah 34.18 suggests

46

that this was a particularly strong ritual, a literal 'cross my heart and hope to die' promise, where the one who breaks the promise must submit to being butchered like the animals. What is extraordinary in this passage from Genesis is that it is God who binds himself with the promise, passing between the animal pieces as a smoking fire-pot and a flaming torch. What it is to cost God to keep not only the letter but the spirit of these his ancient promises to his people is spelled out in today's reading from Luke's Gospel.

Philippians picks up the theme of trust in God's promises. Just as Abram trusts that God will give him a son and a land and an inheritance as incalculable as the stars in the sky, so Paul urges his readers, we too have to trust in the bigger promise. Paul is utterly scornful about those who put their trust in 'earthly things' (Philippians 3.19), but if we are to be as honest as Abram, we will have to admit how much of our security lies here on earth. It is a shock to hear Paul saying that our loyalties declare our citizenship. Where do we really belong? What do our actions, our hopes and our deepest desires suggest about our commitments? Paul does not urge his readers to forget about their bodily, daily needs, but only to long for their transformation. To put comfort and the easy fulfilment of small needs at the top of a list of priorities is to be incapable of understanding the cross. Paul's phrase is harsh in the extreme; he says such people are 'enemies of the cross'. They find God's work of salvation through the cross incomprehensible; it clashes utterly with all their values. Yet, in fact, the only hope there is for the salvation of the body is to learn God's purpose for it. His purpose is rather grander than anything we could design ourselves, but there is no way to it except by trusting in him, even on the cross. Just as God does not laugh at Abram's longing for an heir, so he does not laugh at our needs and desires, but their fulfilment will be his doing, not ours. Abram has the extraordinary and terrifying privilege of seeing the signs of God as he commits himself to his promise. We have seen the Son of God allow himself to be slaughtered like Abram's animals to fulfil that promise.

In the reading from Luke's Gospel, we see our themes coming together. We see in Jesus both the human trust in God and God's own commitment to what he has promised. Nothing is to deter Jesus from the necessary path towards Jerusalem and the cross; nothing is to deter God from what he has bound himself to on our behalf.

# The Third Sunday of Lent

—— ∾ ——

*Isaiah 55.1–9*
*1 Corinthians 10.1–13*
*Luke 13.1–9*

On the face of it, today's readings from Isaiah and Corinthians could hardly provide a greater contrast. The passage from Isaiah is lyrical, joyful, full of assurance, whereas Paul's tone in 1 Corinthians 10 is particularly gloomy and hectoring.

For all kinds of reasons, including the style of writing and the varied references to the historical situation, scholars are now generally agreed that the book of Isaiah is actually made up of the writings of three authors, from different periods. They have all kinds of common themes, so that it makes good sense to bring them together under the heading of Isaiah, which is the name of the first author, at least.

Isaiah 55 is the last chapter of the second section of the book, summing up many of the themes and concerns of chapters 40 to 55. At the heart of this chapter is the picture of God's extravagant invitation to the banquet. There is no cost, all are welcome. Running parallel with that is the theme of forgiveness. There are still those who are trying to *buy* food and wine, although they can see and smell the free riches that are spread out on God's banqueting table. It is almost as if they are afraid to believe in the generosity of God. Surely there must be some catch, they ask? But there are no hidden clauses, Isaiah assures us. The invitation is for all God's people, and through them, for all the world. All who ask for God's mercy will receive it. The only step is to accept God as he is, and trust in his quixotic abundance.

And from this hymn to the love of God, we have to turn to what Paul has to say. The heart of this difficult passage is 1 Corinthians 10.12: 'If you think you are standing, watch out that you do not fall.' The Corinthians obviously believe that they are indeed standing, that they know most of the answers, and that they have entered into God's promises. Paul holds up for them the salutary picture of others who believed themselves so secure that they no longer bothered to attend to the character of God. Perhaps there is not, after all, such a great contrast between Isaiah and Paul. Isaiah reminds us that God's ways are not our ways, and Paul is just recasting that reminder in sterner language. Turning to God is a lifetime's discipline, learning his nature and his will, patiently and humbly, over and over again. The great temptation is to short cuts that lead to more immediate gratification, but as Isaiah asks, 'Why ... spend your money for that which is not bread?' (Isaiah 55.2).

The passage from Luke's Gospel holds Isaiah and Paul together in productive tension. This strange little passage is about both repentance and mercy. Isaiah may seem to stress mercy and Paul repentance, but Isaiah knows that we have to 'return to the LORD' (v. 7) to receive his mercy, and Paul knows that 'God is faithful' (1 Corinthians 10.13) in his desire to hold us in our struggles.

The two halves of Luke's material seem to pull in different directions. Luke 13.1–5 has about it the familiar ring of urgency that is associated with Jesus' ministry. All who meet Jesus are aware that they have come to a crisis point, a point at which they have to take decisions. It sounds as though the people who told Jesus about the death of the Galileans at the hands of Pilate were hoping to provoke Jesus into some kind of violent reaction. If so, they were disappointed. Instead, Jesus faces them with the knowledge of their own mortality. Don't put off life-changing decisions, Jesus urges them, because you may never have the chance again.

But doesn't the story of the fig tree then suggest the opposite? The fig tree is offered mercy and a second chance to prove itself. I suspect that this was a funny story, in Jesus' original telling of it. It may have involved a bit of horseplay with manure, perhaps. Certainly, when you put verses 1–5 together with verses 6–9, you can't help feeling that someone is teasing. Are we in a great rush, or can we take our time? But if what is on offer is the generous mercy of God – call it manure, or call it bread and wine, as Isaiah does – why wait? What possible reason can there be to procrastinate about such an offer?

The Royal Shakespeare Company's production of *The Lion, the Witch and the Wardrobe* has a song in which Aslan invites everyone to the feast. 'Come to the table,' he sings, 'there's plenty of room at the table for all.'

# The Fourth Sunday of Lent

—— ∽ ——

*Joshua 5.9–12*
*2 Corinthians 5.16–21*
*Luke 15.1–3, 11b–32*

Luke, the expert writer, puts the prodigal son as the third of a set of stories about losing and finding. All of the stories emphasize God's joy at finding what had been lost, but the story of the prodigal subtly changes the emphasis. The centre of the first two stories is the action of God. God seeks, God finds, God rejoices and calls others to rejoice. But in the prodigal son, the focus of the story is the response of the two sons. The younger son, the prodigal, has to learn the value of what he once took for granted. He sees his father chiefly as a provider, not a person. The father is there to give the son what he wants and then stand back. Even when the son returns in great need, there is a sort of calculation in his rehearsal of what he will say to his father. He does not say, 'I know my father loves me and will forgive me.' Instead, he is thinking about his own need for food, and how best to get it.

The father's role in the story, unlike that of the shepherd with the lost sheep and the woman with the lost coin, is quite passive. He stays at home and waits, until that pivotal moment in the story when he throws his dignity to the four winds and runs out to hug his son. But notice what Luke tells us about the father's motives. He says (Luke 15.20) that the father is 'filled with compassion'. He does not want the grovelling speech that the son had prepared. Think of the enormous loss of face that the younger son must have been feeling, to have to return in such a way. But the father does not humiliate him further. Instead, he manages to make the son feel that he is doing his father a favour by returning. Does the son recognize that what he needs is not just bread, but also that unfailing love?

But the sting in the tail of this story is the response of the elder son. And, looking again at the opening verses of Luke 15, notice that the

50

audience for these stories is the Pharisees. Clearly, the elder son is the one who really needs to hear what is being said. The elder son does not provoke wild rejoicing and overflowing compassion, but that does not mean that he is not loved. The problem for him, as for the Pharisees – as for us? – is that he cannot believe his father loves him, while at the same time showing such love to one so different from him. Both sons have lessons to learn about the love of the father.

The reading from 2 Corinthians shows that Paul, at least, has understood this message about God. We have here the active, seeking God, who reaches out in Jesus to bring back the lost world. We also have the God who looks at us only with compassion, not wanting to humiliate us or judge us, but only to offer us the chance for a genuinely new relationship. Paul talks quite often in his letters about newness in Christ. He must constantly, particularly at the beginning of his ministry, have faced those who could not forget what he had been. But he knows that God has forgotten it, and made him new.

Paul does not minimize the cost of the new life God offers. He could hardly put it more forcefully. He says that 'he made him [Jesus] to be sin who knew no sin' (2 Corinthians 5.21). You can't just take a wet duster to sin, but God has done the work that we could never have done. Our part is now to accept it, and to be part of it. The next chapter of the story of the prodigal son, according to Paul, is that the younger son goes out of his way to mend the relationship with his brother and then, together, they go out and search for others who need their father's love.

So then, just a few words about the lovely verses from Joshua. These are people who have lived on promises for so long, and are now eating the fruit of the promised land. At last they can forget the past, the only reality they knew in the years of journeying. Now they are home. They can tell you, better than anyone, about the faithful love of God.

These readings are a good choice for Mothering Sunday. They speak of the active, seeking, reliable love of God, which human families can sometimes mirror, faintly. But whether they succeed or fail, they whet your appetite for the lasting love of God.

# The Fifth Sunday of Lent

—— ∿ ——

*Isaiah 43.16–21*
*Philippians 3.4b–14*
*John 12.1–8*

Our Lenten readings have now brought us face to face with what this season is about. We are attempting, with some discipline, to prepare ourselves for Good Friday and Easter. At the start of Lent, with the story of his testing in the wilderness, we see Jesus accepting his calling, with all that will be involved in that. Now at last, in the passage from John's Gospel, some of those around Jesus are beginning to understand where the road to Jerusalem is really leading.

John sets the story of the anointing of Jesus' feet in the home of Lazarus, Martha and Mary. You might expect that they would be the last people to anticipate the cross. They, more than any, have cause to know the power of Jesus, and to believe that death has no hold on him. But Jesus explicitly states that Mary's anointing is a burial anointing, and that she is knowingly performing a prophetic act.

Mary's act is a pivotal moment of loveliness and intimacy between two, other, brutal sets of preparation for Jesus' death. John paints a very physical picture, with the details about Mary's hair, and the fragrance of the perfume, as though he wants us to *feel* the comfort being offered to Jesus. At last, someone accepts and honours what he is to do, rather than denying or misunderstanding. But just before the anointing, we see the Jews planning how they will arrest Jesus, and immediately after the anointing, we see Judas preparing himself to betray.

In keeping with one of John's constant themes, there is no grey area in which we might try to understand either Judas or the Jews. In John's Gospel, there is always a stark choice between light and dark, and Judas has chosen the dark. Perhaps he might have tried to justify his anger at Mary's extravagance – after all, he could point to the many occasions

52

when Jesus taught the importance of caring for the poor. But John allows him no such excuse. Essentially, in all the choices Judas has already made to bring him to this point in the story, he has been setting himself against Jesus.

It is particularly moving to turn from Judas to Paul. Paul is someone who has allowed himself to be changed by God, to be made new, and he knows how things might have been different. He lists all the claims of family, religion, status and personal choice that might so easily have kept him from Christ, and they make an impressive catalogue. Yet what flows through this passage is Paul's overwhelming sense of joy and privilege in knowing Christ Jesus. But even this knowing is not something he prides himself on. No effort of his own, no goodness of his own, has brought him here. It is, from first to last, the work of God in Christ. Paul's great theme, which runs through so many of his letters, is of God's power to make new, to recreate, to justify.

But, of course, the hard side of that, the side that Mary recognizes and Judas will not, is that the only way to be made new is through Christ, and that sharing Christ's way of life leads to the resurrection, but only through the cross. Paul is not advocating that we embrace suffering as a discipline, or because it is good for us, or out of some vague piety but because, whatever happens, we must not be parted from Christ. If clinging to Christ takes you through suffering and death then, Paul proclaims with fierce joy, that is a small price to pay for the enormous privilege of belonging to Christ.

The promise that we can, like Paul, let go of the past and be made new, resonates throughout the glorious poetry of our passage from Isaiah. God reminds Israel there are no dead ends in God, no situations beyond his creative resourcefulness. There is a clear parallel between the power of God that brought Israel out of Egypt, against the massed forces of the mighty Egyptian army, and the power of God to create and recreate. In Isaiah 43.19, God talks about the 'new thing' that he is doing, and the language of newness, of 'springing forth', is reminiscent of the language of the Genesis creation story. We have again one of those insights into the character of God, that God's faithfulness and his inventiveness go hand in hand. It is because God will never give up, never turn away, never abandon what he has made that the power of God to create and raise from the dead is always at work. Be prepared to let go of the old things, God urges, and look out for the 'water in the wilderness'.

# Palm Sunday

— ～ —

*Isaiah 50.4–9a*
*Philippians 2.5–11*
*Luke 23.1–49*

Luke's account of the trial and death of Jesus revolves around images of judgement, and images of truth and falsehood. At the start of the chapter, one trial – the trial conducted by the chief priests and scribes of Israel – has already taken place. It has found Jesus guilty, because the assembled judges desperately wanted him to be guilty. But they are aware that the 'evidence' that they have used to condemn Jesus will not stand up in a trial before Pilate. So they accuse Jesus of leading a revolt against Roman taxes – a clear lie. Just before the Last Supper, Luke shows us that the chief priests and scribes had intended to trap Jesus on just this issue (see Luke 20.19ff.), and that Jesus had avoided the trap.

Pilate then gets his one chance to choose truth, but instead chooses expediency. He sees a way to shift responsibility to Herod, and buries his knowledge that Jesus is innocent.

Herod is a far less clear-sighted and subtle character than Pilate, and he is hoping for a show. He has heard of Jesus as a miracle-worker, and Luke tells us that he questions Jesus for a long time, clearly hoping to make him do magic. When he is disappointed, he behaves like a spoiled child with a broken toy.

The list of those who choose not to see the truth grows longer. Already it contains the Jewish authorities, Pilate and Herod. Now the soldiers and the crowd add their names. The crowd shout out, with a bitter irony of which they are wholly ignorant, that they want the criminal Barabbas released instead of Jesus. Barabbas has actually committed the crimes of which Jesus is innocent and, to add another twist, his name translates as 'son of the Father'. When they have the eternal Son of the Father at their mercy, the crowd choose someone else.

Even the weeping women who follow Jesus on the road to the cross cannot see clearly. Their tears blind them to the fact that what is going on is the judgement of Jerusalem, not of Jesus.

As the onlookers watch the crucifixion, they shout out what they think are witty remarks. 'Save yourself,' they shout to Jesus, 'you were always on about salvation, now do it!' They do not know, of course, that salvation is what the cross is all about. Our salvation.

Throughout this passage, Jesus is totally in command. He answers his accusers when he chooses to, and remains silent when he chooses to. He alone of all the crowds and individuals involved in this story can see the big picture. He knows what he is doing, and he knows what his death will accomplish. Luke makes this clear in the story of the repentant thief whom Jesus forgives, and in the response of the centurion. We are left in no doubt about the power of God, working through the death of Christ.

And if this underplays the terrible desolation that Matthew and Mark show us in Jesus' death on the cross, it is only because it puts all the emphasis on something that is common to all four Gospel accounts of the passion. The path that Jesus follows throughout his ministry leads inevitably to the cross, and it is a path that he chooses freely, out of obedience. Small changes at various stages along the way, little bits of compromise, accommodation, playing to the crowds, using his power to please; all of these could have brought Jesus to a different place. But they would have been at the cost of obscuring his message about God.

The profound passage from Philippians is a meditation on the connection between Jesus' obedience and his divinity. It comes to the extraordinary conclusion that it is only because Jesus is wholly obedient to the Father that we know he is to be worshipped. We know Jesus to be the Son of God because he, unlike us, chooses the path of obedience, even when that leads to the cross. If we use this lens to look back at the ministry of Jesus, we can see how clearly the whole of Jesus' life and death is focused on making the Father visible and present, and how constantly this meant resisting and rejecting the common human urge to power and recognition for himself.

The passage from Isaiah makes the same point. The Servant is a teacher only because he is a listener first (Isaiah 50.4). He listens to God, and so all that he teaches, and all that happens to him, however terrible, will make room for God to be seen and heard.

The reward for the Servant's obedience is vindication. The reward for Jesus' obedience is the chance of vindication for all.

*Easter*

# Easter Sunday

— ～ —

*Isaiah 65.17–25*
*Acts 10.34–43*
*Luke 24.1–12*

Creation and resurrection are mirror images of each other, and they are held together by the nature and purpose of God. At its simplest, God is Life-giver. That has endless implications and ramifications, all of them glorious. In God there is endless inventiveness that can bring newness out of what appeared to be finished; in God, there are no dead ends, a new door can open in what seemed to be a brick wall; in God there is endless patience and resourcefulness that cannot be defeated by even the worst of our sinfulness. All of this is proclaimed today in our three readings.

Isaiah explicitly makes the connection between creation and fulfilment. In the new creation of God, the old can simply be left behind. Israel can at last forget their unfaithfulness and disobedience. They do not have to go on seeking forgiveness, because they are made new. And yet, all the same longings of the old creation are still there. The longing for health and security, for home and food, for family and prosperity have so often led God's people astray, because they have tried to secure them without reference to God. But that does not make those longings wrong in themselves. Indeed, Isaiah says that God rejoices in what he has made, and delights to see his people happy (Isaiah 65.19). The difference is that in this new creation, there will be an intimacy of communication between God and his people that was missing in the old. 'Before they call I will answer,' God says (v. 24).

In Isaiah's vision, the renewed people of God bring blessings for the whole of creation. Similarly, as Peter reflects in Acts, he is beginning to see the enormous implications of belief in Jesus. Acts shows the earliest Christians constantly being nudged into sharing their faith more and more widely. Some are anxious about this, fearing to lose the clarity of

58

the original message, afraid to step outside the bounds of what Jesus himself had done. But Peter recognizes that God has been at work for Cornelius; it has the familiar pattern that Peter knows from the life, death and resurrection of Jesus. He knows that he has been called to preach, and he knows – who better – that the content of his preaching is the forgiveness, the new start, that is offered in Jesus.

Peter's part in witnessing the resurrection is made all the more moving by the fact that the last time we saw Peter in Luke's account, he was weeping bitterly at his betrayal of Jesus (Luke 22.62). Peter had every reason to believe that that was how his relationship with Jesus would end. All the heady excitement of the ministry he had shared with Jesus had been forgotten in his own need for safety. Forgotten, too, was everything Jesus had tried to explain to his friends about the necessary end of his mission. Perhaps 'forgotten' is the wrong word, since all the Gospel accounts suggest that the disciples stubbornly refused to understand what Jesus was saying – it was just too different from what they hoped for.

Certainly, Luke's account of the resurrection, like all the Gospel accounts, starts in darkness and despair. A few of Jesus' friends creep out to give the body the proper care that had been impossible in the horrible press of the soldiers and the crowds and the heat of the day before. None of the disciples who had shared most closely in Jesus' mission are present in this dawn scene. Despair might explain their absence, or perhaps lingering fears for their own safety, or even a degree of self-absorption in their grief. It is, we are told, a group of women who are the first to hear about the resurrection.

'Remember,' they are told, 'remember and understand.' But, away from the dazzling messengers of the resurrection, the women cannot make their explanation convincing to the other disciples. Only Peter goes to check up on their story. Does he go with the beginnings of a wild and desperate hope? Does he go, starting to remember what Jesus had told them, starting to remember all that he had seen and heard in Jesus' company? Does he begin to sense again the living, thrilling presence of God that had been so strongly part of Jesus' mission, and that had seemed such a cruel joke after Jesus' death?

Peter is given a chance to start again. His betrayal of Jesus is not the end of their friendship, as Peter had believed and deserved, but the beginning of Peter's new life, in which Jesus entrusts his gospel to Peter and the friends who had abandoned him at the cross. They had experienced the depths of doubt; who better then to preach the gospel of forgiveness and assurance?

# The Second Sunday of Easter

—— ∾ ——

*Exodus 14.10–31; 15.20–1*
*Acts 5.27–32*
*John 20.19–31*

People are very good at doubting. We seem to be able to move with effortless ease from the utmost certainty to the utmost doubt within moments.

In the reading from Exodus today, just remember what has already happened. Israelites and Egyptians have both seen the terrible plagues that came upon the land, and they have both, eventually, made the connection between the plagues and the enslavement of the Israelites. Pharaoh has finally let the slaves go, and they have moved off, accompanied day and night by the physical sign of God's presence, in the pillar of cloud by day and the pillar of fire by night. Yet, suddenly, Pharaoh changes his mind, forgets all that has happened, and sets out in pursuit of his erstwhile slaves, and they, in turn, forget all that God has done for them, and panic wildly.

What follows reads like God spelling things out in CAPITAL LETTERS. 'Look, you lot,' he seems to say, with affectionate exasperation, as he makes a path through the waves of the sea, 'try to pay attention and remember this for three seconds.' He goes to exaggerated lengths to make it clear to the dimwits – Egyptians, churned up, drowned in the raging torrent; Israelites, feet not even wet. Got it?

Well, for the time being at least, they got the message, and 'feared the Lord and believed in the Lord' (Exodus 14.31). But it doesn't last long.

There is a similar pattern in today's Gospel reading. Again, remember what has gone before. The disciples have seen the power of Jesus, teaching, healing, even raising the dead. They have heard, from Mary Magdalene, about the resurrection. Yet somehow, they are still sitting huddled behind locked doors, frightened and self-pitying. And again, as with the Israelites, God responds with patient humour, and a demonstration that should satisfy even the most hardened doubter.

Into the locked room steps Jesus, whom the disciples had last seen dying in agony. He is clearly the same man – he makes a point of showing them his wounds. He also breathes on them, just in case they should begin to suspect that he was not alive but some kind of ghost.

If the disciples had been able to imagine a conversation with Jesus after his crucifixion, how would it have gone? 'Where were you when I needed you?' perhaps? Or even 'Didn't you listen to a word I was saying all those years?' But there is no mention of the past here. Instead, those who had earned judgement are given the task of judging others; those who had doubted God's power and his promises are given the living, abiding presence of God in the Holy Spirit.

But even that is not enough. Thomas chooses not to believe the combined witness of his friends. He is unconvinced both by their words and by their sudden transformation from defeat to glowing joy. So, just for Thomas, here is the full, unmistakable, physical presence of the crucified and risen Lord. Satisfied, Thomas? Can you manage now to be Convinced Thomas, rather than Doubting Thomas?

Today's passage from Acts suggests that some, at least, of the disciples managed to hold on to their certainty, and never to tire of explaining to others what had been so very hard for them to understand. Can this really be the same Peter, who had been so anxious to distance himself from Jesus at the crucifixion? Yet here he is, suddenly unafraid of arrest and imprisonment. In fact, he is being thoroughly cheeky to the council. 'We're the law-abiding ones,' he says, 'you're the ones who ought to be tried, for misunderstanding our God and killing Jesus.'

But Peter has learned enough about himself to be humble in his witness, too. He knows that it is, ultimately, the presence of the Holy Spirit that guarantees the truth of what he is saying. Although you would think that we have seen more than enough of the power of God to convince us for ever, today's readings suggest otherwise. We will sometimes remember and trust, and sometimes forget and doubt. We will sometimes be able to speak with strength and conviction of all that God has done for us in Christ, and sometimes we will panic and stutter. That is why the real witness to the resurrection power of God is God himself. The Holy Spirit, the Comforter, the Life-giver, the gift to us of God's continuing presence with us, carries on the job of bearing witness to the crucified and risen Christ, quietly and inexorably. God, in his humour and grace, asks us to join in, to tell what we have seen and heard. We can give our testimonies, however feeble, and rely on the power of the Holy Spirit to make God present.

# The Third Sunday of Easter

—— ∽ ——

*Zephaniah 3.14–20*
*Acts 9.1–20*
*John 21.1–19*

This final chapter of John's Gospel is a chapter full of echoes, back to the earthly ministry of Jesus and forward to the life of the Church after the ascension. For example, compare the story of the miraculous catch of fish here in John's Gospel with the stories in Mark and Luke of the calling of Peter, and you will see all kinds of similarities – you might like to look, in particular, at Luke 5.1–11, which is not, according to Luke, the first time that Peter sees Jesus, but is the moment at which he makes a commitment.

In the early stories of the calling of the disciples, the excitement is palpable. They recognize in Jesus something dynamic, and they willingly throw in their lot with him. They expect drama and glory, without too much responsibility – Jesus will tell them what to do. But if the stories at the beginning of the Gospels are the honeymoon period, what we see here in John's Gospel is the commitment 'till death do us part'. Once, Peter thought that being a fisher of men was going to put him in the spotlight, to be admired and loved, but now he has seen Jesus crucified and risen, and he knows that the calling to follow Jesus is grim and costly. John pulls no punches here, clearly linking Peter's call to feed the sheep with the death that Peter is to suffer.

And if Peter initially left his nets to follow Jesus in the throes of a kind of hero worship, he now takes up the charge Jesus gives him without any illusions. He knows that he has betrayed Jesus; he knows what kind of mission Jesus' is – at last; he knows that he will not be able to rely on Jesus to rescue him from tricky or terrible situations. He is prepared for the awesome responsibility of caring for people as Jesus did.

It is characteristic of John's theology that Peter's mission is based on love. In John 21.5, Jesus calls out 'children', to attract their attention in the boat. This is the word that John's Epistles use as the main description of the Christian community to which they are written. In this story, as in the Epistles, there is no doubt that the children are beloved. What is in doubt is how they show that love, which is what brought them into being and is the whole reason for their existence. They are more than willing to accept the love of God, but are they also willing to share it? So when Jesus gives Peter his hard and dangerous task of bringing the Christian community, the Church, into existence, he does not say to Peter, 'I love you and trust you.' Instead he asks, 'Do you love *me*?' It is only when Peter acknowledges that loving God is about giving, not just about getting, that he can play the part that God has for him.

Today's New Testament readings show us the two leaders on whom the Church is built accepting their commission. Paul's meeting with Jesus on the road to Damascus, like Peter's meeting with the risen Christ, is not primarily a joyous occasion. Jesus' words to Paul are almost harsh. Nothing about forgiveness or love, but a ruthless forcing on Paul of the understanding that to persecute his followers is to persecute Jesus. It is, if you like, the other side of Peter's commission, to love Jesus by loving the 'children'. Just as Peter had to learn, at last, to let go of all the illusions of greatness that he had cherished when he started to follow Jesus, so Paul, too, has to let go of all the things he thought he knew and start again. The dazzling light that brings darkness is the symbol of what will happen to Paul, the journey of abnegation that he will have to undertake, letting go of his own sight and learning to see with Jesus' eyes.

Peter and Paul, the founders of the Church, both accept their responsibilities for God's people because they know their own need. Could this be some kind of a parable for the Church? Could it be that we are not actually called always to be *right*, but simply to demonstrate by our own gratitude and love that God can and will forgive? If God can go on loving and forgiving the Church, which has been such a sorry mess for so much of its history, then his power to love and forgive must be enormous indeed.

Over and over again, as Zephaniah bears witness, God has forgiven his people, out of his great love for us. What we have to do is be grateful, and pass it on.

# The Fourth Sunday of Easter

—— ∽ ——

Genesis 7.1–5, 11–18; 8.6–18; 9.8–13
Acts 9.36–43
John 10.22–30

Today's passage from St John's Gospel is part of the escalating conflict between Jesus and 'the Jews'. From the magnificent opening verses of the Gospel, setting out the cosmic significance of the coming of Jesus, John has hammered home the point that there can be no doubt about who Jesus is. His authoritative personality, his miracles and his teaching all make it clear that Jesus and the Father are one. When, here in verse 25, Jesus says that he has already told them who he is we, the readers, know that he has indeed answered their question in all that he has said and done since his coming.

How is it, then, that the religious authorities, the supposed experts, are still asking the same old question? Over and over again in the preceding chapters, they see Jesus' miracles, hear his teaching, question those whom he has healed, and still they can't make up their minds. They are not so completely blinded to the nature of God that they can easily dismiss Jesus, but they have, despite their years of study and devotion, managed to keep God at enough of a distance to make a positive identification difficult. In their heart of hearts, they really do not want Jesus to be telling the truth, and they keep hoping that he will say or do something that will allow them with a clear conscience not to believe.

What is it about Jesus' presentation of God that they so hate? Is it the reality of it, the inescapable *choice* that Jesus lays before them? Most religious people, then as now, manage to tame their God to the point where he doesn't make too much difference to their lives and their choices. They pay him lip-service and carry on regardless. But Jesus won't let people do that. He is God's presence, standing face to face with people, and *making* them (us) decide.

64

The terrible, painful fact that some people choose not to believe runs throughout John's Gospel and, indeed, the Bible as a whole. It is particularly poignant in situations, like the one described here by John, where those who reject God are the ones who should know him best, his own people. So much of the interaction between God and his people that the prophets show us, too, suggests that *thinking* you know God and have got him where you want him is the best possible inoculation against really catching God, the full-blown raging fever of his reality. Any Christian who thinks this is just a warning to 'the Jews' is in trouble.

The story of Noah's ark starts off, in Genesis 6, with the emphasis on those who are about to perish, those who have chosen not to follow God's way. But the story quickly shifts, in those sections we are reading today, to the preservation of the just. The point of the story is renewal, not destruction. Most retellings of the story tend to dwell on the details of life on board the ark while the waters raged around it. But the editor who brings us the final version we have in Genesis is not so easily distracted. His story moves quickly to the climax, when the covering of the ark is removed, and the passengers can get on with what they were saved for, which is the restoration of the earth to its proper fullness and variety of life, but also to its proper covenant relationship with its maker.

Both the story of Noah and Jesus' words in John make it clear that God's purpose is salvation, and that we are created to choose life, though the choice is genuinely ours. But the temptation is to get into a kind of ark mentality and to think that salvation is about getting our people in, into the safety and warmth, and battening down the hatches against the raging world outside. But the point of the ark is the moment where people and animals troop out into the ravaged world to help it start again. The ark is only a good metaphor for the Church if we remember that the point is not to get into the ark, but to let the life of the ark flow out into the world.

The beautiful little story of Tabitha, today's reading from Acts, reinforces Jesus' message in John 10.28, 'I give them eternal life, and they will never perish.' Tabitha is clearly someone who has chosen Jesus, and helped to share his life and love with all around her. She chooses the living God, and her reward is life. Choose life, all three readings beg. The choice is ours, but let us choose life.

# The Fifth Sunday of Easter

— ∼ —

*Genesis 22.1–18*
*Acts 11.1–18*
*John 13.31–5*

The verses from St John's Gospel come at the turning point of the Last Supper. Judas has just left the room, and there is now no going back. A sense of urgency seems to overtake Jesus after this. The supper is over, and Jesus begins to talk, to explain, as though trying to make the disciples understand at last, to impress upon them some of the things that they should already know. But whenever one of the disciples does speak in the verses that follow today's reading, it is only to demonstrate how puzzled they are, and how little they understand, even at this late hour.

The two themes of today's reading from John are related, and are characteristic of all of John's writing. First of all, now that Judas has gone about his business, and the cross is inescapable, Jesus speaks of glorification. In all of John's writing, the cross is the moment of illumination, when God is to be seen in Christ and Christ is to be seen in God. Second, Jesus talks about love, the new commandment that he gives to his disciples. The themes are connected because what is revealed in the cross is the love of God in Christ. In the cross we see that love is the whole nature of God in his dealings with us.

The commandment to love is not exactly new. Most of the Old Testament law is designed to make Israel a loving community, that will treat its members and those who come in contact with it with justice and care. But here in John's Gospel the connection is made explicit and unavoidable. Just as Jesus shows us the nature of God, so we are called to show others that same nature. Just as Israel was designed to be a community that showed the nature of its God, so Jesus' followers are called to be a community from which the love of God, God's very nature, shines out.

66

So what is this love that we are called to receive and transmit? It is, apparently, the love that Jesus has shown to us, his followers. We are to reflect back what we have received and, in doing that, we will be reflecting the God whom we believe in. We will be restoring his image in ourselves, by making ourselves like the Son. We were created in God's image, and now we are to be restored in that image again, by showing the love of the Father and the Son.

This great 'new commandment' can fill us with a great sense of hopelessness and failure, if we do not read John carefully. We know that we are wholly incapable of showing the love of God, but this commandment is given to disciples who don't seem to understand a word Jesus is saying, and who are shortly going to betray him. Jesus' love for his disciples is utterly realistic. He knows the kind of people he has chosen, then and now. They are ordinary, fallible. To these people, Jesus entrusted and continues to entrust himself and his message. They are worthy because they are loved. That is the Christian disciple's only qualification for the great task we are given.

In the story of Abraham's willingness to sacrifice Isaac and in Peter's attempt to explain why he is admitting Gentiles to fellowship, we see people struggling to understand and show the love of God.

Abraham has learned two very important things that most of us never learn in a lifetime: that God comes first, beyond anything else; and that however much we think we love our family or our friends, God loves them more. Abraham knows that God is to be trusted, even when he cannot understand what God is doing. And he trusts God because God is trusting him. God is making Abraham a part of his great purpose of salvation for the world, and Abraham has come close enough to God to know that you cannot bargain about salvation. You cannot say, 'Yes, please, I'll have the salvation, but I won't give anything in return.'

Peter, too, has learned enough about God to recognize the signs of his presence, however unlikely and unpredicted. And so he becomes the means whereby God's salvation comes to Cornelius and his household.

Knowing that we are loved and trusted by God is the beginning of fulfilling this new commandment. We do not have to generate this love ourselves, because it is given to us. Christians are, most fundamentally, people who know that God is love, and we know it, not because we are better at loving than anyone else, but because we know that God has loved us and trusted us, even before we were either lovely or trustworthy.

# The Sixth Sunday of Easter

—— ≈ ——

*Ezekiel 37.1–14*
*Acts 16.9–15*
*John 14.23–9*

The clue to Ezekiel's famous vision of the dry bones comes in verse 11. What Ezekiel has been hearing from the people all around him is a despair that is like death. 'Our bones are dried up, and our hope is lost,' they moan. They are incapable of change or growth because they do not believe in the possibility of life.

God agrees with them about their condition. They *are* lifeless, spiritless, with no home except the shadowy grave. But they need not be without hope. So God takes Ezekiel to the valley full of bones, and makes him prophesy. Just picture it for a moment: the man alone in a valley of dust and death, shouting out, calling upon life and breath and spirit; and seeing the response, as the bones collect themselves, take on flesh and begin to be alive.

It is perfectly clear that this life is not 'natural'. It does not come from the bones themselves, but from God. And the same is true of the people of Israel. In themselves, they have lost the ability to live, but God is going to give them his own breath, his own spirit, so that the life they live will be God's. Their total absence of life and hope is to be remedied by God's gift of his own presence, which is life.

Jesus is talking about absence and presence in the Gospel reading, as well. The whole of the Last Supper is overshadowed by the knowledge that it is the end. The disciples may not quite have taken in what is to happen, and how soon, but they must have picked up the new note in Jesus' teaching after dinner, as he attempts to prepare them for a time when he will not be there.

In this passage, Jesus is setting out the ways in which, as a matter of fact, he will still be with the disciples, come what may. First of all, he will be with them whenever they remember and try to stay faithful to what he has taught them (John 14.23 – 'Those who love me will keep my word'). Next, in trying to continue in love and commitment to Jesus, they will be continuing Jesus' own work of making God present. So, by their love, they can continue the incarnating work of Jesus, and the Father will be present with them, as he was with Jesus. And, of course, since where the Father is, so is the Son (cf. John 14.10), by being the place of God's presence, they are also being the place where Jesus is present (v. 23 – 'my Father will love them, and *we* will come to them and make our home with them').

But, lastly, because Jesus is nothing if not realistic about his followers, he does not expect them to manage this task of loving God and making him present on their own. The Holy Spirit is to come, as a constant enabler of the presence of God (v. 26). Their new life, like that of Ezekiel's dry bones, is not something that they have inside them, waiting to be realized, but is the gift of God.

So, in a kind of circular argument, God is asking them to continue to make him present, as Jesus does, and he is giving them his own life and presence to make that possible. Over and over again, in God's great and gracious plan, we see that we are asked to do and to give what has already been done and given to us by God. We are given forgiveness and asked to forgive, we are given love and asked to love, we are given God and asked to make him a home with us. Our dry bones don't have to generate their own life.

We know what happened next. We know that the disciples went straight from listening to this great promise about the continuing presence of God in Christ through the Spirit to total confusion and despair. But we also know that the promised new life did somehow percolate their dry bones, and that they did rise to the task of sharing God's life and love with the world around them, and that whenever they did, they found that God was there already. For example, in the story of Lydia, as we are told it in Acts 16, we hear that 'the Lord opened her heart to listen eagerly to what was said by Paul' (v. 14). It might have been tempting to think that Paul's fluency and fervour converted Lydia, but the author of Acts is clear that God was at work on both sides of that conversation, making possible what he was asking for. Dry bones can live, with the life of God.

# The Seventh Sunday of Easter

—— ∼ ——

*Ezekiel 36.24–8*
*Acts 16.16–34*
*John 17.20–6*

The verses chosen from Ezekiel for today are a beautiful and encouraging picture of the restoration of Israel, but they urgently need to be read in the light of the verses immediately before and after them. The concentrated, central picture is one of Israel restored at last to life. God searches for his people, scattered among all the nations, rootless and nationless, and brings them home. He himself performs all the ceremonies necessary to wipe away the taint of having lived for so long among idolaters, and he puts his own life in them, so that they are no longer tempted to return to the wicked ways that led to their downfall in the first place. God reiterates his great covenant promise to Abraham and to Moses, but this time, he himself will keep both sides of the covenant, because it will be God's own spirit that enables the people to respond to his promise.

What the verses before make clear, however, is that this is not a desperate strategy on God's part to try to keep his complex plot on course, but a sign of God's eternal and unchanging purpose, which nothing can deflect. God chooses a people to be his own, as a sign of hope to the nations, and nothing can prevent them from fulfilling their function. Even their unfaithfulness and incomprehension becomes a means for God to demonstrate his loving and renewing power. God is holy and glorious, Ezekiel tells us, and nothing will prevent that colossal majesty from becoming visible to the world.

Jesus' prayer in John's Gospel has something of the same force. Again, what is at issue is the glory of God. And, just as in Ezekiel, nothing can compromise the glory of God. The very things that would, logically, deny God's power and reality become the means of confirming them. Above all, in John, the cross of Christ is the moment at which he is glorified, and in which the unity of Father and Son is made visible. So when, in John 17.22, Jesus says, 'The glory that you have given me I have given them', we are bound to conclude that this glory that we share with Jesus is the glory of suffering, and that in obedient suffering, Christians share in the unity of Father, Son and Spirit. This is not to glamorize or spiritualize suffering, but to know, above all, that it cannot ultimately derail the purposes of God. Ezekiel knows that Israel's suffering is sometimes their own fault, and sometimes falls upon them because of their faithfulness to God. Jesus knows that the suffering of his followers will sometimes be because they are running away from the truth and sometimes because they are witnessing to it. Either way it can and will be used to God's loving and life-giving purpose.

Acts is very good at bringing complex and abstract theology to life in practical examples. We have here two connected stories, one in which the glory of God seems to be being declared, and one in which it actually takes root in changed lives.

First of all, Paul and his companions are in the middle of a fruitful mission in Philippi, but their success has its downside. It has attracted the attentions of a kind of stalker, who follows them around, shouting what actually sound like rather flattering descriptions of their work. But although she is acknowledging their connection with 'the Most High God', and their power to offer salvation, she herself is not converted, and her apparent confirmation of their task does not attract others. There is a kind of mechanical recognition of the presence of the divine, without any real willingness or ability to connect with it. This girl has been forced to use her instinct for the numinous as a commercial commodity and so, paradoxically, it has become utterly worthless.

Her witness does not convert, and neither does Paul's exorcism. Instead, these mighty displays land Paul in prison and there, in his weakness and helplessness, the power of God is displayed. How does Paul know, so instinctively, that this is not a moment to stand up and boast? He could have shouted, in the rubble of the prison, standing up, with his shackles in tatters, 'See what my God will do to free me? See how much he values me?' Instead, he chooses to stay captive, almost passive, and to sit and wait by the open door of his jail.

Somehow, the jailer makes the leap between the force that could have been used and the care that actually was. Instantly, he sees the God who channels all his power into love. The glory of God is displayed in that prison cell, not in the broken chains, but in the newly forged bonds of love.

# Day of Pentecost

—— ～ ——

*Genesis 11.1–9*
*Acts 2.1–21*
*John 14.8–17*

The story of the Tower of Babel continues the theology of sin that is found in Genesis 2 and 3, in the story of the Fall. Eve and Adam's desire to seize for themselves a knowledge that properly belongs to God alone is at the heart of their fractured relationship with God. Similarly, here in Genesis 11, the people begin to build their tower so that they can get as near to heaven as possible, and grab a bit of fame and glory for themselves. 'Let us make a name for ourselves,' they decide.

But with this impulse to power also goes a nameless and ill-expressed fear. The people persuade themselves that without their tower, they will be 'scattered abroad upon the face of the whole earth'. As far as we, the readers, can see, there is absolutely no justification for this fear. Who is threatening them? What force will dissipate them? But their instinct is to build high and huddle together.

And, of course, as a result of their actions, the very thing that they had feared actually happens. They are indeed forced apart and scattered over the whole earth, because they can no longer understand each other or work together. The Lord, we are told, 'confused their language'. Perhaps that way they might start to make a little more sense. Their earlier statements and actions might have had a kind of mad logic to them, but they were without any basis in truth. After Babel, they can at least no longer pretend that their system makes sense.

The Acts story of the day of Pentecost is a richly satisfying reversal of Babel. The scattered people of God come together; they had been used to being separated by language, but now God's own words unite them. The messengers of God are people who know they are dependent upon

God. The Holy Spirit comes upon Peter and the other apostles in a powerful and supernatural way, and they cannot even begin to pretend that this is their own doing. If the builders of the Tower of Babel are guilty of trying to be like God, the disciples are only too aware that they are nothing without God's power.

Peter's Pentecost speech sets out the great paradox of God's power. Here are the apostles – simple men, not trained linguists – making themselves heard and understood to the great polyglot crowd. Peter reminds his hearers of the great Old Testament promises of the coming of God's Spirit in power, and claims that this is what they are now witnessing. And in the verses that follow today's reading, the paradox becomes even more pointed, as Peter goes on to connect the power of God with the crucified Jesus.

So today's reading from Acts picks up a theme that is dear to St Paul's heart, as well as much of the Gospels. Over and over again, God chooses as his messengers those who seem inadequate and wholly unsuited for their great task. That's why the story of the Tower of Babel is so illuminating in this context, because it suggests that nothing divides people more quickly from God than a desire for power, and an arrogant determination to rely on themselves. Those who have no illusions about their own gifts might actually be the only ones who are prepared to turn to God and ask for help.

Perhaps that's why Jesus tells his disciples in John's Gospel that the world cannot receive the Spirit of truth (John 14.17). Perhaps the world is too obsessed with its own truth, its own crazily self-authenticating systems, to receive the Spirit whose job it is to unite us with the Father and the Son, to return us to our true dependence upon God.

Jesus does promise his followers a kind of power. Starting from Pentecost, Acts shows us the kind of great works that the disciples are able to do in the name of Jesus. But the point of this power from the Spirit is to point to the Son and, through the Son, to the Father. The Babel-builders wanted power for the sake of self-glorification and self-protection, and it cost them their unity and their ability to relate to each other. The power of God has nothing to do with self-protection and everything to do with restoring unity and communication, which is why the outpouring of the Spirit at Pentecost is so characteristic. It enables Peter and the apostles to communicate; it enables them to make connections, to see the common threads running throughout the history of God's dealings with his people; and it makes them missionaries, longing to share a common life in God, the common life of Father, Son and Holy Spirit.

*Ordinary Time*

# Trinity Sunday

— ∾ —

*Proverbs 8.1–4, 22–31*
*Romans 5.1–5*
*John 16.12–15*

From very early on in the life of the Church, Christians read the figure of 'Wisdom' in Proverbs as a reference to Jesus. They assumed that God had already shown, in hints, characters and patterns of relating, what he would reveal in full in Jesus. Wisdom, in particular, lent herself as a very good introduction to what Christians were claiming about Jesus. Wisdom is a figure who is present with God before anything else is created, and she teaches people God's way in the world.

In the context of the theology of Proverbs itself, of course, written long before the time of Jesus, wisdom is a literary device on the part of the author. To follow the way of 'wisdom' is to live in the world as you should, as its maker intended. It is not, on the whole, a mystical or even deeply religious-sounding book, but its assumption is that if you try hard to find the right way, day by day, and follow the teaching of the wise, you will actually be doing what you were created to do, and you will make the world a better place for yourself and others.

But when Wisdom is personified, as she is in today's passage, the mood changes. This is not the patient, slightly baffled, concentration on doing the best you can, but a sudden insight into the mind of God. Suddenly, instead of the slightly dull and obvious advice of an old gentleman, we are in the presence of God, the source of all wisdom.

At the start of the passage, Wisdom is standing at all the busiest and most noticeable points of the city and shouting. God's wisdom is not a thing reserved only for the few, the intellectual giants. It is available to anyone who has ears to hear. And yet what Wisdom is calling out is sung to the tune that makes the universe dance. She was present as God created the world, and she saw it all unfolding. She shared God's joy in it, and it is this joy, this knowledge of the love of the Creator for

76

his world, that she is sharing as she sings. The knowledge of how to live with joy as a child of God in the world that he has made is what Wisdom offers.

No wonder, then, that Christians saw the connections with Jesus. The first few verses of Romans 5 convey something of that same sense of standing in a world that suddenly makes sense, because we are sure of our rightful place in it. Our place is the one that has been won for us by Christ. Just as in Proverbs the wild delight that Wisdom speaks of has to be filtered through into the minutiae of daily life, so in Romans, the almost unbearable relief of knowing that we are reconciled to God has to be the rock on which we stand, whatever happens in life. Paul wants us to feel the seismic shift in our whole perception of the world, now that we are brought back to God and he wants that to colour everything that happens to us. To live in Christ, as to live by Wisdom, is to live in tune with the world, so that everything that happens, good and bad, deepens our understanding of who we are in relation to God.

But, Paul tells us, we have rather more than a system for recognizing the purpose of God. We have the living presence of God's Holy Spirit, given to us so that we can feel God's love for the world. We are now doing what Wisdom does in Proverbs 8; we are sharing God's love for his world, and feeling his joy in what he has made.

Both of these passages are profound insights into God's Trinitarian nature, but it is the passage from today's Gospel that spells it out. John's image of the Trinity is of a circle in which each figure is only illuminated by the light of the torches that the others are holding. Each desperately wants us to see and love the others. What the torches reveal is both how much they love each other and how alike they are, with a deep family resemblance that makes us look from one to the other with a sense of true recognition. But the circle of light does not exclude us. It spills some of its warmth out to us, the audience. It invites us forward, into the light, and the transforming light begins to make us, too, resemble the main players, not by right, but because of the generous light reflected on us, the light of the Father, Son and Holy Spirit.

# Proper 4

—— ∽ ——

*1 Kings 18.22–3, 41–3*
*Galatians 1.1–12*
*Luke 7.1–10*

This opening section of Galatians has Paul in a very combative frame of mind. Even his formal greetings at the beginning are perfunctory and pointed. Something very dear to Paul is under threat here, and he is riding to its defence. Part of what he is defending is, of course, his own calling and mission. So within the first sentence of the letter, he is hammering home the fact that he is doing only what God has asked him to do. He has no agenda of his own to pursue, nor does he take orders from any 'party' in the church. His sending is directly from 'Jesus Christ and God the Father'. There is also a faint undertone of personal hurt when he says, in verse 6, 'I am astonished that you are so quickly deserting the one who called you.' These are people whom Paul himself has brought to faith in Christ, and he had believed that they would trust him and build on what he had taught them.

But that natural human defensiveness is incidental to Paul's main argument. Much more worrying to him than his own status is the fact that he believes the Galatians are now in danger of losing sight of the gospel, in the confusion of choices that they are presented with. You remember the background story behind the letter to the Galatians? It marks a point in the life of the new church when they have reached a crossroads. They have assumed, with good reason, that to be a good Christian you also have to follow the Jewish law. They cannot deny that God is calling them to preach the good news of Jesus Christ to the Gentiles, but their missionary strategy seems to have been to administer both baptism and circumcision as necessary doorways into the new Christian family.

But Paul is convinced that his mission is primarily to the Gentiles, and that this will have an effect not just on the Gentiles whom he converts, but also on the whole concept of Christianity that his contemporaries have. This enlarged vision of the gospel cannot be contained in the old pots; it requires a radical rethinking of priorities.

One of the many intriguing but unanswered questions that remains about Paul is how he came to this absolute conviction that God does not have entrance requirements to his family; Paul of all people, brought up knowing and loving the law. Just outside the passage set for today, in verse 16, Paul voices his certainty that God's whole purpose in calling him is 'that I might proclaim him among the Gentiles', but he does not tell us if that was his immediate conviction, as he met Jesus on the Damascus road, or a growing understanding of why God is allowing him to be driven out of the synagogues everywhere he goes, out among the others, the outsiders. Paul comes to join the Christian community at a time when this issue of Gentile membership is rife. (You might like to have a look at Acts 9—10, which puts Paul's conversion in context, next to Peter's dream, which appears to speak of the equality of those inside and outside the old covenant rules.) It is hard to remember, now that we know the outcome, how divisive this issue was at the time, but both Acts and Galatians bear witness to the fact. And if the strand in the Bible that talks about the universality of God's love seems to us clearly to predominate, that is because we read it in the light of subsequent history. Galatians suggests that Peter, even with the benefit of his dream, is still uncertain about how widely the principle of inclusion should apply.

So what is it that makes Paul so certain that this is a make-or-break issue for the Church? He tells us in verse 12 that his gospel is based on 'a revelation', and all of his letters bear witness to the fact that he went on testing that revelation against Scripture and through mission, over and over again. He also tests it against his own knowledge that if God can love and save him, the persecutor of the Church, then he can certainly love and save the Gentiles, whose only fault is to be born to the wrong family.

In the light of Paul's work, we can read the story from Luke and the saying from Kings as the clear voice of God, calling us to trust him, reminding us that we do not need to hedge the gospel around with rules and regulations of our own invention. The gospel is God's, and he will give it any protection it might need. Our job is simply to receive it and preach it with gladness.

# *Proper 5*

—— ⁓ ——

*1 Kings 17.17-24*
*Galatians 1.11-24*
*Luke 7.11-17*

We do not always notice the simple compassion of Jesus. We are often so busy looking for the deeper meaning, or finding the application for ourselves that we barely notice the actual motivation in the context of the real situation. Yet compassion is clearly one of the hallmarks of Jesus' personality. Over and over again, the Gospels tell us that Jesus goes out of his way to help the outsider. Jesus lived in a society with, by and large, quite a capacious net for rescuing those in need. Certain things were laid down for Jews through proper observance of the law, and the family operated in a way that we alternately dream of and run from, depending whether we would like to be on the receiving end or the giving end. But even if their net was better mended than ours, still some people fell through it, either because of their race, or because they had no family to care for them. And these people called forth from Jesus unerring love and compassion.

The widow in today's story is one such. She has no husband, and now she has lost her son. We are not told if there was any other family, but we are left with the distinct impression that without her son, the woman will be defenceless. The large crowd following the funeral procession have no intention of taking the son's place. They are here to do the decent thing, and then they intend to fade into the background.

Luke tells us that Jesus looks at the woman and feels sorry for her. What did her face show? Perhaps there was rather more than anxiety about her material future on the woman's face. Perhaps there was the despair of someone who faces not just poverty and poor treatment, but who also faces it alone with no one to love. Whatever it is that Jesus sees, it is enough to make him act.

And what action! The crowds recognize it instantly as the mighty and scary activity of God. They know at once that they are seeing the kind of things their ancestors saw in the prophets. They have been well trained in the Scriptures, and they recognize the signs of God's presence. It cheers them up immensely. Not only do they not have to worry about the widow any more, but they also have a wonderful story to tell, and they can be sure that they – would you believe it – are living in the days when God shows his favour to his people, just like in the stories.

Perhaps some of them, better read, or with better memories, went home and thought further about what they had seen. Perhaps they even remembered the story of the prophet Elijah who also raised a widow's son from the dead. If so, did they notice the differences, as well as the similarities? Elijah's miracle is not noticeably performed out of compassion. He sounds quite cross with God, who is asking all kinds of hard things of him, and is now apparently even making trouble for the very people he has sent to help Elijah. So when Elijah calls upon God, what follows is, in his mind, about the relationship between him, God's prophet, and the wild, hard, exciting God who will not let him go. What God's motives are, of course, we are not told.

But Jesus does not call upon God, and demand, almost petulantly, that the very least God can do, given all that he is asking of Jesus, is to perform a miracle when Jesus tells him to. Instead, Jesus acts out of his own compassion and power, which are, after all, the compassion and power of God. Jesus does not have to wait to see if God is feeling the way he is about the situation. Instead, he acts directly, on his own authority, to give the woman back what she loves and needs most in all the world. This is not about Jesus and God, but about God and the world he made and loves. But the people make the right connection; Jesus may not be doing this to demonstrate how close he is to God, but that is certainly the end result.

And what of Paul? Does God act in love and compassion in calling Paul out of his community and into a life of uncertainty, persecution and glory? Paul certainly seems to think so. When he says that God set him apart before he was born, he is expressing, as deeply and fully as he can, his sense that in meeting Jesus he is coming home. 'This is what I was born for,' he says. Paul responds to the compassion of God with the passion of his life of service.

# *Proper 6*

—— ～ ——

2 Samuel 11.26—12.10, 13–15
Galatians 2.15–21
Luke 7.36—8.3

Nathan the prophet is a good story-teller and a brave man. Though he obviously knows the character of his king well enough to guess David's reaction to his story, yet this is, after all, the king he is talking to.

David has done the most appalling thing. He has taken Uriah's wife, and had Uriah killed. Yet somehow, he has managed to persuade himself that this is a private foible that concerns only himself, and that it has no bearing on the precious relationship between himself and God, on which the whole of his life and his monarchy are built.

Nathan's story rips away the fabric of that deceit, and shows David's actions for what they really are. What is more, it is David who condemns himself, by his outraged reaction to the story. He hears of the rich man who has everything he could possibly want, and who yet takes the poor man's one beloved lamb to feed a traveller, rather than give up one of his own huge flock. He assumes that because he is rich and powerful, he is real in a way that the poor man is not. His needs and desires must be taken seriously, while the poor man can be ignored.

David responds to the story with the righteous anger of a good man who has always fought for justice and for the underdog. He responds as a powerful man, who can ensure that his concept of justice is enforced. But then Nathan says, 'You are the man!' David does not try for one moment to deny it or bluster it out. 'I have sinned against the LORD,' he says.

The reaction of the Pharisee in Luke's story is rather different. Like Nathan, Jesus tells a story to make his listeners see things from a different perspective. But while David is struck to the heart, Simon sees the parallels grudgingly, and he and his guests mutter, trying to find ways of undermining Jesus, so that they don't have to be challenged by what he has said. 'Who does he think he is?' they ask. The rich man, in the story told to David, has discounted the poor man, has decided, no doubt unconsciously, that his poverty makes him in some sense less than human, a being whose feelings need not be taken into account. Simon has done the same for the woman with the ointment. She is merely 'a sinner', not a woman with a history and a desire to change. She has no right, in Simon's estimation, to be a player in the story at all, let alone the central character, the heroine, that Jesus is making her. We don't know if she became one of the group of women who travelled with Jesus and supported him and his followers, but we do know that she recognized her sin and her need, without a prophet to point it out to her, and that she turned to the source of forgiveness.

In Galatians, Paul has internalized these two stories, the one told to David and the one told to Simon, and come up with his own version. He and his fellow Jews are like David and Simon. They believe that they are so central to the story that all other characters are unreal. They believe that their actions, though perhaps not perfect, are nevertheless not too bad. But Paul, like David, has suddenly seen himself in the mirror, in Paul's case, the one held up to him on the road to Damascus. He has realized that all the façade of righteousness and following God's way has been empty.

This is Paul in strikingly humble mode. He makes no attempt to boast about what he has achieved since his conversion, but goes on and on about how believing in Christ is the only good thing he has ever done. Even his attempts to preach the gospel he once persecuted just show how wrong he was when left to his own devices. He just cannot seem to find the words to put strongly enough his conviction that righteousness is not something we are capable of by our own efforts. It is only in giving up his rights in his own life, in being 'crucified with Christ' and so allowing Christ's life to take over in him that he has any hope of being justified, of staying close to God.

If all of today's readings are about forgiveness, God's great and irresistible love reaching out for us, they are also about repentance. Perhaps Paul provides the key. He is prepared to step down from the starring role in his own life, and leave the centre stage for the one who really knows the part, Jesus Christ.

# Proper 7

—— ～ ——

*Isaiah 65.1–9*
*Galatians 3.23–9*
*Luke 8.26–39*

The people in today's reading from Isaiah have apparently got bored with the true God. The chapter opens with God waiting patiently, almost passively, for his people to come looking for him. When they don't, God begins to call out in welcome, but still the people ignore him.

What are they doing that apparently has so much more appeal? Verses 3–5 describe the rituals that the people have invented or adopted from their neighbours, including sacrificing in gardens, meeting in tombs and other secret and scary places, and eating things that are spiced with the taste of uncleanness and deliberate breaking of ancient taboos. The people have made themselves a crazy, busy religion, made exciting by fear and by trespass into the previously forbidden. They have persuaded themselves that, because they are wholly occupied with ritual, they are being 'religious'. They have muddled themselves to the point where they cannot tell the sacred from the profane or the just plain stupid.

Finally, God can stand it no longer. The straw that breaks his back is the misuse of the word 'holy'. Clearly, the people have lost all ability to recognize real holiness, and so to recognize God. They have assumed that, because God did not intervene sooner, he either approved, or was too weak to combat the 'gods' that they had invented for themselves. What is at stake is Israel's whole system of knowing and responding to the living God, but also their own sanity. They can no longer distinguish fantasy from reality. And so God takes action, punitive and terrible, but with the promise of mercy and rebirth at the end.

Just as the people in Isaiah have chosen a world of illusion and madness, and can only be restored to wholeness at great cost, so the

84

story of the demon-possessed man is also about madness and sanity. On the obvious level, of course, it is the naked, screaming man who is mad. Did he choose to live among the unclean dead, as Isaiah's ritualists chose tombs for their rites? Or did others drive him away, and make him take refuge with the dead, whose claim to humanity was now as tenuous as his own? Either way, his life is lonely and pitiful.

But the story now takes a sudden ironic turn, because it is the 'mad' man who recognizes who Jesus is. The people in Isaiah have chosen delusions and made themselves incapable of recognizing God, but the despairing madness of the man in Luke has left him with no illusions at all. He knows what he is seeing.

'What is your name?' Jesus asks. The question creates a little ripple of quiet in the middle of this frantic and noisy story. The man has been shouting; the narrator has been telling, in lurid detail, the awful methods of restraint that have been used on him, and his terrifying response to them; and into this clamour, Jesus speaks. The question treats the man like a human being for the first time in who knows how many years. He has been unclothed, alone, tied up and beaten like a mad dog. Did he once have a name?

But although he cannot now remember what those who once loved him used to call him, Jesus' question marks the turning point in the story. Now Jesus is in command, restoring the human image to this man, as he is to restore it to the whole of humankind.

Why are the local people afraid? Why do they look at the calm, clothed man and beg Jesus to leave? It cannot just be that they are afraid for their livestock. Something about Jesus and his action terrifies them. Perhaps they liked having the mad man there at the outskirts of the village, making them feel sane and in control of their lives. Perhaps they realize that to recognize Jesus is to be on the path to inevitable change. The 'mad' man was desperate enough to welcome change, however drastic, but these 'sane' people are comfortable with their illusion of life, and they do not want it challenged.

In Galatians, Paul tells us that without Christ, we are all in the condition that the demon-possessed man was. We were chained up, naked, living in a world of illusions. But now we are 'clothed' with Christ, sitting at peace and made whole again at his feet. When we gave up our madness, we had also to give up our illusion that we know how to live, how to be human, by ourselves. We gave up the little rituals and fantasies of superiority and control, and admitted that our only hope of being what we are meant to be lies in belonging to Christ.

# *Proper 8*

—— ❧ ——

1 Kings 19.5–16, 19–21
Galatians 5.1, 13–25
Luke 9.51–62

St Teresa of Avila spent many years travelling on God's business, founding and reforming convents. Journeys were both unsafe and uncomfortable in those days, but she was never daunted. But one day, when she was near the end of her tether with weariness, her carriage broke and she fell out of it into the mud. She is reported to have shouted at God, 'No wonder you have so few friends, when you treat them so badly!'

Elijah is in this frame of mind in today's reading, and expresses himself with the same frankness. Remember what he has just been through. He has been preserved through a drought, he has raised the dead, he has confronted the king and killed the priests of Baal, and God has sent fire and rain at his request. But none of this has had any effect (read 1 Kings 17—18 to get the exciting story). The king still hates him, and prefers to worship his wife Jezebel's gods, and Jezebel has sworn to get her revenge for what he did to her priests.

So now Elijah is, frankly, fed up. He walks away from the struggle, into the wilderness, and asks to die. He does not want to fight any more; he does not want to do the hard and thankless things that God has called him to, which have no effect, except to endanger his own life. He no longer wants to be God's prophet, since God does not know how to treat his friends.

Still God won't leave him alone. He sends angels to pester him with food and drink, and Elijah grumpily carries on with his journey to the holy mountain of Horeb. But nothing is going to make him forget his grievance.

God does not try to dispute Elijah's story or defend himself. Instead, he comes to meet Elijah on the holy mountain. Angry and weary as he is, Elijah still recognizes God. He knows that the wind, the earthquake and the fire are sound effects, and it is only when he hears the sound of silence that he stumps out to meet God.

Even now, he is not overawed. In exactly the same accusing monotone, he lays out his sense of failure, despair and resentment of God. And God, who can command drought and fire, earthquake and storm, but prefers the silence, hears his friend Elijah. He allows Elijah to resign. He accepts the charge that Elijah lays against him, and releases him. He does not have to carry on with this dangerous and unremitting work. He can pass it on to Elisha.

Elijah can hardly believe it. When he finds Elisha and passes on his mantle, Elijah obviously believes that the younger man is going to back out. Elisha asks for time to go and say goodbye to his parents, and you can hear the tiredness and disbelief in Elijah's voice when he replies, more or less, 'Oh right, of course you'll come back – not' (19.20). He doesn't really believe that God will let him go. But he has misjudged Elisha, who takes on his new role by killing the oxen that represented his old life. He burns his boats with wholehearted conviction and takes up Elijah's mantle.

There is something very moving about the interaction between God and Elijah in this story. The work is not done, but God recognizes Elijah's need. All through the story, God has taken care of Elijah, feeding him, working miracles at his request, but he does not now say to Elijah, 'Can't you trust me, after all I have done for you?' Instead, he comes to his old friend, in great gentleness, and gives in to him.

No such release awaits Jesus, but then, he does not ask for it. The nearest he comes to a plea for a way out is in the garden of Gethsemane (Luke 22.42), and even then he finds, from somewhere, the strength to make it God's choice, not his own.

His disciples would like pyrotechnics and displays of power such as Elijah was able to call down on his enemies, but Jesus forbids it. He accepts rejection as an inevitable part of being God's friend. His words to those who think they would like to follow him are much harsher than Elijah's response to Elisha's request. Elijah says, out of his gloom and despair, 'Oh, go on then', but Jesus hears the ignorance and insincerity in the voices of those who are making excuses. Elijah is on the verge of freedom, but Jesus has 'set his face to go to Jerusalem' (9.53), and already he is nearly as alone as he will be when he hangs on the cross.

# *Proper 9*

—— ∾ ——

*Isaiah 66.10–14*
*Galatians 6.1–16*
*Luke 10.1–11, 16–20*

Luke 8—10 sets out a very interesting mission strategy. In chapter 8, Jesus himself goes through towns and villages, curing people, and gathering huge crowds to hear his stories and see his miracles. Then in chapter 9, it is the turn of the twelve, who are given instructions very similar to those in today's reading, but without that sense of impending crisis. When they return, they spend some time alone with Jesus, 'debriefing'.

Now it is the turn of the larger group of disciples to try their hand. But what is interesting about all of these stories is how little attention is actually paid to the result of the missions. We hear hardly anything about the numbers of converts made, the preaching techniques, the misunderstandings and abuse. In today's reading, when the disciples return, tired and exhilarated, bursting with stories about what they have done, Jesus deflects them. His words to them are oddly grim, 'Do not rejoice ... that the spirits submit to you, but rejoice that your names are written in heaven.'

There is a sense of great urgency in Jesus' commission to this big group of disciples. They are sent off with a picture to ponder as they hurry through the countryside. Jesus tells them that it is as though, all around them, the fields are full to bursting with food, waiting to be harvested, perfectly ripe. Another day or two and it will rot, or be eaten by the birds and the animals. His listeners would know the frenzy of activity that should be going on but, instead, Jesus points to fields that are eerily empty, as though some great sleeping sickness has spread across the land, and no one is awake to notice what is happening around them.

That is why the mission is so desperately important. There is no time for ordinary precautions or ordinary courtesies – they must not even stop long enough to say 'Good morning', when they pass people on the road. They don't have time to try and win people over. Where they get a positive response straight away, they may stay and preach the gospel; where the first response is negative, they must move on at once. There is no time now to plant, only to gather in.

So why is it that when the disciples come back to Jesus, longing to tell him all that they have done in his name, he suddenly changes the focus? They are on a high, feeling themselves to be in the forefront of a great, successful movement. They have been able to do works of extraordinary power, they are part of the in-group, the future looks rosy. But there is only one future that Jesus is interested in: the coming kingdom of God. So his image of the harvest is the key. This mission is about life. Without the harvest, the people will starve and die. Without the coming kingdom, their lives will be equally worthless. Over and over again in the Gospels, this note of urgency sounds. *Now* is the time of decision. *Now*, as we meet Jesus and hear the gospel, we choose life or death. The harvest won't wait and neither will the kingdom.

The harvest metaphor comes back in Galatians. Clearly there are some in the community in Galatia who would like to hedge their bets, go for a mixed economy, grow a few 'Christian' plants and a few 'traditional' ones, and so make sure they are getting the best of all worlds. But it won't work, Paul tells them. There is only one world. The old one is dead, nailed on the cross. People who are still trying to live in that world are like ghosts, holding on to something that no longer exists. The old dead world had all kinds of standards that are now completely eroded. It was a competitive world, while in this new one, people help each other and bear one another's burdens (Galatians 6.2). It was a world where people measured themselves against each other, rather than looking honestly at their own work and worth (vv. 4–5). It was a world so far from God that people actually thought that God would not notice what they were doing (v. 7).

The new creation comes about through the cross of Christ. There are no other measures in it, no other symbols of power or status. It seems that we simply cannot let go of comparisons, ways of positioning ourselves and others. But Paul is saying that God himself has provided the only thing he recognizes – the cross. The marks of the cross are, paradoxically, the only marks of the new life, the new creation.

# *Proper 10*

— ∽ —

*Deuteronomy 30.9–14*
*Colossians 1.1–14*
*Luke 10.25–37*

Does God actually make things too easy for us? Do we keep looking around for the catch, trying to work out what we are missing, when really the truth is as simple as can be? Our human religious instincts tend to go in for a lot of ritual, membership requirements, secrecy and hierarchy, and churches don't always look very different. But all three of today's readings seem to suggest that God's requirements are devastatingly simple.

Return to God, Deuteronomy says, simply, 'turn to the LORD your God with all your heart and with all your soul' (30.10). No interpreters are needed to show how this is to be done; God is not far away. As they turn back to him, they will find already in themselves the knowledge of his commandments. Their part is one simple movement: turning to face God.

The lawyer who comes to Jesus wants a complicated answer to this question of how to choose God. He knows the simple answer, and he quotes it off pat. But surely that can't be all? There must be more to it than that? He had hoped to come out of the encounter looking clever, but instead he is made to look stupid and, worse than stupid, unfaithful. If choosing God is that easy, what excuse has anyone got for not doing it? So he asks the question, wanting, we are told, 'to justify himself'. He hopes Jesus will produce a long and elaborate formula, with lots of boxes to tick. The lawyer is quietly confident that there will be ticks in most of his boxes already, but he would like this to be public knowledge. In particular, he wants *Jesus* to know how good he is, and say, in an admiring voice, 'Well done. Why can't everyone be like you?'

Instead, Jesus' answer is a story whose point is terrifyingly clear.

Choosing God means choosing people. Choosing God means choosing anyone who needs you. No excuses. The lawyer does not pretend to misunderstand, but we never hear the end of his story. Writing the end of it is our part.

Deuteronomy and the good Samaritan make it all sound so very, very simple. But unfortunately we know it isn't. We are all of us like the lawyer, looking for complicated ways to let ourselves off the hook, or like the people in Deuteronomy, who would like to say 'It's all too difficult, we need someone from heaven, or at least abroad, to explain it to us. It's not our fault that we don't know what to do.' The temptation when faced with this blazing clarity is either to embroider beautiful and elaborate robes to cover it up, so we can't see it too clearly, or just to give up in despair.

Luckily, we have the witness of many generations of people that making the choice is the vital thing. Choosing God, over and over again, however many times our other choices get in the way, is the best we can do. In Colossians, Paul writes with great warmth and generosity and trust to this community of imperfect people who have, despite their imperfections, chosen God. It must have been enormously encouraging for the Colossians to read that Paul knows about their care for each other, and that they are seen as a community where the gospel is alive and well and bearing fruit. It can't always have felt like that on the inside.

But Paul is a very artful church planter. He knows the value of encouragement, but he isn't going to let the Colossians get complacent, or think that their success is their own doing. First, he reminds them that they are part of a wider Christian community – Paul's own prayers are part of what has kept them going, just as our prayers keep others going, and their prayers sustain us.

The prayer that Paul has for the Colossians is utterly comprehensive, and it is also the key for Luke's lawyer and Deuteronomy's bewildered people. We do not have to do this by ourselves. The strength that enables us to live rightly comes from God. God swings into action at the end of today's reading, like Superman to the rescue. What a relief! God rescues us from the darkness, God chooses us, as we are, useless and sinful. This great choice that we thought we had to make, reaching out in our own strength, turning round with great effort to face him, is nothing of the kind. There is no journey to be made – he is here. There is no huge decision to take – we are already part of the kingdom of the Son. All we have to do is say 'Thank you'. It really is that simple.

# *Proper 11*

—— ⁓ ——

*Genesis 18.1–10a*
*Colossians 1.15–28*
*Luke 10.38–42*

From the beginning, human beings have been image-makers, instinctively, compulsively making sense of their world through imagining it. In lives governed by the harshest necessity just to survive, primitive people still painted on the walls of caves or made images out of clay and stone and wood. Some of these images certainly had some kind of 'function' in propitiating or in trying to bind reality by picturing it the way they wanted it to be. But there is an undeniable element of gratuity in these images. It is only because we are by nature image-makers that we can imagine that images are vital and powerful tools for making sense of the world. Animals seem to survive quite well without them.

God, it seems, is an image-maker, too. Paul's great picture of how the whole universe makes sense rests on this starting assumption, that God delights in imagining.

First of all, in his very being, God is image, reflection and transformation, Father, Son and Holy Spirit. God's own self delights in playing with metaphor, image, picture, difference and relation. How would God be if the life of God flowed out into something that expressed it visibly, as opposed to invisibly? How would it be if these first and second images were brought together into a third way of expressing that life and truth, that united but did not coalesce the other two? Something like this kind of creativity and inventiveness that is essential to God comes to us through our understanding of God as Trinity.

But God's creativity is inexhaustible, and it pours out into creation, into something that is genuinely not-God. Paul suggests that this is a natural progression in God's image-making. First, there is the Son, who makes the invisible visible, and then continues to create the whole panorama of life, images of God's creativity, that only make sense when you know their context.

But there is yet another step to this powerful theological canvas that Paul is painting. God the Image-maker then offers himself as the medium, the key for interpreting how all these images fit together and what they mean. He offers himself to be painted on, acted on, played on, destroyed and remade, in the person of Jesus Christ. Without Jesus, Paul argues, the world is a set of apparently fragmented words or chords, but Jesus reconciles them, restoring the harmony, showing the line and shape of all that is.

But, of course, God is an image-breaker as well as an image-maker. If we abstract our powers of imagination from that central source, we can create great and glorious worlds of our own, forgetting that they are, at best, shallow and evanescent shadows of God's. The Colossians once lived in a world of their own making, estranged from God (1.21). To find Jesus, the clue to the image, they had to let go of what they had made themselves. They had to recognize the superior skill of the Creator, and join their efforts to his.

Paul is now a fully commissioned painter in God's school. He is not just filling in the outlines that the Master has laid down, but actually creating a part of the great work himself. He says that he has chosen the same medium, suffering, and that his life is 'completing what is lacking in Christ's afflictions' (v. 24). That is a large boast, but apparently justified. God is an exacting critic, but not a jealous one. He genuinely revels in what we make, what we contribute – after all, he did teach us the skills in the first place. The trouble is that a lot of the time we are trying to make music without sounds, or stories without words or pictures without images. We need the Son, the One who makes visible what is invisible, to give reality to what we create. Otherwise we are creating fantasy worlds, with no meaning and no life.

God the Image-maker comes and looks at what we are making. He looks with piercing generosity and says, 'Hmm, I see what you are getting at. It is nearly there. Why don't you just try *this?*' And he makes a small adjustment, so outrageously original that the whole thing is transformed. Our work and his, joined together to produce something spectacular.

That is what God is doing in today's other two readings. He is suggesting a new way of doing something that will make the whole story different. He is suggesting that things do not have to be as boring as they look. He is suggesting that a small piece of creative thought can change what seemed a foregone conclusion. Abraham and Sarah's canvas and Martha and Mary's symphony are about to explode into genius.

# *Proper 12*

— ∾ —

*Genesis 18.20–32*
*Colossians 2.6–15*
*Luke 11.1–13*

This story from Genesis is often told as though it is about Abraham bargaining with God. Abraham, the generous and merciful, pleads with God, the bloodthirsty and violent, and gradually manages to calm God down and get him to agree to keep the killing to a minimum.

But actually that is not what the story is about at all. In the verses immediately before the reading set for today (17–19), God debates about whether or not to let Abraham in on his plan. You could read this to mean his plan to destroy Sodom and Gomorrah, but it is actually much more likely that it is his larger plan, of how the mighty should treat the weak – a plan that is to come to its fulfilment in Jesus.

So what follows in the conversation between Abraham and God is a lesson from a master teacher. God does not just tell Abraham the plan, but allows him to discover it, and to discover how much it matters, to have his own emotional investment in it. As his own instinct for justice rises, he finds it matched by God's.

It is also another stage in the deepening intimacy between Abraham and God. God allows Abraham to set the pace, and to take the responsibility in what is to happen. There is a kind of teasing pleasure in God's voice as he dares Abraham to test him further and further, waiting for the penny to drop, for Abraham to realize that what he is asking for is what God already wants.

The same kind of learning God's nature is what is going on in Luke's Gospel. Luke's setting for the Lord's Prayer is an interesting one. Matthew has it as part of a discourse on hypocrisy and forgiveness (Matthew 6.9ff.), in the Sermon on the Mount. Luke uses it to talk more generally about prayer.

The chapter starts with Jesus at prayer. There is obviously a quality about his prayer that attracts the disciples and makes them want to learn. They have observed Jesus praying a number of times before, and have begun to realize that prayer is somehow central to who he is and what he is doing. 'Teach us to pray,' they ask. Jesus' response is brief and clear. He teaches them a prayer. He does not teach them about the importance of stillness, or correct posture, or focusing the mind. He teaches them to talk to God, and to bring the whole muddle of our lives, the sublime and the mundane, to God. So in one breath we can ask for the coming of the kingdom *and* our daily bread.

In talking to God, Abraham learns that God is indeed the Just Judge of the earth. And he learns this not as a piece of interesting abstract information but as a dynamic experience, which is to change him. In his indignation at the idea that God might act unjustly, he realizes the value of justice, and that he, too, is called to be just. So, when we pray for forgiveness in the Lord's Prayer, we learn not only that forgiveness matters to God, but that it also matters to us, and we need to share it.

In the reading from Luke, Jesus tells the funny story of the irritating friend to get the disciples to see prayer as something basic, day-to-day. Prayer is not something carefully sanitized, so that we bring to God only what we know he will like. Jesus is encouraging the disciples to bombard God, to tell him everything, to talk to him constantly, to involve him in every part of their lives. Don't shut 'God' and 'prayer' into a small box that only comes out on Sundays, is the message. And as you pester God, as Abraham did, as the persistent friend did to the sleepy householder, you will learn more about God, and about yourself in relation to him.

You might say that the message from all three of today's readings is: 'Go direct to God and accept no substitutes.' It is easy to substitute something else for God, often for the very best of motives. We don't like to show God our anger, or our incomprehension, or our humour, and so we gradually bring less and less of our real selves to prayer. And that means, inevitably, as it would in any relationship, that we know less and less about God and how to recognize him. Abraham had the courage to go straight to God and question him, and Jesus encourages us to do the same. In Colossians, the reader is reminded to go direct to Christ, and not to let anything else, however apparently good, get in the way.

# *Proper 13*

—— ∾ ——

*Ecclesiastes 1.2, 12–14; 2.18–23*
*Colossians 3.1–11*
*Luke 12.13–21*

Today's three readings just are depressing, so brace yourselves. It's partly because the image of the virtuous life that they present is so obviously unattainable, and partly because they seem to epitomize the world-hating morality that Christianity has so often been accused of.

The author of Ecclesiastes can see no point in life. Everything we do is nullified for him by the unavoidable fact of death. Nothing is worth enjoying because it cannot be enjoyed for ever. You might as well simply concentrate on the superficial and ephemeral, since everything is ultimately superficial and ephemeral. What's more, he assumes that this state of affairs is God's doing (Ecclesiastes 1.13), so even the thought of God's eternity is no consolation.

Jesus' words in Luke seem to endorse this gloomy viewpoint. Here again, the emphasis is on death as the ultimate goal, that creeps up on you and makes all your efforts worthless.

And the remedy that Colossians suggests for this state of affairs is hardly more cheering than the ailment. There is a long list of 'vices' which we have somehow to get rid of, or risk the wrath of God (Colossians 3.6). Unfortunately, although we may not have done all the things on the list, we will certainly have done some, and we can have no certainty that we will never again feel anger or greed. How do we 'put to death' what is earthly? And how is that a positive thing to do, one that affirms the goodness of God's creation?

First, by not hurrying away too quickly from what these readings are saying. We can be so eager to persuade people that you can be a Christian and still have a good time that we try to gloss over the need for choice. Some things are incompatible with choosing God. Some things will blunt our palate for God, make us believe that we can be satisfied with less. That is actually the point of what Jesus is saying in Luke. Someone has asked him to arbitrate over a piece of property, and you cannot miss the impatience in Jesus' voice as he replies.

Is Jesus, who 'will come again to judge the living and the dead', really saying he has no right to judge in this case? The story he tells suggests that that is not the point being made here. The rich man has already decided what is important, and he has lived his life by that decision. The 'judgement', then, is one that he has already made. And this is what Jesus wants his listeners to understand. We decide now, day by day, what to value, what to give our heart to. These brothers, fighting over their inheritance, have come to the Judge of all the earth. They have a chance, now, to listen to Jesus and choose the kingdom, or to allow the squabble about money to distract them.

The verses from Colossians then move the argument on a stage. The people who are reading this letter have already made their choice. They have chosen the new life of Christ, to the point where they can emphatically say that the old life is dead (Colossians 3.3). And yet it clings on to them with ghostly and terrible fingers. Despite the choice they have made, both costly and joyful, they are still unable to live Christ's risen life. Over and over again, in all that they do daily, they have to go on making that choice in the small things. That one great decision, to live in Christ, then has increasingly to shape all the smaller decisions, so that each part of their lives demonstrates what they value. The two lists in this reading from Colossians are interesting. The first one (v. 5) seems to concentrate on the big things, the ones that anyone would agree were signs of an immoral life, while the second one (vv. 8–9) goes on to the smaller things, that are easier to forgive ourselves for, but that actually have an insidious and creeping effect on our judgement and on our life together. Colossians makes a forcible connection between these smaller choices and the huge choice for Jesus. Every time we resist anger or malice, the image of God becomes a bit clearer in us (v.10).

So the choice we are being offered is not between a harsh and world-denying morality or a holistic and world-affirming one, but between reality and illusion. The reality is that the world was made by God, and is utterly loved by God. To choose Jesus is to choose to be part of what the world is actually for. It is to choose to be part of God's image, his life that fills the world and redeems it.

# Proper 14

— ∼ —

*Genesis 15.1–6*
*Hebrews 11.1–3, 8–16*
*Luke 12.32–40*

Faith is sometimes presented as necessarily divorced from evidence. If you can prove something, then you don't need to have faith to believe it. But that doesn't seem to be quite what our readings today are saying. They seem to suggest that faith is not an irrational decision to step out into the darkness, but something chosen and calculated on the basis of what is already known and experienced. Faith still has a strong element of risk and uncertainty, but it isn't just plain stupidity.

Abram's venture of faith starts in conversation with God. Those of us who have read Genesis have already had the chance to get to know God a little. We have seen him creating the world, saving Noah and so on. So when, in Genesis 12, the Lord comes to Abram, Abram is already embedded in a story. We are not told about Abram's upbringing, but we are given the list of his ancestors, and his descent from Noah, so we are to understand that the Lord is already known to Abram, at least as part of his heritage. By today's reading in Genesis 15, Abram has tested that initial rather impersonal knowledge a good deal. He has left his land and followed God's promise. So the conversation we overhear has a history to it.

But although things have worked out quite well for Abram, so far, in his dealings with God, that does not make his faith blind. This central thing that God has promised, which is so dear to Abram's heart, but which is also an integral part of the plan that God has outlined to Abram, has yet to happen. Abram still has no heir. But a son is what Abram is really interested in. That was what made it worth taking the risk. The flocks and the wealth are nice, but they are not what he is here for. He doesn't know quite why his son should be vital to God's purposes, too, but he knows that it is so, and that is what binds him to God – they both want and need this one thing.

So when he stands talking to God under the starry night sky, his faith is a complex mixture of what has already gone before and what he longs for. And we are told that God reckons this to him as right-eousness (v. 6). This curious combination of knowing and longing is to be the saving of Abram.

The Hebrews commentary on the story of Abram makes faith the air that Christians must breathe to live. Like Abram, Christians are part of an ongoing story. They come in on a conversation that is already taking place, in which something of the character of the main speaker is already evident. So they are not starting from nothing. And, like Abraham, they are aware that their story, too, will have consequences for those who follow. Hebrews writes that the patriarchs do not see the completion of God's plan, though they see enough to be able to guess, and be excited (v. 13). And they understand enough to be able to live their lives in such a way that they can help generations to come to play their part in their turn. They, like Abraham, live with this mixture of knowing God through what he has already done, and longing to see what is still unknown. Part of what they bequeath to generations to come is that discontent, that restless certainty that what you already know about God and his ways is never enough. Desire and discontent are strange qualities to value, but apparently they are what make God willing to be identified with us, 'not ashamed' to be our God, Hebrews says (v. 16).

So we are beginning to build up a picture of faith. It is based in a knowledge of God, but it is fuelled by longing to know him better, and to see more of what our faithful but enthralling God is up to. What we know for sure is that we have not yet got to the end of what he has in store for us. So faith is about excitement, based on what we have already experienced, not dogged persistence against all evidence.

Luke's story of the waiting servants adds to this feeling of pleasurable tension. These servants know their master, but they also know that he is unpredictable. Not an easy master, then, not one you can please by just doing your ordinary tasks routinely. But if you are prepared to put up with his ways, what fun you will have. Do you know any other master who will come and, laughing, serve you a feast himself in the middle of the night?

# *Proper 15*

——— ~ ———

*Jeremiah 23.23–9*
*Hebrews 11.29—12.2*
*Luke 12.49–56*

Hebrews continues its great description of faith in today's reading. From Moses down to the relatively recent past in the Maccabean revolts, the author of Hebrews reminds his readers of the story that they have inherited. Some of the allusions are clear, and some are harder to pinpoint, but the whole panorama is a vivid and action-packed testimony to the faith of our ancestors.

Today's reading starts with stories of victory – Moses leading the people through the Red Sea, Joshua and his troops bringing down the walls of Jericho, and so on. There are casualties, of course, but only among the baddies. But as the passage proceeds, the outlook for believers gets bleaker. Suddenly, they are the ones who look like the losers. There is talk of torture and horrible death, of losing homes and possessions, and having to wander in the desert, living like animals and on the edge of madness. What starts as a surging, energizing list of victorious heroes for the reader to model herself on now starts to go horribly wrong.

'Hang on,' you can hear the reader say. 'This isn't what I joined up for. You never said faith would lead to all this trouble.'

'But I thought you would have taken that for granted,' the author replies, in bewilderment. 'You do know what happened to our founder, Jesus, don't you? You can't possibly have missed the fact that he died a horrible death?'

'So what are we doing here, then?' the reader demands.

'You are doing what all our ancestors and our Lord himself did,' the author replies, patiently. 'You are living by faith. And that means that your story is partly for other people, not just for yourself.'

Throughout chapter 11, Hebrews is telling the story of faith in the

100

long-term perspective. The individual actors all have some idea that their lives are part of a bigger story and now, Hebrews is reminding us, it is our turn. Like all the great parade of heroes of faith, we have to be prepared to relinquish centre stage, and to see our lives as an episode in the great unfolding plot. That does not make us insignificant, any more than Abraham and Moses are insignificant, but it does change the perspective. This is not an individual sprint we are taking part in, but a relay race, where our job is to run and then pass the baton on safely. Because that is the only way to win the race. We have to win it together. 'They would not, without us, be made perfect,' verse 40 says, because, it adds, this is 'something better'.

The whole story of faith that Hebrews has been telling does take it for granted that it is indeed 'something better' to be part of a whole. To take any one part of the story without the others is to diminish the impact. When we choose faith, we step into a story that already has a strong narrative thread and is full of colourful characters. They lend weight and context to our part of the story, which might otherwise be a little thin and uneventful. For the time that we are on stage, we are supported by a wonderful cast of famous actors, who are generously making us look better by their skill.

But, of course, this is not a play that we can step in and out of. We cannot take off the costume when the scenes get ugly. The reading from Luke today is a fierce reminder that this great story of God's dealings with his world is a story that many people hate and would like to rip apart so they can put some other theme in its place.

The community that forms around Jesus cannot always be harmonious, either in its internal relationships or in its relationships with the rest of the world. To choose to join hands with Hebrews' great cloud of witnesses is to choose not to be part of any other story of the world, and that will sometimes cause division.

So often in Luke, Jesus teaches the importance of peace-making, forgiving, not judging (see Luke 6.27ff., 7.40ff., 11.2ff. to find just a few examples from the chapters immediately before this one). What are we to make of this sudden descent into violence? It sounds like permission for, even a blessing of, strife. But that is why these verses are closely followed by a diatribe about discernment. The crowd pride themselves on being able to forecast the weather or keep themselves out of prison, but can they tell what the real story of the world is? Learning the plot, so that you can be part of it – that is true discernment.

# *Proper 16*

— ⦵ —

*Isaiah 58.9b–14*
*Hebrews 12.18–29*
*Luke 13.10–17*

Can the leader of the synagogue hear himself? Has he any idea what he sounds like? You can feel the silence that ripples out of the crowd as their religious leader tries to persuade them that what they have seen is wrong and an affront to God. He keeps saying to one person after another, 'Surely you can see that there are other days for healings?' He keeps waiting for nods of support, for expressions of indignation against Jesus. But he doesn't get them. The crowd know what they have seen and whose side they are on.

The crowd at the synagogue have seen the woman coming to worship, shuffling painfully to do her duty, bent over as she is. Perhaps they know her well, if she and they are regular visitors to this meeting. They have seen Jesus spotting the woman, something that, apparently, the regular leaders have failed to do for years. They know that what happens is entirely on Jesus' initiative. There is no indication that the woman has come looking for Jesus or for healing. It is he who calls her, not the other way around.

They hear Jesus' words. There is no magic, no incantation, he does not even talk of healing. Instead, what he says is, 'You are free.' They see her straighten up as though he has literally freed her, lifting a great weight off her back, or undoing chains that had kept her bent over. And the woman's response is instant. She wastes no time stretching her cramped limbs, or patting her straightened back. She bursts out into praise of God. Oh yes, the crowd know with utter clarity what they have seen, which is the presence of God.

The presence of God, there in the synagogue, freely offered to an utterly unimportant woman. It gives them all hope. Perhaps worship is not a matter of rules laid down and interpreted by someone else, but is

102

more like the joy and praise pouring out of the woman. Perhaps this is what the sabbath is really about, worship and freedom, not endless worry about whether you've broken some obscure rule without even knowing it.

No wonder the leader of the synagogue gets no response when he tries to whip up the crowd against Jesus. He can hardly deny the logic of Jesus' interpretation of the sabbath, but he hates it. It implies that every single little person in the crowd is of vital importance to God and, if that is the case, then where's the prestige in being a leader? The rejoicing crowd are a mockery of all his years of leadership, carefully training them in dependence. If the sabbath is to be a day when God's free people freely praise him, then half his job, interpreting the sabbath regulations, is gone.

It's not as though Jesus' teaching about the sabbath is so wholly unprecedented. Isaiah said some of the same things. In today's reading, it is clear that the point of the sabbath is to change your daily focus. Without a day on which you remember what you are for, and who your God is, you can just get into the habit of thinking only of yourself and your own needs. Isaiah sees the sabbath as a day that turns you back to God and so away from yourself and towards others. It's a day that keeps on bringing the community back to themselves and their real purpose. And what a purpose it is. They are to 'take delight in the LORD, and ... ride upon the heights of the earth' (Isaiah 58.14).

The desire that the leader of the synagogue has to trivialize the sabbath, to make it something smaller and more controllable is not unknown in Christian circles. Not that 'trivialize' is exactly the word you would use about the Hebrews' description of what is being rejected. But clearly the readers have had a tendency to speak of their encounter with God in terms that are too easily imagined, even if they are meant to be giving due weight to the terrifying holiness of God. They like to imagine themselves cringing in darkness, not worthy to approach God. But Hebrews wants to see them stepping out with confidence into the light of God's city, where they are known and expected, and where the beloved figure of Jesus is waiting for them.

And in case they should start to turn this glorious picture into yet another way of keeping God at a distance, Hebrews reminds them that this confidence is based on their knowledge of God. In the plain daylight of their meeting with Jesus, they can see with total clarity the awesome, loving, wild fire of God.

# Proper 17

—— ≈ ——

*Ecclesiasticus 10.12–18*
*Hebrews 13.1–8, 15, 16*
*Luke 14.1, 7–14*

In this central section of Luke's Gospel it feels as though Jesus is in a kind of first-century *Big Brother*. Everything he does and says is being critically watched, sifted, grafted into other people's fantasies and distorted.

So this is no innocent invitation to dinner. It has been set up to try and trap Jesus, and he knows it, all too well. What is striking is the cool, humorous authority with which he handles the trap. In somebody else's home, surrounded by hostile or thrill-seeking eyes, he makes no attempt to curry favour or play to the crowd. He goes straight on the offensive, turning the spotlight on his watchers. They had expected to watch a spectacle, but now they become the spectacle.

Jesus watches as the guests jostle for position, and he tells two stories about dinner parties, both of them clearly critical of the party he is actually at, and both of them cutting straight to the heart of what it is that the Pharisees and the other community leaders want to know about Jesus. They want to know who he is. They want to know how to position him in their hierarchy of values, so that they know how they can treat him and expect him to treat them. But Jesus won't play this game.

Over and over again in the Gospels we see people coming to Jesus with the same kind of questions about hierarchy and position, about how to measure and order their world and find the best place for themselves in it. And over and over again, Jesus simply refuses to answer in those terms. It is not that he is rejecting one set of hierarchies to replace them with a different set, but that he seems to be trying to get people to start again with a completely different set of assumptions.

In the first of today's stories, there is only one measure, and that is the reaction of the host. The guest has to remember that it is not his dinner party, and he cannot decide for himself who should sit where. The dinner party is given by someone else, and he alone has the right to determine the seating arrangements. In the second, the question is what kind of reward the dinner party is to bring. Is the point of it that it will generate other invitations, brighten up your social life and enhance your status, or might there be another point?

Any of the guests who were still under the impression that these stories of Jesus' were actually about dinner parties is suddenly disillusioned in Luke 14.14. With this mention of the 'resurrection of the righteous' it becomes perfectly clear that these parties are God's party, the kingdom.

And then the stories become really worrying, because Jesus seems to be suggesting to his distinguished audience that they have no idea at all of the criteria that God is using to send out his invitations. No amount of working your way up the religious hierarchical ladder is going to guarantee admission, and if you do get invited, you may find yourself in some very strange company, Jesus implies.

But if, despite all that, you still want to be at the wedding feast, what are you supposed to do? If God's measures are eccentric and anarchic in the extreme, how can we be sure of our invitation?

The answer seems to be that so long as you are asking the question in that way, the response is going to be doubtful at best. How can I make sure that *everybody* gets an invitation, seems to be nearer the mark. And underlying that, how can I live my life so that I would be genuinely pleased to see the local street person sitting at Jesus' right hand at the banquet? How can I learn that including everybody does not devalue my own invitation?

The first step is to remember that we ourselves have done remarkably little to earn our own invitation, so why should we be resentful about God's grace to others? When the poet George Herbert took up the theme of God as host, he reminded us that the banquet is about God's generosity, not our merit.

When invited to the feast, the guest in the poem hangs back, suddenly aware of how dusty he is, and how he has come to the party unprepared, ungrateful and unkind. But Love, the host, is under no illusions about his guests. He knows what he is doing:

> And know you not, sayes Love, who bore the blame?
> My deare, then I will serve.
> You must sit down, sayes Love, and taste my meat;
> So I did sit and eat.
>
> ('Love Bade Me Welcome')

# *Proper 18*

— ∾ —

*Deuteronomy 30.15–20*
*Philemon 1–21*
*Luke 14.25–33*

Which of your letters would you like preserved for a couple of millennia? Philemon is one of the most 'domestic' of the documents of the New Testament, and it is impossible not to read it like an unfinished novel. What happened before the letter? What happened as a result of it? What does it tell us about the main characters?

It does seem clear that the letter is written by Paul on behalf of Onesimus, a runaway slave. We don't know why he ran away, but it looks as though he chose his destination with care. If anyone could shield him from his master's wrath it was Paul. After all, Philemon owes Paul a great deal, and is unlikely to refuse him anything he asks. As far as Onesimus is concerned, it doesn't make much difference that Paul is in prison, since Onesimus is never free, anyway. Perhaps Onesimus had managed to hang around the meetings that happened in Philemon's house, and had heard phrases such as 'no slave, no free, all one in Christ', and decided to put them to the test.

If you read this letter from Onesimus' point of view, has his strategy paid off? Well, yes and no. Although it is an intimate letter, it is still a semi-public one. It is addressed to all the Christians who meet in Philemon's house, and it is talking very openly about Onesimus' failings. It says that he was 'useless' (v. 11), and it makes no attempt to blame Philemon for whatever caused Onesimus to run away. It does not demand that Philemon should free Onesimus, or send him back to Paul. In fact, it is really quite careful not to dictate to Philemon at all. On the other hand, it does publicly ask, in Paul's name, for forgiveness for Onesimus, and so it inevitably makes the members of Philemon's house church into witnesses to how he responds to Paul's requests.

If you read it from Philemon's point of view, it is an absolutely brilliant sleight of hand. It manoeuvres him into a position where he actually has no options at all, while apparently leaving him in charge. It is a very courteous letter, with no hints that only the slaves of bad masters run away. It offers to pay for any damage Onesimus may have done. (But whatever did he do? And how on earth is Paul going to pay for it, from prison, and with no visible means of support other than that provided by his fellow Christians? Is he going to have a whip-round among all his Christian communities to pay Philemon back? Is Philemon really going to put up with that? Doesn't the offer actually force Philemon to waive any financial damages?)

You can't help picturing the meeting between Philemon and One-simus. I do hope that Philemon was big enough to accept Onesimus back in the spirit of the letter. It would have taken a great deal of self-control not to try to make Onesimus feel even slightly guilty.

What I really wanted to do with this reading was to try to write a modern equivalent, but that proved much harder than I had antici-pated. What would be a modern parallel? It would have to be a letter on behalf of someone who is a 'slave', whose 'rights' are not universally acknowledged or defended. Perhaps it could be a letter to a conserva-tive diocese or province, asking for mercy for a gay clergyman, or a female one. Or perhaps to a liberal recipient, asking on behalf of someone opposed to the ordination of women, or a biblical funda-mentalist.

Either way, it would need to ask as Paul does for love, not for justice. Paul asks that Onesimus be treated like a 'beloved brother' (v. 16). All the bigger issues about slavery are noticeable by their absence; this is a 'family' issue. Philemon and Onesimus have to learn to be brothers, because Paul loves them both and, even more, so does God. That is not to say that Christians shouldn't campaign to change laws and societies. Quite the contrary. But the starting point for such campaigning is this domestic situation, in which we are all, whether we like it or not, children of the one Father. It is hard to believe that, if Philemon really managed to love Onesimus like a brother he could go on treating him and viewing him as a slave. Early church commenta-tors gave this story a happy ending, by suggesting that this Onesimus is the one who later became Bishop of Ephesus.

Would that plea have any effect at all in a modern context? Just for a moment, forget about 'rights' and 'justice', and try to believe that this person is a beloved brother or sister.

# *Proper 19*

—— ≈ ——

*Exodus 32.7–14*
*1 Timothy 1.12–17*
*Luke 15.1–10*

The shepherd and the sweeping woman in Luke's stories today are not reacting normally. We are not meant to read these stories and think, 'Ah yes, I would do just that.' We are supposed to question their values and then realize that the whole point of the stories is to question ours.

The scribes and Pharisees are unhappy about the company that Jesus is keeping, and so Jesus tells them these extravagantly exaggerated stories. The shepherd leaves 99 sheep to search for one. But why? Sheep die for all kinds of reasons, and no shepherd can ever expect to get through a whole season without losing a single one. The woman turns her house upside down, looking for one coin, when she has nine other perfectly good ones. And again, everyone knows that coins do go missing, and there is no suggestion that the woman is very poor and cannot afford to lose one, or that the coin is particularly valuable. Both the shepherd and the woman are behaving oddly, just as Jesus is, according to the Pharisees.

In each of these stories, one point is hammered home – God's reaction is wild and exaggerated, just like those of the shepherd and the woman. There is no profligacy in God's housekeeping. He cannot reconcile himself to natural wastage. He is madly happy when someone turns back to him. It is a vivid picture of God, thriftily counting up all the people he has made, anxious that not one should get lost.

But if this is the main point of the story, there is also a secondary one. When the shepherd finds his sheep and the woman her coin, they call in all their friends to share in their rejoicing. How do they react? In the first two stories, we are not told. Did they get into the mood and join in the party, happy just because their friend was happy? Or were

108

they embarrassed and uncomprehending? We really need the third of this collection, the prodigal son, which directly follows on today's reading, to get the answer to that. You will remember how the older brother reacts. The scribes and Pharisees can hardly have missed the point.

But today's three readings take us in a different direction. They allow us to see what happens when the friends of the shepherd and the woman do manage to join in the rejoicing.

The Exodus passage gives us another one of those pictures of God in dialogue with a friend. As when Abraham bargains for the people of Sodom (Genesis 18), so here, God seems to change his mind in talking with Moses. It's as though the shepherd decided to leave the sheep to its fate, but all his friends came round and nagged him until he grudgingly went out to look for it.

Moses makes God change his mind by reminding him what kind of a God he is. He tells God the story of his relationships with Abraham and Isaac, and the promises he made to them. 'This is your character', Moses reminds God, 'and if you act completely out of character now, then everything you did before was worthless.'

Is it God who needs to see what he has always been like? Or is it a moment of sudden clarity for Moses, when he sees God's action all of a piece, and realizes what kind of a God he is dealing with? Certainly, part of the result of the conversation between God and Moses is to bind Moses even more tightly to God's people, annoying and stupid as they are. Read the rest of Exodus 32 to see how angry he gets with them, but also to see how he asks God to visit their punishment on him. Moses has become one of those who would rejoice over the finding of one lost coin.

Even more poignantly, so is Paul. What makes it so moving in this case is that he was once the lost coin himself, and now he longs to find others; he is the sheep turned sheepdog. His experience, too, like that of Moses, is that this is to do with the fundamental character of God. The author says that this is a saying attested by all other Christian authorities (see 1 Timothy 1.15, and cf. e.g. Luke 19.10), 'that Christ Jesus came into the world to save sinners'.

So somebody, at least, was listening to those stories that Jesus told, and got the point of them. Both the point about God, who is like the shepherd or the woman in his total commitment to us, and the point about the reaction of the friends. Now it's our turn.

# Proper 20

—— ∽ ——

*Amos 8.4–7*
*1 Timothy 2.1–7*
*Luke 16.1–13*

Whatever is going on in this strange parable of the dishonest manager? Whichever way you read it, it is confusing. Luke has obviously decided that it is about attachment to wealth, and he has put it with a couple of other stories about the dangers of money, and stuck in Luke 6.16–18 as well, which just heightens the sense of this as a ragbag chapter. You get a picture of Luke, sitting at his desk with a bundle of papers in front of him. He has got the overall structure of his book sorted, and he knows where all the main stories and sayings fit, but now he is left with his file labelled 'miscellaneous'. 'What do I do with these?' he asks himself. 'The old chap who told me the story said he'd been there when Jesus had told it. But I can't help thinking that he must have missed some of it, or wandered off before the end. Jesus just *can't* have told it like this.'

That is certainly the feel of this story. It reads like something that has been wrongly remembered, or had its punchline forgotten, or something. Perhaps the original audience, even, didn't understand it. Several of Jesus' parables were clearly funny in their original context, but have been retold by pious people who believe that religion and laughter have nothing to do with each other. If you read this story as deliberately ironic and unsettling, it begins to make a bit more sense.

For one thing, the audience never quite know where their sympathies are supposed to lie. As the story opens, we have a rich man and his manager. The kind of people to whom Jesus addressed his stories would most naturally have identified with the manager. Verse 1 says that Jesus told this story to his disciples, though later verses in the chapter (see v. 14) suggest that other people were listening in. Either way, this is not an audience made up of the wealthy. Clearly, the rich man owns lots of properties and has put a manager in charge of this

110

one. The rich man himself doesn't seem to live locally, and isn't known to his debtors and tenants. For them, the real source of power, day to day, is the manager. There is also a slight suggestion in verse 1 that the charges being brought against the manager are malicious, and may prove untrue. So the audience settle down to dislike the absentee landlord and feel sorry for the manager.

But then, lo and behold, the manager turns out to be a crook after all. Whether or not he had done anything wrong before, he now sets out to swindle his master. What is his role in the story now? Perhaps he is a kind of comic villain, who still keeps the sympathy of the audience, like Falstaff in Shakespeare's plays. We can see his weaknesses, but they are so like our own that we can't help liking him. Perhaps the audience accepts a general culture in which you do cheat a bit, if the person you are cheating is very rich and not really part of your community. It might be a bit like the assumption in certain circles (though not among readers of this book, I'm sure) that it isn't really immoral not to pay all the taxes you should, if you can get away with it.

But then the story takes another twist when the master acts out of character. If the story is to follow the normal pattern, either the master never finds out, or he finds out and is furious and the manager must either be punished or repent and be reconciled. But here the master congratulates the manager for acting sensibly! What kind of an ending to the story is that? Where's the moral?

Jesus does tell other stories that would seem to question whether the manager had really acted so wisely. Could it be significant that this story immediately follows the story of the prodigal son? When he had spent all his money, where were the grateful friends to take him into their homes? Is the kind of gratitude that the manager is banking on in his master's debtors really so reliable?

Suddenly the story isn't just amusing and abstract, but direct and personal, with the unmistakable ring of Jesus' voice behind it. Who or what are you actually relying on? Take a long hard look at yourself, the things you find funny, the things that you think of as wrong and the things you think don't matter much, where your natural sympathies lie, what makes you feel secure or insecure, who you would turn to in times of trouble. Decision time, says Jesus.

# *Proper 21*

——— ❧ ———

*Amos 6.1a, 4–7*
*1 Timothy 6.6–19*
*Luke 16.19–31*

The people who know about these things generally seem to agree that the Pastoral Letters (1 and 2 Timothy and Titus) were not written by the apostle Paul, at least as they now stand. They have all kinds of good reasons for saying this; for example, the language and theological ideas are subtly different, and it is hard to find a time in Paul's known career that would fit with the references in the letters.

Certainly, the Christian community that is addressed in 1 Timothy sounds like a settled, second-generation church, with a developed set of ministerial functions and a clear sense of church order. Church officials are not just the people in whose houses the community gathers, but bishops and deacons, who have their own households, which are to reflect proper family life (cf. 3.4, 12). None of this is conclusive, of course, and it is very interesting to read two or three commentaries, and see what you think yourself, or read Romans and Timothy side by side and see the differences and overlaps.

But there is a strong sense of a church having to think about the long haul, rather than the first flush of enthusiasm. This is a letter full of largely practical advice on how Christians should relate to each other within the community, with just a few references to the wider world (cf. 2.2). This is a group that is large enough and self-contained enough not to have to think too much about the non-Christian community. Some of them are clearly rather well off – 2.9 reflects a membership that is having to think carefully about appropriate and inappropriate displays of wealth in the Christian context. Although the congregation does contain poorer people and slaves too (cf. 6.1), today's passage is largely addressed to the better-off readers of the letter.

The verse immediately before the beginning of today's reading talks about those who have been teaching that 'godliness is a means of gain' (v. 5). There have always been Christians who see success and material comfort as rewards from God, and clearly this congregation is no exception. The writer does not urge them to give up all their wealth, but to remember where it belongs and what it is worth. It is the love of money, he suggests, that is the danger, because it leads you to value things that are essentially ephemeral. So the wealthy are to use their money for the good of others, and to remember that money and status are not connected, for Christians (see v. 17). The only kind of riches worth having are the ones that lead to 'life that really is life' (v. 19).

The letter sets these struggles with the lure of selfish comfort against the backdrop of God's court. All around us, the author reminds his readers, are those who have already given their testimony, bearing witness to God. At their centre stands Jesus, whose costly witness is the real measure of our own. Every time you make a decision about how to spend, how to live, imagine your actions weighed up in such company, against such a reality, by the 'only Sovereign, the King of kings and Lord of lords' (v. 15).

St Teresa of Avila, a profoundly practical person, wrote in *The Interior Castle,*

> Our Lord asks but two things of us: love for him and for our neighbour ... I think the most certain sign that we keep these two commandments is that we have a genuine love for others. We cannot know whether we love God although there may be strong reasons for thinking so, but there can be no doubt about whether we love our neighbour or no.

Very good and very hard advice. It is a pity that the rich man in today's Gospel never had a chance to meet Teresa, although the story suggests that it would have made no difference. We are not told outright why the rich man deserves to go to hell. We have to infer that it is simply because his riches shielded him to the point where he could ignore Lazarus, starving to death at his gate. The rich man had every excuse not to notice him. He had servants to run his errands, and he probably usually swept through his gates on a horse or in a carriage of some kind. His servants would know better than to let Lazarus bother their master.

The problem with riches is that it is hard to remember how dangerous they are. Insidiously, they get into our systems and make us dependent upon them. Perhaps money should have a kind of Christian equivalent of a government health warning stamped upon it. But we already have 'Moses and the prophets' to warn us.

# *Proper 22*

—— ❧ ——

*Habakkuk 1.1–4; 2.1–4*
*2 Timothy 1.1–14*
*Luke 17.5–10*

This central section of Luke's Gospel is full of very uncomfortable reading. It starts at 9.51, when Jesus 'set his face to go to Jerusalem', and the ministry enters a new phase. Now everything he says and does is being scrutinized with suspicion and hostility by the religious authorities, and he is constantly in the spotlight. Even conversations with the disciples seem to have a wider audience, or else are quickly relayed to others. For example, Luke 16 opens with 'Jesus said to the disciples', but by verse 14, it is the Pharisees, not the disciples, who are reacting to the story. The stories that Jesus tells in this section are provocative and puzzling, often with a sting in the tail. There are only one or two healing stories in the ten chapters that follow 9.51, and even these have an edge to them. Conflict and the expectation of worse are the setting of this whole section.

How do the disciples cope with this situation? They must have picked up the tension and heard the note of urgency in everything Jesus says to them. The verses that come immediately before verse 5 are a terrible warning to be constantly on guard.

So, perhaps not unnaturally, the disciples ask Jesus to 'increase our faith'. A perfectly reasonable request, you might say. If they are going to have to face such conflict they will need all the faith they can get. But Jesus' reply to them is rather short. They don't need *more* faith, they just need to use what they have already got. The smallest possible amount of faith can work wonders, Jesus tells them. Why are they asking for more?

He then puts to them the question about the slave. Would they expect a slave to come in from work and say 'I'm worn out', and slump down on the sofa in front of the telly? Or would they expect him just to

114

get on with his job? Slaves don't expect rewards for doing what they are there for, and neither should disciples.

This seems rather a harsh response to the disciples. You can imagine them raising their eyebrows at each other and thinking that life with Jesus just isn't as much fun as it used to be. But why are they asking for more faith at this moment? Nothing definite has been asked of them yet; they aren't being sent off on a testing task. Why do they suddenly feel the need for more faith? Perhaps what Jesus senses and responds to is that the disciples are asking for faith to act as a kind of strong drug. They want not to feel fear or pain but just to be on a high that will enable them to be unaffected by the tension and conflict around them. They realize that things are coming to a head between Jesus and the religious authorities, and they want some miraculous injection of faith that will insulate them from the unpleasantness around them and allow them to act like the heroes they would like to be. Unfortunately, faith doesn't work like that. Jesus suggests that they already have enough faith to get on with what they are actually being asked to do.

The kind of faith that lets you get on with what you are there for is at the heart of the opening chapter of 2 Timothy. Timothy's faith is a family heirloom, almost as though he has no choice about inheriting it and passing it on. He is under no illusion about faith. He knows it is not a painkiller or a lifesaver, because he knows what it cost Paul, his great hero. But his faith is not given to him so that he can be a hugely important and influential figure, like Paul. Paul is 'a herald and an apostle and a teacher' (1.11), while Timothy is called to be a guardian. He is to guard the gospel by constantly checking it against Paul's own teaching, and he is to guard the people brought under his wing by the gospel. Not glamorous, but still necessary.

Poor Timothy. This first chapter of 2 Timothy gives us a picture of someone who is never seen in his own right. Everywhere he goes in Christian circles he is either known as the grandson of Lois and the son of Eunice or as the disciple of Paul. When he gets something right, people just nod wisely and say, 'Ah yes, that's his mother's influence', or 'Of course, Paul taught him that.' But perhaps he is wise enough just to be grateful for the faith which enables him to do what he has to do, and for the help of the Holy Spirit.

# Proper 23

——— ∿ ———

*2 Kings 5.1–3, 7–15c*
*2 Timothy 2.8–15*
*Luke 17.11–19*

The story of Naaman has got everything. To begin with, the hero is a thoroughly likeable character. (Well, I suppose you could argue that Elisha is the real hero of the story, and no one could call him exactly likeable.) Naaman gets on well with his wife, his slaves and his king, which suggests an unusual gift for friendship. His servants even like him enough to be a little cheeky (see 2 Kings 5.13). But, at the same time, he has ordinary human failings. He is a little too aware of his position, and he does like to be treated with respect.

Next, the story is very funny, specially if you put in the verses that the lectionary suggests you leave out. The King of Israel's response to the request to heal Naaman is pantomime stuff.

And finally, the author has a good eye for scene-setting. There is the intimate scene between Naaman's wife and the slave-girl; there are two contrasting royal courts, with a big king and a little king, and then there is the great set piece, where Naaman with his horses and chariots, his gold and his silver, his slaves and all his finery arrives outside Elisha's mud hut and Elisha doesn't even bother to come out.

Clearly, Elisha means to humiliate Naaman – I did warn you that Elisha is not a nice man, servant of God or no. He could have done it the way Naaman was expecting, with incantations, incense and ritual. At the very least, he could have come out and touched Naaman's leprous hand. Instead he sends his servant out to tell Naaman to take a running jump into the river.

That's what makes Naaman's final response so moving. When his loving servants – a great contrast, by the way, to Elisha's own servant, as you will see when you read the next part of the story – at last persuade Naaman to do as he is told, and he realizes that he is cured,

116

he returns humbly and gratefully to the man of God. There is no sign of a lingering resentment at the way he has been treated. He accepts the implicit rebuke and recognizes what it means. 'Now I know', he says, 'that there is no God in all the earth except in Israel.'

It is this response on Naaman's part that makes him the perfect match for the story we have in today's Gospel. He and the rejoicing leper who remembers that Jesus is the cause of his joy are a good pair. Jesus' response to the leper is much more gracious than Elisha's. Elisha refuses to accept anything from Naaman, or to allow him any gesture that will restore a measure of equality between them. Abject gratitude and an acknowledgement that he is totally in the right is what Elisha is looking for. Jesus, on the other hand, says to the leper, 'Your faith has made you well.' In that sentence, he gives the man back power over his own life, treating him as an equal, fully restored to human relationships. What a gift to a man who was used to being shunned, spending all his life only with other lepers, and with people throwing charity at him and then running away quickly to escape contamination.

But, of course, there is a sting in the tail of this story in Luke's Gospel, because the leper who comes back to thank Jesus is not an Israelite but a foreigner – worse, a Samaritan. It comes as one of a series of stories of Jesus' conflict with the Pharisees and, initially, it lifts the heart. At last we are seeing again the Jesus that we met in the early part of the Gospel, always willing to listen to people and heal them. But when you look back through Luke, in the light of these stories of conflict, you begin to hear the sombre note everywhere, the note struck by people's rejection of Jesus, and his longing for them to hear and understand what he is saying.

All the Gospels agree that although many people either feared or misunderstood Jesus, or both, it was the religious leaders who made an art form of both fearing and misunderstanding him. The very people who had all the clues in their hands to solve the mystery of who Jesus is and what God is doing in him are the ones to be baffled. Perhaps their problem is that they did not realize there was a mystery. They thought they had the solution already. In fact, they thought they were part of it. The temptation to believe that you have got God tamed did not die with the Pharisees. 'Remind them, remind them, remind them,' Timothy is told.

# *Proper 24*

— ∾ —

Genesis 32.22–31
2 Timothy 3.14—4.5
Luke 18.1–8

This odd little parable in Luke gives us the key to all of today's readings: they are about faithful endurance. The story of the judge and the woman is vivid and full of little ironies. The contrast is set up between the judge, who has all the power on his side, and the woman, who doesn't even have a male relative to do her pleading for her, and so is at the bottom of the pecking order. All the same, by sheer persistence, she gets what she wants. The judge, whose title and position arise out of the need to administer justice, doesn't actually care about justice at all. He just wants a quiet life.

So far, so good. But the problem comes when we try to apply the story to the disciples. It is Jesus' remark at the end that brings clarity. 'When the Son of Man comes, will he find faith on earth?' We are not meant to equate the disciples with the woman and God with the unjust judge, but to see two different attitudes. On the one hand, there is the judge, who is lazy and faithless. He does what is right this time, but who knows what will happen next time, if the person who comes to him is less persistent or he has something else on his mind. He is not committed to doing justice, only to living a comfortable life. The woman, on the other hand, is determined that right will be done, and she is not going to give up until it is. She ignores her own low status compared to that of the judge; she ignores all the conventions of when it is proper to approach the judge with her requests; she just goes on and on, indomitably. Which of those two attitudes, Jesus asks, will he find among his followers when the Son of Man comes? Will they have given in to convenience and the desire for a quiet life and gently dropped the stringent demands of the gospel, or will they still be faithful?

Faithfulness is the hallmark of Timothy's ministry. The steady tradition of right belief into which he was born is to be the thread that holds his community together. He has had the luxury of learning the Scriptures (which would, of course, have been the Old Testament, at this point) as a child, and now he is to pass on that gift to others. Clearly, there are people in Timothy's community who have 'itching ears' (2 Timothy 4.3). They like the sound of all kinds of things, and they don't see why they shouldn't choose their own religion by cobbling together lots of different, attractive bits. In response to them, Timothy is to pour out a positive rain of proper teaching. Most 'teach yourself evangelism' courses would recommend careful preparation of your subjects, and finding the right way to communicate at the right time, but Timothy can't wait for that – the situation is too urgent. This is his ministry, his responsibility. The older generation, represented by Paul, is now formally handing on the task to Timothy's generation. In Timothy, at least, they have someone they can trust to be faithful.

Persistence, faithfulness, perseverance are also strongly present in the Genesis story about Jacob's wrestling match. It is such a well-known and well-loved story that it pays careful rereading. In the kind of Sunday-school retellings of it that most of us are used to, so many of the puzzling details are left out.

To begin with, Jacob is on his own at night because he has sent his company on ahead of him to try to appease Esau with a present. He has very good reason to be afraid of Esau, and he wants him softened up before he meets him again. So part of what happens in this story is that Jacob wins a blessing from the stranger (Genesis 32.29), and this blessing is one that he works for himself and earns with pain and effort, unlike the one he stole from Esau by trickery. It leaves him limping, but it also restores in him some sense of his own value. When, at the beginning of Genesis 33, Esau arrives, Jacob doesn't hide any more, but goes out to meet him.

We never find out who the stranger is – though Jacob is convinced that he has met God – and the wrestling itself is strangely inconsequential. We don't even know who won; only that it went on a long time. The vital thing we are told is that Jacob won't give up, even when he is hurt. Like the pestering woman in the parable, and like Timothy, Jacob is rewarded for persistence.

# The Last Sunday After Trinity

——— ∽ ———

*Jeremiah 14.7–10, 19–22*
*2 Timothy 4.6–8, 16–18*
*Luke 18.9–14*

A disciple's tale:

He told another of his stories today. I love his stories – they were
one of the things that made me decide to follow him, really. I just
couldn't bear to miss any of them. They're really funny, and he
sort of acts them out, so that you can see the different characters
as he talks. They make you think, too. Sometimes, when you're
listening, you're sure you've got the point, but hours later, or in
the middle of the night, you suddenly realize that it could mean
something else entirely. We've tried asking him to tell us what the
stories mean. Just occasionally, he'll tell us, but usually he just
grins and says there's no one meaning, and that different people
will hear it differently.

Anyway, the story he told today was about two people praying
in the temple. One was a Pharisee. As soon as he said that, you
could see the Pharisees in the crowd getting red in the face and
waiting to hear what he was going to say. They follow him about
everywhere now, and he's always getting little digs in at them. He
knows they hate him, but are scared to touch him because the
people still think he's wonderful.

So the story goes that the Pharisee has really just come to boast,
not to pray. So we all began to laugh and nudge each other,
because *we* aren't Pharisees, and that bit of the story is not about
us. Then the other man comes in, and starts to pray for mercy,
which he is certainly going to need, because he's a tax-gatherer,
one of the scum that's prepared to work for the occupying army,
and squeeze money out of their own brothers.

But then Jesus says that the tax-gatherer is the one who gets the pat on the head from God.

I don't know why, but that story has really got to me. Is any of it for me? Or is it just a story for Pharisees and tax-gatherers? I don't like either of the characters, but although I hate to admit it, I have more sympathy for the Pharisee. At least he's trying to do good. I know Jesus doesn't care much about fasting, but he's always telling us we have to take care of the poor, and the Pharisee is tithing so that he can share his good fortune with others. And the Pharisee is grateful to God for what he's got. He isn't trying to make out that he owes it all to his own hard work. Whereas the tax-gatherer just stands there and whines. He doesn't even promise to try and change, he just asks for mercy. Why does God like him better?

Am I like the Pharisee? I'm really glad I met Jesus, and had the sense to follow him. I know he's the Messiah, and when he takes over, my family and I are going to do really well out of it. He doesn't like it when we call him 'Messiah', and he looks at us very strangely when we ask how he's going to reward us when he comes to power. My wife thinks it will all end in disaster, and I'll be executed, or end up in jail, but she's just angry because I'm away from home so much now. I just know he's something special, and since I've given up so much for him – my business, my ordinary life, my security – surely he'll do something for me when he turns the Romans out and forms a government?

But does that make me sound just like the Pharisee? I don't understand about the tax-gatherer. I don't even know why he went to the temple at all. It would make more sense if he was promising to give back all the money he'd extorted from the likes of me, but all he's doing is sitting there and crying like a baby. What's so wonderful about that?

In the end, I got so worried about the story that I asked the others what they thought it meant. After a while, one of them asked, 'Would we give up on Jesus if we knew he wasn't the Messiah?' That shut us up, until someone else said that the thing about Jesus is that he makes you love and trust God. If God really is loving and teasing and forgiving, like he is in the stories Jesus tells, then we all have a chance.

Perhaps that's it. You have to want God. Not anything else, just God, just the chance for God to see you as you really are and love you. Perhaps that's it.

# Sundays Before Advent

# The Fourth Sunday Before Advent

—— ∾ ——

*Isaiah 1.10–18*
*2 Thessalonians 1.1–12*
*Luke 19.1–10*

The temptation with today's three readings is to go straight for the story of Zacchaeus. It's warm, vivid and has a happy ending. But the other two readings remind us that Zacchaeus' choice is not the one that everyone makes.

For Isaiah, holiness is the most definitive characteristic of God. The account of his calling as a prophet (see Isaiah 6) shows the splendour and majesty of God, surrounded by his seraphs, his train filling the temple. The contrast between God and the prophet could not be more marked. With such a vision always in his memory, Isaiah can scarcely believe the stupidity and foolhardy pride of God's people, who think they can disobey such a God with impunity.

So, at the start of Isaiah 1 (v. 3), Isaiah points out that even the animals know to whom they belong; only Israel is too stupid to understand what they owe to God. Throughout this chapter, God addresses his people, who are already beaten and sore from the wars they are involved in, but who have still not made the connection between their choices and their sorry state.

Instead, they seem to have turned to ritual. It is as though they are waving some kind of contract in front of God, saying, 'Here, we are fulfilling our part, we have done the sacrifices, the convocations and assemblies, now it's time you did your part.' But God will have none of it. This was not the contract that he signed with his people, but a shoddy forgery. He will not listen to them even when they pray, because their hands 'are full of blood' (v. 15). Their prayers are intended to change God, but they have forgotten that the primary purpose of prayer is to change the one who prays.

God reminds them what they are called for, which is to be a

community that demonstrates love and justice, and so bears witness to the nature of God. Until they return to that calling, everything they say to God is empty words. The choice is theirs – God's forgiveness will be total, but so will his judgement.

2 Thessalonians is uncomfortably full of judgement, too. This community, unlike the one that Isaiah is talking to, do know what they should be. They are commended for their faith and their love, and they have the satisfaction of knowing that their witness is helping others to see God. In other words, they are being exactly what they are meant to be: images, witnesses and mirrors of God. Even though they are suffering persecution, they are not tempted to be like the people of Israel in Isaiah, demanding release and trying to force God to be nice to them. Instead, they accept their fate with gladness, because it gives them even more of a chance to demonstrate their faith and trust.

They know that they are making God's glory visible in their lives now, by their witness, but that the awesome holiness and majesty of God will be revealed fully soon. On that day, these Christians will be ready to take their place with the seraphs, praising God. Their whole lives have been a preparation for that moment, and the hope of it makes all that they are suffering worthwhile.

In such a community, constantly under threat of persecution, you can understand the double emphasis of this section of the letter. On the one hand, Christians need to know that the life they are living now is preparing them for the glorious life to come. It is not their final condition. They also need to know that the costly choice they have made is worth it, and the only way they can know that is by picturing the alternative. What happens to those who do not throw in their lot with Jesus? They have no part in the life to come, and no part in the Lord, who is the only real source of life there is.

This idea that our choices have final consequences is not one we are very comfortable with, but is the unmistakable conclusion to be drawn both from Isaiah and from 2 Thessalonians. Our lives are valuable and meaningful only when they are put into the context of God's whole purpose in creation. Separated from the 'presence of the Lord and from the glory of his might' (2 Thessalonians 1.9), we cease to exist.

Choices have consequences, but in God's mercy, you may have more than one chance to choose. Zacchaeus thought he had made one set of choices, but faced with Jesus, he chooses again. This time he chooses to be what he is created for, a child of Abraham, an inheritor of God's great promise of love and faithfulness.

# The Third Sunday Before Advent

—— ∾ ——

*Job 19.23–7a*
*2 Thessalonians 2.1–5, 13–17*
*Luke 20.27–38*

The book of Job has always inspired strong feelings – hardly surprising, as its themes are suffering and justice. At the heart of the many paradoxes that belief in the God of the Bible presents us with is this one: that God the Creator is utterly loving and yet the world contains suffering and evil. Job is not an 'answer' to this problem – by their very nature, paradoxes are not susceptible to resolution, except by being proven not to be paradoxes at all. But what Job does try to do is to suggest that there are ways of living with this paradox that are religiously and humanly creative and truthful.

Don't be put off by the dramatic setting of the opening of the book. The interchanges between God and Satan are not meant to be doctrinal. They do not tell you about how the relationship between God and evil actually is; they merely set the scene. It is vital to the action that follows that we, the reader, know for sure that Job is utterly innocent. The whole plot depends upon this fact – that Job's suffering is wholly undeserved, and that it demonstrates something that we need to know. So the opening scenes (Job 1—2) show us Satan needling God. If God had a weak point, Satan has found it: he is implying that the whole purpose of creation is undermined from the start. God has made human beings to be utterly free and independent so that they can freely choose to enter into a relationship with God. But Satan suggests that people only love God because of what he can do for them. Their love is no more free and unconditioned than it would have been if God had made robots instead of humans.

What follow is a systematic testing of that idea. Do we indeed love God just for the security and favours he can give us, or do we love him, as he intended, the way Father, Son and Holy Spirit love one another, freely and because we see that God is intrinsically to be loved?

As Job suffers, his family and friends turn from him as one cursed by God. They take it for granted that the point of worshipping God is that he will then protect you. So it must follow that if you are not protected, then that means that you have done something wrong, and God is no longer prepared to shield you and take care of you. They are by no means alone in thinking that the only alternative to divine favour is divine non-existence.

But Job steadfastly rejects that idea. In today's passage, he has reached the end of his tether. In the verses immediately before this, he describes how all those who should love him and support him have actually abandoned him. And yet, he will not pass that emotion on. Those who have relied upon him, and looked up to him as their master, provider, husband, father have turned against him, but still he cannot quite turn against the one who has been all those things for him – God.

Certainly, he is angry with God. He wants a written record of all that he has been through, so that he can present it to God and demand a satisfactory answer. But notice that God is still his whole horizon. It does not occur to him, in his pain, distress and fury, to stop believing in God. And what is it that he wants from God? Does he want justice? Does he want health? Does he want his wealth and his family and his position back? Well, perhaps he does. But more than anything else, he wants to stand in the presence of the living God and hear from him that he is loved and vindicated, and that the relationship between them exists. Job needs to know, above all else, that his Redeemer lives.

This passage demonstrates with utter clarity that Satan has lost – at least, in the case of Job. Job does not believe in God only in prosperity. In despair, it is only God he looks to; not with easy confidence, not with shallow expectation of the return of good times, but with the profound knowledge that it is only God's judgement of his life that matters. He longs to know that God is on his side. Rare man that he is, he does not demand that God's vindication should be shown to all those who doubted. What matters to Job is that he himself should know that God is his witness.

We follow a God who chooses crucifixion as his way in the world. Do we still believe that prosperity is a sign of God's favour?

# The Second Sunday Before Advent

—— ◇ ——

*Malachi 4.1–2a*
*2 Thessalonians 3.6–13*
*Luke 21.5–19*

The material in today's reading from Luke can be found in a very similar form in Mark 13 and Matthew 24, and all are agreed that the temple is the trigger for these terrible sayings. Jesus seems to be warning the disciples about the destruction of the temple in Jerusalem, which did in fact take place in AD 70, on Roman orders.

His disciples couldn't have followed Jesus for all those months without noticing that Jesus' views about the temple and the religious establishment were, at best, ambiguous. But this passage does not suggest that the temple deserves to be destroyed. There is no hint of anger or vengeance in any of these sayings, which somehow makes them more chilling. It is interesting that the disciples immediately assume that Jesus is talking about the end of the world, the time of judgement and consummation. For them, the temple is still so pivotal in their understanding of what God requires that they assume that the only thing that can succeed the temple is God's direct reign.

But although the passage does culminate with the vision of the Son of Man coming in glory to bring redemption (cf. Luke 21.27–8), in Jesus' understanding, a great deal will happen between the end of the temple and the coming of God, and most of it will be horrible.

As so often, the poor disciples are asking for clarification. 'When?' they ask. 'How will we know?' And, as so often, they don't exactly get a straight answer. What they get instead is a method for avoiding distractions. Jesus' advice is odd – they are to be unprepared (v. 14). All around them, the world will be full of people with huge emotions – anger, terror, hatred, fear, anticipation – but they are not to get carried away by all this. They are simply to take it all as an opportunity for mission. Even when things get personal, and they themselves are under attack, they are to keep their hearts fixed on their one main purpose, which is to testify faithfully and to trust in Jesus, both for the immediate words that they are to use, and for their own long-term salvation.

What Jesus is asking for is an almost impossible doggedness and level-headedness, a willingness to set our hands to the task in front of us and forgo the heady excitement of speculation. And in this, of course, he himself is the pattern. What you see in the Gospels – and particularly at this stage, where tension is visibly mounting, and where the terrible climax in Jerusalem is in sight – is Jesus carrying on exactly as before. He still preaches, teaches, heals and urges people towards God and his kingdom. All around him are people trying to work out what will happen, what they should do about it, how they can force events into a pattern. Only Jesus, the cause of it all, carries on, unchanging.

Following the pattern is what is recommended by 2 Thessalonians, too. In this case, the pattern is the apostle Paul, but behind him is the larger template on which Paul modelled himself, Jesus. The letters to the Thessalonians suggest that they, like the disciples in Luke, are tempted to waste their energies in excited looking to the future. What they get is like a glass of cold water in the face. It is all about getting on with their daily work. How annoying for the people who had given up everything to prepare themselves for the end, to wait in stillness for the rapture of Jesus' return, and who are called idle busybodies for their pains. They are trying to second-guess God, or even persuade him to do what they want, instead of just patiently getting on with their lives.

Malachi suggests that following this boring-sounding advice has an extraordinary outcome. It may look undramatic – even, at times, unfaithful – simply to get on with working, praying and testifying when the world around is in chaos, but Malachi suggests following the pattern allows you to see things differently. For the 'arrogant' and the 'evildoers', the presence of God burns like fire. Their lives have been built on straw and they burn like straw. But to God's own people, who have accustomed themselves, faithfully, day by day, to his nature and his will, his presence is like the sun, bringing warmth, healing and life.

Disciples are instructed to follow Jesus under all circumstances, never allowing themselves to be distracted, whatever is going on around them. Then their eyes will be used to spotting glimpses of his light, recognizing him even in shadows, knowing shadows can only be made by the light. So when the sun blazes out, they will be ready for it.

# Christy the King

—— ⟿ ——

*Jeremiah 23.1–6*
*Colossians 1.11–20*
*Luke 23.33–43*

Today's passages might, on a superficial reading, simply be making the fairly standard point that Christ's kingship and authority are a challenge to most human understandings of power. That's a good and important point, and one that needs making repeatedly, since we don't on the whole want to hear it.

But the trouble is that they are now being read by a society that is in a terrible muddle about 'leadership'. So you can't just hold up the standard, worldly model of power and then contrast it with the biblical one, because there isn't a standard, worldly model of power.

There are all kinds of things that suggest that we do not know what we want from our heroes and leaders, we don't know what we are looking for. On the one hand, people beg for strong leadership, but the minute that leadership does something they don't like, they turn round and accuse them of failing to listen to the people and shout that they must remember we are a democracy. Or we set up heroes – sportspeople or actors or models – whose wealth and opportunity we envy, but we seem only to be able to tolerate their success for a short time and then we start to long for them to fail. Their privilege, instead of being an inspiration to us, becomes a challenge, and makes our situation seem worse by comparison, so that we cannot wait to discover that our heroes are secretly deeply miserable people.

In other words, we are fickle and hard to lead and inspire because we have no understanding of our own deepest needs and desires. All we do know is that, whatever they are, they are not being fulfilled.

What might today's passages teach about this situation?

Jeremiah pictures a people whose leadership has left them fragmented and pulling in different directions – very reminiscent of our own

130

culture. The people are scattered and have lost any sense of who they are. They no longer remember that they are God's people and that they belong together in community. For this, Jeremiah roundly blames the leaders, who should have shepherded their people, but instead have allowed them to get scattered and lost. Their punishment is to suffer the fate that they have allowed to come upon God's people. They themselves will be scattered and lost, and they will be leaders and men of power no longer. In their place, God will raise up faithful shepherds, who will restore that lost sense of belonging and security. And then, at last, his people will be ready for the coming of the Messiah, because now they will be in a position to recognize his reign of 'justice and righteousness' (Jeremiah 23.5) for what it is – an echo of God's own nature. In their initial state of distress and alienation, they would not have known 'justice and righteousness' if it had been handed them on a plate.

The Colossians have come to that happy state where they can recognize the rule of God. Indeed, they have taken the next step, the one implied at the end of the reading from Jeremiah, and made the connection between their shepherd and God. They have come to see that Jesus has taken them out of confusion, darkness and submission to false leaders into God's kingdom of free and forgiven people. They have also come to see that he can do this because he is the full reflection of God's own loving and reconciling Kingship.

Jeremiah looks for a time when his people will be rescued, and the Colossians know that they have been already. Luke tells us that the rescuer is a man hanging on a cross. He gives us that supremely paradoxical picture of Jesus, hanging helplessly in pain and near death, yet still the King, opening the gates of his kingdom to the bewildered, misled, barely human rabble around him. As he asks for forgiveness for the crowd, and as he leads the thief into the kingdom, he is, in his agony, still the one whom all 'thrones ... dominions ... rulers ... powers' (Colossians 1.16) must acknowledge as Lord.

The thief has instinctively what Jeremiah's people have to relearn – a sense of God's justice. He recognizes his own guilt and Jesus' inno-cence, and so demonstrates that he can still recognize God. His ability to see the lineaments of God's face and God's rule of righteousness and justice fits him for the kingdom.

To learn to do the same, to be able to recognize the character of God's reign and to long for it, we need to borrow the Colossians' key, which is Jesus Christ, and to look for his likeness day by day until we can recognize and love it.